ETA AND BASQUE NATIONALISM

Spain and the Basque Country

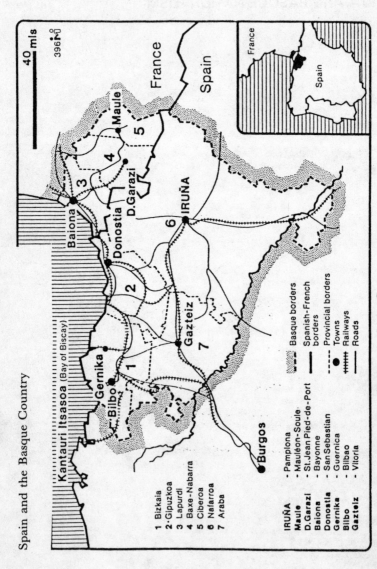

Kantauri Itsasoa (Bay of Biscay)

Maule

France

Spain

40 mls

396 M°

5

4

3

Baiona

Donostia

D.Garazi

IRUÑA

6

Gazteiz

7

2

Gernika

Bilbo

1

Burgos

France

Spain

1 Bizkaia
2·Gipuzkoa
3·Lapurdi
4 Baxe-Nabarra
5 Ciberoa
6 Nafarroa
7 Araba

IRUÑA — Pamplona
Maule — Mauléon-Soule
D.Garazi — St.Jean Pied-de-Port
Baiona — Bayonne
Donostia — San Sebastian
Gernika — Guernica
Bilbo — Bilbao
Gazteiz — Vitoria

Basque borders

Spanish-French borders

Provincial borders

● Towns

+++ Railways

Roads

ETA and BASQUE NATIONALISM
The Fight for Euskadi 1890-1986

John Sullivan

ROUTLEDGE
London and New York

First published in 1988 by
Routledge
11 New Fetter Lane, London EC4P 4EE

Published in the USA by
Routledge
in association with Routledge, Chapman & Hall, Inc.
29 West 35th Street, New York NY 10001

Filmset by Mayhew Typesetting, Bristol, England
Printed and bound in Great Britain by
Biddles Ltd, Guildford and King's Lynn

British Library Cataloguing in Publication Data

Sullivan, J.L.
    ETA and Basque nationalism: the fight
    for Euskadi 1890–1986.
    1. Euskadi ta Askatasuna — History
    I. Title
    322.4'2'09466   DP302.B48

    ISBN 0-415-00366-0

Library of Congress Cataloging in Publication Data
    ISBN 0-415-00366-0

Contents

For Palmira

Acknowledgements

This book is based on a thesis for which I was awarded the degree of Ph.D (London) in 1986. My thanks are due to the many people who helped me by allowing themselves to be interviewed, by obtaining documents and by assisting in other ways. I am particularly grateful to Antolín Amescua, Feliz Aizpurua, María Teresa Castells, Tomás Goikoetxea, Eufemia González, John Hollyman, Blanca Imizcoz, Alison Lever, Antonio G. Pericás, Octavio Rico and Ramón Zulaica.

My greatest debt is to my supervisor Professor Paul Preston, without whose guidance and criticism the work would never have been completed.

I am grateful to my employers, the Western District of the Workers' Educational Association for granting me time off for research and writing during Spring 1980 and Summer 1984.

I am grateful to the trustees of the Isobel Thornley Bequest, University of London, for the financial assistance with the publication of this book.

1

Basque Nationalism from its Origins until the 1950s

Basque nationalism originated in the 1890s in Vizcaya as a response to the rapid transformation of Basque society by the industrialisation which brought massive immigration of workers from other parts of Spain. The immigrants, who came to seek work in the iron mines and steel works, transformed many areas which had once spoken the Basque language, *Euskera*, into Spanish-speaking districts. In their struggle against savage exploitation and harsh working conditions they formed branches of the Unión General de Trabajadores (UGT) and of the Partido Socialista Obrero Español (PSOE).[1] Both the UGT and the PSOE were militantly anticlerical, and were seen as dangerous and immoral by many devout Basque Catholics. The immigrants, apart from their trade union and political activities, merely by speaking Spanish seemed to threaten the stability of traditional Basque society. In addition, many Basques saw the immigrants as morally licentious and consequently as a danger to the ethnically Basque population.[2] Indeed, later nationalist theoreticians argued that Spaniards were racially inferior to Basques.

Until the 1890s the social distinctiveness of the four Basque provinces had produced no nationalist consciousness. The founder of Basque nationalism, Sabino Arana, the son of a Carlist ship-builder, had to invent a name, Euskadi, for the Basque country, design a flag for it, and construct an ideology which would justify the region's claim to independence from Spain. Arana was able to draw on a potent myth which was to be tremendously effective in building a nationalist movement, first in Vizcaya, and later in the other three Basque provinces. The most distinctive feature of Basque society was the language (or group of languages), *Euskera*, which is not Indo-European and has no apparent connection with

1

any other tongue. This fact was enormously helpful in emphasising the distinctiveness of the Basques and justifying their right to
be independent of Spain and France. The singularity of *Euskera*
encouraged the belief that the Basques were a race apart.[3] Naive
versions of Basque history suggested that *Euskera* might be the
language of the Garden of Eden, and the tongue spoken by all
mankind before the disaster of the tower of Babel. The Basques
were thought to be the descendants of Tubal, son of Japhet and
grandson of Noah. It was claimed that they had lived in an
egalitarian, democratic society, where the laws were made by
assemblies of all the citizens, while the rest of the world lived
under tyranny. According to this account, the Basques had fought
for centuries to preserve their independence from foreign con-
querors. In 778, for example, they had defeated the army of
Charlemagne at Roncesvalles. The ancient laws, the *Fueros*, which
were held to be unique to the Basque country, had, it was claimed,
provided a purer democracy than anything existing elsewhere in
the world before modern times.[4] The Basque country, as it had
not, like most of Spain, been subjected to Roman or Moorish
occupation, had escaped the corrupting effect of living under
tyranny, and the contamination resulting from mingling with
those of Moorish or Jewish race.[5].

The Basques had, it was claimed, freely negotiated agreements
which accepted the Spanish King as the lord of Vizcaya and of
other Basque provinces. However, such treaties were not to be
understood as subjection since the King had to rule according to
the ancient laws embodied in the *Fueros*. The racial superiority of
the Basques had been recognised, it was claimed, by a royal decree
granting the citizens of Vizcaya universal nobility. The devout
Catholicism of the Basques, shown by the life of such saints as
Ignatius Loyola and Francis Xavier, was also produced as evidence of their moral superiority over Spaniards. The idyllic
harmony of traditional Basque society was allegedly broken by the
anticlerical and centralising policies adopted by Spanish governments in the nineteenth century. The Basques had seized the
opportunity provided by a dynastic quarrel in 1833 to ally with
Don Carlos, the conservative claimant to the Spanish throne,
supported by the most reactionary forces, in order to preserve
their *Fueros* which were threatened by Liberal governments in
Madrid. The defeat of Don Carlos had resulted in the Basques
being punished by reductions in their rights, although the *Fueros*
remained in modified form. Similarly, after the second Carlist

War of 1873–74, the Basques, once more on the losing side, were
deprived of their customary rights and submitted to the same
centralising laws as the rest of Spain.

In reality the *Fueros* had been granted by the Spanish Crown
and had equivalents throughout Spain before customary law was
replaced by the centralising tendencies of later Spanish governments. Not only had the Basque provinces been an integral part
of Spain, but they had taken a leading part in creating the Spanish
state. It was often pointed out that *Fueros* varied widely in each
province and that there had never been any attempt to create a
unified Basque country.[6] Similarly, the royal decree of 1525
which granted noble status to all the natives of Vizcaya has been
interpreted as a measure to win the support of the population to
the Spanish Crown rather than as a recognition of Basque social
superiority. The *Fueros* did not reflect a primitive democratic
Arcadia, as power remained in the hands of a property-owning
elite, as the franchise was often more restricted than elsewhere in
Spain.[7] Furthermore, the most illustrious Basques had been
servants of the Spanish Crown or the Church.

It was true that the social structure of the Basque country had
been very different from regions such as Andalusia, where large
landowners ruled over downtrodden peasants or landless
labourers. The Basque custom of primogeniture prevented the
extreme fragmentation of land holding which occurred in areas
like Galicia, and encouraged younger sons to leave the land and
serve the Crown as soldiers, sailors or bureaucrats. Good educational standards which produced a high level of written Spanish
accounted for the importance of bureaucrats of Basque origin at
the Madrid court.[8] There seems to have been little conflict
between *Euskera* and Spanish until the late nineteenth century.
Euskera was the language of the home and the countryside, and it
was of no consequence to the authorities that the majority of the
population did not speak Spanish, the language of administration
and public life. *Euskera* was not a written language until the
sixteenth century when Protestant missionaries translated the
Bible and the Catholic Church responded by producing a number
of religious works in that language.

The existence of the *Fueros* was the main evidence produced by
Basque nationalists that the Basques were once a sovereign
people, although the *Fueros* of each province were distinct and the
Spanish Crown had never treated the Basque country as a single
political unit. Nevertheless, the *Fueros* conferred substantial

privileges on the Basques and were popular among most of the population. They stipulated that the Basques were not to be conscripted into the Spanish army, although the local authorities had the duty of raising a militia force. Such an arrangement had obvious advantages for the Spanish Crown in facilitating the defence of a frontier region. The other main provision of the *Feuros*, the exemption from customs duty, was also popular among the mass of the population, and resentment at its abolition was one of the factors which encouraged the growth of nationalism in the late nineteenth century. Until 1837 the customs posts were on the Ebro rather than at the French border or the seaports, so imported goods could be bought cheaply. After the loss of Spain's American empire in the nineteenth century, the rising class of merchants and industrialists, finding the existence of the interior customs barrier detrimental to their interests, petitioned for the customs posts to be placed at the Spanish border.[9] This demand brought the developing bourgeoisie into conflict with both farmers and rural gentry, both of whom benefited from cheap imports.

At the outbreak of the first Carlist War in 1833 most rural areas of the Basque country rallied to the cause of Don Carlos, as the enemy of liberalism. The war was seen by later nationalists as the real beginning of Basque nationalism, and the awakening of the people to regain their ancient rights,[10] although Don Carlos was attempting to conquer Spain for his conservative cause, not lead a separatist movement. The Carlist leadership stressed its conservative ideology, support for the Church and opposition to Liberalism. However, the enormous support for Don Carlos was largely due to the identification of Liberalism with attacks on the *Fueros* and the Church. Local Basque leaders stressed the issue of Foral rights, rather than that of Don Carlos's dynastic claims. The cities of the Basque country supported the Liberal cause of the Queen Regent, María Cristina, and welcomed the defeat of Don Carlos in 1839. In the second Carlist War of 1873–74 the protagonists were the same as in the previous conflict, with the towns and the bourgeoisie backing the central government, while the Carlists retained support of the rural areas. Defeat this time resulted in the abolition of the *Fueros*, leaving the provincial authorities with a vestige of provincial rights, the *Conciertos Económicos*, which permitted them to levy taxes, in order to pay their share of the central government's demands.[11]

The abolition of the *Fueros* was unpopular, even with some liberals who had fought against Carlism because of its reactionary,

4

clerical programme. There were movements urging Foral restorations but these did not evolve into nationalism, until the development of the Vizcayan iron mines brought an influx of immigrants from elsewhere in Spain and produced xenophobic currents in the native population. Sabino Arana drew heavily on nostalgia for the *Fueros* to develop the nationalist ideology, but he also introduced new features to create a modern movement. Arana, influenced by his elder brother, Luis, became a nationalist in 1882 at the age of seventeen and devoted himself to the study of Basque history, language and culture. He spent five years studying in Barcelona between 1883 and 1888 before returning to Vizcaya to begin his political mission.[12]

Although Arana, whose charismatic personality dominated the movement which he founded until his death in 1903, was heavily influenced by his Carlist background, he transformed the Carlist desire for the restoration of the *Fueros* into something quite new — the demand for complete separation of the Basque country from Spain. Arana wanted the restoration of the *Fueros* because he believed that they had once provided the mechanism by which the Basques had governed themselves and could in the future be the means to achieve Basque independence, a programme which had little in common with the Carlist demands for exemption from customs duty and military service. Arana's overriding concern was his belief that the Basque race was in danger of extinction because of an invasion of foreigners whom he considered to be racially degenerate, immoral, non-Catholic and socialist. Basque independence would, Arana considered, make it possible to deny admittance to the Basque country to Spaniards, prohibit intermarriage between them and Basques, restore traditional morality and shut out liberal and socialist influences.

Arana's belief that the *Maketos* (the abusive term he used to describe Spaniards) constituted a danger to the moral health and social purity of the Basques led him to call for measures which would make life uncomfortable for the *Maketos*. Consequently, far from wishing that the immigrants would become culturally assimilated, Arana thought that now worse disaster could befall the Basque race. The most deadly threat which the immigrants presented to the Basques was the social disorder allegedly produced by the PSOE and the UGT. Arana expressed sympathy for the sufferings of native Basque workers, but he attributed their low wages and harsh working conditions to the unfair competition of racially inferior immigrants.

Consequently, Basque workers were urged to organise separately from the immigrants whose expulsion was seen as the way to improve their lot.[13] Arana's substitution of race for language as the distinguishing feature of the Basques did not prevent him from devoting great attention to the revival of *Euskera*, whose main function was to serve as a barrier between the Basques and the *Maketos*. Although Arana's own mother tongue was Spanish, and he learned to speak *Euskera* only when he became a nationalist, he considered that, if Spanish immigrants were to learn to speak it, it would be better that the Basques adopted another language.[14] Similarly, the cultivation of folklore and the encouragement of religious piety served to differentiate native Basques from 'Spanish' immigrants. Nationalists' concern with demonstrating that all of their ancestors had Basque and not Spanish names, and their encouragement of Basque music and dancing, served the same purpose.

Arana's first major work, *Vizcaya por su independencia*, published in 1890, argued that Vizcaya should be independent of Spain,[15] a demand later extended to cover the whole Basque country. Much of Arana's energy went into producing such works, but he also set about creating an organisation to propagate his ideas. In 1893 he addressed a meeting of the Euskalerico group of business and professional[16] men, which had begun by demanding Foral restoration and had evolved towards nationalism. The support of the Euskalericos would have been invaluable to Arana in his efforts to build a nationalist movement, but the members of the group, repelled by his fanaticism and intolerance, refused to join him. However, Arana did begin to build up a following among middle-class people of a similar religious and Carlist background to his own. He consolidated this support by founding the journal *Bizkaitarra* (the Vizcayan) in 1893. In 1894 he founded *Euzkaldun Batzokija* (the Basque Club) as a rival to Liberal, Monarchist and Carlist political associations.[17]

Euskaldun Batzokija was for several years the only organisation which the nationalist movement possessed. Its structure as a social club, rather than a political party, allowed Arana to exercise political control over the movement unfettered by any democratic structure. As Arana's aim to detach the Basque country from Spain was illegal and could have resulted in prosecution, the arrangement helped maintain secrecy. However, a social club was not adequate for the task which Arana had set himself, so in 1895 he formed the Partido Nacionalista Vasco (PNV-EAJ)[18], which elected a regional committee for Vizcaya, although the party's existence was kept secret. The PNV was very different from most Spanish political parties. Far from being merely a machine designed to fight elections, its adherents organised festivals which combined folklore, dancing, religious services and nationalistic politics, a formula which was to be a permanent feature of the PNV's activities. Later PNV leaders were to boast that their organisation was not so much a party as a cultural movement. From the beginning Basque patriotism was equated with loyalty to the PNV.

The PNV soon appealed to a large number of people who shared Arana's feeling that they were threatened by liberalism, socialism and the breakdown of morality, allegedly caused by the Spanish 'invasion'. Inevitably, given Arana's belief that a pre-industrial Arcadia had existed before the massive immigration in the 1880's, the PNV's propaganda emphasised the virtues of rural life. Understandably, idealisation of the countryside appealed to the urban middle-class more than to the farmers, so the party in its early years was strongest in Bilbao. In the rural areas, where the *Maketos* were hardly visible, Carlism remained the leading political force. The PNV's political programme consisted mainly of a demand for the repeal of the law passed on 25 October 1839 restricting the scope of the *Fueros*, following the first Carlist war. The party's lack of a comprehensive programme was more than made up for by the emotional appeal of propaganda which claimed that the Basques were a superior race, and presented a stereotype of the immigrant worker as violent, dishonest and immoral. The social problems associated with rapid industrialisation were all blamed on the *Maketos*, but the PNV's worship of a lost rural paradise did not lead it to decry the process of industrialisation or to attack the capitalists who employed the immigrants. Indeed, Euskadi's high level of economic development was eventually to be produced as an additional proof of Basque superiority.[19]

In the municipal elections in Bilbao in 1896 five PNV supporters were elected. In 1898 Arana himself was elected to the Provincial Council of Vizcaya, although the party's candidate in Guipúzcoa as defeated.[20] Such modest successes were encouraging, but the PNV suffered from severe weaknesses. Most of its supporters came from a Carlist middle-class background and the party had very few capable candidates for public office, nor much influence among industrialists. The PNV greatly increased its strength in 1898 by merging with a section of the Euskalerico group, led by the shipbuilder and shipowner, Ramón de la Sota. The fusion brought the PNV adherents who were wealthy, influential and more highly educated than most of Arana's supporters. Furthermore, the groups merged on Arana's terms, as de la Sota's supporters abandoned their former liberalism and accepted the racism and religious obscurantism which had once repelled them. The support of the former Euskalericos enabled the PNV to launch a daily newspaper, *El Correo Vasco*, in June 1899,[21] which had a much more moderate tone than Arana's previous journals. The tone was influenced by the need to circumvent press censorship, but it also reflected the influence of the former Euskalericos and the enormous difficulties facing a political party in achieving the objective of seceding from Spain.

The Euskalerico group's decision to dissolve itself into the PNV was a result both of its own failure to build any organised support and of the disarray among conservative forces in the Basque country at the end of the nineteenth century. Carlism, which had never been dominant in Bilbao, was in decline, and the most important sectors of big business supported the liberal monarchist, Victor Chávarri, who organised an extensive system of electoral corruption based on local *caciques* (bosses). The monopoly of political power exercised by a tiny group of the richest families of Bilbao through Chávarri's leadership was extremely frustrating for businessmen such as de la Sota, who were not part of the inner circle. Conservative opinion became concerned at the rise of the PSOE which succeeded in having local councillors elected in Bilbao in 1899. The more dynamic sectors of Basque industry needed a party which could achieve mass support and the PNV was the best available candidate. In the municipal election of 1899 five of the party's eight candidates were returned in Bilbao and for the first time it had councillors elected in other parts of Vizcaya,[22] in spite of having hardly any internal organisation. Such electoral success provoked government repression. In September 1899 the Civil Governor of Vizcaya suspended constitutional guarantees on the right to publication and assembly, and closed *El Correo Vasco* and a number of nationalist headquarters.

In May 1902 Arana was imprisoned for five months as a consequence of having sent a telegram to President Roosevelt congratulating him for granting independence to Cuba. In June, the government suspended the PNV's Bilbao councillors. While in prison, Arana made a radical change of direction, which because of his undisputed leadership meant that the PNV's politics also changed. The government's attack on the nationalists forced Arana to reconsider his tactics. After all, if Cuban independence had required the intervention of the United States, it was hardly conceivable that Basque nationalists could achieve their objective by force against the will of the Spanish state. Arana flirted with the idea that an independent Euskadi could be established under the protection of Great Britain, but abandoned it in favour of coming to terms with the Spanish state by calling for autonomy rather than independence. Arana's decision was welcome to the former Euskalericos but was bewildering for his original supporters. Both the liberal and purist tendencies in the PNV were later to present the change as a justification for their own politics. For the most intransigent nationalists the announcement was seen as a legitimate ruse designed to deceive the Spanish government. If the PNV was persecuted for openly proclaiming its nationalism, then the party's doctrine would have to be concealed. Arana's own authority could not be challenged, but as he did not elaborate on his renunciation of separatism in the year between his release from prison and his death from Parkinson's disease in December 1903, his real intentions remained unclear, perhaps deliberately so. In practice, the ambiguity on whether the PNV was committed to complete separation from Spain was to persist throughout the party's existence, and served to preserve its unity by allowing different interpretations of Arana's doctrine.

Although a few months before his death Arana had appointed Angel de Zabala, one of his original followers, as his successor, it seemed that the renunciation of Arana's early doctrine, followed by his death, spelled the end of the Basque nationalism.[23] However, Zabala disobeyed Arana's instructions to create a new organisation dedicated to work for autonomy within Spain rather than independence. The PNV's publications renewed the theme of Arana's early agitation and ignored the *españolista* turn which he had adopted during the last year of his life. As Zabala lacked Arana's charismatic qualities he was forced to share power with the liberal tendency led by de la Sota. Even before Arana's death, the PNV leadership had urged its supporters to vote for the conservative Catholic Urquijo in the elections to the Cortes. In 1906 the liberal wing succeeded in holding a conference which elected a national committee,[24] but Luis Arana, Sabino's brother, who became the party's president, initiated a harsh internal regime designed to maintain the PNV's doctrinal purity. Such intransigence hindered the making of alliances with other conservative forces in order to gain representation in the Cortes and in local government. Yet, as the PNV spread beyond Bilbao and built a more solidly based organisation than most political parties, the doctrinal purity of Zabala and Luis Arana stood in the way of electoral success.

In 1907 when the PNV's moderates supported Fernando Ybarra, one of Bilbao's leading industrialists, in the elections to the Cortes, Luis Arana and Zabala supported a nationalist candidate.[25] In practice, the PNV was split into two tendencies, each with its own journal, *Euskalduna*, backed by de la Sota, and *Aberri* (Fatherland) supported by Luis Arana. The moderate tendency triumphed at the PNV's Assembly held in 1908 at Elgoibar, where a manifesto was adopted which did not advocate secession from Spain, but merely a return to the situation existing before 1839, and stated that the party would engage only in legal activity. In the future, having one grandparent with a Basque name was deemed sufficient to qualify for membership of the PNV, a considerable modification of the party's racial criteria, which had hitherto demanded that all four grandparents should have Basque names.[26] Ramón de la Sota, who directed one of the most dynamic financial and industrial groups in Spain, became the PNV's President and the key figure in its evolution towards moderate positions after 1908. In 1909, de la Sota organised a movement of shipowners and shipbuilders in support of the protectionist measures advocated by the conservative leader, Maura. Such an economic programme was compatible with advocating Basque autonomy, but hardly with secession from Spain.

Industrialists such as de la Sota benefited greatly from the 1914–18 war as the combatants required goods and transport, while the Spanish market did not have to face foreign competition. When in 1917 Santiago Alba, the Minister of the Economy, tried to tax war profits de la Sota led a movement opposing the measure.[27] De la Sota's strategy of allying with other conservative forces was highly successful in 1917, when the PNV did well in both national and provincial elections. The *españolista* evolution of the PNV was highly unwelcome to the purists, and particularly to Luis Arana. In 1910 the party had changed its name to Comunión Nacionalista Vasca (CNV), an indication of both clerical influence and Carlist tradition. In 1916 Luis Arana and a small group of his followers briefly resigned from the CNV, because they disagreed with both the moderate, scarcely nationalist, policies of the organisation and with the pro-Allied stance favoured by de la Sota who had important business contacts with England.[28] The coexistence of intransigent nationalists and advocates of autonomy within the Spanish state inside the same organisation was facilitated by the social conservatism and religious piety which united both tendencies. Luis Arana himself had, in spite of his hatred of all things Spanish, stood as a candidate as part of a coalition with non-nationalists.

Another example of an endeavour which united both tendencies inside the PNV was the creation in 1911 of a trade union for native Basque workers, Solidaridad de Obreros Vascos (SOV) (later STV-ELA).[29] SOV was one of a number of similar attempts elsewhere in Spain to form Catholic unions intended to preserve workers from socialist contagion, none of which was nearly as successful as SOV. Many native Basque workers, especially those employed in small enterprises, identified with their Basque employers rather than with the *Maketos* in the UGT. Nationalist employers such as de la Sota supported the SOV, which was the dominant union in his Euskalduna shipyards. The founding of the SOV was partly a consequence of the PNV leaders' alarm at the success of a general strike called by the UGT in 1910. The SOV was explicitly anti-socialist and in its early years recruited only those workers whose Basque names indicated their racial purity.

The Comunión Nacionalista's evolution provoked dissent among many of its young members who, supported by Arana and Zabala in their journal *Aberri*, in 1921 formed a breakaway party which revived the name of the PNV.[30] The new party reiterated Sabino Arana's original ideas, making little effort to adapt them to changed times. Its paper *Gudari* (soldier) even revived Arana's concern about the moral risks inherent in modern dancing. *Gudari* rejected socialism but was concerned that nationalism should recruit workers and win them away from the class struggle. Although the PNV's ideology was unoriginal it did introduce several new organisational features, such as the formation of mountaineering groups which became bastions of orthodox, radical nationalism. The PNV was influenced by the Irish nationalist movement, from which it took the idea of women's groups which were to become an important feature of the party. The PNV's concern with social and labour questions was

11

illustrated by an article written by its leader Eli Gallastegui in 1923, protesting against an armed assault by the police on the headquarters of the Communist Party. Gallastegui's article provoked a sharp attack from the CNV, which accused him of anti-nationalist behaviour by encouraging class struggle.[30]

In 1923 General Primo de Rivera carried out a military coup which forced both the PNV and CNV into clandestinity and lost the CNV the support of moderate bourgeois elements. The mountaineering groups in the PNV were better able to avoid police surveillance than the larger, but less active, CNV. Illegality encouraged a desire for unity which led to a reunification conference at Vergara in November 1930 as the dictatorship was ending.[31] The ideological basis of unification was a victory for the more orthodox nationalism of the PNV, as it reiterated that the new party (which retained the name PNV) adhered to the doctrine of JEL ('God and the Old Laws'). The congress of Vergara did not produce a united nationalist movement, as a group immediately broke away to form *Acción Nacionalista Vasca* (ANV) which declared itself to be non-confessional.[32] ANV, nearly all of whose members were drawn from the urban middle class in the environs of Bilbao, was an attempt to adapt nationalism to industrial society. It attacked the PNV's racism and declared that those who came to work in Euskadi were also Basques, yet it made the familiar nationalist attack on the immigrants' morality and demanded that native workers be given preference in jobs. The ANV wanted Euskadi to become an independent centralised state, not a federation of provinces, each with its separate Foral rights,[33] an issue which divided Basque nationalism throughout its existence.

The fall of the monarchy in 1931 presented great opportunities for the PNV. Although the Basque nationalists had not been party to the pact of San Sebastián, signed by most of the anti-monarchist forces, including the Catalan nationalists, in August 1930, they could reasonably hope to be granted the autonomy which Catalonia had been promised. The PNV's unity was made easier by the fact that the leaders of the party were nearly all young men who had played no part in the disputes which had caused the 1921 split. These new leaders belonged to the middle bourgeoisie and were of very similar political views. They included the party's President, José Antonio Aguirre, whose family owned a chocolate factory in Getxo,[34] José María Leizaola, a lawyer from San Sebastián, Manuel Irujo, a barrister from Navarre, and Telesforo

12

Monzón, a more aristocratic figure from Vergara, in Guipúzcoa. None of them had anything like the financial or political standing which de la Sota had possessed when he was the PNV's President. The PNV formed an electoral slate with the Carlists and other Catholic forces to contest the municipal elections of April 1931, which precipitated the fall of the monarchy. The electoral alliance triumphed easily in all four Basque provinces. In spite of their conservative politics, the PNV's leaders welcomed the establishment of the Republic, which it was hoped would concede many of the party's demands. In June, together with the Carlists, it organised an assembly of local councillors in Estalla, Navarre, which approved the draft of an autonomy statute.[35]

The PNV's influence was shown in clauses of the draft statute such as that which required ten years' residence in the Basque country as a condition for acquiring citizenship rights. The proposed autonomous Basque state was to have a government elected indirectly by the municipal authorities, which would take over most of the functions hitherto carried out by the Spanish state. It was to have full responsibility for religious affairs, a proposal completely unacceptable to the Spanish left which feared that a reactionary, clerical Basque government would be a creature of the Vatican.[36] In June, in the Republic's first parliamentary elections, the PNV-Carlist alliance had fourteen representatives returned to the Cortes, in sharp contrast to the results elsewhere in Spain, which were a triumph for the left. The consequent alarm on the left was increased by the statements which the newly elected members of the Cortes made in July, at a huge rally in Guernica, before their departure for Madrid, where they pledged that they would fight for the religious rights of the Basque race. Antonio Pildain, canon of Vitoria Cathedral, and member of the Cortes for Guipúzcoa, attacked the injuries suffered by the Church and declared that Africa began at Madrid.[37] In the Cortes the nationalist-Catholic representatives opposed those parts of the Constitution, then being drafted, which provided for a secular state. They refused to vote for the Constitution, because of its secular nature, and left the debating chamber before it was approved in October 1931.[38]

Although the socialists and republicans feared that an autonomous Basque government dominated by the PNV would be a hotbed of reaction, they were prepared to grant an autonomy statute similar to that which was to be implemented in Catalonia. Such a statute would be less far-reaching than that proposed at the

13

assembly in Estella, since the Cortes had ruled that for an autonomous region to regulate its own religious affairs would be incompatible with the new Spanish Constitution.[39] The government set about drawing up a statute which would be in accordance with the Constitution. For most of 1932 and 1933 the PNV endeavoured to get the essential points of the Estella Statute accepted. To the extent that the PNV tried to come to terms with the left, it precluded an alliance with the Carlists whose main motive for wanting an autonomous community had been the prospect that the power to regulate its own religious affairs would counteract the anticlericalism of the Madrid government. At an assembly held in June 1932 in Pamplona to consider the Statute the majority of the delegates from Vizcaya, Guipúzcoa and Alava voted in favour of forming an autonomous Basque region within the Spanish state, but the mainly Carlist delegates from Navarre voted against by 123 votes to 109.[40] The vote demonstrated the strength of Carlism in Navarre, and ended its alliance with the PNV. Consequently, Basque nationalists had to face the fact that the autonomous regions which they wanted would not include Navarre.[41]

At the same time that the PNV's alliance with the Carlists broke down, its relationship with the Spanish government worsened, because of what was seen as the Republic's persecution of the Church. The government's decision to subject the monastic orders to state regulation provoked violent protests in the Basque country, which in early 1933 led to the arrest of several hundred people, including a PNV leader, Telesforo Monzón, and to violent clashes between members of the PNV and PSOE.[42] Nevertheless, throughout most of 1933, it seemed that progress was being made in reconciling nationalist aspirations with the requirements of the republican Constitution. In August 1933, in Vitoria, another assembly of municipal councillors accepted a revised autonomy statute, and elected a committee to supervise a referendum, which was to approve the proposals before they were presented to the Cortes.[43] In the referendum held on 5 November 84 per cent of the electorate in Guipúzcoa, Vizcaya and Alava accepted the Statute. However, progress towards achieving Basque autonomy had by then encountered a new obstacle. The government led by the republican Manuel Azaña resigned in September and the elections held on 15 November produced a right-wing majority in the Cortes and a government headed by Lerroux, the conservative leader of the Radical party.

The PNV's leaders were optimistic that the provisions of the Statute, obtained with so much difficulty from their traditional enemies on the left, would be accepted by a government which should be favourably disposed to themselves, the strongest opponents of socialism in the Basque country. In the elections, the party had stood on its own, now that its alliance with the Carlists had ended, and had emerged as the strongest force with twelve members in the Cortes.[44] However, the Cortes refused to grant the Statute on the pretext that in Alava, where abstention in the referendum had been heavy, only a minority of the population had voted in favour. Faced with such intransigence the PNV's leaders were forced to look for allies on the left. When in July 1934 the government refused to implement the Statute which had been agreed for Catalonia, and the Catalonian deputies left the Cortes in protest, the PNV deputies went with them in a gesture of solidarity.[45]

Nationalist dissatisfaction with the Spanish right was increased when forty right-wing parliamentarians proposed that the law for the tax on wine should be changed. The proposal, which was strongly opposed in the Basque country, would, if adopted, have unilaterally altered the *Conciertos Económicos* which regulated that tax, to the detriment of Basque interests.[46] Clearly, a Cortes which could consider removing existing privileges was unlikely to give the Basque country more self-government. Although a commission of experts was appointed to study the Statute which had been approved in the referendum of November 1933, the statements made by leading right-wing politicians, such as Gil Robles and Calvo Sotelo, showed hostility to conceding real autonomy. Calvo Sotelo's statement in November 1935 that he would prefer that Spain should be 'red rather than dismembered'[47] was shared by a substantial section of the right-wing parties and by many army officers. The government's dispute with the Basque nationalists was just one aspect of the growing tension which was to culminate in Civil War in 1936. In October 1934, the inclusion of three members of the right-wing CEDA (Confederación Española de Derechas Autónomas) led by Gil Robles in the government provoked an insurrection in Asturias, supported by an attempted general strike throughout Spain. Although the PNV's activists and the nationalist union STV-ELA remained neutral, their offices were closed and many of their members imprisoned.[48] The PNV members in the Cortes voted in favour of the government in the aftermath of the Asturias rising, but,

15

nevertheless, the party's leaders were losing hope of obtaining an acceptable autonomy statute.

The commission appointed by the Cortes to study the question of Basque autonomy never reported, because the President dissolved the government in December 1935, and called elections in February. As Spain lurched towards civil war the PNV's leaders were faced with a difficult choice of allies. The left parties were prepared to concede an autonomy statute, but the PNV's members shared the terror of other conservative Spaniards at the prospect of the violence and anarchy which they thought a left victory would bring. The dilemma was to produce contradictory responses by PNV members in the prelude to, and early days of, the military rebellion against the Popular Front government elected in February 1936. In the February elections, the PNV stood alone resisting pressure from the Vatican to make an alliance with the 'Spanish' right.[49]

The spokesmen of the left parties continued to attack the PNV for its clericalism and its collaboration with the right-wing government which had ruled since 1933. However, despite this hostility, the PNV's leaders knew the only forces which were likely to grant Basque autonomy were those which supported the Popular Front, so it now had a vested interest in the survival of a democratic Spain. The abandonment of the demand for independence caused some of its members in the mountaineering association, the Mendiguizales, led by Eli Gallastegui, to found a journal *Yagi Yagi* (Arise) to maintain the purity of Sabino Arana's doctrine.[50] The journal represented an ideological current rather than an organisation and indicated the rejection by some nationalists of their party's evolution towards acceptance of the Republic and away from an alliance with the right. The prospect of class struggle being unleashed by a victory of the Popular Front in the election was as frightening a prospect for PNV supporters as for conservatives elsewhere in Spain. Although the Party's statements proclaimed that class struggle was a product of Spanish injustice and immorality, PNV supporters knew that Bilbao was a stronghold of the left parties and that many socialist workers were ethnically Basque.

The conspirators who were preparing the insurrection which on 18 July was to unleash the Civil War had attempted to involve sections of the PNV. In April, when Telesforo Monzón met with supporters of the Falange and other right-wing forces in San Sebastián, the Party was invited to participate in the forthcoming rebellion. Monzón was, reluctantly, prepared to accept a military dictatorship, but pointed out that although the PNV had a strong organisation its members were unarmed. The party was provided with a small amount of weaponry in return for its expected support for the rebellion.[51] When the military rebellion started, the PNV's reaction differed in each province. In Vitoria, the capital of Alava, Landaburu, the PNV member of the Cortes welcomed what he described as a crusade of regeneration. He appealed to Aguirre, the PNV's president, not to resist the rebel army when it entered Vizcaya, but to limit his action to protecting buildings and people. Landaburu's reaction was partly due to the strength of the rebels in Alava, and also to the influence of the Archbishop of Vitoria who sought an alliance between the PNV and the military rebels.[52] After the rebels had consolidated their power in Alava, PNV emissaries were allowed to go to Bilbao, which was still in government hands, to negotiate with their national leadership in an attempt to obtain the party's neutrality.

In Navarre the rebellion was so immediately successful that the local PNV had little opportunity to take a position on it. In Bilbao, where there was no military rising, it issued a statement on 19 July opposing the rebellion. In San Sebastián, the PNV's leaders also issued a statement opposing the rising, but took no part in the first days of confused fighting between improvised militias of the workers' parties and the forces supporting the rebellion.[53] Left-wing activists were exasperated at the sight of the PNV fortifying churches and their own headquarters against the imaginary threat from the armed workers, who were fully occupied in a bloody struggle with the insurgents defending the María Cristina hotel.[54] Nationalist inactivity in San Sebastián meant that the *Junta* set up to defend the Republic was dominated by working-class parties and trade unions.

Within a few days the PNV moved more firmly into the republican camp, but nevertheless concentrated on building up its own detachments, rather than attacking the rebels.[55] The nationalist leader, Andrés Irujo, suggested that the workers' detachments should concentrate on attacking the rebels in the city of San Sebastán because as urban dwellers they would be more effective street fighters, while the PNV militia should hold themselves in reserve outside the city. The workers' leaders feared that if they agreed to Irujo's suggestion they would be caught i a trap. Later, when Irujo announced, after the evacuation of S Sebastián had been decided, that he would stay in the city to f on, the left leaders suspected that he intended to negotiate with the rebels and insisted that two PNV representatives accompany the rest of the *Junta* in their retreat towards Vizcaya.[56]

When San Sebastián was evacuated on 13 September, shortly after rebel forces from Navarre arrived, the PNV's supporters could congratulate themselves on avoiding a pitched battle which would have cost lives and damaged property. As the republican forces continued to retreat towards Vizcaya the power of the nationalists within the republican alliance increased. On 1 October the Spanish government approved the long awaited autonomy Statute, and a few days later Aguirre was sworn in as the President of an autonomous Basque government at an impressive ceremony in Guernica. In the first weeks of the Civil War, the political situation in much of the Basque country had resembled that in the rest of Republican Spain, as the workers' parties had formed *Juntas* which had taken control of political life. Now the PNV became the dominant political force in the Basque country, because, although Aguirre's government included socialists, republicans and a communist, most important ministries were in the hands of members of his party.[57]

The PNV's hegemony had a profound effect on the way the war was conducted in the ten months before the rebel troops occupied Vizcaya. As the northern front was cut off from Madrid, the precise limits of the autonomy Statute were hardly relevant. There was no attempt at socialisation of industry and large firms continued to operate with scarcely any state control. Drastic measures, including the closure of its printing press, were taken against the anarcho-syndicalist union, the CNT, when it criticised the Basque government.[58] The existence of such a government dominated by Catholics was welcome to the more conservative elements in the republican camp, as it enabled the independent workers' forces to be brought under State control more easily than elsewhere in Spain.[59] Although there was agreement between moderate Spanish Republicans and Basque Nationalists on their attitude to the revolutionary forces, there was conflict over the Basque country's attitude to the rest of the republican territory. For the Madrid government, the regions of Santander, Asturias and the Basque country, all cut off from Madrid, constituted a single military unit, whereas for the Basque government's leaders they did not. There was constant friction between the high command of the Basque government and the regional command of the republican army over the conduct of the war and the Basque government's refusal to send adequate supplies to Santander and Asturias.[60] The PNV leaders' main concern was to alleviate the suffering which the war inflicted on the Basque people. When, on 26 April 1937, German planes destroyed Guernica, the small town in Vizcaya which was regarded as the historic seat of Basque democracy, sympathisers of the Spanish Republic throughout the world saw the bombing as the outstanding symbol of the struggle between democracy and Fascism. For some Basque nationalists it was both a crime of Spain and her German ally against Euskadi, and a warning of the consequences of a war which was not going well.

In Spring 1937, as Franco's troops advanced into Vizcaya, the central government considered that a fortified Bilbao could be defended, just as Madrid had been. Prieto, who in May had become War Minister, sent a telegram to the Basque government demanding that this should be done, but Aguirre and his colleagues were tempted by the attempts of the Vatican and the Italian government to negotiate a separate peace using a Basque priest, Alberto Onaindía, as an intermediary.[61] If Bilbao was defended, there would, inevitably, be heavy loss of life and destruction of property. If the city was captured, the war in Euskadi would be over, and the alliance with the 'Spanish' left, always unpopular with large sections of the PNV, could be terminated. Basque consciences would be clear, as the nationalists would have defended their country as long as possible. Such a view appeared treacherous to both the central government and the 'Spanish' left in the Basque country as the fall of Bilbao would expose the flank of the republican forces, and free the enemy to concentrate its attack elsewhere. The 'Spanish' left considered that, if Bilbao was captured, the Basque army should fall back on Santander and continue the war. Doubts over nationalist intentions were strengthened in May when the central government intercepted a telegram from the Vatican to Aguirre, containing peace offers. [62]

In mid-June, when, after a fierce battle, the insurgents captured the mountain of Artxanda overlooking Bilbao, and an attack on the city was imminent, the socialist leaders and the army commanders wanted to sabotage war industry. Leizaola, the chief Basque government representative, as Aguirre had by then been evacuated, disagreed and made sure that well-armed detachments of the PNV's *Ertzaina* (police) were on hand to prevent sabotage by the 'Spanish' republican troops. On 19 June Franco's forces captured a city with a greater capacity for war production than any they had previously possessed.[63] The fall of Bilbao and the retreat into Santander were seen as serious reverses rather than a final defeat[64] by the soldiers in the left battalions, but for many nationalists the departure from Vizcaya meant that they were now unwilling participants in a purely Spanish war. As the pressure for a separate peace intensified, Aguirre tried to persuade the republican government of the desirability of transporting the Basque forces to Catalonia, to act as a moderate force which would help restrain what he saw as left excesses, but his proposals were rejected.[65] The Francoist forces began their attack on Sandander, facing an army the nationalist part of which was reluctant to continue the war. The death of the popular commander, Saseta, accentuated nationalist demoralisation.

In a pact negotiated between the Italian government and Ajuriaguerra, the PNV's chairman, the Basque troops fell back to the small coastal town of Santoña in Santander, where, on 26 August, they embarked on ships which, they believed, would be allowed to leave the harbour. However, the Italian officers reneged on the agreement and the troops were ordered to disembark and were taken prisoner.[66] As the promised concessions did not materialise, the nationalist troops and political activists were treated almost as harshly as their 'red' allies, and executions commenced as soon as Spanish troops took over from the Italians. The surrender greatly weakened the republican forces in Santander and was bitterly resented by non-nationalists.[67] After Santoña, the war was over for the nationalists, although many left-wing Basques fought on until Sandander and Asturias were overrun. Curiously, a PNV leader, Manuel de Irujo, continued as a minister in the Spanish republican government. The fierce repression, and the betrayal of the agreement made with the Italians, persuaded the Basque leaders in exile to renew their allegiance to the Spanish Republic. The impotence of the non-nationalist components of Aguirre's government was shown by the fact that they had been neither consulted nor informed of the negotiations undertaken by the PNV's leaders.

After the fall of Vizcaya, the entire Spanish Basque country was subjected to the repression which already prevailed in Navarre, Alava and Guipúzcoa. Thousands of nationalists were killed or imprisoned, just as were supporters of the left parties. The military governor of San Sebastián issued an order prohibiting the use of *Euskera* and, as late as 1947, the Minister of Education forbade its use in a bulletin of the women's section of Catholic Action.[68] The mood of the new regime was expressed by José María de Areilza, who was appointed Mayor of Bilbao, in a speech in the bull-ring on 1 July 1937. Areilza declared that Euskadi no longer existed and that Vizcaya was once again conquered for Spain. Elsewhere in Spain the clergy had been, in the main, supporters of the rebellion against the republic. In contrast, in the Basque country, seventeen priests were executed, hundreds were imprisoned, and many more were transferred to other parishes because of doubts about their loyalty to the new rulers.[69] The repression softened after the early years, but the use of written Basque remained outlawed. In some rural areas of Guipúzcoa and Vizcaya, the use of *Euskera* could not be prohibited as most people were not fluent in Spanish, but Basque speakers were often humiliated in their dealings with officials and supporters of the regime. Nationalist politics and Basque culture could find expression only in exile, so Basque hopes for the attainment of democracy became centred on the intervention of the powers who were about to declare war on Germany.

During World War II, the PNV's network of activists gathered information for British Intelligence, in Madrid as well as in the Basque country.[70] For a militant such as Joseba Elósegui, as for the PNV's exiled leadership, the Allied struggle against Franco's allies was a continuation of the war which had begun in 1936. Aguirre, who had escaped to the United States after having lived clandestinely in Germany, declared that the cause of America was the cause of the whole world.[71] Basque nationalists helped Allied airmen and escaped prisoners of war who had managed to cross the Pyrenees, because, understandably, they believed that an Allied victory would restore the freedom which they had lost. Such support for the allies was shared by most of the 'Spanish' left, including the PCE, after Germany's attack on the Soviet Union in 1941. The PCE and many left activists worked with Allied agencies, and the republican leaders were also fervent supporters of the anti-Fascist war.[72] Such political agreement produced a rapprochement between the PNV and the Spanish Republican government in exile, and consequently, an abandonment of the demand for complete Basque independence, although Manuel Irujo, who had set up a Basque National Council in London, drew up plans for a future Basque state which was to include parts of Aragon. The prospect of an Allied victory, which it was hoped would lead to a removal of the Franco regime, strengthened the tendency towards co-operation between nationalist and 'Spanish' political tendencies. In March 1945, most of the parties with strength in the Basque country signed a pact in Bayonne which reaffirmed the legitimacy of the autonomous government formed in October 1936.[73] The declaration provoked revulsion from intransigent nationalists, such as Telesforo Monzón, who refused to accept the authority of the Spanish Republic.

The optimism of the PNV's leaders at the close of World War II was demonstrated by their creation of armed units, trained by American advisers, stationed at the French-Spanish border. However, as the Allies' relations with the Franco regime improved, it became obvious that they would not support an invasion, so in 1947 the units were disbanded.[74] In 1947, a general strike in Bilbao, supported by both the PNV and the republican forces, posed the sharpest threat to the dictatorship since the end of the Civil War. Although the PNV and the Basque government in exile supported the strike, such industrial action was a difficult tactic for a party which included both industrialists and workers in its ranks. The repression following the strike severely weakened the PNV. Thereafter, overt resistance was confined to daring feats such as that carried out by Joseba Elósegui, who hung an *Ikurriña* on the spire of the pro-cathedral of San Sebastián at Easter 1946.[75] On several occasions during 1947 and 1949 a young PNV activist, José Joaquín Azurza, managed to broadcast a tape-recorded message by President Aguirre.[76]

Such actions were rare and hardly important enough to cause great concern to the local police or civil administration. It appeared in the late 1940s and early 1950s that Basque nationalism posed even less of a threat to the Spanish government than did the illegal working-class organisations either in the Basque country or elsewhere in Spain. Such a conclusion underestimated the cultural resilience of the nationalist movement. Although Basque publications were prohibited, the spoken language survived in the rural areas, and many of the lower ranks of the clergy retained their nationalist convictions. In the privacy of their families many Basques continued to celebrate nationalist festivals, absorb nationalist sentiments and nourish the memory of their period of autonomy.[77] Such cultural survivals, which appeared merely nostalgic, were eventually to produce dramatic consequences. The PNV in exile, and its exiguous representation within the Spanish Basque country, continued its policy of co-operation with the exiled Spanish republicans, in the hope that one day a democratic Spain would grant autonomy to Euskadi. However, as the years passed and this strategy produced no success, radical nationalists such as Monzón and the remnants of *Yagi Yagi* rejected the compromises which the exiled Basque government made with the Spanish republicans. Such hostility to Spanish republicans was supplemented by a renewed hostility to the *Maketos* as economic revival brought a new wave of immigrants to Euskadi. Ceferino de Jemein, one of the PNV's leading writers, spoke in 1957 of the immigrants in a tone reminiscent of Arana, describing them as a mass of degenerate 'Koreans', indifferent to how they lived and parasitic on Euskadi.[78] The prospects for Basque nationalism appeared bleak as neither reliance on the United States, alliance with the Spanish Republic, nor a retreat into cultural nationalism offered any prospect of advance.

REFERENCES

1. Juan Pablo Fusi Aizpurua, *Política obrera en el País Vasco 1880-1923* (Madrid, 1975), passim.
2. Juan José Solozábal, *El primer nacionalismo vasco* (San Sebastián, 1977), passim.
3. Martín de Ugalde, *Síntesis de la historia del País Vasco* (Barcelona, 1977), pp. 11-59.
4. Manuel Irujo, *Inglaterra y los Vascos* (Buenos Aires, 1945), pp. 8-9 and 209; Federico de Arteaga, *ETA y el proceso de Burgos* (San Sebastián, 1978, pp. 41-50.
5. Sabino Arana Goiri, 'La pureza de raza' in L. Haranburu (ed.), *Obras escogidas, Antología política* (San Sebastián, 1978), pp. 192-8.
6. Salvador de Madariaga, *Spain* (London, 1942), p. 181; Arteaga, *ETA*, pp. 147-78.
7. Maximiano García Venero, *Historia del nacionalismo vasco* (Madrid, 1979), pp. 69-94.
8. Javier Corcuera Atienza, *Orígenes, Ideología, y organización del nacionalismo vasco 1876-1904* (Madrid, 1979), pp. 28-9.
9. Francisco Letamendía (Ortzi), *Historia de Euskadi. El nacionalismo vasco y ETA* (Barcelona, 1977), p. 81.
10. Eduardo de Uriarte, *La insurrección de los Vascos* (San Sebastián, 1978), passim.
11. Emilio López Adán 'Beltza', *El nacionalismo vasco 1876-1936* (San Sebastián, 1977), pp. 31-2.
12. Venero, *Historia*, pp. 243-51.
13. Arana, 'Los Chinos en Euskeria', *Obras Escogidas*, pp. 181-2.
14. Arana, 'Errores Catalanistas', *Obras*, pp. 185-91.
15. Arana, 'Vizcaya por su independencia', *Obras*, pp. 11-42.
16. Arana, 'Discurso de Larrazábal', *Obras*, pp. 43-9.

17. Larronde, *El nacionalismo vasco, su origen y su ideologia en la obra de Sabino Arana Goiri* (San Sebastián, 1977), pp. 182–97.

18. The Basque title of the PNV is Eusko Alderdi Jeltzalea (EAJ) ('patriotic Basque followers of the doctrine of JEL'); JEL is an acronym for *Jaungoikua eta Lega Zarra* ('God and the Old Laws'). The followers of the PNV referred to themselves as *Jelkides*, advocates of the JEL doctrine.

19. Arana, 'Conócete a ti mismo', *Obras*, pp. 211–20.

20. Larronde, *El nacionalismo Vasco*, pp. 307–9.

21. Corcuera, *Orígenes*, pp. 448–57.

22. Corcuera, *Orígenes*, pp. 457–61.

23. See *El Liberal*, 26 Nov. 1903, cited in Corcuera, *Orígenes*, p. 569.

24. Beltza, *Del carlismo al nacionalismo burgués* (San Sebastián, 1978), p. 165.

25. Ortzi, *Historia*, p. 151.

26. Larronde, *El nacionalismo vasco*, Apéndice VI, pp. 391–2.

27. Ortzi, *Historia*, p. 159.

28. Stanley G. Payne, *El nacionalismo vasco, de sus orígenes a la ETA* (Madrid, 1974), p. 114.

29. Policarpo de Larrañaga, *Contribución a la historia obrera de Euskalherria* (2 volumes) (San Sebastián, 1976–77), passim.

30. Beltza, *El nacionalismo vasco*, pp. 182–3.

31. Garcia Venero, *Historia*, pp. 472–3.

32. José Luis de la Granja, *Nacionalismo y II República en el país vasco* (Madrid, 1986), passim.

33. Ortzi, *Historia*, pp. 176–7.

34. Eugenio Ibarzábal (ed), *50 años de nacionalismo vasco, 1928–1978* (San Sebastián, 1978), pp. 375–92.

35. José Antonio de Agirre y Lekube, *Entre la libertad y la revolución 1930–35* (Bilbao, 1976), pp. 51–84. (The author's name is usually spelt Aguirre.)

36. Juan Pablo Fusi Aizpurua, *El problema vasco en la II República*, (Madrid, 1979), p. 73. For the text of the Statute see Fernado Sarrailh de Ihartza (Krutwig), *Vasconia* (Buenos Aires, 1962), pp. 425–9.

37. Agirre, *Entre*, pp. 104–5.

38. Ortzi, *Historia*, p. 183.

39. Martin Blinkhorn, '"The Basque Ulster": Navarre and the Basque Autonomy Question under the Spanish Second Republic', *The Historical Journal*, no. 3 (1974).

40. Agirre, *Entre*, pp. 269–302.

41. Martin Blinkhorn, *Carlism and crisis in Spain 1931–39* (Cambridge, 1975), passim.

42. Agirre, *Entre*, p. 356; Ortzi, *Historia,* p. 188.

43. Ibid., pp. 364–81.

44. Ibid., pp. 402–8.

45. Ortzi, *Historia*, p. 193.

46. Agirre, *Entre*, pp. 461–4.

47. Richard A.H. Robinson, *The Origin of Franco's Spain* (Newton Abbot, 1970), p.219.

48. Agirre, *Entre*, pp. 544–58.

49. Paul Preston (ed.), *The Coming of the Spanish Civil War* (London,

1978), pp. 169–70.

50. See interview with *Yagi Yagi* supporter Trifón Echeberria in Ibarzábal, *50 años*, pp. 117–29.

51. José María Gil Robles, *No fue posible la paz* (Barcelona, 1968), pp. 710–11.

52. Manuel Chiapuso, *El gobierno vasco y los anarquistas. Bilbao en guerra* (San Sebastián, 1978), pp. 147–56; Ander Landaburu, *La causa del pueblo vasco* (Paris, 1956), p. 14.

53. Author's interview with Luis Arbella, a participant in the fighting in San Sebastián. San Sebastián, 1 April, 1980; Manuel Chiapuso, *Los anarquistas y la guerra en Euskadi. La comuna de San Sebastián* (San Sebastián, 1977) passim; Miguel de Amilibia, *Los batallones de Euskadi* (San Sebastián, 1978), p. 25.

54. Interview with CNT leader, Miguel González Inestal, in Ronald Fraser, *Blood of Spain. The experience of Civil War 1936–1939*) (London, 1979), p. 190; author's interview with Aniceto Gallurralde, CNT secretary for San Sebastián at the time of the rising, San Sebastián, 9 August 1981; Chiapuso, *Los anarquistas*, p. 95.

55. Author's interview with J. Elosegui, San Sebastián, 27 March 1980.

56. Amilibia, *Los batallones*, p. 15.

57. José Luis y José María Arenillas, *Sobre la cuestión nacional en Euskadi* (Barcelona, 1981), p. 104; Hugh Thomas, *The Spanish Civil War* (Harmondsworth, 1971), p. 370.

58. Chiapuzo, *El gobierno vasco*, pp. 142–5.

59. For an account of this process, especially in Catalonia, see Burnett Bolloten, *The Grand Camouflage* (London, 1968), passim.

60. Chiapuso, *El gobierno vasco*, p. 117.

61. Alberto de Onaindía, *Hombre de paz en la guerra* (Buenos Aires, 1973), passim; José Antonio de Aguirre, *El informe del Presidente Aguirre al gobierno de la República* (Bilbao, 1978), passim; also José Antonio de Aguirre, *Freedom was Flesh and Blood* (London, 1944), pp. 57–9.

62. Payne, *El nacionalismo vasco*, p. 247; José Antonio de Aguirre y Lekebu, *De Guernica a Nueva York pasando por Berlin* (Buenos Aires, 1944), pp. 31–9.

63. Amilibia, *Los batallones*, pp. 159–63; Chiapuso, *El gobierno vasco*, pp. 200–20.

64. Author's interview with Antolín Amescua, a UGT militant whose battalion fought on until the enemy forces occupied Asturias, San Sebastián, 4 August 1981.

65. Aguirre, *De Guernica*, pp. 59–61.

66. Interview with Luis Sansinenea, one of those captured at Santoña, in Ibarzábal, *50 años*, pp. 195–213; Aguirre, *De Guernica*, pp. 62–5.

67. Author's interview with Luis Arbella, PSOE member and political commissar in Santander in 1937, San Sebastián, 1 April 1980.

68. Dr. de Azpilikoeta, *Le Problème Basque* (Paris, 1938), cited in Jokin Apalategi, *Los Vascos de la nación al estado* (San Sebastián, 1979), p. 180; Ortzi, *Historia*, p. 270.

69. Ortzi, *Historia*, p. 251.

70. Beltza, *El nacionalismo vasco en el exilio 1937–1960* (San Sebastián,

1977), p. 14.

71. Author's interview with Joseba Elósegui, San Sebastián, 27 March 1980; Aguirre, *De Guernica*, pp. 381-7.

72. Hartmut Heine, *La oposición política al Franquismo* (Barcelona, 1983), pp. 95-107.

73. Author's interview with Luis Arbella; José María Garmendia and Alberto Elordi, *La resistencia vasca* (San Sebastián, 1982), pp. 168-9.

74. Garmendia and Elordi, *La resistencia vasca* (San Sebastián, 1982), p. 178.

75. Author's interview with Joseba Elósegui; Joseba Elósegui, *Quiero morir por algo* (Bordeaux, 1971), pp. 316-20.

76. Author's interview with José Joaquín Azurza, San Sebastián, 18 March 1980; Garmedia and Elordi, *La resistencia vasca*, p. 181.

77. Author's interview with Mario Onaindía, Vitoria, 26 March 1980.

78. Gregorio Morán, *Los Españoles que dejaron de serlo* (Barcelona, 1982), p. 261.

2

ETA's First Steps 1951–1967

In the 1950s the Basque country, like the rest of Spain, was changing rapidly as the Spanish economy began to recover from the effects of the Civil War and political isolation. Both the economic recovery and political factors helped to consolidate the system. When the Allied victory in 1945 left the Franco regime dangerously isolated, it seemed to many of Franco's opponents that his regime could not survive the defeat of Nazi Germany and Fascist Italy, and that the Allies would restore democracy in Spain. In fact, the Allied powers made no serious attempt to remove Franco, and with the intensification of the Cold War, the United States came to see Franco as a valuable ally. In 1953, when Spain signed a pact with the United States which granted America military bases in return for economic aid, Spain's economic and diplomatic isolation was ended.

In the 1960s other influences were to help break down Spain's isolation, as tourism brought foreign exchange and foreign customs, while economic growth in Western Europe provided the opportunity of emigration for Spanish workers. The Basque country, as one of the most industrialised parts of Spain, underwent massive economic expansion, with an increase in demand for labour which could not be met locally. Consequently, there was a huge influx of immigrants from other parts of Spain coming to seek work in the Basque country. Immigration had been continual since the 1890s, but a booming economy was soon to increase the numbers to record figures, with inevitable strains on Basque culture and society.[1] While the absence of freedom of speech, assembly and association distinguished Spain from most of Western Europe, none the less the Franco regime of the late 1950s was very different from the savage dictatorship which had been installed after the nationalist victory in the Civil War. The regime seemed more secure than ever before, and so was able to permit a relaxation of repression.

These economic and political developments presented grave problems for Basque nationalism. While both the Basque government in exile and the PNV were seen by many Basques as their legitimate representatives, the possibility of nationalism regaining power seemed remote. The difficulty was underlined in an influential book by a PNV leader, Landaburu, which recognised that many Basques, including traditional PNV supporters, were prospering under Franco. Such people retained a cultural identification with the nationalist movement, although they had long since abandoned any kind of struggle against the Franco regime.[2] These contradictions within Basque society produced a crisis inside Basque nationalism, whose most important expression was the formation of the *Ekin* group by students of Bilbao University in the early 1950s.[3] The title of the group indicated the nature of *Ekin's*, and later *ETA's* differences with the PNV. *Ekin* means 'to begin', and for the young men who formed the group its creation implied the rejection of the now obsolete and irrelevant PNV.

Ekin members were mainly from nationalist families. In spite of this, they had no contact with the PNV, which they considered had done little since Franco's occupation of the Basque country in 1937.[4] Therefore they thought it was necessary to begin anew. Such an interpretation of history appeared perverse to supporters of the PNV, such as Mikel Isasi, the Party's liaison officer with EGI, who pointed out that *Ekin's* founders began their work only a couple of years after the general strike of 1951, which the nationalists had helped to organise. Severe repression after the strike had weakened the PNV,[5] but its supporters considered that, far from being dead, the party and its youth wing, Eukzo Gastedi (EG), later EGI, were alive and active.[6] PNV supporters were involved in efforts to preserve *Euskera*, and they encouraged Basque customs and folklore through participation in popular festivals, dance groups and choirs. They worked actively in the *Ikastolas*, the illegal Basque language schools, while sympathisers among the clergy used the opportunities provided by the Church's relative freedom to promote Basque culture.[7] This might not have been recognised as political activity by political parties elsewhere, but the PNV had always had a conception of politics which included social life and culture. PNV supporters had fought and died for their cause in the Civil War, when that had been the realistic and appropriate thing to do. In the different circumstances of the 1950s, when armed struggle was no longer possible, the PNV worked in a less dramatic, but equally committed, patient and tenacious way. Moreover, the autonomous government continued to exercise its functions in exile but in close touch with the interior.[8] In the opinion of PNV supporters, the Basque government was neither a relic nor an instrument of the PNV, but the legitimate representative of the Basque people. Political forces which had not existed at the time of the Civil War were welcome to become part of it.

The *Ekin* group, while not challenging the principles of the tradition of the PNV, were highly critical of its conduct of the struggle against Spanish oppression. Their criticisms were expressed most cogently by José Luis Alvarez Emparanza (Txillardegi), the son of the owner of a printworks, who was the dominant intellectual figure in *Ekin*. Txillardegi considered that the existence of the Basque people was threatened in the same way that it had been when Sabino Arana had founded the nationalist movement. The response of the PNV to this acute danger was quite inadequate. Participating in cultural events and producing bulletins describing the oppression of the Basques did nothing to avert the imminent danger of cultural extinction. For Txillardegi, *Euskera* was the key to the survival of the Basques as a distinct people, and he felt astonished that people could consider themselves nationalists while failing to speak, study and propagate it.[9] He also felt that the exiled Basque government had become a relic which represented the generation which had been defeated in the Civil War, but not those who did not remember that struggle.[10] Of the twelve people involved in the discussion group which decided to set up *Ekin*, only seven took the step of forming a clandestine organisation. The group's activities were confined to discussions, and the production of educational material based on Catholic social theory, and whatever nationalist and Basque cultural material they could obtain.[11] *Ekin* benefited from the hermetic cultural and social conditions in the Basque country, which made surveillance by outsiders difficult. The group could expand through personal contact with trusted people from ethnically or culturally Basque backgrounds. The temporarily reduced intensity of repression made the task of creating a nationalist movement possible even though clandestinity remained essential.

Ekin was, inevitably, drawn towards the PNV as there were no clear political differences between the two groups. In 1956, on the occasion of the World Basque Conference, *Ekin* members José Manuel Aguirre and Benito del Valle went to Paris and talked to José Antonio Aguirre, the leader of the exiled Government. It was agreed that *Ekin* should fuse with the PNV's youth group, EG, which now became known as EGI.[12] There were distinct advantages in the fusion for both sides. The PNV obtained a group whose intellectual level was much higher than that of existing EG members. In consequence, *Ekin's* activists could be used to educate EG's members. On the other hand, the fusion with EG (now EGI) gave *Ekin* access to young people, especially in villages, and to circles much wider than the university. The groups were complementary in other ways. EG was activist and scarcely clandestine. Its nationalism was traditional, emotional and untutored. *Ekin* would be able to provide education and theory.[13]

However, difficulties soon emerged. The *Ekin* members were suspicious because EG was not really a clandestine organisation. They considered that it had drifted into being merely a folklore group tolerated by the police.[14] Nor was suspicion confined to one side. The PNV always considered itself as *the* party of the Basque people, not just one political party among others. A group of students who formed their own organisation instead of simply joining the PNV seemed to be behaving with a degree of arrogance, so relations within the united organisation were strained from the beginning. Juan Ajuriaguerra, the main PNV leader in the interior, who was particularly hostile to the *Ekin* group, stated that the PNV would not admit *Ekin*, but would accept those individual members whom it considered worth having.[15] In later years, Ajuriaguerra expressed surprise that a group of people whom he had considered as cautious intellectuals should eventually take up armed struggle.[16] Juan Ajuriaguerra and Mikel Isasi believed that *Ekin's* leaders were arrogant in discounting the PNV's record of struggle,[17] while *Ekin's* founders stressed the need for a more active resistance to Spanish oppression.

The tensions between the two groups were intensified by mutual allegations of being agents of the United States intelligence agencies. The allegations were partly the consequence of the PNV's peculiar structure. There were parallel groups in the interior, the PNV organisation led by Ajuriaguerra, and the '*Servicios*', under the direct control of José Antonio Aguirre, the head of the Basque government in exile in Paris.[18] The '*Servicios*' was an intelligence organisation created during the Civil War which was kept in existence during the Second World War to help the Allied war effort. After 1945, the *'Servicios'* continued to work with the US government. The PNV's reliance on American support was understandable during the early years of the Franco regime. The PNV was a conservative, Catholic party committed to parliamentary democracy, similar in many ways to the Christian Democratic parties favoured by the United States in several European countries, and Aguirre was an admirer of American society and government. When relations between the United States and Russia deteriorated at the end of the Second World War, the PNV supported the United States. The alliance which developed between the Spanish and American governments placed a strain on this relationship. In 1951, when the PNV helped to organise a general strike, which was very well supported, the United States authorities were informed, as they had been about similar efforts in the past. Ajuriaguerra became suspicious that, now that the United States government regarded Franco as an ally, information given to the Americans would be passed on to the Spanish authorities. Consequently, he saw the PNV's allegiance to the United States as a mistake which endangered the security of all Franco's opponents.[19]

José Mitxelena, the chief of the *'Servicios'*, considered that while it was regrettable that the Allies had not honoured their promises to the Basques, if the Cold War was ended by the defeat of Russia, the Americans would no longer need Franco and could finally fulfil their obligations. Consequently, continued co-operation with the USA was essential. The logic of this strategy led Mitxelena to be bitterly hostile to left-wing or activist tendencies. Curiously enough, in the light of ETA's later development, Ajuriaguerra suspected that the *Ekin* group were in direct touch with Mitxelena and the American State Department. Txillardegi, for his part, considered that the PNV was manipulated by the CIA.[20]

Within EGI, the *Ekin* group advocated a policy of liberation through armed struggle, but had no immediate proposals for the launching of such a struggle. The split from the PNV which led to the creation of ETA was caused, not by disagreement over whether violent methods were justified or not, but by incompatibility between a group of activists and a party which saw Basque festivals and cultural events as, in themselves, directly political activities. The growing tensions between the people who had come from *Ekin* and the PNV leadership produced no clear political debate or sharply differentiated positions. In later years, ETA members found it hard to explain why disagreements which did not seem to be fundamental had produced a split.[21] Although the accounts by *Ekin's* founders failed to describe any fundamental political difference between *Ekin* and the PNV, they depicted a climate of suspicion where people on each side were suspected of acting as agents of the American intelligence services. Increasing antagonism, expressed in a highly personal way, made co-operation impossible in local branches which normally functioned as groups of friends. The very lack of clear political divisions which could have been rationally debated made the atmosphere worse. The immediate event which was to make the *Ekin* group leave the PNV occurred when Benito del Valle, a founder of *Ekin*, was expelled from EGI by the PNV's Vizcayan provincial committee on the rather vague grounds of suspected disloyalty. The expulsion did not necessarily herald a purge of the *Ekin* group, as the PNV had a federal provincial organisation. Nevertheless the action was the culmination of a period of ill-feeling which convinced the *Ekin* group that there was no future for them in the PNV, and that they needed to form an independent organisation.

Subsequent statements by ETA's founders have left the reasons for the break with the PNV unclear. For example, Julen Madariaga, a founder member of both *Ekin* and ETA, complained of the PNV's conservatism and its cantonalism (the party's organisation was based on provincial autonomy rather than on a centralised structure for the whole of Euskadi). His distrust was later strengthened by his belief that, after the split, PNV supporters revealed names of ETA members to the police.[22] In another version of ETA's origins published in 1969, Madariaga omitted to mention *Ekin's* stay in the PNV altogether, and stated merely that *Ekin* changed its name to ETA in 1959.[23] Txillardegi, who had been accused by a PNV member of being an agent of the '*Servicios*', subsequently came to believe that the '*Servicios*' were trying to provoke disunity within the ranks of the nationalist movement.[24] In an account written in 1971 aimed at a new generation of dissident EGI members, Txillardegi complained of the slanders which Ajuriaguerra had directed at *Ekin*/EGI members, accusing them of being 'communists, Buddhists and smugglers', and of being infiltrated by the police. Txillardegi also claimed that *Ekin*/EGI was becoming socialist from 1956 onwards, which, if true, would certainly have led to a conflict with the conservative PNV.[25] However, the organisation's statements provided no evidence for Txillardegi's claim. PNV activists attributed ETA's foundation to a generational conflict. The young men who formed ETA were, it was claimed, rebelling against their parents.[26]

In 1959 the PNV appeared even more than the PSOE to be a relic of the past, as its social base seemed in practice to have come to terms with Francoism. Most opponents of the Franco regime regarded the PNV as an archaic survival, even as late as the 1970s, but the emergence of ETA from its ranks, and the PNV's own revival after Franco's death, showed this view to have been mistaken. The PNV's role as a cultural and social movement rather than just a party justified its claim to forty years of exemplary resistance to Francoism, while its opponents could charge that it simply went to sleep. The PNV maintained an organisation in Euskadi, although its activities were rather sparse, after the strikes of 1951. The context of intense cultural activity in which it operated allowed it to continue in existence with a level of political presence hardly sufficient to keep most political parties alive.[27]

The dissident *Ekin*/EGI members for some time maintained that they were the real EGI, but eventually decided that they needed their own identity, so ETA (*Euskadi ta Askatasuna*, Freedom for the Basque country) was formed on St Ignatius's Day, 31 July 1959. Most people chose either ETA or the PNV according to their commitment to a group of friends, rather than individual conviction, in a pattern which was to prove the rule in subsequent ETA divisions.[28] This group allegiance was largely determined by the Basque institution of the *cuadrilla*, a group of friends of roughly the same age who would spend most of their time together, drinking in bars, having meals, or mountain-climbing. In years to come, a *cuadrilla* would often be almost indistinguishable from an ETA group. This social network was to be an enormous advantage to ETA, whose activists were never merely isolated individuals. On the other hand, loyalty to the *cuadrilla* made a deep political understanding almost impossible, as political divisions could not be allowed to split the group, whose members tended to follow the lead of the most dominant member.[29]

In the villages especially, friends, neighbours and acquaintances who understood little of ETA's politics would be prepared to support ETA members who were imprisoned or were forced into exile. In contrast, members of 'Spanish' political organisations, such as the PCE, were socially isolated and even ostracised. ETA's later adoption of a Marxist ideology did not lead most nationalists to see ETA members as defectors from the nationalist cause. A local environment where ETA members were supported, and respected, by people with a variety of political views, and of different social positions, discouraged the growth of specific and therefore divisive ideas. In the 1960s and 1970s, as ETA gained support, the Basque country became highly politicised while, at the same time, the level of political knowledge remained extremely shallow.

Much of the activity of ETA consisted of distributing small lapel badges of the Basque flag at popular festivals and cultural events.[30] ETA, like the PNV, enjoyed the advantage that the cultural world of the Basque country was closed to the police and to state authority generally. ETA recruited members from the mountaineering groups which were a popular feature of Basque life. Cultural and social activities linked to the Church provided a useful milieu, as did the movement to revive *Euskera*. Most of all, the close-knit relationships of kinship and peer groups provided a protection against informers and police detection[31] which activists trying to reconstruct the Socialist Party, the Communist Party or other left groups did not have. Basque nationalists benefited from the general easing of repression in the 1950s. Contrary to the claim made by some nationalists, there was never any serious attempt to prohibit the use of spoken Basque. In fact this would have been impossible in rural areas where some older people could speak very little Spanish. Nevertheless, in the eyes of the regime's ideologists, *Euskera* was dangerous, precisely because it was a symbol of nationalism. Until 1976 the use of Basque names at baptisms or on gravestones was forbidden.[32] Schools in Basque-speaking areas taught only in Spanish, as they had done since public education had existed.

The Church was the main refuge for Basque culture, as the clergy drawn from rural areas of Euskadi remained a stronghold of Basque feeling. Thus the church hierarchy never encouraged any attempt to persecute Basque speech, as priests in predominately Basque areas would have been unable to carry out their pastoral duties properly if they had not spoken *Euskera*. Not surprisingly, the Church was the first to take advantage of the slackening of repression by producing Basque language journals and religious broadcasts in *Euskera*.[33] The creation of the Basque language schools which had begun early in the 1950s owed a lot to the clergy. These schools — the *Ikastolas* — soon ceased to be clandestine, although they continued to be persecuted by the authorities, and the movement which supported them was eventually to involve thousands of people. The revival of Basque language and culture in the 1960s provided a soil where ETA could grow. In May 1960, 339 Basque priests signed a letter to their bishops asking for support for the rights of the Basque people.[34] No other part of Spain displayed such a high level of opposition to the regime by the clergy. ETA's impact on the world outside the circle of PNV sympathisers was tiny until the summer of 1961. Its main activities still consisted of educational and cultural meetings in fairly restricted nationalist circles, and the distribution of miniature Basque flags (*Ikurriñas*) at cultural events. Some propaganda was distributed, but this had to be done extremely carefully, as even strong nationalists were, understandably, nervous about accepting illegal propaganda.[35] ETA's main publications in its early years consisted of *Ekin's* documents and the *Libro Blanco*, a sprawling collection of texts on security, religion and assorted topics intended for internal education.[36]

This situation began to change in the spring of 1961, with the publication of *Zutik*, which was to become ETA's regular journal. Most issues of the publication were duplicated, sometimes in Spain, sometimes in France, and an elaborate network was organised to distribute it. In the future, *Zutik* was to be ETA's main voice, and its pages revealed ETA's internal developments and disagreements, although early issues showed no clear divergence from the PNV. In April 1961 the journal was dedicated principally to a pious account of the social ideas of José Antonio Aguirre, to commemorate his death.[37] An equally respectful account of the life of Jesús María Leizaola, who had succeeded Aguirre as head of the Basque government, was published in the Venezuelan edition of *Zutik*, which since 1960 had been published by a group of exiles.[38] Txillardegi, assisted by other founders of ETA, such as Xavier Imaz, was the main influence on *Zutik* in its early years.

The PNV could be forgiven for seeing ETA as a movement of impatient youth, lacking any firm basis for its split from the parent organisation. Perhaps the clearest expression of the ideology of the early ETA was provided by a speech which Txillardegi delivered in Paris in 1961, where he called for the formation of a National Front of all patriotic elements. It was necessary, he declared, for older people to realise that young people must be represented and that the Basque resistance should realise that the world had changed since the defeat in 1937.[39] Txillardegi's speech was to some extent a confirmation of the PNV's belief that ETA was the product of a generation gap (although Txillardegi was then 30 years old). Accordingly, it might have been possible for the PNV to have kept ETA's allegiance by adopting a more conciliatory attitude. However, it would have been difficult for the PNV formally to accept the necessity of an organised National Front, as the Basque government in exile believed itself to be fulfilling the functions which Txillardegi outlined for that Front. The PNV was prepared to accept that new forces had come into existence since 1937 but insisted that such forces should seek to incorporate themselves into the legitimate government, although by 1961 that body appeared as a ghostly relic of a half-forgotten past, almost as absurd as the exiled Spanish Republican government. It was not attractive to young people, especially after the death in 1960 of the *Lendakari* (leader) Aguirre, a charismatic figure whose death left a vacuum which could not easily be filled.

There was little, apart from activism, to differentiate ETA from its parent during the first two years of its independent existence, as its publication proposed nothing more radical than Christian Democratic measures such as minimum wages and family allowances. Both the PNV and ETA carried out wall daubings and the defacement of memorials commemorating Franco's victory in the Civil War. ETA's commitment to armed struggle did not have any practical consequences until July 1961, when it attempted to derail a train carrying Civil War veterans to a rally celebrating the 25th anniversary of Franco's rising. That exploit, which first brought ETA to public attention, was disastrous for the organisation's structure. Scores of people were arrested, a number of whom were sentenced to long terms in prison, and many others escaped to France. Although, in theory, ETA had adopted a more closed organisation than EGI or the PNV, it was not prepared for the repression which left the organisation paralysed and dismantled. The decision to derail the train was made by Julen Madariaga, as ETA did not have the organisational structure which could, collectively, have decided to take such an action.[40] In a pattern which was to recur throughout ETA's history, a military action was to have disastrous consequences for those involved in propaganda, cultural, or educational work. In turn, the rethinking made necessary by the increased repression was to change ETA's political ideas.

The picture of the average ETA militant given by the descriptions of those arrested was of a young man, from a nationalist family, ethnically Basque although not always completely so, without a university education, but carrying out some skilled job in industry or commerce.[41] These backgrounds were slightly more humble than those of ETA's founders. This general picture of an average ETA militant remained remarkably constant over the years.

In addition to the shock of having their organisation dismantled by the police, ETA's refugees, on arriving in France, had to come to terms with the hostility of the PNV. Despite the bitterness over the EGI split, most people in ETA had considered themselves part of the nationalist family. Faced with this hostile reception, the refugees in France realised that ETA had to reorient itself. They began to make preparations for ETA's First Assembly, which was held in May 1962 at a Benedictine abbey in the French Basque country.[42] The fact that ETA existed for almost three years without having a congress indicated not merely organisational looseness, but its lack of a clear boundary, not only with the PNV, but with the Basque ethnic community generally. Until the First Assembly not only did ETA have no clear structure, but the activities of its members were not clearly distinguished from those of other Basque nationalists. Its members would make propaganda while participating in Basque cultural events in the same way as would other nationalists who had no connection with ETA.[43] The repression following the attempted derailment showed the inadequacy of such a loose organisation. Most of those imprisoned found, on their release, that ETA had become a very different organisation from the one they had joined.[44] The main achievement of the First Assembly was to adopt a Statement of Principles, and to create a more organised structure than that which had existed until then.

The Statement of Principles was a two-page document demanding independence and unification of the French and Spanish Basque country in a democratic state which would guarantee freedom for all religions. The Statement also supported a Federal Europe, and declared that immigrants would neither be expelled nor segregated, as long as they did not act against the Basque national interest. In the future independent Euskadi there would be freedom of speech for all those who did not attempt to impose a dictatorial regime, whether fascist or communist. *Euskera* would be the sole official language, although French and Spanish would be recognised provisionally. Basic industries would be nationalised, trade unions and co-operatives encouraged, and there should be grants for students above the age of 16.[45] Although such declarations did not mark any sharp break with the ideas of the PNV, the holding of the First Assembly and the creation of a more structured organisation did. The founding members of ETA and *Ekin*, although now exiled in France, remained as ETA's leaders. With the creation of a tighter organisation composed of young men with a fervent commitment to create an independent Euskadi, ETA's members discovered that the ideas which they had taken from the PNV and from *Ekin* were a poor guide to developing a strategy in an industrialised society in the 1960s. Restoration of the *Fueros*, participation in cultural events, and idealisation of a golden age had little relevance to much of the Basque population, whether immigrant or native; ETA's attempt to reconcile its original ideas with social reality soon led to disagreements and divisions.

One of the biggest areas of disagreement concerned the attitude which should be taken towards the immigrants. ETA's changing and contradictory responses to this problem were reflected in its publications, particularly *Zutik*. Basque nationalism had arisen in the late 19th century, and had revived in the 1950s, because of the threat which the immigrants were seen to present to the Basque culture and way of life. ETA had originated in a culture which hated all things Spanish, yet it had to come to terms with the fact that half the 'nation' was foreign, being either immigrants or the children of immigrants.[46] In addition large numbers of ethnically Basque people were culturally Spanish. A degree of anti-immigrant feeling and a preoccupation with Basque social distinctiveness was a necessary component of Basque nationalism. Yet a movement whose base was confined to the ethnically Basque part of Euskadi's population, and which looked on the 'Spanish' opposition to Franco as an enemy, condemned itself to a permanent minority position. Although ETA's Second Assembly held near Bayonne in March 1963 produced no ideological change, ETA began to move towards an acceptance of the immigrants as Basques, or at least potential Basques. In 1963 and 1964 ETA began to publish articles sympathising with the plight of those who had been forced by poverty and unemployment to leave their homes and seek employment in Euskadi. This growing sympathy for the immigrants went hand in hand with the development of socialist ideas. Eventually, sections of ETA came to regard immigrant industrial workers as part of the vanguard of a movement which had arisen out of resentment at their existence.

ETA was never to resolve the question of what attitude to take to the immigrants. Complete acceptance of them would have cut ETA off from grass roots nationalist feeling and would have pushed it in the direction of alliances with the 'Spanish' left. In the future, those tendencies within ETA which fully accepted the immigrants tended to substitute the demand for autonomy for that of independence, and bilingualism for that of a completely Basque-speaking Euskadi. ETA's new tolerance of the immigrants produced the recognition that they were subject to considerable discrimination and racist abuse at the hands of traditional nationalists, who now described them as 'Koreans' rather than *Maketos*. In April 1963, *Zutik* was largely devoted to the immigrant problem. In an article, 'The Problem of the Immigration', the attitude was adopted that the immigrants must show that they respected Basque rights before they themselves could expect to receive respect.[47] This ambiguous formulation could mean either that an immigrant should merely have to be tolerant of a language and customs with which he was unfamiliar, or that he was required to learn the Basque language and adopt Basque customs. Later in the same year an article in *Zutik* adopted a distinctly positive attitude to the immigrants, recognising that immigration was a general phenomenon throughout the world, and not the result of a plot by Franco, as many nationalists believed.[48] Immigrants, it was argued, should be accepted, and should join with the ethnically Basque people in their struggle for liberation. This position did not, in principle, conflict with that of the PNV, as the battle for a racially pure Euskadi had long since been lost, but in practice PNV supporters did not accept that the native population were at all responsible for the immigrants rejection of nationalism. Indeed, for many PNV supporters, all of the 'Spanish' teachers and administrative workers were enemy agents.[49]

In practice, the PNV was often more flexible than some of its more chauvinistic statements suggested, as the 'Spanish' origin of some of its adherents demonstrated. Its failure to integrate the immigrants was due to ordinary middle class snobbery as much as to racialist beliefs. In addition, the PNV's deep implantation in cultural and folklore activities, which gave it such resilience, was not an effective method of integrating people unfamiliar with Basque culture.

ETA, as a modern phenomenon, was almost forced to take a more welcoming attitude to the immigrants than did the PNV, although such a development laid it open to the charge of having become 'Spanish'. On the related topic of the attitude to be taken towards 'Spanish' political forces, ETA was more Catholic than the Pope. The PNV was castigated for having, in 1937, carried on the war outside Euskadi, for having served in the Spanish Republican government in the company of communists, and for having made pacts with 'Spanish' political parties. In contrast, ETA declared it would have nothing to do with agreements such as the pact of Bayonne, signed by the PNV together with 'Spanish' parties in 1945, which had accepted Basque autonomy rather than total independence.[50] ETA's evolving differences with the PNV included rejection both of the PNV's racism and emphasis on folklore and of its willingness to accept autonomy within the Spanish state. Such differences in the 1930s had produced both the modernising ANV and the intransigent *Yagi Yagi* groups.[51] ETA was to retain both, ultimately incompatible, criticisms of the PNV in the same organisation.

The renewal of the labour movement opposition to the Franco regime[52] aroused little interest on ETA's part for several years. ETA did, of course, support the right of workers to join trade unions, but did not yet see the working class as the key agent of change. Nor did the 'Spanish' left see the early ETA as a potential ally, as workers in Bilbao and other industrial centres were not greatly interested in the activities of young radical nationalists. This was hardly surprising in view of the history of conflict between nationalism and socialism. The PNV's hostility to the 'Spanish' labour movement had been reciprocated by the Socialist Party, and to a lesser extent the Communist Party, except for the Civil War period. Although the propaganda of the Spanish Nationalist forces during and after the Civil War claimed that they were fighting against 'red separatism', the 'reds' and the 'separatists' in the Basque country were two distinct forces with separate social and ethnic bases. If the revival of the 'red' opposition to the regime, manifested by the strike wave of 1962, did not at first have any great effect on ETA, the position was soon to change. ETA's organisational separation from the PNV made it more receptive to developments outside the traditional nationalist community. Nevertheless, it was difficult for an organisation which had originated in the conservative, anti-socialist, PNV to cross over to the socialist camp. The bridge towards socialist positions was to be provided by the anti-colonialist struggles of the time, particularly in Algeria and Cuba.

Those struggles, seeming to combine socialism and nationalism, appeared for a time to overcome the traditional divide between nationalists and socialists. Nearly everyone in ETA enthusiastically supported Fidel Castro, and later the leaders of the Vietnamese FLN, but the synthesis of nationalism and socialism, which appeared to provide ETA with a unifying theory, did not last for long. For some ETA members, identification with Third World struggles led to acceptance of the claim that Euskadi was a colony and that the way to national liberation lay in a guerrilla struggle, based on Algerian, Cuban or Vietnamese models. Other members realised that the Basque country, one of the most industrialised parts of Spain, was not part of the Third World. They became attracted to a socialist perspective, based on the working class, which in Euskadi was mainly composed of immigrants, or their children, who were among the least nationalist sections of the population.

In the years following the First Assembly, ETA tried to reconcile different strategies. Its journal, *Zutik*, carried articles extolling traditional Basque patriotism,[53] and others supporting the Cuban revolution. Eventually, ETA was to suffer a split between the supporters of a Marxist strategy based on the working class, including the immigrants,[54] and a coalition of advocates of a Third World guerrilla strategy, and others such as Txillardegi who maintained the traditional nationalist rejection of all things Spanish. The basis of the guerrilla strategy was to be provided by the book *Vasconia*, written by Federico Krutwig, under the pseudonym of Fernado Sarrailh de Ilhartza. *Vasconia*, published in Buenos Aires in 1962,[55] was important both for its contents and for the impression it made on ETA and on others, even though its length (638 closely-printed pages) must have reduced the number of its readers. Its importance for ETA lay in its attempt to provide a theory of Basque nationalism which would be adequate for the modern world, and specifically a strategy of guerrilla warfare, based on the experience of Third World national liberation movements. ETA first heard of *Vasconia* through denunciations of the book in the Spanish right-wing press, which presented its author as ETA's leading theoretician, a false accusation which was later to become true.[56] The extreme violence of Krutwig's language made the book an easy target for attack. So did the racist concepts which harped back to the ideas of Sabino

Arana. The PNV's press responded with outrage to *Vasconia*, and to newspaper allegations that ETA remained a branch of the PNV and that Krutwig's book expressed the party's ideas. An article in *Alderdi*, the PNV's journal, and a statement by the party's Guipúzcoa provincial committee bitterly attacked *Vasconia* and its author, accusing him of being a coward whose objective was to discredit the PNV. Furthermore, the statement complained that while declaring himself a defender of the Basque race, Krutwig did not have a drop of Basque blood in his veins.[57]

Alderdi's observation that Krutwig was of non-Basque origin was true, as although born in Vizcaya in 1922 he was of mixed Italian and German descent. Although virulently racist[58] his main preoccupation was with language. He had been a member of *Euzkalzaindia* (the Academy of the Basque Language) in Vizcaya from 1942 to 1953, where he worked to create a unified literary language which would supersede the various Basque dialects.[59] He had gone into exile in 1953, after making a speech which violently attacked the Basque clergy for their failure to preach in *Euskera*. Krutwig's belief in the key role of language was to form the basis of an alliance with Txillardegi, who had held similar views since the founding of *Ekin*. ETA's first reaction to *Vasconia*, while less hostile than that of the PNV, was not enthusiastic. In a review of the book, Txillardegi welcomed its appearance, but objected to the virulence of its criticism of the PNV.[60]

Vasconia argued that Euskadi was more oppressed than the colonies which had been subjected to European imperialism, and that the only way to achieve independence was through a war of national liberation, beginning with small guerrilla actions.[61] Krutwig drew this conclusion from his analysis of the anti-colonial struggles following World War II, notably in Algeria. He did not claim that the war of liberation would take exactly the same form in Euskadi as in Africa or Asia, as the much higher levels of skill and education of the population in Euskadi would make it much harder for the occupying forces to carry out repressive policies.[62] Nevertheless, the process of the liberation struggle was seen as essentially the same as that which Krutwig thought had taken place in Algeria.

Krutwig's enduring contribution to ETA's strategy was his theory of the cycle of action/repression/action, which held that, where popular protest against injustices met with oppression, the revolutionary forces should act to punish the oppressors. The occupying forces would then retaliate with indiscriminate violence, since they would not know who the revolutionaries were, causing the population to respond with increased protests and support for the resistance in an upward spiral of resistance to the dictatorship. Krutwig's examples of the kind of actions which the resistance should undertake were both colourful and sadistic. He insisted that it would be necessary to use torture against the torturers of the occupying forces.[63] The families of torturers should be killed, while terrorism should be employed against the police and administrators of the oppressor state. Nor should the war be confined within the nation's frontiers. Families of embassy staff should be kidnapped or killed and passenger ships should be blown up. The USA should be punished for its support of the Spanish dictatorship. American troops should be slaughtered. It was irrelevant whether an individual Yankee was guilty or not, as the United States was an ally of the oppressor.[64]

As the armed struggle escalated, there would be a development of a parallel system of administration, which would gradually take over the functions of the colonial power. The high level of education in Euskadi would make it easier to create a parallel administration than in other colonial countries. After independence had been won the old colonial administration should be expelled. Krutwig warned that as a system of dual power developed, the Spanish government was likely to offer talks. If this should happen, it was essential that the revolutionaries should beware of giving in to the weariness with violence of the general population. Nothing less than complete independence should be accepted. Those Spanish immigrants willing to integrate themselves into Basque society would be welcome to remain in the new, independent Euskadi, but those not willing to do so would be expelled.[65] Krutwig believed that in the Basque country the memory of primitive communism which had once existed would make it easy to introduce a communist system where industrial and agricultural pursuits would be combined in communal enterprises. Spain would be in a catastrophic situation after Euskadi and Catalonia became independent, but that was of no concern to the Basques.[66]

The influence of *Vasconia* on ETA became apparent with the publication of the booklet, *Insurrección en Euskadi*, written by José Luis Zalbide, an engineering student and leading member of ETA, in 1963 under the pseudonym of K. de Zumbeltz.[67] *Insurrección en Euskadi* was largely a condensation of the parts of

Krutwig's book which dealt with armed struggle. It concentrated on the guerrilla struggle ignoring the philosophical and historical questions examined by Krutwig, and reiterated Krutwig's theory of action/repression/action. Successful guerrilla actions, Zalbide argued, would make the enemy forces lash out blindly in their rage against attackers whom they were unable to identify, so they were bound to commit atrocities and attack innocent people. The general population, which would have, until then, been passive, would retaliate by supporting the armed resistance forces. Zalbide saw the objective of the guerrilla forces as being to create chaos and to destroy the legitimacy of the oppressor rather than physically drive the enemy troops out of Euskadi. He accepted that, as Euskadi was highly industrialised, the urban guerrilla would be more important than the war in the countryside, and he repeated Krutwig's injunctions on the need to create a parallel system of administration.[69] Like Krutwig, he believed that the high level of education in Euskadi, and the existence of large numbers of people with administrative experience, would make this task much easier than it had been in underdeveloped countries. In the later stages of the revolutionary war, the guerrillas would probably control large sections of the country, so that by the time independence was achieved the secret parallel administration would be ready to take over, quite smoothly. Any shortage of administrators would be met by the return of educated Basques now living abroad.

Zalbide, like Krutwig, mixed broad strategic conceptions with detailed instructions on the best methods of armed attack. The best time would be around midnight — the guerrillas should attack under cover of darkness and would then have until dawn to make their escape.[69] Sometimes the attackers should terrify the enemy with shouts, while at other times they should attack in complete silence. Sometimes the enemy should be surprised by guerrillas dressing in their own uniforms, and then opening fire at point-blank range. On the march there should be no smoking or talking and lights should not be carried.[70] Zalbide's thesis was adopted as ETA's policy at the Third Assembly, which was held in April and May 1964. Yet the ideas expounded there had little relevance to the actual activities of wall daubing and cautious agitation which ETA practised. ETA did not have the resources, training or arms even to begin the kind of campaign proposed by Krutwig and Zalbide. Its first armed robbery, which took place in September 1965, was unsuccessful and led to Zalbide's arrest.[71]

The eventual turn to armed struggle was to be sparked off by circumstances which had little to do with Krutwig's theory.

One important organisational change initiated after ETA's First Assembly was the creation of *liberados*, full-time activists who lived in clandestinity and devoted all their energies to the organisation.[72] Such a development substantially increased ETA's need for money. So too did the regular publication of *Zutik*, whose production and distribution became ETA's central activity. The most obvious source of finance was contributions from nationalist supporters, who could be expected to give financial aid to ETA, without necessarily sharing all its views, or even understanding what they were. Such contributions were at first completely voluntary, but an element of compulsion began to emerge.

In September 1964, ETA announced that, as all Basques had a legal and moral duty to support the resistance to the oppressor, ETA would forcibly ensure that people carried out this duty, just as a government of an independent country would insist that citizens paid their taxes.[73] However, ETA in 1964 lacked the infrastructure and perhaps the will to impose any systematic forced contributions to its funds, although there were specific incidents of bringing pressure on individuals to make them donate money.[74] For example, in November 1964 ETA responded to allegations by a prominent exiled PNV member, Ramón de la Sota, that it had tried to extort money from him, charges which had resulted in the expulsion of leading ETA members from the French Basque country. According to ETA, there had been no attempt at extortion. De la Sota had, at first, volunteered to give money to ETA, and had wanted his sons to be accepted as members. A sudden change of mind on his part produced a confrontation.[75] As a result of de la Sota's allegations, Txillardegi, Julen Madariaga and Benito del Valle were expelled from the French Basque country, and were no longer able to directly oversee ETA's activities. In August 1965, when ETA announced that it intended to acquire the resources it needed to carry on the struggle for national liberation, assurances were given that such requisitions would be carried out very carefully, and that nothing would be taken from anyone who could not afford it.[76]

The expulsion of ETA's founders from the French Basque country accentuated the tendency, initiated by the flights into exile in 1961, for the actual leadership to be exercised by younger men. This new leadership was consolidated at ETA's Fourth

Assembly, the first to be held in the interior, in summer 1965, which adopted a socialist ideology, and set up a Political Office to carry out most of the functions hitherto performed by the Executive. Zalbide had, in 1965, become ETA's dominant figure and the leading contributor to *Zutik*, whose contents reflected his own melange of nationalist, socialist and Third Worldist ideas.[77] Besides Zalbide, the leaders in the interior were grouped around the Political Office, whose leading members were Patxi Iturrioz, a founding member of ETA, and Eugenio del Río, a younger man with a non-nationalist background, whose influence grew in 1965 and 1966. The ascendancy of Iturrioz and del Río, which increased after Zalbide's arrest in September 1965, and the flight of other key members consolidated the Marxist tendency, which was to concentrate on socialist propaganda and industrial agitation, to the dismay of ETA's founders.

The new interior leadership in the Political Office was greatly influenced by the rising tide of working-class struggle which amounted to the reconstitution of the labour movement, after the long years when the repression had made any permanent organisation practically impossible. The Worker's Commissions, which had arisen in the strike wave of 1962, became permanent, structured, although clandestine organisations.[78] It was hardly surprising that the Political Office, based in San Sebastián, which contained people with a higher intellectual level than most of ETA's members, should see the working class as the main force in overthrowing the dictatorship. After all, young men of rather similar backgrounds in the Basque country and elsewhere in Spain were joining the PCE or the Frente de Liberación Popular (henceforth FLP), an organisation originating in a left Catholic milieu, in an attempt to assist working-class struggles. ETA's interior leadership now sought to intervene on this terrain, although the attempt to do so presented a number of difficulties. The working-class movement in the Basque country had a tradition of organisation going back to the founding of the UGT and the PSOE in the late nineteenth century. Since its beginning, the labour movement had been bitterly attacked by the Basque nationalists. Indeed, the formation of the PNV was largely a reaction to the rise of the socialist and trade union movement.

There seemed little likelihood that workers, especially in Spanish speaking areas, would accept the leadership of a radical nationalist group with no history of involvement in industrial struggle. Nor could ETA bring much, except commitment, to

46

such a struggle, as its middle-class social composition and implantation in the smaller towns and rural areas hardly qualified it to lead such activities. Moreover, involvement in trade union work inevitably put the National Front of all patriotic Basques, both workers and employers, into question. While both ETA and the PNV supported the rights of workers to join trade unions, the social base of both organisations could hardly be enthusiastic about strikes, which would harm all employers, whether they were supporters of the PNV or of Franco's regime. The key sectors of the working class were Spanish-speaking and generally indifferent to one of ETA's basic objectives, the revival of the Basque language. Nor did the demand for the unification of the four Spanish Basque provinces with the French Basque country, to form an independent Euskadi, spark any interest among industrial workers in Bilbao or elsewhere.

Inevitably, involvement in the working-class struggle was to change ETA's method of working. This was soon apparent in the organisation's journal *Zutik*, which began to be filled with socialist propaganda and articles supporting the workers' struggle.[79] These were, naturally, written mainly in Spanish, the language of the group at which they were directed. ETA's tradition provided it with no clear strategy for intervention in such struggles, a failing which placed it at a disadvantage with its competitors in the PCE and even the Euskadiko Sozialisten Batasuna (ESBA), the Basque branch of the FLP. ETA found the theory it needed in a group of then fashionable writers, Andre Gorz, Lelio Basso, Ernest Mandel and Serge Mallet, who sought a way to awaken the working-class movement from the passivity caused by the long boom following World War II, through a strategy of radical or structural reforms, as opposed to mere wage demands. That strategy was intended to avoid, on the one hand, the danger of incorporation into the capitalist system produced by orthodox social democratic practice, and on the other hand the utopianism of demands to seize power.

Such demands, which would have appeared fanciful in the Spain of the 1940s and the 1950s, seemed by the mid-1960s to be much more plausible because of the considerable liberalisation which was taking place in many areas of Spanish society. For example, the press law introduced in the spring of 1966 by the Minister of Information and Tourism, Manuel Fraga, considerably increased the ability of the press to report and comment on events. Responding to such developments, ETA's interior leadership adopted a more open style of work. In 1965 and 1966 *Zutik* changed from being a journal filled with a mixture of short news reports, items on Basque culture and emotional attacks on the Spanish occupation, to provide some rather impressive analysis of the changing political and economic situation, in both the Basque country and the rest of Spain.[80] The possibility of the Spanish and Basque capitalists removing Franco, while retaining the capitalist system, was discussed, as was the need for the working class to be prepared to fight this potential new capitalism.

In their efforts to understand the social reality of the Basque country, the leaders of the Political Office were forced to reject some of the basic tenets which ETA shared with other Basque nationalists. As Euskadi was an industrial society, class struggle was more relevant than guerrilla war. If the working class was the key force in society, ETA had to accept the fact that the core of it was either immigrant or culturally Spanish, and did not, for the most part, see ETA as relevant to its struggle. The Political Office leaders were drawn to the conclusion that it was impossible to overthrow the regime which oppressed the Basque people unless there was a revolution throughout Spain. Attempts to win working class and immigrant support had to cope with the existence of virulently chauvinistic attitudes towards the immigrants within the nationalist community.

The logic of their analysis led ETA's interior leadership not only to abandon the elitist strategy of armed minority action in favour of one of mass struggle, but to attack the notion of unity with the Basque bourgeoisie,[81] and to support the Workers' Commissions. Acceptance of the immigrants as full members of Basque society necessarily clashed with the traditional nationalist view that they were oppressors of the Basque people. The realisation that Euskadi's liberation depended on the overthrow of the Franco regime implied that it was necessary to ally with 'Spanish' forces both in Euskadi and in Spain as a whole. Once these conclusions had been accepted, little remained of ETA's original objectives. The defence of *Euskera* became a matter of fighting for equality of treatment with Spanish, and the demand for the unification of the French and Spanish Basque country became irrelevant. As ETA seriously tried to recruit immigrants, it was faced with its own heritage of the virulent chauvinism so forcibly expressed by Basque nationalism's founder, Sabino Arana. The radically changed contents of *Zutik* became the main point of contention in the dispute which was to culminate in the split which

ETA suffered at the Fifth Assembly at the end of 1966.

From his exile in Belgium, Txillardegi watched the development of ETA and particularly of the contents of *Zutik* with growing alarm. In his view, the leadership in the Political Office were betraying all that ETA had stood for. Their advocacy of a Marxist-inspired class front made the formation of a National Front of Basques of all social classes impossible. Txillardegi was appalled at what he regarded as *Zutik's* abandonment of any concern with Basque culture and language. It seemed to him that ETA was being transformed from a patriotic movement, dedicated to national liberation, into a dogmatic communist party. His criticism, expressed at first in letters to the Political Office, and later in the journal *Branka*,[82] centred on the growing Marxist tone of *Zutik*, the neglect of the language question, and failure to press for the formation of a National Front for the reunification of Euskadi, including Navarre and the French Basque country. Txillardegi based his case against the leaders in the Political Office principally on the contents of *Zutik*, which had, he alleged, ceased to be a patriotic nationalist organ. Its contents showed that the interior leadership had become traitors to Euskadi.[83]

Txillardegi had, from exile, continued to write for the journal, but none of his articles were published after early 1965. He had been angered by an article in *Zutik*, published in May 1965, which argued that the reactionary ideology of many nationalists prevented the integration of immigrant workers into the patriotic movement.[84] Throughout 1965 and 1966 Txillardegi's criticism of the Political Office intensified. He alleged that their obsession with Marxism and neglect of the Basque language were converting ETA into a 'Spanish' organisation. The first reaction of the interior leadership to Txillardegi's criticism was conciliatory. In a communication sent to him in March 1966, they accepted that they had been at fault in neglecting the Basque language, but denied that ETA had become dogmatically Marxist.[85]

The explanations of the interior leaders did not satisfy Txillardegi, who now began to make his criticism public. In a number of articles, he alleged that ETA had been taken over by Euskadiko Sozialisten Batasuna (Basque Socialist Unity) (EBSA), the Basque wing of the FLP, and demanded that the people who, he claimed, had infiltrated ETA be expelled.[86] Txillardegi demanded a reiteration of the ideological principles adopted at ETA's First Assembly in 1962, which stated that ETA's first task was to strengthen the Basque language. This would also be the main priority of a future government of an independent Euskadi, which would ensure that after a transitional phase, all teaching, press, radio, television and administration would be carried out exclusively in *Euskera*. As Basque was not yet adequate for all specialised and technical needs, the teaching of languages such as Russian, German, English and Esperanto would be encouraged. Txillardegi argued that the future independent Euskadi should include parts of Rioja, Jaca (in Aragon) and Béarn. Anti-immigrant chauvinism by the native population would be prohibited, as would all acts by the immigrants which were objectively imperialist. In Txillardegi's view, immigrants who retained their Spanish language and culture, or supported a Spanish political party, were behaving in an imperialist way.

Txillardegi's criticism grew harsher as he became more convinced that the line of the Political Office was not produced by error, but was explained by 'Spanish' infiltration and takeover of ETA's interior leadership. Txillardegi argued that some activists, once they discovered the class struggle, forgot all about cultural and ethnic oppression. Such people, he declared, embraced Marxism as a religion and failed to make any examination of the actual conditions of Basque society. Interestingly, in view of Txillardegi's later alliance with those advocating guerrilla warfare, he criticised advocates of such a strategy for Euskadi as abstract dogmatists. It would be a grave error to convert ETA into a Marxist-Leninist Party. It should remain a broad movement with room for different tendencies within it. As Txillardegi, supported by ETA's other founders, came to the conclusion that the interior leaders in the Political Office had betrayed ETA's principles, he began to work towards their removal. In the struggle to gain control of ETA, the old leadership had the advantage of their prestige as founders of the organisation. However, their condition as exiles made it very difficult to win adherents among the activists in the interior. The interior leadership had succeeded in building up a much more structered organisation than had existed in ETA's early years and had gathered around them a cadre of militants whose intellectual level was quite high. ETA was beginning to go beyond the stage when its principal activities consisted of wall-daubing, defacing of monuments to Franco's victory, and participation in cultural events.

ETA's founders knew that their own ideas were much more in tune with the simple patriotism of the average ETA member than the Marxist theories of the interior leadership. However, to gain control over ETA, the old leadership had to get in touch with the base. The problem was accentuated by the shortage of capable and politically sophisticated people among their supporters. As Txillardegi and his associates were not themselves able to go to the Spanish Basque country, they made contact in the summer of 1966 with several younger exiles who resented the failure of the Political Office to develop the armed struggle. The main activist in the campaign was a medical student from Navarre, José María Escubi, who crossed the border with several other exiles loyal to himself, in order to create an opposition to the interior leadership,[88] in spite of the fact that a police record should have disqualified him for underground work.

Escubi found his main allies in the brothers José Antonio and Juan María (Txabi) Etxebarrieta. José Antonio, the elder brother, who was not then an ETA member, was one of the few people capable of providing a political challenge to the leadership of the Political Office.[89] With the help of the Etxebarrietas and the returned exiles, Escubi set about organising an Assembly. When Iturrioz, the only member of the interior leadership who had been elected to the executive at the Fourth Assembly, in 1965, met the other members of the executive in France, he was told that he was expelled on the grounds of having abandoned ETA's principles.[90] Escubi, acting in the name of the exiled leadership, organised the Fifth Assembly, which began on 7 December 1966 at a church hall in Gaztelu in Guipúzcoa, where the parish priest was a sympathiser, and later a member, of ETA. The Assembly had not been preceded by a political discussion at the base, or by the election of delegates. In many cases, Escubi selected the participants on no other grounds than that they were activists.[91]

Supporters of the Political Office were surprised that none of its members were present at the Assembly, and even more so that the first item on the agenda was the ratification of the executive's expulsion of Iturrioz. They asked that Iturrioz should be allowed to present his case against expulsion, and when this request was refused, they declared that the Assembly was fraudulent and consequently refused to take part in it. The majority of those present accepted the legitimacy of the Assembly and voted for Iturrioz's expulsion.[92] The minority, who for reasons of security were prevented from leaving the premises, were kept in a separate room where they discussed how they would carry on with the struggle in spite of the coup which had occurred. Escubi and the Etxebarrieta brothers were successful in establishing their claim to

51

be ETA's authentic leaders. The supporters of the Political Office still considered themselves the genuine ETA, although it was soon apparent that Escubi's coup, although based on fraudulent selection, did represent the feelings of the majority of grass-roots activists.

The minority who adopted the name of ETA-Berri (the new ETA) continued with their socialist propaganda and participation in the Workers' Commissions, regarding folklore activities and wall-daubing as contributing little to the creation of the revolutionary Marxist party which they believed was necessary to achieve an independent socialist Euskadi. They argued that the group which had, by undemocratic means, taken control at the Fifth Assembly, had no right to consider itself the official organisation.[93] The majority at the Assembly sometimes called themselves ETA-Zaharra (the old ETA), sometimes ETA-Bai (ETA-yes), to distinguish themselves from ETA-Berri, whom they saw as having tried to liquidate the organisation. However, they generally used the title ETA without suffixes, as they were anxious to establish that there was only one genuine ETA, and generally referred to ETA-Berri as the '*Likis*', i.e. liquidationists.[94] The Marxist or '*españolista*' tendency, ETA-Berri, considered that their own evolution towards Marxist positions was a logical development from ETA's adoption of socialism at the Fourth Assembly in 1965, and continued to move away from ETA's original nationalism. The evolution of ETA-Berri was demonstrated in a pamphlet published in early 1967, shortly after their expulsion, which attacked the ideas of their former comrades, as expounded in the documents adopted at the Fifth Assembly.[95]

According to the ETA-Berri pamphlet, the majority at the Fifth Assembly had deviated from the socialist line adopted at the Fourth Assembly. ETA-Berri's members continued to consider themselves popular nationalists as distinct from the conservative nationalists of the PNV and, in their opinion, of the rival branch of ETA. The resolutions adopted at the Fifth Assembly were criticised for containing an idealist vision of the Basque people as an ethnic group whose essence lay in the Basque language. In contrast, ETA-Berri, it was declared, would continue to fight for *Euskera*, not least because the unjust discrimination against it constituted an obstacle to working-class solidarity. ETA-Berri would fight to achieve working class unity and would struggle against the reactionary and chauvinistic tendencies which existed within the ethnically Basque population. The pamphlet, while it maintained ETA-Berri's claim to be nationalist, based itself on the actual Basque population, both native and immigrant, Basque and Spanish speaking. This political stance was to lead ETA-Berri towards unity with Marxist groups elsewhere in Spain.

Another pamphlet published early in 1967 developed ETA-Berri's conception of popular nationalism,[96] by emphasising the importance of the working class, while continuing to call for a patriotic front which would include professional people and small employers. ETA-Berri's concentration on industrial and economic struggles brought it, inevitably, into conflict with employers, whether supporters of the PNV or of Spanish centralism. Consequently, ETA-Berri continued its move away from nationalism, free from the need which the rival branch of ETA had, to devise formulae which would win support from the conservative base of the PNV. While its opponents' charge that ETA-Berri had ceased to be nationalist was largely justified, the organisation continued to present itself from 1967 to 1969 as the legitimate ETA. ETA-Berri made no attempt to deny the changes in ideology which had taken place but maintained these had not been the result of a coup, as Txillardegi and Krutwig alleged,[97] but had happened over a long period, as a result of experience in struggle.

In August 1969 ETA-Berri's version of *Zutik* announced that it would henceforth abandon the title ETA-Berri, and would no longer use *Zutik* as the name of its journal. The organisation was renamed Komunistak (The Communists) which also became the title of its journal. The change had been preceded by a lengthy period of criticism of the whole Basque nationalist tradition.[98] An article in the first issue of *Komunistak* made a ferocious attack on the racism of the founder of the nationalist movement, which was bound to cause outrage among nationalists whether of left or right.[99] In the next number José Uribe attempted to settle accounts with ETA's traditions through an examination of the rival branch of ETA; Uribe's article criticised the fetishisation of *Euskera*, the racist tone of ETA's publications and the absurdity of the claim that Euskadi was a colony. He argued that the rival branch of ETA (now the only ETA) gave a socialist tone to the traditional racism of the nationalist movement.[100]

On abandoning nationalism the leaders of ETA-Berri had no clear attitude to the various factions on the 'Spanish' left, contrary to the claims made by their enemies within ETA that they were pawns of the FLP/ESBA group. One of the charges made against the leaders of the Political Office, before their expulsion from

ETA, was that they supported the PCE's line of participation in the elections for workplace representatives to the official *Sindicatos*. In fact, the early ETA-Berri always had differences with the PCE, but its criticisms were made at first in moderate tones. For example, on the fiftieth anniversary of the Russian Revolution, the Soviet bureaucracy was subjected to mild criticism.[101] Following the student revolt in May 1968 in France, and the Russian invasion of Czechoslovakia in August of the same year,[102] Komunistak adopted a Maoist ideology and denounced the Soviet leaders and their Spanish supporters as counter-revolutionaries.

Komunistak, after merging with several tiny dissident communist groups from other parts of Spain, became the Movimiento Comunista de España (henceforth MCE) in 1972.[103] Adoption of Maoism involved an acceptance of the need to build an alliance of all patriotic Spaniards to fight against the subjection of Spain to American imperialism. The charge that they had exchanged Basque for Spanish patriotism had, belatedly, come true. The MCE had considerable success in the early and mid 1970s in building a revolutionary organisation with some influence in the working class. In the closing years of Franco's rule it was the third largest of the Maoist parties in Spain, and was strong in Vizcaya and Guipúzcoa. Unlike its main rivals, the MCE survived the transition to parliamentary democracy, retaining a base in the Basque country, but in the process abandoning the harsh criticism of nationalism which had produced ETA-Berri's expulsion.

ETA-Berri's evolution would not have surprised those who had expelled its leaders at the Fifth Assembly. For their part, those who accepted the legitimacy of the Assembly saw themselves as continuing the struggle which had been temporarily diverted by Spanish 'infiltration'. The Assembly, after ratifying the expulsion of the leaders of the Political Office, proceeded to elect a new Executive. From the beginning of the proceedings, it was apparent that there were differences between the tendency inspired by Txillardegi and the younger activists who had co-operated to overthrow the leadership of the Political Office. Txabi Etxebarrieta was elected President of the Assembly in opposition to Xabier Imaz, the most prominent member of the Txillardegi tendency in attendance. The Assembly went on to agree on a communiqué about the dissidents who had been removed from office, and to approve an account of the proceedings.[104] It would have seemed that Txillardegi's efforts to remove Marxist and *españolista* tendencies from ETA had been completely successful. Specific decisions on the organisation and structure of ETA were left to the second part of the Assembly, which was held in March 1967 at Guetaria in Guipúzcoa, in a building belonging to the Jesuits.

By the second part of the Assembly, the alliance between the Txillardegi faction and the younger activists led by Escubi and the Etxebarrieta brothers disintegrated. The tendency formed by Escubi's supporters and the Etxebarrieta brothers considered themselves Marxists, and although their 'Marxism' did not lead them to make any serious analysis of Basque society, it was difficult to combine even the most superficial Marxist rhetoric with an alliance with Txillardegi. The young men who now formed ETA's leadership felt to some extent that they had been manoeuvred into acting in the interests of Txillardegi's faction. Their opposition to ETA-Berri's Marxism did not prevent them feeling passionately identified with communist leaders such as Che Guevara.[105] Global Struggle.

The Assembly rejected the documents drawn up by the Txillardegi tendency, the *'Grupo Socialista'*[106], and went on to adopt a number of documents which reflected the ideas of José Antonio Etxebarrieta and Krutwig, both of whom had joined ETA in late 1966.[107] The Assembly accepted the *Informe Verde*, which committed ETA to a strategy of guerrilla war and to an ideology of Marxist-Leninism. It was decided that the organisation would be divided into four Fronts dealing with the political, cultural, socio-economic and military areas of struggle. The most important theoretical innovation which the Assembly adopted was the conception of the *Pueblo Trabajador Vasco* (PTV), the force which was to carry out the Basque revolution. The PTV, or 'Basque working people', were defined as those who earned their living in the Basque country and supported Basque aspirations.[108] The concept of the PTV was a necessarily ambiguous formula which was intended to exclude the big bourgeoisie, but include the small employers who formed an important part of the nationalist community. The concept did little to clarify ETA-Bai's (henceforth simply ETA) attitude to the immigrants who formed such a large part of the Basque population. Were the immigrants part of the PTV? The answer seemed to be 'yes and no'. The formula, while too favourable to the immigrants to be accepted by the Txillardegi tendency, was seen by opponents as a modern version of the traditional racist categorisations of Basque nationalism.[109] In fact, ETA wished to gain the support both of workers who were economically exploited, and of the predominantly conservative Basque nationalist community. The former leadership of the Political Office who now formed ETA-Berri had identified with the workers' struggle exclusively and had soon ceased to be nationalist. The question of what an immigrant had to do to gain entry to the PTV was deliberately left unclarified.

Most of the founding leaders of ETA (Txillardegi, José Manuel Aguirre, Benito de Valle and Xabier Imaz) resigned shortly after the second part of the Fifth Assembly, as did the organisation's representatives in Mexico,[110] alleging continuing 'Spanish' infiltration of ETA. Txillardegi's alliance with the young men who were soon to launch a campaign of violence had always been opportunist. His perceptive assessment of the realities of an industrialised society made him, in some ways, closer to the leadership which he had been instrumental in overthrowing. However, his realisation that a commitment to class struggle, in a country where the labour force included so many immigrants, necessarily led to the abandonment of the National Front forced him into an alliance with the advocates of armed struggle. Txillardegi was in the future to be involved in several similar alliances arising from further splits in ETA.

The dominant leaders of ETA after the Fifth Assembly were Escubi and Txabi, the younger Etxebarrieta brother. The older brother, José Antonio, was an important intellectual influence and a leading contributor to *Zutik*, but his poor health prevented him from playing a more active role.[111] Krutwig was elected to the Executive Committee in spite of having been a member of ETA for only a few months. However, the operational leadership remained in the hands of Escubi and Txabi Etxebarrieta, supported by new leaders such as Patxo Unzueta, a Bilbao university student and close friend of Txabi. The political analysis produced by the new team was grossly inferior to either Txillardegi's accurate assessment of the social base of nationalism, or to ETA-Berri's study of the labour movement. However, the confused and contradictory nature of ETA's ideology did not prevent it from becoming the crucial factor in Basque politics in the late 1960s, as a result of the campaign of armed struggle which began in 1968.

REFERENCES

1. L.C. Núñez, *Clases sociales en Euskadi* (San Sebastián, 1977) p. 163.
2. Landaburu, *La causa del pueblo vasco* (Paris, 1956), pp. 115–116.
3. J.L. Alvarez Emparanza (Txillardegi), *Ikastaroak formanzia koadernoak IPES*), No.1 (Bilbao, 1980).
4. For Txillardegi's background see interview in Eugenio Ibarzábal, *50 años de nacionalismo vasco 1928-1978* (Ediciones Vascas, San Sebastián, 1978).
5. Author's interview with Mikel Isasi, Bilbao, 14 March 1980.
6. Author's interview with José Joaquín Azurza Aristeguieta, San Sebastián, 18 March 1980.
7. 'Escuela y academia de danzas vascas en Hernani', *Alderdi Documentos Y* (San Sebastián, 1979/80), Vol. 1, p. 59.
8. 'Reunión del Gobierno de Euskadi in Bayona', *OPE*, 23 March 1959, in *Documentos Y*, Vol 1, p. 56.
9. Txillardegi, in Ibarzábal, *50 años*.
10. Txillardegi, 'De Santoña a Burgos', in *Documentos Y*, Vol. 1, pp. 21-23.
11. Txillardegi, in Ibarzabal, *50 años*; see also interview with Txillardegi in *Garai*, September 1976.
12. Txillardegi, in Ibarzábal, *50 años*.
13. Interview with Julen Madariaga, founder member of Ekin and ETA in *Punto y Hora*, 18 to 24 August (1977), 14; 'El Grupo Ekin y los primeros pasos', by ETA founding member Jon Nicolas, in *Documentos Y*, Vol. 1, pp. 25-32.
15. Txillardegi, in Ibarzábal, *50 años*; also 'Testimonios personales', *IPES*, No. 1.
16. Ajuriaguerra interview, in Ibarzábal, *50 años*, pp. 339-45.
17. Author's interview with Mikel Isasi.
18. Ajuriaguerra, in Ibarzábal, *50 años*; J.M. Garmendia and A. Elordi, *La resistencia vasca*, pp. 263-4.
19. E. Ibarzábal, 'Asi nació ETA', *Muga*, No. 1, June 1979.
20. E. Ibarzábal, *Muga*, June 1979.
21. Benito de Valle and Julen Aguirre, *Punto y Hora*, 27 July and 8 Nov. 1979; Ibarzábal, *Muga*, No. 2, September 1979.
22. J. Madariaga, *Punta y Hora*, 18-24 August 1977 and 13-27 July 1984.
23. J. Madariaga, 'Lutte Révolutionnaire en Euskadi', in *Documentos Y*, Vol. 9, pp. 385-95.
24. Txillardegi in Ibarzábal, *50 años*.
25. Txillardegi, 'De Santoña a Burgos', in *Documentos Y*, Vol. 1, pp. 21-3.
26. Author's interview with Sr Azurza, San Sebastián, 18 March 1980.
27. For the PNV's early cultural activities see Corcuera, *Orígenes*, pp. 216, 423-66.
28. Author's interviews with Sabino Arana, a founder member of ETA, Vitoria, 16 March 1980, and Patxo Unzueta, a leader of ETA from 1967, Bilbao, 13 March 1980.

29. Author's interview with Mario Onaindia.

30. Author's interview with Sabino Arana.

31. Interview with Sabino Arana.

32. Author's interview with Elizabeta Bazkara, Bilbao, 14 March 1980.

33. L.C. Núñez, *Opresión y defensa del Euskera* (San Sebastián, 1977), passim.

34. 'Escrito de los 339 sacerdotes vascos', in A. de Onaindía (ed), *Ayer como hoy* (St. Jean de Luz, 1975), pp. 227–43.

35. Author's interviews with Sabino Arana, Vitoria 16 March 1980, and Iñaki Sarasketa, San Sebastián, 26 March 1980.

36. 'Libro Blanco', in *Documentos Y*, Vol. 1, pp. 151–298.

37. 'José Antonio Aguirre y lo social', *Zutik*, April (1961).

38. 'Leizaola: hombre del destino', *Zutik* (Caracas), No. 12, undated.

39. 'La juventud vasca ante el 7 de Octubre', *Zutik* (Caracas), No. 15, undated.

40. Author's interview with Ildefonso Iriarte Otermín, one of those arrested following the attempt on the train, San Sebastián, 14 July 1980.

41. See *Zutik* (Caracas) (undated) for details of the accused.

42. J. Nicholas, 'Notas a la primera asamblea', in *Documentos Y*, Vol. 1, pp. 522–3.

43. Author's interview with Sabino Arana.

44. Author's interview with Ildefonso Iriarte Otermín.

45. 'Euskadi ta Azkatazuna — principios, Mayo de 1962' in *Documentos Y*, Vol. 1, pp. 532–3.

46. See Núñez, *Clases sociales*, Ch. 7 'Inmigración'.

47. 'El problema de la inmigración', *Zutik*, No. 11, April 1963.

48. 'Carta a un coreano', *Zutik*, No. 12 (undated).

49. See 'Carta a los coreanos', *Gudari* (Soldier) No. 20, 1963, journal of Eusko Gaztedi.

50. 'A todos los Vascos de buena fe', *Hoja suplementaria de Zutik*, No. 10, April 1964.

51. See Chapter 1, p. 16.

52. L. Ramírez (Luciano Rincón), *Nuestros primeros veinticinco años* (Paris, 1964), passim.

53. 'El sentimiento de nacionalidad', *Zutik* (Caracas), No. 16 (1961).

54. I. Goitia, 'Algunas precisiones sobre Euskadi', *Ruedo Ibérico*, No. 25, June–July 1970.

55. *Vasconia*, passim.

56. *El Español*, 22 Feb. 1964: *La Voz de España*, San Sebastián, 12 Feb. 1964.

57. *Alderdi*, March 1964.

58. See *Vasconia*, p. 322. .

59. 'Ayer y Hoy de F. Krutwig', interview in *Muga*, No. 2, Sept. 1979, P. 51.

60. 'Vasconia', *Zutik*, No. 16 (undated).

61. *Vasconia*, pp. 296, 329–36 and 340.

62. *Vasconia*, p. 337.

63. *Vasconia*, p. 339.

64. *Vasconia*, p. 340.

65. *Vasconia*, p. 382.
66. *Vasconia*, pp. 375–82.
67. K. de Zumbeltz, *La Insurrección en Euskadi* (Bayonne, 1964), passim.
68. K. de Zumbeltz, *La Insurrección en Euskadi* (Bayonne, 1964), pp. 30–32.
69. K. de Zumbeltz, *La Insurrección en Euskadi* (Bayonne, 1964), p. 41.
70. K. de Zumbeltz, *La Insurrección en Euskadi* (Bayonne, 1964), p. 41.
71. *Zutik*, No. 34, September 1965.
72. Author's interview with Sabino Arana.
73. 'Dinero, dinero y más dinero', *Zutik Berriak*, September 1964.
74. See *Zutik*, No. 22, undated, but in 1964.
75. '"Patriota" desenmascarado', *Zutik. Boletín de Noticias*, 30 November 1964.
76. 'Comunicado al pueblo vasco', *Zutik*, No. 32, August 1965.
77. See 'Carta a los intelectuales', written by Zalbide, *Zutik*, No. 30, June 1965.
78. N. Sartorius, *El resurgir del Movimiento Obrero* (Barcelona, 1975), passim.
79. See *Zutik*, from No. 32, August 1965, onwards.
80. For example, 'Reflexiones sobre la actual situación en el Estado Español', *Zutik*, No. 42, summer 1966.
81. J. Fernández (Patxi Iturrioz), 'Unidad si pero. . . qué unidad?', *Zutik*, No. 41, undated; 'Revolución socialista y unidad obrera', *Zutik*, No. 43, undated.
82. *Branka* was a semi-official journal of ETA edited by Txillardegi.
83. 'Informe político de la dirección de ETA', 26 November 1965; 'Segundo Informe envíado al ejecutivo', 19 Dec. 1965; 'Asunto extremadamente grave', 16 March 1966; 'A todos los militantes', 19 March 1965; all reprinted in *Documentos Y*, Vol. 4, pp. 422–68.
84. J. Fernández (Patxi Iturrioz), '¿De quién es la culpa?', *Zutik*, No. 29, May 1965. For Txillardegi's reply see *Segundo informe*.
85. 'Segundo informe envíado al ejecutivo', 19 December 1965; 'Contestación del comité ejecutivo a Jean' (Txillardegi), 24 March 1966; in *Documentos Y*, Vo. 4, pp. 470–3.
86. *Asunto extremadamente grave*. See also 'A todos los militantes de ETA', in *Documentos Y*, Vol. 4, pp. 422–68.
87. 'Crisis Ideológica', in *Documentos Y*, Vol. 4, pp. 439–42.
88. See the report of one such emissary, 'Santi', in *Oficial a todas las delegaciones*, Bayonne, 28 November 1966, in *Documentos Y*, Vol. 5, pp. 532–4.
89. Author's interview with Patxo Unzueta, Bilbao, 13 March 1980.
90. 'Comunicado de expulsión de Mikel', in *Documentos Y*, Vol. 5, p. 133.
91. Author's interview with Patxo Unzueta.
92. Interview with Unzueta.
93. J. Liskar, 'Euskadi: el proletariado y la cuestión nacional', *Acción Comunista*, No. 11, August 1969.
94. Author's interview with ETA activists Iñaki Garcia Aranberri, Ondarroa, 19 March 1980, Iñaki Sarasketa, San Sebastián, 17 March

1980, Patxo Unzueta, Bilbao, 13 March 1980.

95. 'Examen crítico de las posiciones ideológicas adoptadas por un grupo de militantes de ETA; in *Documentos Y*, Vol. 5, pp. 275–85.

96. 'Viva la revolución nacional', in *Documentos Y*, Vol. 5, pp. 327–37.

97. Txillardegi, 'La evolución del imperialismo español en Euskadi', *Branka* No. 6, 1969. *Documentos Y*, Vol. 5, pp. 308–21.

98. *Zutik*, No. 45, No. 48, No. 50 (ETA-Berri), undated.

99. 'Sabino Arana: un racista fuera de serie', *Komunistak*, No. 1, undated.

100. J. Uribe, '¿Qué es ETA-Bai?', *Komunistak*, No. 2, June 1969.

101. 'En el 5° aniversario de la Revolución de Octubre', *Zutik*, No. 52 (ETA-Berri), undated.

102. 'Chekoslovakia — toma de postura', *Zutik*, No. 60 (ETA-Berri), undated.

103. T. Díaz, 'Conciliaciones del lo irreconciliable', *Komunistak*, No. 3, November 1969.

104. 'Posiciones ideológicas aprobadas por la V Asamblea', in *Documentos Y*, Vol. 5, pp. 168–77.

105. Author's interview with Patxo Unzueta.

106. 'Proposición de cursillo de tendencia socialista' in *Documentos Y*, Vol. 7, pp. 25–37.

107. 'Informe Verde Revisado', 'Ideología oficial de Y' in *Documentos Y*, Vol. 7, pp. 57–99.

108. See 'Pueblo Trabajador Vasco', *Zutik*, No. 44 (ETA-Bai), January 1967.

109. See '¿Qué es ETA-Bai?', *Komunistak*, No. 2, June 1969.

110. 'Al Comité ejecutivo de ETA — carta de dimisión de Txillardegi', 14 April 1967, 'Carta-renunciando de la delegación de ETA en México', 15 May 1967, in *Documentos Y*, Vol. 7, pp. 101–2.

111. Author's interview with Patxo Unzueta.

3

The Beginnings of Armed Struggle: Spring 1967 to Autumn 1970

The departure of Txillardegi and his supporters put the leadership of Etxebarrieta and Escubi firmly in control of ETA-Bai (henceforth simply ETA). Julen Madariaga was the only prominent founder to remain a member after the second part of the Fifth Assembly.[1] The prospects for accomplishing the task of ending the Spanish occupation appeared daunting, as ETA was neither a mass organisation nor one steeled in the experience of armed struggle. Its main activities had consisted of very rudimentary propaganda such as wall-daubing.[2] Attempts at more ambitious feats such as the derailment of a train in 1961,[3] and the robbery of a bank messenger in 1965,[4] had ended in disaster. The leadership which had been expelled had attempted to develop socialist ideas and trade union agitation, but in doing so had antagonised both ETA's founders and its traditional base. In addition ETA's special relationship to the PNV had been endangered by a number of its actions, ranging from attempted extortion from members of the PNV[5] to adoption of a Marxist ideology and advocacy of armed struggle.

Although ETA was a tiny organisation, whose resources were pitifully inadequate to accomplish the task of winning Basque independence, its leaders considered that they had the potential support, strategy and organisation to succeed. In particular, they believed that the theoretical innovation provided by the concept of the *Pueblo Trabajador Vasco* (PTV) provided a formula which would enable ETA to overcome the false dichotomy between the struggle against national and social oppression. The PTV was declared to be both the victim of Spanish oppression and the force which would create an independent, socialist Euskadi.[6] Although the concept of the PTV was expounded many times in ETA statements, it was never clarified. According to interpretation it could be taken to mean:

a) all of the Basque people minus the 'oligarchy';
b) the ethnically Basque population, plus those immigrants who chose to incorporate themselves into it. The criteria for incorporation were themselves obscure. Learning to speak *Euskera* was an important condition, as was joining in the struggle for national liberation;
c) the working class and its allies, irrespective of ethnic or geographical origin.

The utility of the PTV concept lay in its capacity to mean different things to different people, and thereby enable ETA to slough off the racist connotations of traditional Basque nationalism and yet remain within the nationalist camp. The concept was often derided by ETA's critics, as a tortuous attempt to combine 'left' phraseology with a desire for an alliance with the social strata sympathetic to the PNV. ETA's leaders were sure that their ideas would win more support than ETA-Berri's exotic theories, expressed in long articles influenced by writers belonging to the New Left.[7] ETA's own general theory, elaborated by Krutwig, who had joined ETA and been elected to the leadership at the Fifth Assembly, saw Euskadi as a colony, comparable to Third World countries. The pattern of guerrilla war which had achieved independence for Algeria and was currently being carried out in Vietnam was also seen as appropriate for Euskadi.

ETA's new leaders also had a strategy, tactics and a form of organisation drawn from their interpretation of the experience of Cuba, Vietnam and Algeria. In order to mobilise the population against Spanish oppression it would be necessary, they argued, to form a National Front, which would include all social classes except the oligarchy. The ideological underpinning of the need for a National Front was expressed in the formula of the *Frente Nacional Vasco*[8] (FNV) which provided for an alliance with those capitalists who were sympathetic to the PNV. ETA's evolution towards becoming an organisation with a definite ideology of its own made alliances necessary in order to achieve co-operation with the diverse forces which, while they would have fitted comfortably into the early ETA when it was itself a broad social movement, could hardly belong to a Marxist organisation. While the formula of the PTV represented an overture to sympathisers of the

PNV, it also expressed a desire to incorporate immigrant workers. Such workers were seen as either part of the PTV, or at least potential members of it, if they showed willingness to incorporate themselves into Basque life and national aspirations.[9]

Although ETA's leaders had allied with Txillardegi and his supporters in the struggle to depose Iturrioz and del Río, they had no wish to abandon the work of industrial agitation, which from their point of view was perfectly compatible with the struggle for national independence.[10] This orientation was expressed in ETA's journal, *Zutik*, whose main contributors and editors in 1967 and most of 1968 were the Etxebarrieta brothers, and the team of people grouped around Escubi who had organised the expulsion of the leaders of the former Political Office.[11] *Zutik* attacked these leaders for their abandonment of nationalism and for their rejection of the National Front, but the journal also emphasised the need for a socialist revolution and criticised the conservatism of the PNV.[12]

ETA's leaders attacked the ETA-Berri group for becoming creatures of 'Spanish' political parties.[13] However, they themselves could not help but be influenced by the changing reality of Spain in the late 1960s. Although workers' attempts to organise independently of the official *Sindicatos* were repressed more strongly than they had been in the mid-1960s, the general trend in Spanish society was towards a growing liberalisation, even though the process was uncertain and constantly subject to reversal. This liberalisation was itself a result of the gradual disintegration of the Francoist system as it proved incapable of fulfilling the needs of Spanish capitalism. Practically all sections of Spanish business were strongly in favour of entry into the EEC and this had been government policy since the early 1960s.[14] Yet entry was not likely to be granted while Spain lacked the rights of association, assembly and free speech. Powerful forces within Spain's economic and political elites understood that EEC entry required a move towards a more democratic system and were prepared to pay the price. In addition, the brutal repression which had consolidated the Franco dictatorship in the aftermath of the Civil War was no longer adequate to control the working class in a more industrialised and urbanised Spain.

The Church was one of the first sections of the alliance, which had triumphed in the Civil War, to begin to take its distance from the regime.[15] Several bishops made statements supporting workers' rights and the Church-sponsored workers' groups.

Hermandad Obrera de Acción Católica (HOAC) and Juventudes Obreras Católicas (JOC) began to become involved in workers' struggles. In the Basque country, where a large section of the lower clergy had always been opposed to the Franco regime, such tendencies were stronger than in most other parts of Spain. Activists from Christian organisations formed the illegal trade union groups, Acción Sindical de los Trabajadores (AST), which subsequently became the Maoist Organización Revolucionaria de Trabajadores (ORT).

Just as the attempt to adjust to the reality of the 1960s produced tensions within the economic elite and the Church, so it did among the opposition. In spite of ETA's theory that the struggle in Euskadi was similar to those taking place in the Third World, it could not help but be influenced by the movements taking place among the opposition, which were producing a more varied political scene than had existed in the 1950s. Txillardegi's attack on the leaders of the Political Office had presented them as infiltrators acting on behalf of the 'communists'. The 'communists' in Txillardegi's view were a vague category which included both ESBA and the PCE.[16] His hostility to those forces was a continuation of Basque nationalism's long-standing hatred for the 'Spanish' labour movement. In fact Txillardegi's picture of a unified 'Spanish' communist movement which included both the PCE and ESBA was terribly distorted. ETA's former leaders, now in ETA-Berri, had not been greatly influenced by the PCE, partly because that party's analysis of Spain's political, social and economic situation reflected the world of the 1930s rather than the 1960s. The resemblance between the politics of ESBA and that of Iturrioz and del Río was not a product of ESBA's 'infiltration' but of common influences which led both groups to look towards contemporary European social theorists to provide an explanation of the modern world. In the early 1960s the PCE itself suffered from disagreements between its leadership who continued to see Spain as an impoverished, backward country ruled by a tiny Franco clique, with hardly any basis of support in society, and those such as its most capable theoretician, Fernando Claudín, whose attempt to come to terms with the social change since the Civil War resulted in his expulsion in 1965.[17]

The falsity of Txillardegi's belief in the existence of a unified communist ideology which could be used to divert Basque patriots from their struggle for national liberation was shown by the fact that his main allies in the struggle against the Political Office considered themselves to be communists. However, the communism of Escubi, the Etxebarrieta brothers and Unzueta did not at that stage lead them to sympathise with ETA-Berri's abandonment of nationalism. Instead, Marxism was redefined, so that the struggle for national liberation was declared to be the main communist priority. ETA's 'communist' leaders' analysis of the world was only slightly more sophisticated than that of the PCE.[18] However, some of them later graduated to employing Marxism as a method of analysis rather than as a source of rhetoric. The growth of Maoism in the late 1960s influenced ETA, understandably, because of its ideology combining nationalism and armed struggle, but as Maoism made no analysis of Basque or Spanish reality, its influence was not destructive of nationalist myths.

ETA's formula for carrying out the various aspects of the struggle was to set up a structure of separate Fronts, based on what was believed to be the model adopted by the Vietnamese in their struggle against the French and the Americans. There were to be four Fronts: Military, Political, Cultural and Economic (or Workers'). This structure was supposed to improve security as the militants of a particular Front would not be conversant with the activities of the others.[19] However, the actual tasks of the various Fronts were not clear, even in theory, and ETA veterans of that period were rather uncertain as to where the division of labour lay.[20] The functions of the Political and Workers' Fronts seemed to be particularly confused. This was less true of the Cultural Front, which had the task of encouraging and strengthening all aspects of Basque culture, such as learning and teaching *Euskera*, participating in Basque festivals and folklore events, helping the *Ikastolas* and learning about Basque history and literature. Such activities had been central to ETA from its beginning and, while by 1967 most of them were no longer actually illegal, they were often obstructed by the authorities and closely watched by the police. The activities of the Cultural Front were carried out partly in co-operation, partly in competition with the PNV, ELA and Txillardegi's sympathisers, grouped around the journal *Branka*, originally a semi-official organ of ETA. The combination of a fairly well-defined field of activity, and the lack of a distinct and separate line on Basque culture, resulted in ETA using activities such as folk dancing mainly as areas of recruitment, sometimes to the irritation of other enthusiasts for Basque culture, who resented ETA's attempts to recruit members.[21] In practice, the Cultural Front ranked low in ETA's hierarchy. It did not direct the strategy of the struggle, as did the Political Front, nor did it carry out the dramatic actions of the Military Front. According to Krutwig's theory, the spiral of action/repression/action would often be set off by a low-level activity such as the founding of an *Ikastola*, but the higher, more violent levels of struggle would not be carried out by the Cultural Front.[22]

The cultural sphere, where ETA, like the PNV, was able to propagate its ideas and recruit to its ranks was also an area where ETA competed with the PNV, Txillardegi's group, and the splinters of ELA, the nationalist trade union. The journal of the Cultural Front, *Kemen*, tried in 1969 to outline a theory which distinguished ETA from these competitors, but with only limited success. According to *Kemen*, the Basque right wing idealised an imaginary Basque past, and believed that Basque culture could simply be restored, whereas in reality culture was constantly changing. The influence of the Basque right in the *Ikastolas* and the *Escuelas Sociales* (adult discussion groups organised by the Church) had the effect of creating a myth about Basque culture and idealising the supposedly perfect character of ancient Basque democracy. For ETA, in contrast, Basque culture would have to be constantly recreated.[23]

ETA's criticism of the cultural practice of the PNV agreed with the strictures made by Txillardegi ever since the founding of *Ekin*. He had then argued that the attempt to reduce culture to folklore and religious piety was reactionary. Yet, in practice, it was difficult for ETA to differentiate itself from other nationalists in the *Ikastolas* and *Escuelas Sociales*. The Cultural Front did not, for example, seem to have much success in bringing Basque culture to immigrant workers. Contact with workers was generally made through the Economic Front, which although originally a fund-raising agency was transformed into the Workers' Front, a body carrying out industrial agitation. The task of the Political Front was to work out the political line of the organisation, something which did not require the participation of many activists. In practice, the position was even more confused, as activists would move from one Front to another and carry out tasks supposedly belonging to different Fronts at the same time. There was uncertainty as to whether the Fronts were organisational divisions within ETA, or merely fields of activity. In retrospect, some ETA members saw them as aspirations rather than organisational structures.[24]

The activities of the Workers' Front had unintended consequences, as waging a class struggle meant working with and trying to recruit immigrants. The immigrant workers were seen as, potentially, both friends and enemies because their presence as bearers of an alien language and culture was thought to be damaging to Basque life, while their condition as exploited labourers made them enemies of the employers. Immigrant workers could choose to become Basque by integrating into Basque life, participating in the class struggle, and thereby become full members of the PTV, irrespective of their ethnic origin.[25] Such a qualified welcome could hardly be inviting to workers who saw themselves as having moved from one part of Spain to another, not as having emigrated to a foreign country. In addition, the stress on individually choosing to be Basque did not fit well with the collectivist orientation of those workers attracted to the illegal trade union movement.[26] The Workers' Front was also handicapped by the survival of virulent chauvinist attitudes within ETA. Inevitably, ETA members working in that Front tended to emphasise socialist propaganda and industrial agitation, rather than traditional nationalist concerns.

ETA's activities in the workers' movement bore fruit to some extent in Vizcaya, in 1968 and 1969, when it was claimed that ETA had several hundred members concentrated in the heavy industries of greater Bilbao.[27] Paradoxically, that success was partly due to the fact that repression increased after August 1968 when normal legal rights were suspended because of the State of Emergency. The Workers' Commissions, and particularly their Communist Party leadership, had taken advantage of the limited increase in toleration of opposition by the Franco regime up to 1967 to gain positions as elected workplace representatives within the structure of the official *Sindicatos*. However, the growing strength of the workers' movement provoked a reaction from the government which led, on several occasions, to the declaration of States of Emergency, when citizens' legal rights were suspended. One such State of Emergency, declared throughout Spain at the beginning of 1967, coincided with the long and bitter strike at Laminaciones de Bandas in Bilbao.[28] The government move to a more repressive policy, which reflected internal differences on how best to deal with the workers' movement, convinced many people on the left that the PCE's concentration on winning positions within the *Sindicatos* was mistaken. In the new climate, the Communist Party lost some ground to more militant tendencies, one of which was ETA, while the Workers' Commissions became less open organisations and, in the Basque country, tended to turn into alliances of clandestine political groups.

ETA's Military Front had, in theory, quite specific tasks. In the long run it was to direct the guerrilla army which would prepare the people for an uprising against the occupying power. In the short term, it was to back up the people's struggle by intervening when mass action had reached its limit.[29] It was to punish informers, agents of the regime and other enemies of the people. The long-term aim to launch a guerrilla war was never to materialise, and the nearest attempt to achieve it was carried out, not by ETA itself, but by the Grupo Autónomo, also known as Las Cabras (the goats). Las Cabras was formed by Francisco Javier Zumalde, who had been entrusted with military affairs after the Fourth Assembly of ETA in 1965. Zumalde was opposed to political action and had decided views on military matters, seeing the task of ETA as being to train for guerrilla war. He took his supporters on long route marches, prepared caches of provisions in the mountains, and generally behaved like an army commander in charge of manoeuvres. As Zumalde was extremely cautious about initiating violent activities, the elaborate manoeuvres of Las Cabras went largely undetected. The group's written material was mainly for internal consumption and was extremely sparse and simplistic, consisting mainly of instructions on maintaining security, denunciations of informers, glorification of the moral values prevailing in the Basque countryside, religious justifications of the right to violent resistance against oppression, and instructions on methods of sabotage.[30]

It was only because of intensive police activity following the State of Emergency in 1968 that the group's activities were discovered. Zumalde had to flee into exile in August 1968 and a number of his supporters were arrested in November and December of the same year,[31] with the result that the group went out of existence, and a number of its supporters drifted back to ETA. Zumalde himself never thought that he had split from ETA, but merely that he had disengaged from politics, to continue faithfully the organisation's original task.[32] The existence of Las Cabras, largely irrelevant to the history of either ETA or the Basque country, was nevertheless indicative of the social and community basis of radical nationalism. Zumalde had succeeded in maintaining a political group enacting a boy scout fantasy with the firm social base of the mountaineering groups which were so popular in the Basque country. The defection of Zumalde led to the Military Front being reconstituted under the leadership of Jon Etxabe, who while sharing Zumalde's view that the 'peasants' were the core of the Basque people, operated from a base in the French Basque country and did not indulge in Zumalde's mountaineering exploits.

The difficulties of achieving the contradictory objectives of building a workers' party, constructing a National Front, and launching a guerrilla war were not as apparent in 1967 as they later became, not least because none of the tasks which ETA had set itself were being carried out on any sizeable scale. Indeed, ETA's human and material resources were woefully inadequate for either trade union agitation or armed struggle. However, the growing strength of the illegal workers' movement provided a field for the activities of the Workers' Front. ETA's leaders, like their predecessors, now in ETA-Berri, were strongly influenced by the rise of the workers' movement and particularly by the strike at Laminaciones de Bandas in Bilbao in 1966–67, which produced a widespread support movement. ETA benefited from the fact that the Workers' Commissions, although strongly influenced by the Communist Party, remained a fairly broad and open organisation.[33] The PCE itself looked quite favourably on ETA, as representative of the new forces which were moving into opposition to the Franco regime.[34] Txabi Echevarrieta was given the post of propaganda secretary in the Workers' Commissions of Vizcaya, although he was a student not a worker.

Much of the Workers' Front propaganda activity was similar to that carried out by non-nationalist left-wing groups. While the distinguishing feature of ETA was to be the armed operations of its Military Front, the first steps towards creating an armed force were rather modest. This was hardly surprising in view of the lack of resources available, yet the armed campaign could not be delayed for too long. ETA had been committed theoretically to a campaign which would launch a guerrilla war since the appearance of Zalbide's *Insurrección en Euskadi* in 1964. In addition, as one of the main charges against the ETA-Berri tendency was that it had abandoned the strategy of armed struggle, the failure to begin such a struggle would have made ETA's new leadership appear inept. In the spring and early summer of 1967, ETA carried out several successful bank robberies and planted bombs which damaged various official buildings and monuments.[35] These actions hardly amounted to the launching of a guerrilla war but they had psychological importance in demonstrating that ETA was serious about its intentions. An indication of ETA's new attitude was the *liberados'* (full-timers) custom of carrying arms when on a mission, although at first this had more psychological than military importance. The entire military training of Iñaki Sarasketa, a member of ETA's leadership, had consisted of firing one shot from a pistol, and this seems to have been fairly typical.[36]

The robberies and attacks on buildings and symbols of the regime were a small problem for the police compared with the sharp rise in workers' struggles in 1967 and 1968. The incidents which ETA reported were often quite minor. For example, the setting fire to some police vehicles in Bilbao,[37] the destruction of a plaque commemorating the death of Franco supporters during the Civil War, the throwing of a fire bomb at a police station,[38] and threats to police informers were all considered important enough to be included in ETA's propaganda. As ETA wanted to combine mass activity with armed struggle, it would often make its attacks around key dates, such as May Day or Easter, when the PNV would call demonstrations for *Aberri Eguna* (the day of the Basque fatherland).[39] ETA's actions, which were intended to accentuate the atmosphere of tension, were fairly small-scale and even the daubing of patriotic slogans was still considered worthy of report on ETA's publications throughout 1967,[40] but the level of violent actions slowly mounted. In December 1967, several ETA members were wounded when the police discovered an attempt to plant explosives at the offices of the *Sindicatos* in Eibar and Elgoibar.[41] The likelihood of bloodshed was illustrated by the capture of Sabino Arana, an ETA *liberado*, in Vitoria in February 1968, when he fired a pistol at a policeman and missed, in an unsuccessful attempt to escape.[42]

The action which produced ETA's first martyr, and started the process which was to make the organisation the key force in Basque politics, was rather similar to that which led to Arana's capture. It also illustrated the gulf between ETA's theories on guerrilla war and its lack of resources or preparation to launch such a struggle. In June 1968 Txabi Etxebarrieta and another *liberado*, Iñaki Sarasketa, travelling by car, were stopped by a Civil Guard on traffic duty. Txabi was carrying a pistol, as was by then customary among ETA's *liberados*. Possession of such a weapon would, if detected, have led to a long prison sentence. Txabi, in order to avoid such a fate, shot and killed the Civil Guard. Shortly afterwards, when the police caught up with the fugitives at Tolosa, Txabi was immediately shot dead. Sarasketa escaped, but was captured soon afterwards.[43] The repercussions of Txabi's death were greater than anyone could have imagined, as it was regarded as cold-blooded murder by many Basque people. Masses were said for him in many churches and these became occasions for denouncing the regime. A number of factors combined to make Txabi's death one of the key events in ETA's struggle. He was ETA's first martyr, the victim of a brutal, summary execution, and ETA's publications made many people familiar with the life and personality of a talented and sensitive young man.[44] Txabi had been one of the main theoreticians of the strategy which produced his own death. Unlike many of his supporters Txabi was not merely a fighter, but a writer and an activist in the Workers' Commissions.

Sarasketa was first of all sentenced to life imprisonment but, as this was considered too lenient by the military authorities, he was re-tried and sentenced to death. The sentence was later commuted because of his youth (he was 19 years old). The agitation against Sarasketa's sentence, and the demonstrations of grief at Txabi's killing, combined to intensify the spirit of protest and helped to bring a knowledge of ETA's activities beyond the fairly narrow circle of its sympathisers up till then. These events drew many people into politics. For example, the lawyer Juan María Bandres, who later became a prominent leader of a political party originating in ETA, undertook the legal defence of Sarasketa, mainly because of family friendships.[45] Txabi's life illustrated the dynamic and the functioning of ETA, and the demonstrations which followed his death showed the importance which ETA's martyrs were to have throughout the organisation's history. Txabi had been the main creator of the organisational scheme which divided ETA into different Fronts, yet his own diverse activities should, theoretically, have been carried out by separate people in different Fronts. The shot which killed the traffic policeman started the process of armed struggle, which was in theory to be carried out by the Military Front. The killing of Txabi seemed, for some time, to have been the spark which started the armed struggle which he had advocated. His death was followed by an intense campaign of violence, but this proved impossible to sustain and declined after the spring of 1969.

The real achievement marked by his death was the considerable support for ETA shown by wide sections of the population. The emotional scenes at the many funeral services held for him[46] demonstrated that his 'Marxism' had not separated him from the Basque Catholic population, many of whom identified with ETA

71

without understanding its ideas. There were demonstrations in protest at Txabi's death not only in the Basque-speaking, conservative areas, but also in factories where most of the workers were immigrants. However impossible the long-term coexistence of conservative Basque nationalism and left-wing socialism in the aftermath of Txabi's killing, his theoretical construction, the PTV, appeared feasible.

In November of the previous year Che Guevara had been captured, and later murdered, in the mountains of Bolivia, where he had been leading a guerrilla band. Txabi had, like all of ETA's leadership, been a fervent admirer of Guevara and the circumstances of both deaths seemed to his friends remarkably similar.[47] The resources of Che Guevara and his comrades were tiny compared to those which his enemies possessed, but ETA's leaders, nevertheless, believed that Che's followers would eventually triumph. Justice was on their side and so, potentially, were the mass of oppressed people. The same was, they believed, true for ETA in Euskadi. ETA's leaders' horror at Txabi's death impelled them to launch a reprisal which was to bring down a ferocious repression on their organisation. It was decided that the retaliation should take the form of killing the notorious police chief Melitón Manzanas. In early August 1968, Manzanas was shot in the doorway of his house in the border town of Irún, by a gunman who then escaped.[48] The event was undoubtedly popular among large sections of the population,[49] as it demonstrated ETA's power to strike back at the oppressor of the Basque people. Furthermore, as the killing of Manzanas was followed by a wave of shootings, bombings and robberies, ETA seemed well on the way to carrying out the campaign of violence to which it had committed itself at the Fifth Assembly.

The campaign, however, was not the beginning of a people's war. Nearly all the attacks were carried out by full-time activists, who were themselves the leaders of the organisation. Nor was it based on mass activity, although it benefited from the support of many people who provided information and shelter to activists. On the occasions where people who were not *liberados* were involved in armed struggle, the separation of activities between different Fronts which ETA's theory prescribed was not observed. For example, in April 1969 in the incident which produced the second death sentence on an ETA member, Iñaki Garcia Aranberri and Andoni Arrizabalaga, both from the Basque-speaking coastal town of Ordarroa on the border of Vizcaya and

Guipúzcoa, planted a bomb in a police vehicle. García Aranberri was not a member of the Military Front and his previous ETA activities had consisted mainly of distributing propaganda in rural areas.[50] Both men were savagely tortured and in October 1969 Arrizabalaga was condemned to death, but his sentence was commuted to life imprisonment as a result of a massive protest movement. Immediately after the assassination of Manzanas a State of Emergency was declared in the province of Guipúzcoa, which allowed the police a free hand in their treatment of suspects.[51] As the police investigations were brutal and arbitrary, hundreds of innocent people were arrested and physically assaulted.[52]

The scale of the repression produced a wave of protest even greater than the one which had followed Txabi's death. The protests included strikes by workers and also demonstrations by substantial numbers of priests and lay Catholics, such as one in Vizcaya, in February 1969, when hundreds of people occupied a church in protest against the repression.] A similar occupation took place in March at the cathedral in San Sebastián, and 500 Basque priests asked the Spanish Episcopal Conference to condemn the State of Emergency.[53] Even more alarmingly, from the government's point of view, some bishops also criticised the repressive measures, Mgr. Cirarda, the Bishop of San Sebastián, going so far as to publish a pastoral letter criticising the State of Emergency. In April, when the police arrested the Vicar-General of Bilbao, accusing him of helping ETA, the bishop opposed the arrest, alleging that it was a breach of the Concordat with the Vatican.[54] Repression did little to break ETA's campaign of violence, but the police eventually had some success in capturing ETA activists. In late 1968 José María Dorronsoro, an ex-seminarist and ETA *liberado*, was arrested.[55] In January 1969 two others, Gregorio López Irasuegui, and Francisco Javier Izco, were captured when they made an armed assault on the women's prison in Pamplona in an attempt to rescue López Irasuegui's wife, María Aránzazu Arruti.[56] All of these were later to be accused of armed rebellion at the Burgos Trial in December 1970, where Izco was alleged to be the one who had actually shot Manzanas. The State of Emergency, which had existed in Guipúzcoa since August 1968, was extended in January 1969 to all of Spain for a period of three months.[57] In March four more *liberados*, who were to be among the accused at Burgos, were captured.

In April 1969 the police achieved their greatest success in their fight against ETA when they captured a number of *liberados*, including Mario Onaindía, who was to become one of ETA's most famous leaders, in their Bilbao hiding place.[59] Those arrested made up, with Izco, Dorronsoro and López Irasuegui, the core of ETA's military leadership, and were accused at the Burgos trial of being responsible for the killing of Melitón Manzanas, as well as other serious crimes. The *liberados* had been based in a flat in the Calle de Artecalle, in the old town of Bilbao, where police had been observing their movements for some time. One *liberado*, Mikel Echevarria, was able to escape in a taxi, although he had been wounded in a shoot-out when the police attacked. The driver of the taxi, Fermín Monasterio, was found shot dead some distance away, the first civilian to be killed by ETA, although a communiqué insisted that the bullets which killed him were of 9mm calibre and therefore had been fired by the regulation weapon of the Civil Guard.[59] After the arrests at the Calle de Artecalle and elsewhere, the nucleus of ETA's full-time military activists was dismantled. The ending of the State of Emergency on 25 March seemed to show that ETA was no longer much of a problem for the Franco regime. The failure of the armed campaign was apparent to Escubi who had been the main person responsible for launching it. Escubi was able to escape to France, where he examined the lessons of the failure of ETA's military struggle. Since late 1968, he had been critical not of armed struggle as such, but of continuing a campaign of violence when ETA lacked the political and organisational capacity to benefit from it.[60] His deepening criticism of the armed struggle, which he had done so much to launch, was to lead him to abandon ETA in 1970.

Echevarria was able to escape to France, helped by a number of people who provided him with shelter. The police arrested hundreds of people, including a number of priests, in connection with his flight. This popular backing which was to become strikingly apparent at the Burgos trial showed that the really important effect of ETA's actions was to provide heroes and martyrs to whom the people could rally. The capture or flight of the *liberados* who had formed ETA's leadership until Spring 1969 was a stunning blow which forced the organisation to re-examine its strategy. The effects of the arrests and flights into exile had in any case practically destroyed ETA's ability to carry out military activities. Once again organisational problems impelled ETA in a new political direction. The new leadership which was formed after the capture of the *liberados* in the Calle de Artecalle was based on the Workers' Front in Bilbao and included a number of University students.[61] ETA's presence in San Sebastián and the industrial areas of Guipúzcoa had suffered from the effects of the expulsions which had taken place at the Fifth Assembly, and the effects of police repression had temporarily weakened it in the villages.

ETA's new leaders were strongly influenced by the struggles of students and workers in May 1968 in France and believed the strikes of Spanish workers could lead to a revolution. Henceforth mass activity, particularly by the Workers' Front, was to be given priority over the armed struggle of specialised groups. The failure of the military offensive left ETA with two main strategies. Firstly, the strengthening of the National Front (FNV) through a movement emphasising Basque unity, described as the BAI campaign,[62] which was to unite patriots of varied class backgrounds and political beliefs; and secondly, a turn to the working class, leading to the transformation of ETA into a workers' party. These two objectives were not seen as incompatible.[63] So the organisation's publication carried articles which tried to reconcile Marxist doctrine with the heritage of Sabino Arana. The new analysis, written by Unzueta and endorsed by the men who were to be the leaders of ETA for several years, was seen by them, in retrospect, as a crucial step in ETA's progress from being a confused populist organisation paying lip-service to Marxism to becoming a genuinely communist group. Yet it reaffirmed the populist theory adopted at the Fifth Assembly, made a bitter attack on the 'Spanish' organisations who, effectively, comprised the labour movement in Euskadi,[64] and defended the concept of the *Pueblo Trabajador Vasco* and the need for an alliance with the patriotic sectors of the bourgeoisie.[65] Unzueta made a fervent call for workers' unity but the 'Spanish' left were attacked for destroying that unity, by denying the reality of Basque national identity and, allegedly, bringing fascist and imperialist aberrations into the workers' movement.[66]

ETA's leaders thought that the working class was capable of initiating struggles, but not of carrying them through, unaided, to a successful conclusion. At a given stage ETA's specialised military detachments would have to intervene, by carrying out acts of sabotage and kidnapping those managers whose actions had harmed workers' interests. It was recognised that ETA's interventions in industrial struggles would intensify state repression against the workers, but this, it was claimed, would have the beneficial effect of opening their eyes to the nature of the Spanish state, and would encourage them to take more drastic action.[67] This process described was, in fact, a reiteration of the action/repression/action spiral first proposed by Krutwig in *Vasconia*. It bore little relation to ETA's actual practice and was never put into operation by the leadership which advocated it. Those who eventually did carry out such actions were to regard its authors as traitors. The 'Spanish' left's advocacy of the right of the Basques to national self-determination was dismissed as meaningless, because self-determination was not something which could be granted by a future Spanish socialist government, but had to be achieved in struggles against the Spanish state. The 'Spanish' left's criticism of the Basque National Front (FNV), as an instrument of the bourgeoisie to divide the workers, was rejected as denying the national oppression of the Basque people.

None of the policies or theories adopted at the Fifth Assembly were rejected, and the publication of the articles met with no immediate opposition. The harsh attacks which were made on ETA-Berri and other 'Spanish' organisations would certainly have done much to disarm criticism from anyone who feared a repetition of the adoption of *españolista* positions, but this was not the only reason for ETA's attacks on the 'Spanish' groups in the labour movement. Whereas ETA's participation in a National Front could be part of a division of labour between itself and more conservative forces, it had no distinct constituency in the working class, and its attempts to build a base of support there would entail bitter competition with the 'Spanish' forces which did not have such a base. Although continuing to support the strategy of building the National Front, *Zutik 51* displayed a real hostility to the PNV, which combined with a genuine commitment to working class struggle was, eventually, to take most of those who, in 1969, were ETA members out of the nationalist movement.

ETA's expectation that a National Front, with considerable potential support from the PNV and other non-working class forces, would be led by a working class in which ETA and other nationalist forces had very little strength appeared absurd to non-nationalists, particularly to the ETA-Berri tendency, who saw ETA's socialist rhetoric as a smokescreen hiding both its desire for an alliance with the PNV and its extremely ambiguous attitude to the immigrants.[68] Yet the left-wing tendencies, which were to emerge in ETA in the next few years, saw the publication of *Zutik 51* as marking a crucial stage in the abandonment of chauvinism and a turn to mass action, in preference to the violent activities of élite groups. *Zutik 51* explicitly upheld the need for specialised military formations, but these were to function in the service of the mass movement. ETA's leaders' uneasy mixture of socialism and nationalism began to attract criticism from its exiled members who had access to literature previously unavailable, and time to study. However, during 1969 and 1970 most of the members in the interior and in prison were happy with the direction in which the organisation was going. Prisoners such as Sabino Arana, Iñaki Sarasketa and Iñaki Garcia Aranberri managed to follow the evolution of ETA, through smuggled communications and news brought by relatives on visits to prison.[69] Young members, even in villages, who were themselves rebelling against the stifling conservatism of their environment accepted the attacks on the PNV.[70]

ETA's leaders did not consider that they had to choose between involvement in the working class and socialist struggle, or of participation in the nationalist movement, as both were, in their opinion, necessary parts of the overall struggle. At the same time that the leadership was proclaiming the need to transform ETA into a Marxist party, it declared that 1970 was to be the year of the National Front,[71] aimed at consolidating the prestige which ETA's heroes enjoyed among a wide layer of people, and of winning over the members of EGI, the PNV's youth group, who were once again becoming disillusioned with the inactivity of their parent organisation. To this end ETA produced the journal *Batasuna* (Unity), five issues of which appeared between April and June 1970. The first issue reported enthusiastically on indications of support for a National Front from diverse nationalist forces, while criticising Komunistak (the former ETA-Berri) for its dismissal of Sabino Arana as a racist.[72] ETA's attempt to unite the class struggle with the national struggle led it to produce the slogan *Batasuna Langile* (workers' unity) for demonstrations on May Day 1970.[73] But in the factories workers' unity meant, overwhelmingly, the unity of non-nationalist forces.

A concept such as the *Pueblo Trabajador Vasco* had little relevance to the working-class struggle in which ETA had become involved, so the organisation began to substitute the term 'working class', thereby abandoning a concept which had been an essential ingredient in the organisation's mixture of socialism and radical nationalism. Industrial agitation brought the realisation that the strikes taking place in Bilbao were part of a struggle happening throughout Spain. Propaganda had, if it was to be effective, to be written mainly in Spanish. This necessity pointed the way to ETA's substituting the demand for equality of treatment for *Euskera* for that of the creation of a monolingual Euskadi. The adoption of the demand for the right to national self-determination rather than simply calling for Basque independence was another related development. The decision to transform ETA into a revolutionary Marxist party would, if carried through consistently, have had the effect of turning ETA members in the villages into isolated individuals, separated from their neighbours by their adoption of an exotic doctrine. The basis of ETA's strength in the unity of *cuadrillas*, neighbours and relatives would have been destroyed.

The leadership which replaced those who had been arrested, or had fled abroad in 1969, felt itself to be provisional and dependent on the approval of the former leaders in prison and of Escubi in exile.[74] It was also under pressure from Etxabe, the head of the Military Front, and from other exiles such as Krutwig and López Adán (Beltza), who suspected that the internal leadership was repeating the 'Spanish' deviation of ETA-Berri. The attempt to win the approval of these divergent critics led ETA's interior leadership to behave in a contradictory manner, combining socialist propaganda with limited attempts to restart the armed struggle, mainly by organising robberies. The BAI campaign, which was intended to develop a patriotic alliance, was criticised by Escubi and his supporters as a reversion to the bourgeois politics of ETA's founders. Yet ETA's interior leadership thought they had carried out their tasks fairly well. The membership had grown despite the repression and for the first time the Workers' Front had some influence in the workers' movement, particularly in Vizcaya. Most important of all, the prestige ETA had gained through its military activity was being successfully used to construct a National Front which would, it was hoped, win support from people who had traditionally supported the PNV.

This strategy was reflected in a document, *A todos los makos* (to all the prisons), written by Patxo Unzueta, the interior leaders' dominant political thinker.[75] Escubi and his co-thinkers thought that the document showed a relapse into ETA's traditional nationalism.[76] The fact that a key statement, analysing ETA's situation and perspectives, which attempted to justify the leadership's policy against attacks from its critics was addressed to the prisoners showed their prestige and importance within ETA, as well as their growing numbers. The interior leadership believed that ETA was making considerable progress in the task of constructing the Basque revolutionary party, and in harnessing the majority of Basque capitalists to the chariot of the socialist revolution. According to Unzueta, the immediate task in Euskadi was to fight for popular rather than socialist objectives,[77] but, once the popular forces led by the working class achieved national liberation, the transition to a socialist revolution would be inevitable. *A todos los makos* dealt with the apparently inherent contradiction of building a working-class party and a National Front embracing people of all classes, by arguing that the consolidation of one was dependent on the growth of the other. ETA, it was claimed, had been forced by circumstances to act as the Front of which it was, in theory, only one component. The early ETA, which had itself been a broad movement, had necessarily contained within itself a diversity of political ideas. Now, as the National Front developed a real existence, ETA would be able to fulfil its part as the vanguard communist party.[78]

A todos los makos wrestled with the awkward problem of the immigrant composition of the Basque proletariat, which was to bedevil all attempts to create a synthesis of nationalism and socialism, and argued that ETA had to promote bilingualism, rather than advocate a monolingual *Euskera*-speaking Euskadi. While maintaining the formula of the PTV, the document gave it a left-wing slant by defining it as consisting of all those who sold their labour power in Euskadi.[79] Taken with the abandonment of the aim of monolinguism this conception would have made all workers part of the PTV, as entrance would cease to depend on individual choice and effort. Such a definition, which failed to differentiate between ethnic Basques and immigrants, could not fail to be rejected by upholders of ETA's traditional nationalist ideology.

A todos los makos argued that the vanguard would not be formed by ETA merely changing its name. The putative party would represent all Basque workers. The, perhaps deliberate, ambiguity of the formulation stopped just short of saying that ETA was willing to be part of a regroupment with other parties. The effects of the repression following the assassination of Manzanas had, it was claimed, strengthened ETA instead of weakening it. Not only had there been a considerable growth in membership, especially in the industrial areas of Bilbao, but ETA's prestige was extremely high.

The PNV was much less hostile to ETA than in the mid-1960s and its youth movement, EGI, was under strong ETA influence. The 'Spanish' left, particularly the PCE, spoke in very warm terms of ETA and was anxious to make an alliance. The Workers' Front had finally succeeded in winning some influence in the factories, while the intellectual level of ETA's publications had advanced considerably from the simple-minded rhetoric of the group's early years. The modest satisfaction expressed in the report to the prisoners appeared, at the time, to be justified.

A todos los makos observed that the Communist Party had, for the first time in its history, called for support for the *Aberri Eguna* (Day of the Basque People) demonstration, an event hitherto dominated by the PNV. In addition, EGI was talking with ETA, as were some individual members of the PNV. ETA's claim to influence such diverse forces seemed a remarkable achievement, but Unzueta and his companions were aware that they faced great problems. Preparations were under way for the trial of the ETA members responsible for the wave of violence, including the killing of Manzanas. The trial was to take place at Burgos, capital of the military region in which the Basque country fell, at the end of the year. ETA's leadership had the task of mounting a campaign in Euskadi, and mobilising public opinion in Spain and abroad to try and save the lives of their comrades.[81] The interior leadership was aware that their conduct was coming under heavy fire from leading members in exile. Criticisms based on adherence to traditional Basque nationalism were made by Krutwig; by López Adán (Beltza), an important leader in the interior until his flight into exile in 1967, who combined traditional nationalism with anarchism;[81] and by Jon Etxabe, the head of the Military Front, who favoured a strategy of guerrilla war, based on the farmers, against the interior leadership's line of building an industrially based Marxist party. Etxabe was also bitterly hostile to any rapprochement with 'Spanish' forces, either in Euskadi or elsewhere in Spain. In practice, Etxabe and the Military Front, based in France, were acting on their own account from early 1970.

ETA's interior leadership were less concerned about Etxabe's criticisms than those of their mentor Escubi, who after escaping to France in the spring of 1969 had become highly critical of the policies which he had done so much to develop. Escubi and his exiled supporters formed Red Cells to study Marxism and develop an adequate strategy, which would enable Euskadi to achieve national liberation and socialism. ETA's interior leadership believed that their own political line was compatible with that of the Red Cells and hoped that the forthcoming Sixth Assembly should confirm their position and declare support for their policies. The Fifth Assembly had elected a National Committee, the *Biltzaar Ttippia* (BT) (literally 'small assembly'), to be the supreme authority between assemblies, but this had never been a functioning leadership and the majority of its members were in exile in different parts of Europe. Effectively, leadership had been exercised by an executive committee, the *Komite Ejecutivo Táctico* (KET), created by Escubi and composed of the leading members in the interior.

By 1970, as a result of death, exile, imprisonment and defections, the composition of the KET had itself changed drastically. After the arrests in the spring of 1969, the members of the new KET, effectively the third leadership team since the Fifth Assembly, aware of their youth and inexperience, were anxious to win the approval of the former leaders, in exile and in prison.[82] The KET's achievements had indeed been considerable as ETA had an organised structure and a greater strength in the workers' movement than ever before. The campaign in support of the prisoners had touched a chord among many different sections of the Basque people, including PNV supporters, priests and workers. EGI seemed on the point of seceding from the PNV to unite with ETA, a development which would have greatly increased the strength of the organisation.[83] The Red Cells agreed that the 'principal contradiction' in Euskadi was between the oligarchy and the people. However, while accepting the need for an alliance with the petty-bourgeoisie which followed from this theory, the Red Cells thought that, in practice, the interior leadership risked subordinating ETA to the politics of the petty-bourgeoisie, represented in Euskadi by the PNV. This, it was argued, repeated the error, which the PCE made at an all-Spanish level, of confusing the popular democratic revolution with the socialist one. The Red Cells thought that the attempt to ally with middle-class sectors, while necessary, had gone too far, producing a turn to the right.[84]

ETA's interior leadership accepted that they had been guilty of some right-wing deviations, but believed that their mistakes had been corrected. They saw the decision to transform ETA from a social movement into a revolutionary Marxist party not as an arbitrary step, but as a logical continuation of the evolution which had taken place at the Fourth and Fifth Assemblies. As the creation of such a party had to be based on a real understanding among the membership, ETA instituted a thoroughgoing debate in 1969 and 1970, by publishing many internal documents, by anonymous individuals and groups. Nearly all the contributors to the discussion had in common an acceptance of 'Marxism' and were strongly influenced by Mao, Castro and the leaders of the Vietnamese Liberation Front. Most of the documents, which contained more rhetoric than analysis of either the Basque country or ETA, placed a further barrier between the organisation and social reality. Nevertheless, the problems which had faced ETA from its beginnings — its relationships with the 'non-monopoly' capitalists, and specifically with the PNV, the immigrants, and the Spanish opposition to Franco's regime — were all discussed, albeit in a highly abstract form, as was the economic relationship between Euskadi and Spain.

Perhaps the most coherent argument for ETA continuing as a broad cross-class movement was given in the document *Paten-kutzat*, which accepted the key role of the working class, but argued that the Basque revolution had to be popular rather than socialist because in Euskadi the oligarchy, rather than the bourgeoisie, was the dominant class.[85] Consequently, it was argued, ETA should continue to be a Front of all the popular classes. The workers should play a secondary part in the next period of struggle and should not put their own interests before those of the National Front as a whole. According to the author of *Paten-kutzat*, there were very few communists in ETA, nor was ETA's membership mainly working-class. The leadership might attack the bourgeoisie, but this meant little to ordinary members. There was a need, he argued, for an organisation representing all the anti-oligarchy sections of the population and also for a party of the Basque proletariat. ETA, for the moment, had to fulfil both functions. The approach suggested by *Paten-kutzat* would have allowed ETA to incorporate Marxist terminology, while pursuing its traditional goals. The assertion that Euskadi was ruled by an oligarchy justified the building of a National Front and the postponement of specifically working-class demands and struggles to the indefinite future.

Most contributions to the pre-Assembly discussion accepted the need for both a revolutionary party and a National Front, and accepted that the immigrants formed part of the Basque people. None of the documents called for the abandonment of armed struggle, although most of them recognised that Euskadi was not part of the Third World. The documents, apparently, reflected the ideas of much of the membership, not just those of the students in Bilbao.[86] The writers' belief in the possibility of gaining support both from the nationalist community and from immigrant workers was a reflection of their own situation. Nearly all ETA members were young men from ethnically Basque families, and many combined study with paid employment. Their experience of a society undergoing rapid social change and their identification with anti-colonial struggles made them reject the distinction between social revolution and national liberation.[87] Although appeals to the authority of Mao, Castro and Stalin did little to clarify the dilemmas faced by ETA, there was agreement on a left-wing version of the theories adopted at the Fifth Assembly in 1967, especially on the concept of the PTV. An exception to this was a contribution by Beltza, written in February 1970, which criticised an article published in *Kemen*, ETA's theoretical journal, in October 1969.[88] Beltza, from his exile in Brussels, had watched ETA's evolution towards 'Marxism-Leninism' with dismay. His article combined anarchist and nationalist criticism in a bitter attack on the concept of the vanguard party, which the interior leadership wanted ETA to become. Beltza argued that the May 1968 rebellion in France showed the possibility of carrying out a libertarian revolution without such a party. The hostile tone of his contribution foreshadowed his resignation from ETA soon afterwards.[89]

Among the material circulated was a document, *Notas al problema nacional*, which made a scathing attack on the entire Basque nationalist tradition, pointed out its roots in anti-immigrant chauvinism, and denounced its part in persuading Basque workers to subordinate their own interests to that of the Basque bourgeoisie.[90] Julen Madariaga cited the publication of *Notas . . .* as proof of the interior leaders' treachery, alleging that it had been written by Escubi.[91] In fact, *Notas . . .* did not represent the ideas of the interior leadership. It had been written by a member of Kommunistak for use in the *Escuelas Sociales* and had been circulated because of the interior leadership's desire to have the widest possible discussion. A better guide to their thinking was provided by a document written in June 1970, *Algunas notas . . .*,[92] which argued for the abandonment of the attempt to form a National Front with the patriotic bourgeoisie. The document, written by the Bilbao leadership, was a rectification of another document also written by themselves three months before, which argued the same case less strongly.[93] The publication of the second version of *Algunas Notas* . . . did mark some leaders' break with nationalism, although this was to be neither permanent nor consistent.

The attempt to balance between the tradition of armed struggle and working-class solidarity produced a curious, but significant, action when the proceeds of a robbery carried out in July 1970 were donated to the families of building workers who had been killed by the police during a demonstration in Granada. The money was discreetly accepted by the families, but could not be acknowledged because of the inevitable police reaction. The robbery showed that ETA was capable of continuing the armed struggle, while the Robin Hood gesture of donating the money to the workers of Granada demonstrated the group's socialism and internationalism.[94] Several bank robberies had taken place in 1970, but such actions were intended to serve the financial needs of the organisation rather than being the main focus of the struggle. The support which ETA had always enjoyed among the section of the lower clergy was now reinforced by the development of a more critical attitude to the Franco regime by the Church hierarchy, when Bishop Cirarda of Bilbao refused in June 1970 to hold a service to commemorate the anniversary of Franco's troops capturing the city.[95]

The interior leadership thought they had carried out the task which had been entrusted to them and that the criticism they were receiving from both right and left was unjustified. They considered that they had steered a middle course between ETA-Berri's abandonment of the national struggle and the traditional chauvinistic nationalism of ETA's early days. However, it seemed to Krutwig that ETA's leaders were repeating the history of ETA-Berri almost exactly, in subordinating the national to the class struggle, and that the reason for their treachery was the same, namely infiltration of ETA by 'Spanish' communists.[96] Krutwig's criticisms were supported by Beltza and Julen Madariaga as well as by Txillardegi, who, although he had resigned from ETA in 1967, influenced its supporters through his editorship of the journal *Branka*. ETA's leadership were rather contemptuous of the criticism from Txillerdegi and his supporters, regarding it as representing a stage of ETA's thinking which had been overcome, even before the Fifth Assembly. Txillardegi and Beltza were, after all, no longer members of the organisation, while Krutwig, who did remain a member, had lived peacefully in exile without ever taking part in the violence which he theorised about. The criticisms made by Escubi and the Red Cells were, on the other hand, taken much more seriously. The forthcoming Assembly would, it was thought, clear up much of the misunderstanding and consolidate ETA's evolution towards becoming a revolutionary Marxist party.[97]

The hopes of the interior leadership were to be bitterly disappointed. Far from bringing about agreement, the Assembly produced a division into three mutually hostile organisations, ETA-VI, ETA-V and the Red Cells. Before the Assembly held in Itxaso, in the French Basque country, in late August and early September 1970, the interior leadership went to a great deal of trouble to prepare as representative a meeting as possible. The Red Cells were given eleven delegates out of a total of thirty-three, a figure which reflected their prestige as veterans, rather than their activity, now confined to study circles in exile. Krutwig, Etxabe, Madariaga and their followers saw the concessions to the Red Cells as one more proof of Escubi's manipulation of the Assembly. Once having made the arrangements, the interior leadership discovered that Etxabe, Madariaga and other former leaders were boycotting the Assembly and plotting to overthrow them. Madariaga did attend, but his involvement with the plotters had become known and the Assembly voted to expel him. Madariaga's expulsion signified a split between the interior leadership and the previous leaders, who represented the line of the early ETA. Some of those who supported the right-wing tendency known to their opponents as the 'Milis', and to themselves as ETA-V, had ceased to be members of ETA some time before, so their boycott of the Assembly merely ratified an accomplished fact.[98]

The interior leadership were surprised by the intensity of the differences which developed between themselves and the Red Cells after Madariaga was expelled. Although aware that the Red Cells were bitterly critical of what they saw as their comrades' capitulation to nationalism, particularly as expressed in *A todos los makos*, this was not seen as grounds for a split, as the interior leadership had themselves subsequently criticised the document and had accepted many of the strictures made by the Red Cells. The break with nationalism was shown in the main statement adopted by the Assembly which called for the recognition of the right to self-determination, rather than for independence, and pointed out the advantages for the working class of large, centralised states. The National Front of all patriotic Basques was not mentioned, although its formation had been seen as one of ETA's main tasks.[99] None of these developments satisfied the Red Cells who had come to the conclusion that ETA was incapable of being transformed into the revolutionary workers' party which they saw as necessary. ETA, in their opinion, was by its nature a petit-bourgeois organisation, which would always tend to adopt policies reflecting its own class position. This was demonstrated by the failure of the interior leadership to abandon the idea of the Basque National Front (FNV), which the Red Cells saw as an inherently anti-working-class concept. The Red Cells' members knew that they would be unable, from exile, to control ETA's activities, and they suspected, rightly as it turned out, that the interior leadership would relapse and re-adopt policies which it had now formally renounced. Accordingly the Red Cell members resigned and formed a separate organisation.[100]

The right-wing military tendency, who saw the evolution of the interior leadership as a simple repetition of the ETA-Berri story, where honest Basque patriots had been outwitted by cunning Spanish infiltrators, issued a manifesto accusing the interior leadership of being '*Españolistas*', and consequently expelling them. They declared the Sixth Assembly illegal, alleging that the five surviving 'orthodox' members of the Central Committee (BT) elected at the Fifth Assembly — Krutwig, Beltza, Arregui, Madariaga and Etxabe — were the only legitimate leadership.[101] The right-wing manifesto attacked the leadership which had emerged at the Assembly as liquidationists, '*Españolistas*', and followers of Escubi, refusing to acknowledge that Escubi and his supporters had also broken with the interior leadership and now formed a quite separate organisation. The manifesto reiterated that the Basque revolution would be made in Euskadi, and that *Euskera* was to be the sole language of the future independent Basque state.[102] This line was reiterated in an article by Etxabe, the Military Front leader, in the publication *Kemen*, where he repeated the standard explanation of deviationism in terms of 'Spanish' infiltration. Escubi's group who Etxabe, apparently, believed had organised the Sixth Assembly, had, he alleged, links with either the PCE or the Maoist groups, Voz Obrera (VO) or the Partido Comunista International (PCI). Escubi, who had once been a good patriot, had — it was claimed — lost his way because he had turned to politics.

According to Etxabe, the *Españolistas*' desire for unity of the working class at the level of the Spanish State was incompatible with nationalism. They had embraced communism, ignoring the fact that the communists, who had invaded Hungary and Czechoslovakia, were also fascists. As for the Spanish working class, so idolised by the '*Españolistas*', they also were imperialists, who supported their government's oppression of Euskadi, just as American workers backed theirs in Vietnam.[103] Etxabe called for the formation of a National Front which would include all patriotic elements, whether of Christian or other tendencies. The flirtation of the '*Españolistas*' with the communists was, he declared, as ridiculous as had been the inclusion of the Socialist Party in the Basque government in exile. Etxabe was particularly incensed by ETA's decision to hand over the proceeds of a robbery to the families of three building workers shot dead by the Civil Guard in Granada, which, he declared, was robbing the Basque resistance to aid Spaniards. Krutwig wrote another article in similar vein, where he also explained the evolution of the interior leadership as being a result of Spanish infiltration, which he alleged could be deduced from their phraseology, which could not have been produced by Basques. The liquidationist group were, he alleged, Trotskyist, just like ETA-Berri, as was shown by their denial of the theory of national liberation as a necessary stage before social liberation.[104] The nationalist movement had once again been infiltrated by those who wished to destroy it.

The split by the right-wing tendency merely confirmed the existing situation. Etxabe and his group had been acting in practice as an independent organisation since the beginning of the year. Nationalists such as Etxabe had been prepared to tolerate a 'Marxism' which had functioned as an ideology justifying the armed activity of an armed vanguard. However, the Marxism now advocated by both the interior leadership and the Red Cells would have abandoned the nationalism which had been the reason for ETA's existence, and the rejection of the National Front of all patriotic Basques would have alienated most of ETA's potential supporters. The great majority of ETA activists in the Spanish Basque country supported the Sixth Assembly leadership. Although the level of political understanding of these members was low, they did not want to return to the racist, conservative line expounded by Etxabe. A statement of support for the decisions of the Sixth Assembly by all the Burgos prisoners helped to confirm its legitimacy.[105] The Sixth Assembly leadership was severely shaken by the defection of Escubi and his followers, and to a much lesser extent by the split led by Krutwig, Etxabe and Madariaga.[106] However, their resolve to continue with the struggle was unshaken. They had the enormous responsibility of leading the campaign to save the lives of their comrades who would soon be brought to trial on charges which included the killing of Melitón Manzanas. While this was a formidable task, the interior leadership (henceforth ETA-VI) had more resources to carry it out than ever before. The ideology of the organisation had changed enormously since the Fifth Assembly, but the determination to create a socialist Euskadi by an effort of will remained.

REFERENCES

1. Interview with Madariaga in *Punto y Hora*, 18–24 August 1977.
2. Author's interview with Sabino Arana, Vitoria, 16 March 1980, and Iñaki Sarasketa, San Sebastián, 26 March 1980; see *Zutik*, January, March and June 1964, 4 January 1965, 30 November 1965.
3. *Zutik*, November 1961 and December 1961–January 1962.
4. *Zutik*, 30 November 1965 and January 1966.
5. 'Noticias de Euskadi', *Zutik*, 1 January 1965.
6. 'Pueblo Trabajador Vasco', *Zutik*, No. 44, January 1967.
7. Author's interview with Patxo Unzueta.
8. 'El socialismo vasco y el frente nacional', *Zutik*, No. 44, January 1967.
9. *Ideologia oficial de Y, Documentos Y*, Vol. 7; 'El Batasun Eguna y la unidad Obrera', *Zutik*, No. 47, September 1967.
10. Author's interview with Patxo Unzueta and Iñaki Sarasketa.
11. See 'Ha muerto J.A. Etxevarrieta', *Berriak*, No. 14, February 1973.
12. 'Situación económica de España y de Euzkadi', *Zutik*, No. 45.
13. Goiri (a pseudonym of Txabi), 'Situación del socialismo vasco y el Frente Nacional', *Zutik*, No. 44, January 1967.
14. Max Gallo, *Histoire de l'Espagne Franquiste*, 2 vols (Paris, 1969), p. 407.
15. Luis Ramírez (Luciano Rincón), *Nuestros primeros veinticinco años* (Paris, 1964), Chapter 12, 'La rebelión del clero'.
16. For an ESBA criticism of both branches of ETA see 'Estado de excepción', *Batasuna*, No. 3, undated.
17. Fernando Claudín, *Documentos de una divergencia comunista*, (Barcelona, 1978), passim; Fernando Claudín, *Santiago Carrillo. Crónica de un Secretario General* (Barcelona, 1983), pp. 151–77; Jorge Semprún, *Autobiografía de Federico Sánchez* (Barcelona, 1977), passim; Gregorio Morán, *Miseria y grandeza del Partido Comunista de España, 1939–1985* (Barcelona, 1986), pp. 378–403.
18. Author's interview with Patxo Unzueta.
19. *V Asamblea de ETA, Segunda sesión (Actas)*.

20. Author's interviews with Iñaki Sarasketa, San Sebastián, 26 March 1980, Iñaki Garcia Aranberri, Ondarroa, 19 March 1980, and Sabino Arana, Vitoria, 16 March 1980.

21. Author's interview with Elisabet Baztarretxe and Josu Bravo, PNV activists in the 1960s, Bilbao, 14 March 1980.

22. 'Espiral acción-represión', *Zutik*, No. 50, December 1968.

23. 'Frente Cultural', *Kemen*, September–October 1969

24. Author's interviews with Sabino Arana, Iñaki Sarasketa and Iñaki Garcia Aranberri, quoted above.

25. 'Batasuna: Frente Nacional Vasco', *Zutik*, No. 50, December 1968.

26. Author's interview with ETA-Berri leader Javier Ortiz, San Sebastián, summer 1968.

27. Author's interview with José María Iriarte (Bikilia), a leader of the Workers' Front in 1969–70, San Sebastián, 17 August 1981.

28. 'La huelga de Bandas. . . .', *Horizonte Español 1972*, 2 Vols (Paris, 1972), Vol. 1, pp. 64–74.

29. 'Espiral acción-represión', *Zutik*, No. 50, December 1968.

30. *Dedicado a los que en silencio cumplen con la mas ingrata de las misiones*, and *Del derecho de los súbditos a la resistencia*, *Documentos Y*, Vol. 6, pp. 433–8 and 455–509.

31. 'Consejos de guerra en Burgos', *Berriak*, No. 8, 28 July 1971.

32. Interview with Zumalde in *La Voz de España*, San Sebastián, 29 and 30 December 1979.

33. 'Luttes ouvrières en Espagne', *Frères du Monde*, No. 60.

34. 'La lucha antifranquista en Guipúzcoa', *Mundo Obrero*, September 1968.

35. *La acción-represión en Euskadi*, *Documentos Y*, Vol. 7, pp. 518–23.

36. Author's interview with Iñaki Sarasketa, San Sebastián, 26 March 1980.

37. *Zutik-Berriak* undated, perhaps June 1967.

38. *Zutik-Berriak*, 21 April 1967.

39. Author's interviews with Sabino Arana, Vitoria, 16 March 1980, and Iñaki Garcia Aranberri, Ondarroa, 19 March 1980.

40. 'Gazteiz (Euskadi)', *Zutik-Berriak*, 21 April 1967.

41. *La acción-represión en Euskadi*, *Documentos Y*, Vol. 7, pp. 518–23.

42. Author's interview with Sabino Arana, Vitoria, 16 March 1980; *Manifesto-Aberri Eguna 1968*, *Documentos Y*, Vol. 7, pp. 471–7

43. Interview with Sarasketa; *La Voz de España*, 9 June 1968; 'El primer martir de la revolución', ETA statement on Txabi's death, *Documentos Y*, Vol. 7, p. 484.

44. 'Biografía', *Iraultza*, 1968; 'Txabi asesinado', *Zutik*, No. 44 (Caracas), 7 June 1968.

45. Interview with Sarasketa.

46. *Horizonte Español*, Vol. 1, p. 120.

47. 'Nuestras armas', *Zutik*, No. 49, July 1968; 'Ha muerto el Che Guevara', *Zutik*, No. 47, undated.

48. *La Voz de España*, 3 August 1968.

49. 'Manzanas, una muerte providencial', *Gudari*, No. 48, 1968.

50. Interview with García Aranberri.

51. *Horizonte Español 1972*, Vol. 1, pp. 121–2.

52. *Branka* (undated — French edition) gave a total of 1,953 arrests. *Documentos Y*, Vol. 8, p. 226.
53. *Horizonte Español 1972*, Vol. 1, p. 142.
54. *Horizonte Español 1972*, Vol. 1. p. 151.
55. Miguel Castells and Franciso Letamendía, *Burgos, Juicio a un pueblo* (San Sebastián, 1978) p. 31.
56. 'Detenciones en Pamplona', *Zutik- Berriak*, January 1969; *Horizonte Español 1972*, Vol. 1, p. 36.
57. *Horizonte Español 1972*, Vol. 1, p. 138.
58. *Información al PTV*, ETA leaflet, *Documentos Y*, Vol. 8, pp. 281–2; author's interview with Mario Onaindía, Vitoria, 25 March 1980.
59. '*Información al PTV*'.
60. *Rapport M*, (undated), *Documentos Y*, Vol. 8, pp. 55–61.
61. Author's interviews with José María Iriarte (Bikilia), a leader of the Workers' Front, San Sebastián, 17 August 1981, and Patxo Unzueta, Bilbao, 13 March 1980.
62. 'BAI: *Batasuna* (Unity), *Askatasuna* (Freedom), *Indarra* (Strength)'; BAI is the Basque word for 'yes', *Hojas Batasuna*, *Documentos Y*, Vol. 7, pp. 363–77.
63. Interviews with Patxo Unzueta and Bikilia.
64. 'Líneas generales de una estrategia a largo plazo', *Zutik*, No. 51, March 1969.
65. 'Líneas generales. . ..', *Zutik*, March 1969.
66. 'Líneas generales. . ..', *Zutik*, March 1969.
67. 'Un paso hacia la unidad del PTV', *Zutik*, No. 51, March 1969.
68. '¿Qué es ETA Bai?', *Kommunistak*, No. 2, June 1969.
69. Interviews with Sabino Arana, Iñaki Sarasketa and Iñaki Garcia Aranberri.
70. Author's interview with one such member, José Miguel Goiburu (Goiherri), a future leader of ETA-V, San Sebastián, 5 August 1984.
71. Editorial: '1970 año del Frente Nacional Vasco', *Gudalde*, No. 3, undated.
72. *Batasuna*, undated and unnumbered.
73. 'Batasun Eguna', *Batasuna*, No. 3; 'Batasun Langile', *Batasuna*, No. 4, undated.
74. Author's interviews with 'Bikilia' and Patxo Unzueta.
75. *A todos los Makos*, *Documentos Y*, Vol. 9, pp. 367–75.
76. *Crítica al informe de los Makos* (a communication from the cell in Clermont-Ferrand), *Documentos Y*, Vol. 9, pp. 378–80.
77. *A todos los Makos*.
78. *A todos los Makos*.
79. *A todos los Makos*.
80. Interview with Unzueta.
81. *Sobre el trabajo: Estructura, militancia y disciplina*, *Documentos Y*, Vol. 9, pp. 212–22.
82. *Comunicado de aclaración de ETA*, *Documentos Y*, Vol. 9, pp. 460–4.
83. *EGI Batasuna*, published by dissident EGI members in 1970, *Documentos Y*, Vol. 9, pp. 23–30.
84. *Crítica al informe de los Makos*, *Documentos Y*, Vol. 9, pp. 378–80.
85. *Patenkutzat*, *Documentos Y*, Vol. 9, pp. 102–6.

86. Author's interviews with Unzueta and 'Bikilia', cited above.

87. Author's interview with Mikel Orrantia, Bilbao, 13 March 1980.

88. Beltza, *Sobre el trabajo: Estructura, Militancia y Disciplina, Documentos Y*, Vol. 9, pp. 217–22.

89. See *Zeltan Ari*, No. 1, 7 June 1970.

90. *Notas al problema nacional, Documentos Y*, Vol. 9, pp. 233–55.

91. *Zutik* (ETA V) No. 57, October (1970).

92. *Algunas notas. . ., Documentos Y*, Vol. 9, pp. 304–49.

93. *Algunas notas. . ., Documentos Y*, Vol. 9, pp. 263–71.

94. *Tres asesinados y varios heridos graves en Granada por las fuerzas de represión fascistas, Documentos Y*, Vol. 8, p. 461.

95. *Horizonte Español 1972*, Vol. 1, p. 201: *Zutik* (Caracas, undated) No. 91.

96. F. Sarailh and P. Zugasti, *Comentarios y proposiciones ante la próxima asamblea, Documentos Y*, Vol. 12, pp. 99–115; Federico, *Sobre la situación actual, Documentos Y*, Vol. 9, pp. 465–74.

97. Interviews with Unzueta and 'Bikilia'.

98. 'El desarrollo de la VI Asamblea', *Zutik* (ETA VI), No. 52, May (1971).

99. *Proposiciones generales, Documentos Y*, Vol. 9, pp. 430–6.

100. See 'Desarrollo de la VI Asamblea', *Saioak*, No. 3 (1971).

101. Federico (Krutwig), *Sobre la situación actual*, undated but probably September 1970, *Documentos Y*, Vol. 9, pp. 465–74.

102. *Manifesto, Documentos Y*, Vol. 9, pp. 451–2.

103. J.J. Etxabe, 'Carta abierta a todos los militantes de ETA', *Kemen* (undated).

104. *Sobre la situación actual, Documentos Y*, Vol. 9, pp. 465–74.

105. *Documento de los presos de Burgos, Documentos Y*, Vol. 9, pp. 199–217.

106. *Comunicado de aclaración, Documentos Y*, Vol. 9, pp. 460–4.

4

The Burgos Trial

The long awaited trial, by a military court, of sixteen members of ETA, which started in Burgos on 3 December 1970, was undoubtedly the most crucial event in ETA's history. The trial, and the very strong campaign to save the lives of those six accused who were condemned to death, had the effect of bringing the ideas of ETA-VI before the entire population of the Basque country, and indeed of the world. Before the trial the accused were unknown, but by its conclusion children in the street could recite their names in the same way that they could those of the members of the football teams Atlético de Bilbao and Real Sociedad de San Sebastián,[1] The enormous public response to the trial, which included strikes, demonstrations and occupation of churches, showed that the accused were not simply isolated members of a terrorist band, as the Spanish press suggested.[2] On the contrary, ETA-VI's activities enjoyed the sympathy of large numbers of people who did not share all of their ideas. The theory of action/repression/action, which had appeared to be rather discredited in 1969 and most of 1970, seemed valid once more.

The charges against the prisoners presented a picture of a daring campaign of armed struggle. Jean-Paul Sartre thought that ETA resembled both the anti-German resistance movements which had arisen during World War Two, and the anti-colonial struggles in the Third World since.[3] As the offences which the prisoners were charged with were committed during the campaign of armed struggle launched by Escubi in 1968/1969, observers learned nothing about the developments within ETA since spring 1969, which had culminated in the decision, taken at the Sixth Assembly in the autumn of 1970, that the organisation should be transformed into a Marxist party. The fact that ETA had split into several parts was not generally understood, and the contradictory press statements which were issued by ETA-V and ETA-VI only added to the confusion.

The arrest of many leading ETA members in 1969 had been a big victory for the police, and had considerably reduced ETA's campaign of violence. In a sense, the trial could be seen as merely a sequel to the crushing of ETA's offensive of 1968/69. However, the trial of nationalists for crimes which could result in death sentences created problems for a government which was anxious to establish that Spain was a normal western country which was gradually liberalising and qualifying for eventual membership of the Common Market. In 1963 there had been an international scandal when a PCE underground organiser, Julián Grimau, had been executed for crimes which he was alleged to have committed during the Civil War.[4] The government could not have been happy about the prospect of executing any more of its political opponents. The death sentences passed on Sarasketa and Arrizabalaga in 1968 and 1969 had both been commuted to terms of imprisonment, perhaps as indication that the authorities feared the repercussions of killing ETA members. By the time Franco realised how embarrassing a show trial of civilians by a military court would be, a sudden cancellation would have been taken as a sign of weakness.[5]

Another way of avoiding publicity would have been to take advantage of the fact that two of the accused were priests, and persuade the bishops to request that the trial be held '*in camera*', as was provided for by the Concordat with the Vatican. The bishops of Bilbao and San Sebastián, however, refused to exercise this right, leaving the authorities with no alternative but to go ahead with an open trial held in the presence of foreign journalists.[6] The bishops' decision not to co-operate with the government was, in itself, an indication of the disintegration of the alliance which had triumphed in the Civil War. The authorities had to drive a wedge between ETA and the traditional base of nationalism if they were to succeed in getting the majority of the Basque people to accept that the accused were terrorists, rather than Basque patriots. The prisoners were handcuffed together throughout the trial, as if to show how dangerous they were, but the attempt to depict the accused as desperate criminals was unsuccessful. For a majority of Basque people, the sixteen prisoners were legitimate successors to those who had fought for Euskadi in the Civil War. The support shown for them through strikes and demonstrations made the authorities declare a State of Emergency in Guipúzcoa, the most nationalist of the Basque provinces, just after the trial opened.[7]

The charges which the prisoners faced gave a vivid impression of the functioning of ETA in the period up to April 1969. They had carried out a spectacular series of actions which included causing explosions both in official buildings and commercial premises, armed robbery, illegal possession of arms, preparing and distributing propaganda, and planning the assassination of Melitón Manzanas.[8] Most of the accused were *liberados* (full-time ETA members), and the charges against them presented a picture of a group of people who, under the leadership of Escubi, had worked together as a team,[9] even using as a common base the flat in the Calle de Artecalle, in Bilbao, where a number of them had been arrested. These methods of organisation employed bore little resemblance to the structure of separate Fronts, carrying out different functions, decided on at the Fifth Assembly. The accused together with others, who had managed to avoid arrest, had been the real leadership of ETA, and the core of its activists. For example, the prosecution alleged that the decision to assassinate Melitón Manzanas had been made by some of the defendants rather than by any superior body.[10]

The sixteen prisoners were fairly representative of the social base of ETA throughout its existence. Nearly all were from Vizcaya or Guipúzcoa and there were, apart from the two priests, several ex-seminarists. Some had been manual workers, but the majority followed lower-middle-class occupations, such as technicians, teachers and clerks. None were farmers, although they tended to come from smaller towns rather than cities. The names of several showed them to be of mixed Basque/Spanish origin, and none were from an upper-class background. Most were quite young; for example, Jesús Abrisqueta Corta, was already a *liberado*, although he was only nineteen at the time of his arrest in April 1969. Even more striking, in view of their status in the organisation, most of them had not been members at the time of the Fifth Assembly in 1966/67, a good indication of how police action made it impossible for ETA to establish a stable leadership inside Spain.[11] The lower rate of violence since most of the accused were arrested seemed to indicate that the government was well on the way to defeating ETA. Yet the outcome of the trial was a moral and political defeat for the Franco regime. This was partly due to the conduct of the prisoners who succeeded to a remarkable degree in turning their trial into a condemnation of the regime by describing the torture to which they had been subjected by the police. The fact that the numerous foreign journalists who attended the trial reported the prisoners' description of the tortures which had been inflicted on them showed that the government had made a mistake in staging a show trial.

The defence lawyers played a very effective part in helping the accused to present the trial as a political assault on the Basque people.[12] ETA's new 'internationalist' spirit led it to engage the political activists Peces Barba, a PSOE member from Madrid and a future President of the Cortes, and Sole Barbera, a PCE member from Catalonia. José Antonio Etxebarrieta, brother of Txabi and himself a prominent ETA theoretician, defended Izco de la Iglesia, who was accused of killing Manzanas. Some of the others were in the future to become key supporters of ETA. Juan María Bandrés, who had previously defended Sarasketa, Txabi's companion at the time of his death,[13] was later to become a Senator for an electoral alliance linked to a branch of ETA. Miguel Castells, who was not at the time particularly nationalist, was to become a leader of a political organisation linked to ETA, as was Francisco Letamendía, a younger man, who defended Itziar Aizpurua. Bandrés, Castells and Letamendía were not obvious candidates for the part of leaders of revolutionary nationalist organisations. All three were from comfortable upper-middle-class backgrounds, Castells being the son of San Sebastián's *Notario Público* (Public Registrar) and the brother-in-law of José Ramón Recalde, a former leader of ESBA, whom Txillardegi had seen as the sinister mastermind responsible for the 'infiltration' and take-over of the ETA leadership in 1965 and 1966.[14]

The key role which lawyers played at Burgos and in later trials was partly due to their function as substitute spokesmen for ETA. The Burgos trial was the best opportunity which the organisation had ever had to expound its ideas to the public. ETA's combination of enjoying enormous public sympathy, while having little organised structure, made the lawyers' role extremely important. Through skilful questioning of their clients and constant objections to the military judges' conduct of the trial, and by press conferences aimed at foreign journalists, the defence lawyers aided the prisoners to expound ETA's ideas and to denounce police torture and oppression of the Basques.[15] The official press campaign of denunciation of ETA, and the repression which extended to the families of the lawyers, had a tremendously radicalising effect on them.[16] Letamendía, for example, although not a sympathiser of ETA before the trial, went into exile shortly afterwards and became a leading member of ETA-VI.[17]

Itziar Aizpurua, one of the three women among the accused, set the mood which was to dominate the trial when she described how her political consciousness was awakened by observing both the hardship suffered by the immigrants in Deva, her native village, and the discrimination against the native population by the refusal to allow children to speak *Euskera* in school and by the authorities' prohibition of Basque cultural events.[18] José María Dorronsoro declared that the peasants in Euskadi were exploited by the oligarchy, just as were the peasants in Andalusia, and also stated that he was a Marxist-Leninist. Eduardo Uriarte Romero spoke of his early upbringing in Seville and declared that the Basque, French and Spanish people were all exploited by the oligarchy.[19] Victor Arana described how he had had to go to work at the age of fifteen following the death of his father. Arana's mother received no pension although her husband had contributed to the appropriate fund during his thirty years of employment with the same firm. The official *Sindicato* had done nothing to help the widow to obtain her rights. This event had made a strong impression on Arana and had been one of the main reasons for his joining ETA.[20]

Similar statements made by many of the accused seemed to show that ETA had been transformed into a Marxist-Leninist organisation which, while it confined its activities to Euskadi, sympathised equally with the oppressed elsewhere in Spain, and had completely abandoned anti-Spanish chauvinism. Such declarations, on the face of it, seemed calculated to alienate the Catholic small town milieu which had been the traditional base of Basque nationalism, and from which most of the accused themselves came. The official ideology of the forces which had risen against the Republic in 1936 was that Spain was threatened by 'red separatism'. 'Red separatism' had been a concept invented by the Franco regime's propagandists, whereas in reality the alliance between the conservative PNV and the working-class forces supporting the Republic had always been uneasy. The declaration of the prisoners, combining nationalism and Marxism-Leninism, indicated that 'red separatism' now really existed.[21]

Some of the accused in their declaration to the court took a more traditional nationalist stance. For example, Gregorio López

Irasuegi declared that he considered himself a prisoner of war, gave his name and position in ETA, and refused to answer any more questions, claiming that this was his right under the Geneva Convention.[22] However, López Irasuegi's response, while it might be more welcome to traditional nationalists than declarations of Marxist-Leninism, did not indicate any split among the prisoners, all of whom supported the leadership which had been elected at the Sixth Assembly a few months before. All of the prisoners were determined to seize the opportunity presented by the trial to inform the world of how the Basque people were oppressed. Joaquín Gorostidi declared that ETA was not a terrorist organisation, but a movement of national liberation. The bombs which had been planted at various monuments and official buildings were not intended to create terror but to draw attention to the oppression suffered by the Basque people, and to initiate the spiral of action/repression/action which would lead to national liberation. He also denied that ETA was a separatist organisation. On the contrary, as it was internationalist it supported the struggle of other nations against oppression. ETA's struggle, he declared, was breaking one of the links of the imperialist chain, and thereby helping the struggle of the oppressed elsewhere.[23]

However, the declarations of commitment to Marxism and to the necessity of a working-class revolution had little connection with the activities which the prisoners were charged with. Few of them had had any direct involvement in working-class struggle and nearly all were from the ethnically Basque middle class. Their 'Marxism' consisted, essentially, of a belief in the need for a struggle of oppressed people throughout the world. José María Dorronsoro's statement that a peasant in Andalusia was as oppressed as one in Euskadi was unwelcome to most nationalists, but hardly amounted to a Marxist analysis. The prisoners' statements seemed to indicate that they, and their organisation, had moved away from nationalism in the same way as had ETA-Berri, but most of them were eventually to return to the nationalist fold.

Juan Echave, one of the priests among the accused, denied that there was any contradiction between his vocation and his membership of ETA, declaring that a priest had the duty to seek solutions to the people's political, economic and cultural problems, as well as ministering to their religious needs. Echave declared that ETA was internationalist and that its commitment to international solidarity was particularly appealing to him as he had, at one time, considered dedicating himself to missionary work abroad.[24] He declared that he still considered himself as the parish priest of his village and that his bishop had not indicated that he was to be dismissed. He also gave a detailed account of the tortures which he claimed the police had inflicted on him. Abrisqueta, the youngest of the accused, described how he had been continually tortured over a period of days.[25] Francisco Javier Martínez also denied that ETA was a separatist organisation. On the contrary, it was internationalist and supported the struggle of the proletariat wherever it took place. The prosecution continually complained that most of the prisoners' evidence was not pertinent to the case, and the presiding officer ordered the accused, on a number of occasions, to confine themselves to answering the questions put to them.[26] Nevertheless, aided by the complaints of their lawyers, those examined in the first few days of the trial succeeded in their objective of describing both their maltreatment at the hands of the police and the reality of oppression in the Basque country.

The prisoners' evidence was, from the authorities' point of view, giving the world an appalling picture of the Franco regime. A respite was provided when, on 7 December, the trial was interrupted for a day because, it was announced, one of the presiding officers was ill.[27] The delay may have been produced by the need to consider the damage which the prisoners' statements were causing. Although the discretion of the Spanish press could be relied on, the trial was being extensively covered by the foreign press, whose reports were much more revealing. When the trial reconvened the following day, the President of the Court announced that, in future, the accused must confine themselves to answering the questions put to them.[28] It was however too late for the authorities to avoid the debacle which the trial had become. The change in the conduct of the trial became apparent when Izco de la Iglesia, the alleged killer of Manzanas, answering the questions of his lawyer, started to describe the treatment he had been subjected to at the hands of the police. When he was told to desist, his lawyer, Etxebarrieta, accused the judges of obstructing the defence.[29] The change in the President of the Court's attitude made the subsequent conduct of the trial more typical of the proceedings of a military court than it had been earlier with the tolerance with which the first prisoners' statements had been received.[30]

In response to the more rigorous treatment, three of the accused refused to answer questions, declaring they were prisoners of war, and appealing to the Geneva Convention. It seemed that the very effective tactics of the accused acting as the accuser, through lengthy statements from the dock, were no longer permitted and that the rest of the trial would be an anticlimax. However, when the last prisoner to be called, Mario Onaindía, gave evidence, events took a new turn. When Onaindía started to make a speech protesting against the oppression suffered by the Basques, the President of the Court ordered him to be silent. Onaindía attempted to grab an axe and move towards the table where the members of the tribunal sat. Amidst general pandemonium several officers drew their swords and the police their revolvers. Onaindía was overpowered as the rest of the prisoners, who were handcuffed together, rose to their feet and sang *Eusko Gudariak*, the Basque soldiers' anthem.[31] The proceedings were suspended and the court cleared, but the incident had been witnessed by the foreign journalists who were present, and was widely reported.

When order was restored the court reconvened, but this time with the press and public excluded. The prisoners' lawyers, who had wanted the bishops of Bilbao and San Sebastián to testify, now, in protest, declined to call any defence witnesses.[32] The trial, which had looked like being lengthy now proceeded quickly. On 9 December the prosecutor made his submission, demanding sentences of death for six of the accused and lengthy prison terms for the others. The prisoners were then asked if they had anything to say before the judges retired to consider their verdict. All of the accused made defiant statements, many of them in both Spanish and *Euskera*, declaring that the trial had been a farce, shouting 'Revolution or Death' and declaring their solidarity with the socialist revolution in Spain as well as in Euskadi.[33]

The high drama of the courtroom scenes was followed by a long period of tension, while the military judges retired to examine the written evidence and consider their verdict. Anxiety was increased by the knowledge that ETA-V, which had kidnapped the German Consul in San Sebastián two days before the trial opened, had threatened to kill him in the event of any of the accused men being executed. When the sentences were announced more than two weeks later, on 28 December, they were predictably severe. María Aránzazu Arruti, already serving a prison term for previous offences, was absolved, but the sentences imposed on her comrades ranged from twelve to ninety years. However, these verdicts were overshadowed by the horrifying fact that six of the accused were condemned to death. Three of them received double death sentences.[34] The effect of this was to increase the campaign of protest, in a desperate effort to get the penalties revoked. The three principal Basque bishops went to Madrid in an unsuccessful attempt to meet Franco, in order to plead for clemency.[35]

ETA-VI's leadership was convinced, long before the trial opened, that its main task was to save the lives of those comrades who were likely to be sentenced to death.[36] Their responsibility was enormous and the campaign which they launched was an example of the strategy which Unzueta had outlined in *A todos los Makos*. The potential support for the prisoners included all the heterogeneous forces to whom ETA had tried to ally itself and give direction. These included the 'non-monopoly' capitalists, who formed part of the traditional base of the PNV, and the activists in the illegal labour movement, nearly all of whom were non-nationalist. ETA-VI now saw mass mobilisation as the only way of saving their comrades' lives. The organisation's attempts to produce such a mass mobilisation were fairly successful, as nationalists, as well as the PCE, the MCE and other left-wing groups, were anxious to build the broadest possible alliance.[37] In any case, the left organisations had their strength in the workplaces, where nationalists were weak, so the likelihood of clashes which could divide the campaign was limited.[38] The government's concern about the scale of the protest movement which the trial had produced was expressed in a confidential document circulated among the leaders of the Movimiento (formerly the Falange) which found its way to the clandestine opposition press.[39] ETA-VI's involvement in the campaign, necessarily, forced its members to engage in very open forms of activity. This, in turn, brought intensified police repression, with the result that many of the leadership had to go into exile. ETA-VI's activists suffered the worst of both worlds, as they belonged to an organisation identified with armed struggle, while at the same time they were attempting to build a mass movement. Nevertheless, the organisation considered the campaign a success, as it had won the support of a wider spectrum of the population than could have been mobilised on any other issue.[40]

The popular backing for the accused in the Basque country greatly surpassed even that which had occurred after Txabi's death. In addition to demonstrations by clergy and congregations in traditional Basque areas, there were strikes in factories with a predominantly immigrant labour force. A young man had been shot dead early in December by the Civil Guard, during a demonstration in Eibar, the home of two of the prisoners.[41] The government's declaration of a State of Emergency, in Guipúzcoa, was an indication of the scale of the protests. The Workers' Commissions and other illegal organisations called a general strike on 3 December, the opening day of the trial, which paralysed many of the industrial centres in Vizcaya and Guipúzcoa.[42] In some places the strikers erected barricades. The government responded by concentrating thousands of armed and plain-clothes police in the centre of the main towns. It was announced that more than a hundred people had been arrested in the course of the day. In spite of the massive police presence, groups of people in San Sebastián tried to burn down the offices of the official newspapers, in protest at the lying version of events which they had published.[43]

According to the authorities the protests were manipulated by the communists. The PCE was certainly very active in the campaign and it had issued a joint statement with ETA-VI in October, calling for a general strike to start as soon as the trial began.[44] This was to be an embarrassment to ETA-VI as traditional nationalists were puzzled by it, while Etxabe's breakaway group which now described itself at ETA-*Askatusuna ala hil* (Freedom or Death) saw it as one more proof that ETA-VI had been infiltrated by 'Spanish' agents. The scale and militancy of the demonstrations confirmed ETA-VI in its belief that such activities were more important than the spectacular ones for which their comrades were being tried.

ETA-VI's leaders believed that the campaign had helped to achieve two of ETA's objectives, unity of the working class and unity of the Basque nation, but once the trial was over, the Workers' Front and the National Front proved as hard to build as before. ETA-VI's campaign was not confined to the Basque country, as its leaders were aware that the trial had aroused considerable opposition both in Spain and abroad, and they worked hard to get support outside Euskadi. In Euskadi, ETA-VI mounted an enormous publicity campaign by means of leaflets and broadsheets, in spite of the tremendous dangers and difficulties involved in distributing illegal propaganda. ETA's leaflets called on the people to show their support for the prisoners by going on strike, keeping children away from school, and boycotting entertainments. Owners of shops, bars and similar establishments were asked to close their premises.[45] Such leaflets carried declarations from the prisoners which not only expressed their willingness to die for their country, but their commitment to socialist revolution.[46] Sometimes, appeals for the prisoners were mingled with demands for higher wages and trade union rights. Propaganda was distributed in factories and on the streets, using the network of *cuadrillas*; ETA-VI co-operated, uneasily, with other tendencies in the campaign. The propaganda achieved an amazing response. Not only did ordinary Basques demonstrate and fight back against attacks by the police, but the struggle took spontaneous forms involving people who had no connection with illegal organisations.[47]

The trial was both a problem and a challenge to the PNV. The friendly attitude which the PNV had adopted to ETA in its early days had steadily worsened as ETA had moved towards socialism and guerrilla action. The welcome return to orthodox nationalism, marked by the expulsion of the ETA-Berri tendency, had been illusory, as the new ETA leadership had reaffirmed ETA's Marxism, to the disgust of the PNV. In addition, ETA was acting as a pole of attraction for the PNV youth in EGI, which was in danger of splitting once again.[48] The PNV had, itself, flirted with the idea of adopting armed struggle, under the pressure to compete with ETA, but had abandoned the idea after two EGI members were killed transporting explosives on April 1 1969.[49] However great the PNV's misgivings about giving support to an organisation which had now become a serious rival, it really had no choice but to mobilise its members in support of ETA's prisoners. Long before the trial the PNV's press had published articles implicitly sympathetic to ETA.

The government in exile, dominated by the PNV, called for a general strike in protest against the court martial.[50] Even if the party's leaders had been cynical enough to instruct its members to stand aside from the campaign of support for the prisoners, their members would not have obeyed. PNV activists were representative of a large sector of the Basque population and shared its anguish at the prospect of young Basques being executed. An extreme example of a PNV supporter's identification with ETA's fighters was provided by an incident in September when Franco had attended the opening of the world pelota championships. A middle-aged man, Joseba Elósegui, wrapped in flames, threw himself from a balcony above Franco in an unsuccessful attempt at suicide. The incident was widely reported, but its significance was not fully understood outside the Basque country. Elósegui was known as a distinguished Basque patriot with an outstanding record of resistance to the Franco regime. Elósegui, who was later to become a PNV senator, had been a commander in the Basque army at Guernica when it was bombed by German planes in 1937, and had been sentenced to death on being taken prisoner.[51] When Franco's army occupied Euskadi, he was exchanged for an enemy prisoner and subsequently fought in the republican army in Catalonia. Later he had worked with the Allies in German-occupied France, and had gone to carry out clandestine work for the PNV, inside Spain.[52] Elósegui's willingness to give his life for his ideals was in character with his previous history and sprang from the same despair which in 1946 had impelled him to hang an *Ikurriña* on the spire of San Sebastián's pro-cathedral.[53] He had been encouraged by the rise of a new opposition to the regime in the 1960s and was appalled at the prospect of the Burgos prisoners being executed, although he did not agree with their violent methods, which he felt would not achieve their objective.[54] His gesture demonstrated the frustration of a natural activist who could find no other way to express his solidarity. Elósegui's self-immolation reflected the depth of sympathy for the prisoners in the nationalist community, and the more general resentment at police repression. Other PNV members, in less dramatic ways, did all they could to save the lives of the prisoners, despite their puzzlement over the Marxist statements which had been made during the trial.

The PNV was not the only nationalist group which mobilised on behalf of the prisoners. Supporters of Txillardegi's journal, *Branka*, were active in the campaign, as were members of ELA, the nationalist trade union. Etxabe and his comrades in ETA-V were also determined to intervene in order to save the prisoners' lives and to demonstrate that they themselves, and not the leadership elected at the Sixth Assembly, were the legitimate ETA. ETA-V was confronted by a dilemma as a result of the scale of the demonstrations in support of the Burgos prisoners. While many people sympathised with Etxabe's racism and anti-Marxism,[55] ETA-V had no organised presence within Spain. Although ETA-V regarded the interior leadership, who had been confirmed in their positions after the Sixth Assembly, as traitors and liquidators of the same type as those expelled at the Fifth Assembly in 1966/67, the fact that the prisoners supported the decisions of the Sixth Assembly gave it legitimacy in the eyes of the great majority of ETA's supporters. ETA's heroes, some of whom might soon be martyred, were beyond criticism. The mingling of socialist propaganda with appeals to save the lives of the prisoners was an alarming continuation of the policies which ETA-V had criticised. In addition, the fact that 'Spanish' organisations in Euskadi and outside had thrown themselves into the struggle to save the Burgos prisoners threatened to obscure what ETA-V felt to be the nature of ETA's national mission. ETA-V was in danger of being pushed aside, as its leaders, dispersed throughout Europe, were incapable of challenging ETA-VI.

Etxabe and his supporters made their presence felt just before the trial opened, at the beginning of December, by a daring stroke — the kidnapping of Herr Beihl, the German Consul in San Sebastián, who was held hostage to ensure that the death sentences demanded by the prosecution were not carried out.[56] The effect of the kidnapping was to increase police repression still further and to add to the climate of tension. ETA-V's weakness was counterbalanced, to some extent by the support it received from conservative nationalists, such as the prominent PNV member Telesforo Monzón, a former minister in the Basque autonomous government, and Father Larrazábal, a well-known French Basque nationalist. Monzón, as president of the refugee organisation *Anai Artea* (Between Brothers), acted as spokesman for the kidnappers and as an intermediary with the press. The kidnapping allowed ETA-V to compensate for its organisational weakness and obtain a hearing for its views through statements by Monzón and Larrazábal and through interviews with foreign journalists. The political attitudes which emerged from these interviews had little resemblance to the statements being made by the Burgos prisoners. For example, two ETA-V leaders who informed a French journalist that Beihl would be killed if any of the prisoners were executed emphasised that their organisation was anti-Spanish, rather than anti-Franco, that it was engaged in a struggle against colonialism, and that it wished to create a Basque National Front, which would include those whom the Marxist-Leninists in ETA-VI described as the bourgeoisie.[57] The kidnapping was a considerable propaganda success, which enabled ETA-V to become known to a wider audience. Beihl was released unharmed on Christmas Eve, before the sentences had been announced.[58]

ETA-VI adopted a very hesitant attitude to the kidnapping which their rivals had carried out. Its leaders issued a statement denying that ETA was responsible, reiterating the primacy of mass action rather than armed exploits, yet refusing to condemn the action as such. ETA-VI's leaders even announced that if the Spanish government gave in to ETA-V's threats and allowed their comrades to be released from prison in exchange for the German Consul, they had the organisation's permission to accept.[59] ETA-VI's failure to repudiate a kidnapping which was aimed as much at challenging its own authority as it was at influencing the Burgos trial showed an uncertain attitude to minority armed action. In theory, ETA-VI had evolved to a point at which its leaders considered such actions to be counter-productive and saw the group around Etxabe as reactionaries, whose chauvinism was an obstacle to the unity of the Basque People. ETA-VI's failure to denounce a kidnapping which was vital in building the prestige of ETA-V was criticised by some of its members.[60] Later, kidnapping was to become one of ETA's most important methods of struggle.

Support for the prisoners was not confined to the Basque country, as there were demonstrations in many parts of Spain,[61] particularly in Catalonia, where a number of intellectuals occupied the monastery of Montserrat and issued a call for the right of national self-determination which received the support of the Abbot.[62] There were violent clashes with the police in Barcelona, and in Madrid the university was closed in an effort to prevent demonstrations of support. The government responded to the campaign by suspending article 18 of the Constitution, thereby giving the police a free hand to deal with those involved in the protests. In an address to the Spanish parliament, the Prime Minister, Carrero Blanco, emphasised that the government was determined to maintain order, and would not give way to pressure from outside. He also praised Spain's 'organic democracy', a clear indication that the government had no intention of abolishing the Francoist structures embodied in that Falangist concept.[63]

The demonstrations which took place throughout the world presented the Spanish government with a grave problem. Suddenly, foreign newspapers were full of reports from the Basque country, an area which few people had previously heard of. Dockers in France and Italy refused to load Spanish ships and two demonstrators in Milan were killed by the police.[64] In an unprecedented gesture the Vatican published an article in its daily newspaper *Osservatore Romano* asking that the Spanish government should exercise clemency in its treatment of the Burgos prisoners.[65] The feeling that powerful foreign interests were exercising illegitimate pressure on Spain was greatly resented by right-wing Spaniards and was reflected in the Spanish press, yet the regime could not be indifferent to the opinions of foreign governments, nor to the reports of the trial in the foreign press, radio and television. The Spanish press was particularly outraged by the coverage given to the trial by French television, which had been very sympathetic to the accused.[66] Sánchez Bella, the Minister of Information and Tourism, also denounced the 'anti-Spanish' campaign in the foreign press and television.

The authorities responded to the propaganda defeat which was being inflicted on them by organising a number of 'spontaneous' meetings in Burgos, Madrid and other cities. The opposition could point out that such demonstrations were officially organised and stage-managed, in the same style as those which had been a prominent feature of the regime's early years. This was largely true, but the demonstrations also revealed the growing divergences within the ruling alliance, and the resentment felt within the Falange at the dominant role in the government of members of the right-wing technocratic religious association Opus Dei.[67] For example, at an enormous rally held on 17 December at the Plaza de Oriente in Madrid, attended by Franco and Prince Juan Carlos, participants carried slogans which attacked Opus Dei as well as liberal elements in the Church.[69] The main theme, of this and similar demonstrations, was solidarity with Franco personally rather than with the government, as several cabinet members were known to have been against holding the trial in that way.[69] The growing fragmentation of the Franco regime was also shown by the presence of ultra-right-wing groups, such as Fuerza Nueva, which had been formed in reaction to the liberalisation of the 1960s. A bizarre manifestation of the right-wing mobilisation was the appearance of anti-ETA, and anti-liberal, slogans painted on walls. In Spain painted slogans such as 'Red Bishops to Moscow' were an unconvincing way of persuading the public that the regime had massive popular support.[70]

The Church's growing divergence with the regime was a clear indication that most of the Church hierarchy no longer considered Franco's rule a guarantee of stability, although a number of priests retained their early enthusiasm for it. The army's response to the storm surrounding the Burgos trial was more complicated. Anger at the prisoners' disrespectful attitude to the military court produced ultra-right-wing reactions, while on the other hand some officers felt that the government was to blame for using a military court to try people for actions which should have been dealt with by a civilian one, and thereby diverting the people's anger against oppression and corruption against the army. General García Valiño, who as Captain-General of the Madrid military region had had to confirm the death sentence on Julián Grimau, wrote to General Garcia Rebull saying that, in his opinion, it was a mistake to use the army for such trials. He believed that a military trial threatened to lose the army the respect of the people. General Diez Alegría, Chief of the General Staff, was known to hold similar views.[71]

The trial also sparked off resentment further down in the military hierarchy. Young officers were holding meetings where discussions, originally about the invidious position in which the army had been placed, led on to wider issues of the army's role in Spanish society and the officers' own career prospects. Thousands of officers signed a manifesto outlining their grievances, which was sent to Franco, who was already aware that such meetings were being held.[72] An announcement that the armed forces were to be granted wage rises was, perhaps, a response to military grievances.[73] Although the secrecy inherent in a military institution made it difficult to interpret the mood of the army officers,[74] the possibility of a captains' revolt aroused a good deal of interest. The contents of the declaration were hardly revolutionary, as it stressed its authors' loyalty to Franco, and the need to maintain law and order. However, the declaration also called for an end to corruption and the resignation of the government, both of which demands were interpreted as attacks on Opus Dei.[75] In 1969 Franco had finally named Prince Juan Carlos as his successor, a decision which had been opposed by the Falangist and Carlist factions in the regime, and had angered many monarchists who saw Don Juan, the Prince's father, as the legitimate heir to the throne. The appointment of a cabinet dominated by Opus Dei members was also disliked by the regime's traditional supporters, who made capital out of the involvement of that organisation's supporters in a fraud perpetrated by the Matesa company. These circumstances combined to give the Burgos trial a significance which would hardly have been envisaged when the decision to hold it had been taken.

The divergences within the regime, so apparent at the pro-Franco demonstrations, also emerged, cautiously, in the Spanish press and more openly in interviews in the foreign press. *ABC*, the traditionally monarchist journal, describing the demonstrations in favour of Franco held in the Plaza de Oriente, claimed that they

showed the almost unanimous support for Franco, and the rejection of anarchism, terrorism and chaos.[76] *Arriba* was more
restrained. It welcomed the Pope's plea for clemency but pointed
out that he was being scrupulously respectful of the sovereignty of
the Spanish state, and was not trying to bring pressure on the
legitimate authorities.[77] The Catholic daily, *Ya*, reflected the
position of the bishops, stressing that demonstrations and
disturbances benefited only the extreme left and right, and pointing out that the bishops' conference had condemned violence from
wherever it came.[78] Such a measured attitude was anathema to
the fervent supporters of Franco, who saw it as equating the
violence of ETA with the legitimate punishment which the State
imposed on criminals. Although most newspapers objected
strongly to the pressure which foreign opinion was putting on the
Spanish government, they did not actually call for the death
sentences to be carried out. Apart from the Fascist groups, most
of the right was, reluctantly, prepared for Franco to exercise
clemency.

On 30 December Franco signed reprieves of all six death
sentences. The announcement was hardly unexpected,[79] but
nevertheless it was greeted with overwhelming relief by people in
the Basque country. A decision to carry out the executions would
have created an insurrectionary situation, particularly in those
areas from which the condemned men came. Putting down such
outbreaks would undoubtedly have resulted in considerable bloodshed and continuing unrest. In addition, executions would have
been badly received by foreign governments, by the Church, and
by most of the population, so they would hardly have been possible, without a more general move to turn back the clock to the
policies of earlier years.[80] Franco's prudent decision was interpreted by supporters of the regime as an act of clemency by a
government which had the backing of the great mass of Spanish
people, and was unaffected by the support campaign or by international pressure. Undoubtedly, many of those who attended the
pro-Franco demonstrations must have been disappointed that the
death sentences were not carried out, and suspicious that Carrero
Blanco's government was surrendering to the pressure of the
hated liberal democracies. Their fears were surely justified. A
regime which, at the end of the Civil War, had consolidated its
rule by scores of thousands of executions, yet now felt unable to
execute men convicted of killing a police officer, had suffered a
massive political defeat.

For the Carrero Blanco government, the trial had proved a hideous mistake which put a question mark over Opus Dei's formula of an authoritarian, technocratic regime, which rejected parliamentary democracy and civil liberty, while trying to phase out the fascist elements who had given the Franco regime much of its character in its early years. The campaign in support of the Burgos prisoners had also been a mobilisation for the democracy which the government was unwilling to grant. The demonstrations in support of Franco did show that there were still many people who were prepared to fight tooth and nail to prevent Spain from becoming a decadent, 'inorganic' democracy. However, the fact that the predominant tone of these demonstrations was not friendly to the cabinet, but rather eager to return to the policies and style of the regime's early years, presented the government with additional problems. The Bishops' brilliant tactics in taking their distance from the regime, which upset many right-wing Catholics, showed very clearly that the majority of the Church hierarchy were no longer confident that the regime could provide a viable future for Spain, or protect the Church's long-term interests. Traditionalists such as Madrid's bishop Mgr. Casimiro Morcillo, who used his Christmas sermon to attack the regime's opponents, were clearly in a minority.[81]

ETA-VI's leaders saw the reprieves as a victory which had been forced from the regime by mass mobilisation, and as a vindication of its strategy of combining the struggles for national and social liberation, and of relying on the mass movement, instead of the violent actions of an armed vanguard. The cost to the organisation had been heavy. Not only had the Burgos prisoners been sentenced to enormously long terms of imprisonment, but many other activists had been arrested, or had been forced to flee into exile. However, ETA-VI's leaders believed that their organisation had made considerable advances on the way to becoming the revolutionary party which would lead the Basque revolution. For the first time a mass movement had been mobilised behind ETA's demands. The campaign around the trial had also raised the political level of many thousands of people, and had provided ETA-VI with a basis with which to go forward.[82] ETA-VI's leaders had, they believed, followed the example of the Chinese and Vietnamese revolutionary leaderships in uniting nationalist and socialist struggles. In addition, they had won support of all the Burgos prisoners for the changes which had taken place in ETA's policy since they themselves had been imprisoned. The small group of people around Etxabe, who formed ETA-V, had, it believed, been reduced to the stunt of kidnapping the German Consul, because of its lack of support among the Basque people. The support shown for the prisoners outside Euskadi showed the absurdity of Etxabe's chauvinism, and the success of the campaign indicated that Escubi's pessimism about ETA-VI was unjustified. In the event, ETA-VI was to have a less successful future than its leaders supposed.

REFERENCES

1. Author's interview with Patxo Unzueta, Bilbao, 13 March 1980.
2. *Le Monde*, 12 Dec. 1970.
3. Preface to Gisèle Halimi, 'Le Procès de Burgos' in *Zutik (ETA-V)*, No. 61.
4. Max Gallo, *Histoire de l'Espagne Franquiste*, Vol. 2, pp. 369–72; Jorge Semprún, *Autobiografía de Federico Sánchez* (Barcelona, 1977), pp. 194–212; also, Fernando Claudín, *Santiago Carillo, Crónica de un secretario general* (Barcelona, 1983), p. 155.
5. Edouard de Blaye, *Franco and the politics of Spain* (London, 1976), p. 281.
6. *Horizonte Español 1972*, Vol. 1, p. 230.
7. *Le Monde*, 6–7 Dec. 1970.
8. Prosecution statement in *Burgos: Juicio a un Pueblo*, pp. 26–50.
9. See *Le Monde*, 30 Dec. 1970 for a summary of an interview with Escubi in *Politique Hebdo*.
10. *Burgos: Juicio a un Pueblo*, passim.
11. *Burgos: Juicio*, passim.
12. *Burgos: Juicio*, passim.
13. See Chapter 3.
14. *Asunto extremadamente grave* in *Documentos Y*, Vol. 4, p. 463.
15. Kepa Salaberri, *Sumarísmo 31/69: El proceso de Euskadi en Burgos* (Paris, 1971), pp. 168–235; Gisèle Halimi, *El Proceso de Burgos* (Caracas, 1972), passim; Arteaga, *ETA y el Proceso de Burgos*, pp. 303–9.
16. See *Gudari*, No. 48, 1968.
17. Interview with Patxo Unzueta.
18. Salaberri, *Sumarísmo 31/69*, pp. 181–6.
19. *Le Monde*, 6, 7 and 8 Dec. 1970.
20. Salaberri, *Sumarísmo 31/69*, pp. 186–90.
21. Inscriptions on Civil War monuments in the Basque country often referred to the defeated as '*hordas rojas separatistas*'.
22. *Le Monde*, 10 Dec. 1970.
23. Salaberri, *Sumarísmo 31/69*, pp. 211–14.
24. Salaberri, *Sumarísmo 31/69*, pp. 215–8.
25. *Le Monde*, 8 Dec. 1970; Salaberri, *Sumarísmo 31/69*, pp. 178–81.
26. Salaberri, *Sumarísmo 31/69*, pp. 153–254.

27. *Le Monde*, 8 Dec. 1970.
28. *The Times*, 9 Dec. 1970; *Burgos: Juicio a un pueblo*, pp. 225–8.
29. *Le Monde*, 10 Dec. 1970.
30. De Blaye, *Franco*, p. 294.
31. Author's interview with Mario Onaindía, Vitoria 26 March 1980 .
32. *Le Monde*, 10 Dec. 1970.
33. *Le Monde*, 11 Dec. 1970.
34. *Le Monde*, 29 Dec. 1970.
35. *Le Monde*, 30 Dec. 1970.
36. Author's interviews with Patxo Unzueta, and with 'Bikilia', San Sebastián, 7 Aug. 1981.
37. 'Hemos salvado a los de Burgos', *Mundo Obrero*, 23 Jan. 1971; 'Una actitud digna y valiente', *Zer Egin?*, No. 10, Dec. 1970.
38. *Documentos Y*, Vol. 10, pp. 84–9.
39. See 'El consejo nacional del movimiento y las crisis de diciembre', *Mundo Obrero*, 28 March 1971.
40. Interviews with Patxo Unzueta and 'Bikilia'.
41. *Le Monde*, 2 Dec. 1970.
42. *Le Monde*, 5 Dec. 1970.
43. *Pueblo*, 4 Dec. 1970. Quoted in Salaberri, *Sumarísmo 31/69*, pp. 158–9.
44. *Euskadi ta Askatasuna (ETA) y Partido Comunista de Euskadi llaman al paro general*, in *Documentos Y*, Vol. 9, pp. 481–2.
45. *Llamamiento al pueblo de Oñate*, in *Documentos Y*, Vol. 10, pp. 73–6.
46. *Sumario 31* (leaflet); *Ante la represión fascista una llamada al pueblo* (leaflet), both in *Documentos Y*, Vol. 10, p. 77; *The Times*, 14 Dec. 1970.
47. *Le Monde*, 2 Dec. 1970.
48. Author's interview with Patxo Unzueta; *Carta a los Makos*.
49. *Alderdi*, 3 June 1983.
50. *The Times*, 7 Dec. 1970.
51. Elósegui, *Quiero morir*, pp. 146–88.
52. Elósegui, *Quiero morir*, pp. 286–313.
53. Elósegui, *Quiero morir*, pp. 316–320.
54. Author's interview with Joseba Elósegui, San Sebastián, 27 March 1980.
55. Charles Vanhecke, 'Le renouveau du nationalisme Basque', *Le Monde*, 11 Dec. 1970.
56. *The Times*, 3 Dec. 1970; *Le Monde*, 2 and 3 Dec. 1970.
57. See interview with two ETA-V leaders by Jean Lacouture, 'On veut nous tuer parce que nous faisons peur', *Le Monde*, 16 Dec. 1970.
58. *Le Monde*, 26 Dec. 1970.
59. *Communicado de la dirección nacional de ETA*, in *Documentos Y*, Vol. 10, p. 117; see also *Berriak*, No. 3, 27 Jan. 1971.
60. 'Critica a *Berriak*', *Keman*, April 1971.
61. *Le Monde*, 12 Dec. 1970.
62. *Le Monde*, 15 and 17 Dec. 1970.
63. *Le Monde*, 21 and 22 Dec. 1970.
64. *Le Monde*, 15 Dec. 1970.
65. *Osservatore Romano*, 25 Dec. 1970, quoted in Halimi, *El Proceso de Burgos*, p. 255.

66. *La Vanguardia*, 19 Dec. 1970.
67. De Blaye, *Franco*, pp. 308–11.
68. *Le Monde*, 19 Dec. 1970.
69. *Le Monde*, 19 Dec. 1970.
70. In spring 1971 the slogan '*Obispos rojos a Moscú*' could still be seen painted on the main bridge across the river Urumea in San Sebastián.
71. *Le Monde*, 13 Dec. 1970.
72. Marcel Neidergang, *Le Monde*, 29 Dec. 1970.
73. *Le Monde*, 25 Dec. 1970.
74. Julio Busquets, *El militar de carrera en España* (Barcelona, 1967), passim.
75. *Le Figaro*, 23 Dec. 1970, quoted in Salaberri, *Sumarísmo 31/69*, p. 255–7.
76. 'El común denominador', *ABC*, 18 Dec. 1970.
77. 'Nota de la Santa Sede', *Arriba*, 27 Nov. 1970.
78. *Ya*, 27 Nov. 1970 and 3 Dec. 1970.
79. See *The Times*, leading article, 31 Dec. 1970.
80. *Le Monde*, 1 Jan. 1971; De Blaye, *Franco*, p. 321.
81. De Blaye, *Franco*, p. 314
82. Author's interviews with 'Bikilia', Ramón Zallo and Patxo Unzueta.

5

The Return to Radical Nationalism

Part I: The decline of ETA-VI

It will be recalled that the leadership which had its position confirmed at the Sixth Assembly were optimistic about the future. They had, they believed, done well in mounting the campaign which had probably saved the lives of six of their comrades. ETA-VI was considerably stronger and its prestige was, following the trial, incomparably greater than ever before, among all sections of the Basque population. The agitation in support of the Burgos prisoners had demonstrated the organisation's ability to win support both from traditional nationalists, and from the 'Spanish' groups, in the illegal labour movement. Practically all of ETA's prisoners (not only those involved in the Burgos trial) supported the ETA-VI leadership. The leadership saw their own strategy as a direct continuation of the decisions adopted at the Fifth Assembly, not as a deviation similar to that of ETA-Berri.[1]

The main problem facing ETA-VI was the repression, consisting of arrests, beatings and searches, which had intensified as a result of the agitation surrounding the Burgos trial. Many of the ETA-VI leadership were forced to go into exile, in a repetition of a pattern which was now becoming familiar. The repression benefited ETA-VI in some ways, by providing a large pool of people who were outraged at the oppression, and were drawn towards ETA-VI as the most intransigent opponent of the Franco regime. However, the repression also made it impossible to maintain a continuous leadership in the interior, and made it difficult for the exiled leadership to keep in touch with the rank and file inside Spain. The defection of Escubi and his followers was a severe blow, but ETA-VI's leaders believed Escubi was mistaken in characterising the group as incurably petty-bourgeois,[2] and that ETA-VI was shaking free of its petty-bourgeois origins. The split of the small group around the Military Front leader Etxabe (known to ETA-VI members as the 'Milis') was seen as less of a problem. Etxabe and his supporters were trying to go back to the primitive nationalism of ETA's early years, and were not merely denying the advances registered at the Sixth Assembly, but those at the Fifth also, so they were seen as having little future. The main people associated with it were, in contrast to Escubi, of very little consequence. Txillardegi had resigned from ETA early in 1967, Krutwig had lived in comfortable exile abroad and López Adán (Beltza) was exiled in Brussels.[3] The components of the 'Milis' (henceforth ETA-V) were thought to have no common basis of agreement, and were, therefore, not seen as serious rivals of ETA-VI in the task of building either the National Front, or the workers' party.

ETA-VI's leaders' attempts to form the National Front were hampered by the fact that the communiqué which they had signed with the PCE in October 1970 had not been well received by many of their rank and file, or by sympathisers. The communiqué was useful ammunition for ETA-V, in its claim that ETA-VI had become a 'Spanish' organisation. ETA-VI's leaders attempted to extricate themselves from the dilemma by explaining that the statement was originally to have been signed by a number of other organisations. In a note of self-criticism, a member of ETA-VI's executive committee argued that as the revisionist and opportunist attitude of the PCE provoked anti-communist reactions in the Basque population, co-operation with that party had not, in fact, contributed to the internationalist education of the Basque people, since they were still dominated by bourgeois nationalism.[4] The self-criticism was rather disingenuous, as the nationalist community was not opposed to association with the PCE because of revulsion at that party's departure from Marxist orthodoxy, but because it was 'Spanish' and communist.

The leadership of ETA-VI continued to vacillate between the incompatible aims of attempting to transform their organisation into a communist party, and building a National Front of all patriotic Basques. The leadership's belief that both objectives were compatible was put to the test in January 1971, when a number of nationalist organisations (including Branka, ELA, ELA-Berri and ETA-V) called a meeting to discuss the formation of a National Front, but did not invite ETA-VI. The leaders of

ETA-VI responded by producing a leaflet denouncing the attempted exclusion, in view of their organisation of the killing of Manzanas, and the fact that they had more members in prison or in exile than any other group.[5] The leaflet, while it attacked those involved in the ETA-V split, did not clarify whether ETA-VI was opposed to the creation of the Front or merely angry at its own exclusion from it.

ETA-VI was invited to a later meeting where it was provisionally accepted as a participant, on condition that its representatives withdrew the attack which had been made on the founding meeting.[6] ETA-VI's leaders agreed to do so, and published a statement saying that Etxabe and his associates were neither right-wingers nor traitors, but Basque patriots.[7] The statement remained critical of Etxabe and made a distinction between his policies and those which Beltza and Krutwig expressed in the journal *Gataska*. It expressed a wish for an alliance with the people in ETA-V, an attitude which was quite at variance with ETA-VI's recent politics. ETA-VI's willingness to ally with the Basque right caused some dissension among ETA-VI's members, as the organisation was by now deeply divided on the desirability of a National Front.[8] In the event, ETA-VI's retraction was not sufficiently far-reaching, so it was once again excluded from the talks.[9] This exclusion narrowed the base of the Front considerably. The purpose of the FNV was to consolidate the popular movement among nationalists of various shades which had flourished during the Burgos trial, yet a Front which excluded the organisation to which all the prisoners belonged would have been incomplete, to say the least. The repeal of the death sentences had had the effect of ending the massive demonstrations, so the proposed Front no longer benefited from the impetus which these demonstrations had provided.

ETA-VI's expulsion from the talks did not mean that the remaining participants were united. The PNV withdrew from the discussions as it was reluctant to create an organisation which, once established, would have placed the government in exile, in which the PNV was the dominant force, in a difficult position. Whereas the exiled government was supposed to represent the whole Basque population, the version of the National Front proposed by Txillardegi and others would have been confined to *Abertzales*, i.e. those who favoured complete Basque independence, and would consequently have excluded parties such as the PSOE and PCE. The chauvinism of some participants was shown by their demand that the discussion should take place entirely in *Euskera*, although it was pointed out that this would effectively exclude a number of those already present.[10] With the withdrawal of the PNV and ETA-VI the proposed National Front was reduced to a rump around ETA-V, and ELA-Berri, a breakaway from the historic nationalist trade union, Monzón and Txillardegi, with little influence in society and none in the workers' movement.[11]

In 1972 neither ETA-V, Txillardegi nor ELA-Berri had the organisational strength or the prestige which would have made a National Front led by them a plausible rival to either the PNV or to ETA-VI. However, Txillardegi's efforts to create an alliance of the social forces represented at the discussions met with considerable success in later years. Even if its apologies had been acceptable, ETA-VI could hardly have remained in an organisation which excluded the PCE, MCE and all others with any strength in the labour movement. ETA-VI's original reaction of eondemnation towards the proposed National Front was much more in tune with the line which it had followed for most of 1970, and with its pretensions of having become a Marxist-Leninist Party. The demands of the participants consisted of reunification of the French and Spanish Basque country, the creation of a completely Basque-speaking country, and independence,[12] all demands which were unacceptable to the workers' movement, which ETA-VI aspired to lead. ETA-VI's subsequent attempts to participate in united nationalist activities were consistently rejected by the other *Abertzale* forces, as when its members were prevented from participating in a hunger strike in Bayonne, held in protest at the harassment of Basque refugees in France.[13] In the view of Txillardegi, Etxabe and the PNV, they were no longer part of the nationalist community.

ETA-VI's leadership's hope that the Red Cells could be won back to the organisation encouraged them to play down the extent of the disagreements which had led the Red Cells to resign at the Sixth Assembly. ETA-VI did not publish an account of the result of the Assembly until May 1971, eight months after it had been held,[14] by which time it had become clear that the Red Cells had made an even sharper break with nationalism than had ETA-Berri four years earlier. The Red Cells, in their journal *Saioak*, had subjected the whole tradition of Basque nationalism to a withering criticism, and called for the unity of the working class both in the Basque country and throughout the world.[15] ETA-VI, *Saioak* declared, was inherently a petty-bourgeois organisation which could not be transformed into the communist party which was necessary to lead the revolution.[16] *Saioak*'s supporters were, in spite of the high quality of their analysis, unable to repeat the success of ETA-Berri in building a communist group in Euskadi. Unlike those involved in the earlier split, *Saioak*'s supporters had not been involved in industrial struggle. They were refugees in France whose main contribution to ETA's struggle had been the unleashing of the armed campaign of 1968/69. *Saioak* wished to persuade socialists from a variety of political origins to come together to create a revolutionary Marxist party. However, most activists inside Spain remained loyal to their own organisations in spite of the poverty of their political analysis. Consequently *Saioak* collapsed, thereby removing a possible rival to ETA-VI, although its criticism of ETA-VI's political zigzags remained as a permanent embarrassment.[17]

The Red Cells, and subsequently *Saioak*, were sociologically very much part of the tradition which they criticised so virulently. The core of the group consisted of Escubi, and those activists such as Xabier Bareño, José María Bilbao and Mikel Azurmendi, who had helped Txillardegi to remove Iturrioz and Del Río. At the Sixth Assembly, all but one of the Red Cells' delegates had resigned from ETA, while none of the delegates from the interior had joined them, thus showing a pattern of conduct on both sides, typical of group loyalty to a *cuadrilla* rather than the deviations which one might have expected to have been produced by political discussion. Having resigned from ETA, the Red Cells were cut off from any regular contact with members of an organisation involved in struggles in Spain.

The fact that ETA-VI was involved in workers' struggles compensated for its political incoherence. Once excluded from the National Front it turned rapidly to the left and devoted its energies to the workers' movement. ETA-VI's attraction to the workers' struggle was influenced by the rise in such activity in the early 1970s, both in Euskadi and elsewhere in Spain. The number of strikes rose sharply and they were accompanied by mass demonstrations, which were suppressed by the police, who on several occasions killed workers taking part in them.[18] The strength of the Workers' Commissions continued to increase in spite of arrests and trials of their leaders. ETA-VI's concern with the labour movement was reflected in its press, which devoted much of its space to strikes in Madrid, Barcelona, Asturias and

Galicia during 1971. In September in Madrid a building worker, Pedro Patiño, a PCE member, was shot dead by police[19], and in 1972 there were more strikes in Madrid, Asturias, Bilbao, Barcelona and Vitoria. In El Ferrol, in Galicia, in March 1972 the police opened fire on a demonstration, killing two and wounding twenty-three people.[20] The movement reached its peak in 1973 in Pamplona, where there was virtually a general strike.[21]

The government's reaction to the rise in working-class struggle was contradictory. On the one hand, the police readiness to shoot strikers indicated that the opposition's hopes of liberalisation were unrealistic. On the other hand, the government continued to try to reform the *Sindicatos* in order to make them, to some extent, responsive to workers' aspirations, by introducing, early in 1971, a trade union law which was supposed to achieve that purpose. However, the regime met with very little success in persuading workers that the *Sindicatos* were effective instruments for pursuing working-class demands. In the elections for *Sindicato* workplace representatives in the spring of 1971, abstention was high, in spite of the PCE's strong support for participation.[22] ETA-VI, like most other left groups, urged the workers to boycott the elections.[23]

Not only workers were sceptical of the value of the *Sindicatos*. A section of capitalists were becoming convinced that they would have to accept genuine workers' organisations, particularly the Workers' Commissions, although the police continued to arrest its leaders. The division, within the Spanish bourgeoisie, over whether or not to deal directly with the Workers' Commissions was part of the wider question of whether the political institutions which Franco had created were appropriate to meet the needs of Spanish capitalism in a period when the post-war boom seemed to be faltering all over the capitalist world. In 1971, Franco was 78 years old and in poor health. The more hard-core Franco supporters hoped that the Prime Minister, Carrero Blanco, not Prince Juan Carlos, would be Franco's real political heir, and that he would ensure that the Francoist regime would continue to function. Other important political figures, such as José María de Areilza, a former ambassador to the United States, disagreed, believing that the combination of economic uncertainty and working-class militancy was a recipe for social unrest and made contact with the Communist Party and the Workers' Commissions.[24] The more liberal representatives of Spanish capitalism believed that it was necessary to broaden the base of the system and to make concessions to the working class and other forces pressing for change. If this was not done, basic economic struggles would, it was believed, become politicised.

Important representatives of big business such as Joaquín Garrigues Walker were coming to accept that a parliamentary democracy was the best form of government to cope with the economic crisis. As there were no real democratic bourgeois parties in existence, a transition to a parliamentary democracy would require a pact with the illegal socialist forces, particularly the PCE. The PCE had, for some time, been trying to persuade liberal capitalists to accept the 'pact for liberty' which was its recipe for liquidating the dictatorship, but outside Catalonia this initiative had met with little response. There were important differences between the PCE and the liberal capitalists, as the PCE opposed the monarchy and held that the people of Euskadi and Catalonia had the right to decide whether they wished to secede from Spain. Even if the liberal capitalists had been prepared to accept this, there was little likelihood that the army would accept a republican or federal Spain. In the early 1970s the PCE and the liberal sectors of the regime moved towards accepting the compromise which was to bring about the transition to a parliamentary democracy.[25]

The PCE's leadership were not themselves free agents in so far as most of the party's members would have been unhappy about accepting the monarchy. In addition, the forces to the left of the PCE might seize the opportunity presented by a rising tide of class struggle in order to gain ground from it. ETA-VI was, as it abandoned its nationalist ideas, becoming one of the groups which challenged the PCE's strategy. ETA-VI threw itself into the strike movements, seeing them as being incomparably more important than ETA-V's interventions, which consisted largely of planting bombs in public buildings.[26] ETA-VI was concerned to fight against the PCE attempts to moderate the struggle so that agreement could be reached with the more liberal wing of Spanish capitalism. ETA-VI, in contrast, hoped that the struggle would produce directly elected committees which would serve as organs of workers' power.[27]

ETA-VI's leaders maintained that, contrary to *Saioak*'s claims, its activists were not imprisoned by the group's past, nor were they incapable of changing. *Saioak*'s contention implied that the initials 'ETA' carried a force of their own, which was able to prevent the organisation from becoming a Marxist party. ETA-

VI's leaders argued that the group had accepted the need to transform itself into such a party, and would proceed to carry out its decisions.[28] The obstacles to building a revolutionary party included the middle-class origins of most of ETA's activists, the dominance of the PCE in the workers' movement, and the impossibility of an organisation which concerned itself only with Euskadi playing a leading part in struggles which erupted all over Spain. As ETA-VI's leaders came to accept that Euskadi could not become free while the rest of Spain remained subject to the Franco dictatorship, they began to seek unity with Marxist forces in other parts of Spain, in order to create an organisation which could challenge the dominance exercised by the PCE.

The decision taken at the Sixth Assembly to convert ETA-VI into a workers' party had, at first, few specific consequences, as the abandonment of a strategy based on guerrilla actions was not replaced by the adoption of any clear alternative. ETA-VI remained a decentralised Federation of *cuadrillas* whose activists in one district would participate in the Workers' Commissions, while those in another would not. Those who did participate in them had no common approach or centralised direction.[29] The real cement which continued to hold ETA-VI together was the familiar mixture of activism and nationalism. ETA-VI had decided to create a workers' party, yet it had no clear formula to distinguish its version of such a party from others whose claims were longer established.[30] The enormous impetus given by the Burgos trial enabled ETA-VI to survive throughout most of 1971, in spite of the contradiction of seeking an alliance with the PNV while trying to build a workers' vanguard in the factories.

The abandonment of armed struggle prejudiced ETA-VI's attempts to recruit members, as young people found ETA-V's efforts to continue guerrilla activity more romantic and exciting.[31] As ETA-VI moved, hesitantly, towards becoming a revolutionary Marxist organisation, its leaders found that recruiting activists, training them and determining the priorities of the organisation all clashed with the tradition of ETA as a broad popular movement. As ETA-VI gradually came to be seen as a non-traditionalist organisation it lost most of what had been ETA's traditional base of support among priests and in the Basque cultural milieu. Its commitment to the aim of building a workers' party did not have much effect in altering its predominantly middle-class social composition. ETA-VI's leadership were united in their rejection of anti-Spanish chauvinism, their commitment to mass action rather than armed activities by an armed vanguard, and their struggle to prevent most of the membership from joining ETA-V. Apart from that, the leadership had little ideological consistency, with the result that the organisation tended to zigzag from one policy to another. Once having abandoned nationalism it made little sense to insist on having an autonomous strategy for Euskadi, when intervening in struggles which were part of a movement taking place throughout Spain. Yet to unite with groups outside Euskadi would have jettisoned the remnants of the organisation's claim to be the legitimate heir to ETA's tradition. These contradictions produced an organisational paralysis throughout 1971,[32] which was all the more frustrating in that it coincided with a strike wave in many parts of Spain, which enabled other left-wing groups to grow.

ETA-VI's leaders recognised that although the level of strikes in Euskadi was very high, the political level of the mass movement was much lower than had been reached in Catalonia. ETA-VI was determined to provide the leadership of the workers' movement, but although it had several hundred committed activists who were prepared to put the effort and sacrifice once devoted to nationalism into the working-class struggle, it was not a proletarian organisation. Although *Zutik* now presented ETA-VI as communist, its middle-class composition and the concentration of its members in ethnically Basque towns and villages which had in the past been ETA's greatest strength was a disadvantage in building a workers' party. Some of ETA-VI's leaders knew that time was not on their side as, if the working class failed to give a revolutionary lead to the rest of society, many of the combative sections of white-collar workers, professional people and independent businessmen, who had been drawn away from chauvinistic nationalism under the influence of ETA, would relapse and become fellow-travellers of the PNV.[33] Attempts to translate general revolutionary slogans into a definite strategy were by late 1971 beginning to produce splits in the organisation.

Once having rejected the alliance with Basque capitalists exemplified by the Frente Nacional Vasco (FNV) ETA-VI was reluctant to accept the same strategy at an all-Spain level, as advocated by the PCE, the leading force in the workers' movement. ETA-VI agreed with most other left forces that the elections for workplace posts in the official Sindicatos should be boycotted.[34] In 1971 it had no clear attitude to the Workers' Commissions, the main emerging trade union, but tended to favour the creation of 'red groups' of militants, instead of attempts to organise the whole workforce.[35] Nor did ETA-VI have the experience or the structure to transform its considerable base of activists into a trade union ginger group. These weaknesses contrasted strongly with the strength of the PCE, which, although less dominant in the Basque country than in other industrial centres, was nevertheless a disciplined, cohesive force whose members belonged to it because of their acceptance of a recognised set of ideas. ETA-VI's members had not, in general, joined the organisation because of their beliefs on how trade union struggle should be carried out, although most of them now accepted that that struggle was crucial. Nor was ETA-VI able to make a selection of activists as it lacked any coherent theory.[36] The group solidarity which, by involving groups of friends in the organisation, had so greatly strengthened ETA as a populist movement, was a disadvantage in the attempt to become a political party based on the working class.

While ETA-VI could differentiate itself from the PCE, simply by being more militant, and presenting more radical demands, this was not enough to distinguish it from the more left-wing, Maoist groups, such as Kommunistak (formerly ETA-Berri) and the ORT, another Maoist group which had originated in *Vanguardia Obrera* a Catholic Workers group initiated by the Jesuits. Kommunistak, for example, favoured a revolutionary bloc (i.e. an alliance between the groups to the left of the PCE). ETA-VI was quite unable to make any considered analysis of such proposals, nor did a strategy emerge from experience, as some members hoped. By 1971, although ETA-VI considered that it was no longer a broad national liberation movement but a group which was in the process of transforming itself into a revolutionary party, it remained unclear whether ETA-VI was to be a mass party or a Leninist vanguard. It was also uncertain whether the organisation still favoured the creation of a state independent of Spain and the unification of the French and Spanish Basque country. Nor did ETA-VI have a consistent attitude to Basque culture, to the language question, and more generally to the middle-class milieu from which it had sprung. In its search for partners, ETA-VI was repelled by the Maoism of the larger left groups, such as the PCE (i), the ORT and the MCE. Not only did these groups blindly support the Chinese government, which was becoming friendly to both the United States and conservative regimes in the Third World, but their political analysis was extremely crude and sectarian. The MCE had long since abandoned the critical Marxist ideas which had caused its leaders' expulsion from ETA, in favour of Maoist rhetoric.

Such questions presented difficulties enough in themselves, but ETA-VI had additional problems to contend with. The exiled leadership were developing their ideas rapidly, under the influence of literature which had not been available to them inside Spain, and through contact with French and Spanish Marxists. The rank and file in the interior were bewildered by their leaders' exhortation to read Lenin, Mao and Trotsky. ETA-VI's problems were intensified by continual arrests, particularly of a number of the interior leadership in Bilbao in March 1972.[37] The inability of ETA-VI to transform itself into a Marxist party produced disagreements among its leaders, at a meeting of its *Biltzaar Ttippia* in February 1972. ETA-VI inherited a tradition where the function of theoretical formulae was to obscure the differences between incompatible tendencies. As ETA-V slowly began to gain ground in the nationalist milieu and ETA-VI failed to develop a strong base in the factories, some members of the leadership started to question this tradition. They urged an adoption of Trotskyism and regroupment with the Liga Comunista Revolucionaria (LCR), the Spanish section of one of the rival Fourth Internationals — a small group with little support either in the Basque country or elsewhere in Spain, which had emerged from the break-up of the FLP in 1969.[38] However, its creation marked the reappearance of Trotskyism in Spain after an absence of thirty years. The Spanish Trotskyist group — Izquierda Comunista[39] — under the leadership of Andrés Nin[40] had been one of the largest communist organisations which had accepted Trotsky's analysis in the early 1930s. However, the Izquierda Comunista had broken with Trotsky in 1933[41] and in 1935 had merged with another dissident communist group to form the Partido Obrero de Unificación Marxista (POUM), leaving Trotsky with only a tiny group of supporters, who were unable to maintain an existence after Franco's victory.[42]

The proposal that ETA-VI should adopt a distinct Trotskyist identity alarmed other members of the leadership, less because of a positive rejection or understanding of Trotskyism than because of their knowledge that the effect of an open debate within the ranks of the organisation would be devastating for activists who would not understand the disagreements. The minority of 'anti-Trotskyist' leaders (henceforth the 'Minos') who included

Francisco Letamendía, a defence lawyer at the Burgos trial, were in favour of the gradual transformation of ETA-VI into a Marxist party, which would take a position on issues as they arose, creating a strategy and educating the membership in the process. The revolutionary theory which ETA-VI needed would, the 'Minos' claimed, have to be based on an analysis of facts and experiences which were, so far, not available. The 'Minos'' own solution to ETA-VI's crisis lay in the adoption of a 'Transformation Tactic' which would, they hoped, convert ETA-VI into a revolutionary Marxist party on the basis of lessons derived from experience rather than from what they saw as an arbitrary leap in the dark.[43] The majority of the leaders' choice of the Trotskyist option was facilitated by their rejection of the growing moderation of the PCE and by the disarray of the Maoist groups, who found it more and more difficult to justify China's pro-American positions.[44] By 1972 Maoism was much less attractive than it had been in 1969, when ETA-Berri had first adopted it. For example, the contention of the MCE, and other Maoist groups, that the Soviet Union was ruled by a fascist, bourgeois dictatorship appeared implausible to ETA-VI's leaders. ETA-VI were, as fervent supporters of the Vietnamese struggle for independence, critical of the limited aim China gave to the Vietnamese, which they felt compared unfavourably with that given to the conservative military dictatorship in Pakistan.[45]

At a meeting of an enlarged *Biltzaar Ttippia* of ETA-VI, held in July 1972, a majority of the leadership proposed that there should be thoroughgoing discussion by the whole membership, on whether ETA-VI should merge with the LCR. The 'Minos' demanded that an Assembly should be held immediately to decide on the question. The differences proved irreconcilable[46] and the 'Minos' formed a separate organisation, which they claimed was the legitimate ETA-VI, and proceeded to hold an Assembly, in November 1972, which they described as the second part of the Sixth Assembly (the first part having taken place in August/September 1970).[47] The 'Minos' had more people inside Spain than did the 'majority' faction, so they considered themselves the legitimate ETA-VI, in spite of having been in a minority on the *Biltzaar Ttippia* of the united organisation.

ETA-VI's 'Minos' were united only in rejecting the decision to unit with the LCR. Although this rejection was shared by a majority of the membership inside Spain, it was an inadequate basis for survival as an independent group. ETA-VI's 'Minos' made no criticism of Trotskyism, nor did they clarify whether they were, in principle, determined to remain an independent group which confined its activity to Euskadi. The ETA-VI 'Minos' Assembly adopted an elaborate programme described as a 'Tactic of Transformation' which outlined how the organisation would intervene in the workers' movement, as well as in students' groups, neighbourhood organisations and the co-operative movement.[49] The 'Minos' announced that they would change the name of their publications to avoid confusion between themselves and the 'Majority' tendency. After this seemingly promising beginning, ETA-VI's 'Minos' promptly collapsed, having produced one issue of *Zutik*, their theoretical organ, and two issues of an agitational journal. ETA-VI 'Minos' had several hundred members when it split from ETA-VI and it was acknowledged to have played a prominent part in the strikes in Pamplona in 1973.[49]

The apparent modesty of the 'Transformation Tactic' obscured the determination to avoid difficult issues and pushed the organisation back towards the empiricism which had characterised ETA throughout most of its history.[50] The split between 'Minos' and 'Mayos' did not reflect any great sociological differences between the two groups, as both were mainly ethnically Basque and middle-class. Those such as Unzueta, José Vicente Idoyaga and Ramón Zallo who formed the leadership of the 'Mayos' had adopted Trotskyism after a study of Marxist theory. When the 'Minos' collapsed many of its members joined the PCE, bringing to that organisation a substantial cadre, which included Roberto Lertxundi, later to become the Party's General Secretary in the Basque country. Very few became supporters of ETA-V, but their best known theoretician 'Peru' (Francisco Letamendía), following a sojourn in Paris and writing of a history of the Basque country, became a sympathiser of ETA-Político-Militar, one of the branches of the, by then, divided ETA-V.

The 'majority' faction of ETA-VI held their version of the second half of the Sixth Assembly in December 1972, when it was decided to seek unity with the LCR and membership of the Fourth International. ETA-VI 'Mayos' brought about 300 members to the unified organisation which took the name of ETA-VI-LCR.[51] The LCR had more than twice as many members as the ETA-VI 'Mayos' before the fusion, few of them in the Basque country, although these included Luciano Rincón, perhaps Spain's most brilliant political writer. Given the relative populations of Euskadi and the rest of Spain the united organisation was very much stronger in the Basque country than elsewhere. The retention of the name ETA-VI did not, judging from the statements adopted at ETA-VI 'Mayos' seventh and last Assembly held immediately before its fusion with the LCR, indicate that the organisation's members were half-hearted about its abandonment of nationalism.[52] The programme which was adopted showed that ETA-VI 'Mayos' had unreservedly dedicated itself to intervention in working-class struggles. The group had reacted to the sharp rise in strike activity since 1970 by assuming that the dictatorship might soon be overthrown, and that the working class should prepare for a situation of dual power. The duty of revolutionaries, according to ETA-VI-LCR, was to encourage the creation of militant, unitary, organs of struggle in the workplace. These should not be mere transmission belts for the revolutionary party, but genuine attempts to build a wide base of support, in the Workers' Commissions and elsewhere. In contrast to the Maoist groups, ETA-VI 'Mayos' was aware that it was not a mass party but a group of a few hundred people, which had not yet found a way to get the support of many workers.[53]

It considered that revolutionaries should not set up sectarian Workers' Commissions as rivals to those influenced by the PCE, but should struggle to win a hearing in the mass organisations. ETA-VI 'Mayos'' (henceforth ETA-VI) stress on mass organisation, as opposed to armed struggle, did not mean that it had adopted pacifist positions. The Assembly noted the overthrow of the government of President Allende in Chile as an example of the folly of relying on pacts with capitalists. ETA-VI declared that it was necessary for the working class to prepare for violent confrontation by creating defence groups in the Workers' Commissions, the carrying out of propaganda actions by armed groups and, eventually, the creation of armed and trained fighting detachments.[54] The Assembly adopted the slogan of the 'free union of the people subject to the Spanish State', a formula which expressed ETA-VI's rejection of independence as an ideal, but acceptance of the democratic right of the Basque people to choose to become independent of Spain if they so wished. Although secession was seen as improbable and undesirable, revolutionaries should, it was argued, raise the demand for the right of national self-determination as a way to educate people in Marxist method.[55]

The slogan 'free union of the people subject to the Spanish

State' clarified the possible ambiguity in the demand for the right
to self-determination and was intended to prevent the national
questions from being a source of disunity for the workers' movement. The Assembly noted that the rival 'Minos' faction of ETA-
VI had virtually collapsed, arguing that this was due to its leaders'
refusal to take a position on any question.[56] ETA-V was
criticised for failing to carry out any mass work. It was pointed out
that although five of its members had been killed by the police
within a year, there had been no mass demonstrations comparable
to those which had taken place in protest against the killing of, and
death sentences imposed on, ETA members in the 1960s.

Now that the unity of the working class became one of ETA-
VI's main preoccupations, it became alarmed at the reactionary
influence which the PNV and ELA exercised on the ethnically
Basque population through their work in the *Ikastolas*.[57] ETA-
VI's insistence on the need to prepare for eventual armed struggle
was less a reflection of its origin as an armed movement than an
acceptance of the orthodox communist position that socialism
would not be achieved without a revolution, and of the influence
on the Fourth International of the guerrilla movements in Latin
America. Fusion with the LCR, and affiliation to the Fourth
International, had surprisingly few specific consequences. The
organisation, although very critical of the Chinese leadership,
remained an admirer of the Cuban and Vietnamese ones. The
most positive aspect of the adoption of the LCR's version of Trotskyism was shown in the LCR-ETA-VI's emphasis on workers'
unity. While the organisation continued to criticise the PCE's
policies, it avoided the hysteria, ultra-leftism and China-worship
of its Maoist competitors. ETA-VI's absorption into a party
organised throughout Spain, and its rejection of alliances with
Basque capitalists, showed a move from nationalist to communist
positions which was very similar to that made by ETA-Berri in the
late 1960s. However, the organisation's strength continued to be
in the ethnically Basque middle class. The lack of implantation in
the workers' movement, and disappointment at the frustrated
hopes for socialist revolution after the transition to a parliamentary democracy in 1977, was after 1980 to lead ETA-VI's
successor, the LCR-LKI, to relapse into the nationalist positions
it had once fiercely rejected.[58]

Part II: The rise of ETA-V

During the time that ETA-VI was moving away from nationalism, the tiny group around Etxabe were endeavouring to re-establish ETA's original principles and their own claim to be the custodian of its tradition. Initially, their efforts were much less successful than had been those of the leadership elected at the Fifth Assembly in combating a similar '*españolista*' danger. Although the leaders of ETA-V considered themselves as the legitimate heirs of ETA's tradition, the ETA-VI leadership had the backing of most of the organisation and particularly of its imprisoned members. ETA-V did not have the membership, the prestige nor the organisation to mount an effective challenge to its rivals. Although the main participants in ETA-V were united in attacking the 'treachery' of the ETA-VI leadership, they themselves were not a homogeneous group. Etxabe was against 'politics' as such, and saw himself as simply a patriot fighting for the liberation of Euskadi from Spanish rule. Talk of class struggle smacked of treason to him, as it threatened to divide the Basque people.[59] Txillardegi, who described himself as a 'socialist humanist', also had very conservative and chauvinistic ideas. He continued to believe that the crucial element in the survival of the Basque people lay in the strengthening of *Euskera*, and he had been sceptical about the possibilities of launching armed struggle in Euskadi, when it had first been seriously proposed in the mid-1960s. Both Txillardegi's and Etxabe's political ideas had more in common with those prevailing in ETA's earliest years than with those which were adopted at the Fifth Assembly.

In contrast, Krutwig, Beltza and Julen Madariaga had been strong supporters of the decisions taken at the Fifth Assembly, where Krutwig had been one of the main theoreticians. Krutwig presented his criticism of ETA-VI in Marxist terms, alleging that it was un-Marxist to stress class struggle before national liberation was achieved. Once the stage of national independence had been achieved, class struggle would become legitimate and desirable.[60] In addition to their ideological differences, the leaders of ETA-V were handicapped by the fact that they were exiled in France, Italy and Belgium. Etxabe had led the Military Front from the French Basque country, but Krutwig had never taken an active part in ETA's activities. López Adán and Madariaga had been activists, but were no longer so. Given the organisational and political weakness of ETA-V, it is hardly surprising that ETA-VI's leaders did not see their rivals as a serious threat. ETA-V's main accomplishment in 1970, the kidnapping of the German Consul, Herr Beihl, was seen as a publicity stunt, while their choice of conservatives such as Telesforo Monzón and Father Larrazábal as intermediaries in that affair showed, in ETA-VI's view, the falsity of ETA-V's claim to ETA's socialist heritage.[61]

However, ETA-V's primitive nationalism was to prove, in the long run, more in tune with ETA's traditional social base than was ETA-VI's Marxism. ETA members had always been drawn, predominantly, from the ethnically Basque sector of the population, mainly from families who supported the PNV. As ETA-VI began to move away from nationalism and to split into factions, a trickle of the activists transferred their allegiance to ETA-V.[62] The theoretical shift toward Marxism, which had been registered at the Fifth Assembly, had not been accompanied by any systematic Marxist education, which would have enabled ETA-VI's rank and file to translate rhetoric into practice. ETA-V was much better placed than ETA-VI to participate in the formation of the National Front. The PNV, which would have been an essential partner in such a Front, was unenthusiastic about either group, but more at home with ETA-V than with the '*españolista*' ETA-VI. Other advocates of the National Front such as the supporters of Txillardegi's journal *Branka*, ELA-Berri, the breakaway from the historic nationalist trade union, and EGI, the PNV's youth group, which was once more in conflict with its parent organisation all preferred ETA-V to ETA-VI. ETA-V did succeed in getting other organisations to sign joint statements, generally confined to strictly nationalist demands. In one such joint appeal, issued for the Easter nationalist celebration, Aberri Eguna, in 1972, the signatories called on the Catholic Church to re-organise its ecclesiastical boundaries, so that both the French and Spanish Basque country would be part of the same diocese.[63]

As ETA-V slowly began to recruit new members its founders resigned and lapsed into inactivity. In the summer of 1971 Etxabe, the Military Front leader, resigned to be replaced by his deputy, Eustakio Mendizabal (Txikia), a former seminarist,[64] thereby removing a leader whose chauvinism had become an embarrassment. As the Military Front was, in practice, the only functioning part of ETA-V, Txikia became the group's leader. He proceeded to launch a campaign of armed struggle which was to result in many arrests and several deaths, including his own. The ideology which ETA-V needed had to reconcile the essentials of traditional Basque nationalism with the versions of Marxism which were current in the early 1970s. The bulk of this theory was provided by Beltza and Krutwig in pamphlets and in articles published in the journal *Gathazka* which was produced in Belgium. In one such contribution, *Estrategia y tática*, it was argued that, as modern research had shown that forms of thought depended on the language used, Basque socialism must be led by people who spoke *Euskera*, and that there must be a struggle to restore it as the language of the whole Basque country.[65] In the same work it was argued that a Basque socialist party must be very wary of making any alliances with 'Spanish' forces. The PNV might be able to make pacts with the PCE, because the difference in the parties' social objectives made it unlikely that their politics would be confused, but a Basque socialist party was in much more danger of being subordinated to the strategy of Spanish socialism, so such an alliance was highly dangerous.[66]

Young supporters of ETA-V seized eagerly on the writings of Krutwig and Beltza for justification of their desire to return to the primitive nationalism of the original ETA. The failure of such theories to analyse modern Basque society, or to provide a viable strategy for the liberation of Euskadi, was a positive advantage. *Gathazka* and ETA-V's version of *Zutik* were smuggled across the border and reprinted by local activists. The other reading of ETA-V's activists in the early 1970s was eclectic. It depended on accident and the whim of the censor whether activists read Stalin on national self-determination, Frantz Fanon or Che Guevara.[67] Such varied writings did not provide a strategy for ETA-V, but they did provide a rationalisation for the existing priority given to armed struggle. An example of the theory which activists welcomed was provided by *Principios del nacionalismo revolucionario*, where Krutwig and Beltza argued that only those who spoke *Euskera* were fully Basque, and that those unable to do so, usually through no fault of their own, had a duty to learn it.[68] The conclusions of the theory were that the Basques' enemy was Spain, not capitalism in general, *Euskera* was the only genuine language of the Basque country, there was a need for a National Front of patriotic Basques of all social classes, and the violent action of an armed vanguard was a vital part of the national liberation struggle.[69] In substance, the analysis of Beltza and Krutwig provided a basis for a return to the ideas of ETA's early years, while justifying these ideas by reference to Marx, Lenin, Trotsky and Kropotkin. In the 1970s the authority of traditional '*sabiniano*' nationalism had to be supplemented by that of more advanced writers. Beltza and Krutwig specifically rejected the notion propounded by ETA-VI that 'anyone who sold his labour in the Basque country was a Basque' as ridiculous.[70] The majority of Spanish immigrants in Euskadi, they insisted, were Spanish, not alienated Basques. The authors also specifically rejected demands for bilingualism, claiming that for a revolutionary to propose the coexistence of *Euskera* and the language of the conqueror was as ridiculous as to demand the coexistence of labour and capital.[71]

In the villages the existence of a dense network of family and friends made the distribution of such illegal literature much easier than it was for 'Spanish' groups in the cities. The same network facilitated recruitment. Sympathisers would initially be given some simple task such as wall daubing to perform, before being entrusted with more important missions. The line between being a sympathiser and a member of ETA-V was not well-defined, especially in the villages. The distribution of clandestine propaganda was an activity which was also carried out by members of ETA-VI and of people in 'Spanish' groups. However, those ETA-V members engaged in such comparatively humble tasks knew that they belonged to the organisation which was carrying on the armed struggle, initiated by the heroes of the Burgos trial. New recruits to ETA-V felt a strong identification with ETA's tradition while remaining remarkably ignorant of the details of the organisation's history. The romantic appeal of belonging to an organisation which combined the glamour of armed struggle with a rejection of the conservative social attitudes of the PNV gave ETA-V a great advantage over ETA-VI. The repression of the late 1960s had awakened a deep feeling of Basque ethnic identity, which extended to people from Carlist families. In an example of this Basque patriotism a group of Basque Carlists were arrested at the end of 1970 in Burgos province, where they were trying to interrupt the transmission of Franco's end-of-the-year broadcast to the nation.[72] Armed struggle, after having been out of favour since 1969, was beginning to revive to the advantage of ETA-V.

Beltza and Krutwig's polemic against the 'stencil revolu-tionaries' who believed in propaganda rather than armed action was very popular among young men who craved for dramatic activity. Apart from the contributions of Krutwig and Beltza, the main theoretical influence on the early ETA-V was the booklet *Fines y medios en la lucha de liberación nacional*, written by the imprisoned Zalbide in 1969, under his pseudonym of K. de Zumbeltz. *Fines . . .* was essentially a treatise on forms of military struggle and organisation, with little political content.[73] ETA-V's own publications were very sparse in its early years. As it disputed the claim of ETA-VI to the titles of ETA's journals, it began, in October 1970, to publish its own version of *Zutik*.[16] ETA-V's journal was very lightweight and its main purpose was to establish the group's claim to be the genuine ETA. The first issue consisted solely of an article by Julen Madariaga which attacked the leadership of ETA-VI, by attributing to them an article written by a member of Komunistak.[75] Another issue consisted entirely of ETA-V's statement on freeing the German Consul, Herr Beihl.[76] When ETA-V attempted to make a more thorough criticism of their rivals in ETA-VI, their lack of intellectual resources compelled them to print an article by Txillardegi, and reproduce an article by Jean-Paul Sartre, originally published as a preface to a book on the Burgos trial. Sartre restated the argument that Euskadi was a colony, which ETA had adopted at its Fifth Assembly.[77]

ETA-V's leaders were concerned that some naive patriots were willing to accept ETA-VI as participants in a National Front,[78] and were critical of ETA-VI's talk of fascist oppression which implied opposition to the Franco dictatorship rather than to the Spanish State, and were particularly annoyed at ETA-VI's calls for solidarity between workers in struggle in various parts of Spain, which they argued was analogous to calling for solidarity between Germans and Russians during the German occupation.[79] ETA-V continued to insist that Euskadi was subject to foreign military occupation as a result of being defeated in three wars. In a repetition of Txillardegi's allegations against Iturrioz and del Río it was suggested that ETA-VI was a product of infiltration by the PCE,[80] although ETA-V's leaders knew that their rivals in ETA-VI were of impeccably Basque and nationalist origin.

ETA-V's attempts to become accepted as the legitimate organisation were hampered by the firm statement supporting the leadership of ETA-VI which had been signed by all of the accused in the Burgos trial, and had met with the approval of the organisations' other prisoners, who tried to keep up with developments in the outside world through information provided by visitors and by smuggled communications.[81] Most of the prisoners in 1970 shared the contempt of the ETA-VI leadership for the split led by

Etxabe and Krutwig. The argument that those elected to the Biltzaar Ttippia at the Fifth Assembly in 1967 were the only legitimate leadership would hardly be convincing for the accused at the Burgos trial, who had themselves constituted the effective leadership of ETA up until their arrest in 1969, with no better constitutional claim than that of those who had replaced them. The chauvinism expounded by Etxabe, which contrasted so strongly with the statements of solidarity with the Spanish working class which the prisoners had made during the Burgos trial, could hardly be accepted by them. Nor were the prisoners impressed by Txillardegi's claim to represent ETA, in view of his resignation from the organisation in the spring of 1967.[82] Beltza had also resigned from ETA in 1970.[83] Krutwig and Madariaga, although they had remained members, had not participated in the struggle inside Spain since the Fifth Assembly.

For most supporters of the accused at the Burgos trial, who understood little of the organisation's ideological struggles, the prisoners' statements gave ETA-VI legitimacy. However, by late 1971, as it became clear that ETA-VI was making little progress in its attempt to become a Marxist organisation, the prisoners found themselves in the unenviable position of being no longer the unchallenged representatives of the Basque struggle for liberation. The Marxism of ETA's prisoners had generally not extended to more than sympathy with the oppressed and a hostility to the 'oligarchy'. ETA-VI's leaders' adoption of a political strategy which few of the prisoners were able to understand threatened to create conflict within the nationalist community. The censorship made it difficult for the prisoners to make a serious study of their organisation's Marxist ideas.[84]

As ETA-V slowly began to fill the political space occupied by ETA in the early 1960s, some of the prisoners transferred their allegiance. The public adhesion to ETA-V early in 1972 of Zalbide, ETA's main leader until his imprisonment in 1965, together with Onaindia and Uriarte, heroes of the Burgos trial, was a symptom of a development affecting a majority of prisoners.[85] The change of allegiance presented great difficulties for people who had previously rejected the political conceptions of Etxabe and his supporters. The move was made easier by Etxabe's resignation, but still required a considerable political somersault. Those prisoners who made statements transferring their allegiance from ETA-VI to ETA-V reiterated their original support for unification of the French and Spanish Basque country, stressed the importance of transforming Euskadi into a Basque-speaking state, rejecting bilingualism, and emphasised the need for a National Front.[86]

The prisoners criticised ETA-VI for having an un-Marxist conception of the national question, which led it to ignore the need for alliances with other social classes, such as the national bourgeoisie which had shown itself to be objectively revolutionary by the stand it had taken at the Burgos trial. The correct Marxist stance, the prisoners argued, was to create a National Front and fight for an independent sovereign Euskadi, as a necessary stage before the socialist revolution.[87] The prisoners' ingenious formula for reconciling socialist rhetoric with support for ETA-V was to provide that organisation with the theory which replaced the primitive nationalism, and anti-communism, of Etxabe and Txillardegi. The adherence of a number of prisoners to ETA-V was an absolutely essential factor in establishing that organisation's legitimacy. Although the leadership of ETA-VI could be accused of treachery, any attempt to criticise the heroes of the Burgos trial would have been counter-productive. As ETA-V's leaders were reluctant to attack the Marxist rhetoric and declaration of solidarity with the Spanish working class voiced at the Burgos trial, a statement such as that made by José María Dorronsoro, that a peasant in Andalusia was as oppressed as a peasant in Euskadi,[88] had to be explained away, by claiming that it had been taken out of context. In 1971 and 1972 ETA-V recruited some ETA-VI activists who had become alarmed at that organisation's gradual abandonment of nationalism. A few members of the, now dismantled, Las Cabras group, such as Imanol Pagoaga, and a large number of individuals, radicalised by the repression and the campaign of the Burgos trial, also joined ETA-V. The new recruits tended to be of more rural origin than those who had joined ETA in the late sixties, and their low political level shocked ETA-VI members whom they encountered in prison.[89]

ETA-V's slow growth in numbers received a huge boost in spring 1972, when it united with EGI. Practically all of EGI's several hundred activists went over to ETA-V, leaving the PNV with a tiny rump, and giving ETA-V a real base inside Spain.[90] The PNV's failure to retain control of its youth organisation was hardly surprising. EGI had revived, in the late 1960s, partly as a result of the growing politicisation of the Basque country which had followed from the killing of Manzanas, ETA's campaign of violence, and the Burgos trial. As EGI became a more active organisation, ETA's activities provided a model to emulate. For example, EGI would hang *Ikurriñas* on the highway and steal material to produce propaganda. The general repression which ETA's campaign produced made EGI's work of maintaining its own structure hazardous, and made it necessary for it to adopt a similar kind of organisation.[91]

The rapprochement which the interior leadership had hoped for before the split at the Sixth Assembly had been frustrated by ETA-VI's adoption of Marxist positions.[92] As ETA-V sought to build up contacts inside Spain, they found that EGI was receptive to their message. Múgica Arregui, the dominant figure in EGI who had been committed to ETA-V's line for some time before the fusion, was to be one of the main leaders of the united organisation. From mid-1971 ETA-V started preparing to resume the armed struggle. The first steps consisted of carrying out robberies to provide the money needed to obtain arms and to maintain a network of *liberados*. The organisation was not yet ready to undertake actions comparable to the killing of Manzanas or the bombings of public buildings which had been carried out in 1969. Nor did ETA-V yet directly attack the police. However, such confrontations were soon to occur as armed *liberados* carried out their missions, with consequent loss of life on both sides. ETA-V was, by the end of 1971, in a position to begin to launch a campaign of armed struggle, which started slowly, but escalated with the kidnapping of the industrialist Lorenzo Zabala in January 1972.[93]

Zabala, the chairman of the company Precicontrol in Eibar, was involved in a dispute with his employees, originally over their request for a wage increase. There had been a strike which had lasted several months before the kidnapping. When ETA-V announced that Zabala would be executed unless the company re-employed all the sacked workers, and accepted the claim for a wage increase of 250 pesetas per week, the company agreed and Zabala was freed. The kidnapping was seen by ETA-V as a model of the process of action/repression/action, first elaborated by Krutwig and Zumbeltz, and adopted as ETA policy at its Fifth Assembly. The workers, not ETA, it was claimed, had initiated the struggle, but had been unable to win it on their own because of the force of repression. Therefore ETA's intervention was justified, and was complementing the workers' struggle rather than substituting itself for it.[94] Zabala was ethnically Basque, and had no known political connections, so the action was presented as a socialist one. Although Zabala was the second person to be kidnapped by ETA-V, the incident was the real start of a tactic which was to become one of its main activities. When Herr Beihl, the German Consul, had been kidnapped in December 1970 the action had appeared to many as a publicity stunt, which would have been unlikely to result in his death. In contrast, kidnapping for ransom, and to support labour disputes, was to be used many times in the future. Using the armed struggle to intervene in labour disputes allowed ETA-V to take up the strategy which had been abandoned in 1969, and at the same time defend itself from the charge that it was merely a middle-class military organisation.

By 1972 ETA-V's publications had abandoned the chauvinistic tone which had marked them in 1970 and 1971. The organisation readopted the political line it had followed in the period after the Fifth Assembly. The struggle for national liberation was held to be compatible not only with socialism but also with internationalism, as ETA's joint declaration with a number of foreign nationalist organisations showed.[95] Beltza's claim that Euskadi was a colony was criticised,[96] and the PNV was attacked, as was ELA, the moderate Basque trade union.[97] However, ETA-V continued to believe that the creation of an independent Basque state must precede the struggle for socialism. Consequently, armed struggle was vital, as was the creation of a National Front which would include all those forces opposed to the Spanish 'oligarchy'. In practice, the organisation's theory had little relationship to its activities. It had hardly any strength in the factories and consequently its main interventions in industrial struggle consisted of exploits such as planting bombs in the offices of the official *Sindicatos*.

The theory that there was a progressive national bourgeoisie which was a potential ally of ETA-V in its struggle against the oligarchy gave no guide to intervention in industrial struggle. In the interior of Guipúzcoa and Vizcaya, where ETA-V was strong, the oligarchy was noticeably absent. Industrialists tended to be Basque, often of fairly humble origins, and were frequently supporters of the PNV. Where their opinions and background were suitable, they could be counted as members of the PTV. The kidnapping of an ethnically Basque industrialist like Zabala upset the PNV and endangered the creation of the National Front. The increase in ETA-V's activities resulted, inevitably, in casualties among their members, in incidents such as that which produced the death of ETA's first martyr, Txabi Etxebarrieta. In April 1972, shortly before the Aberri Eguna demonstrations, an ETA-V *liberado*, Jon Goikoetxea, was killed in a clash with the police at Elizondo, near the French border, where he had made a clandestine border crossing.[98] ETA-V alleged that Goikoetxea had been shot in the back and issued demands to the people to call a general strike, close bars and other commercial establishments, boycott the press, and have demonstrations of protest in all localities.[99] Such a demand, which had not been preceded by any mass campaign or involvement in industrial issues, was symptomatic of an attitude which was to be dominant throughout the history of the organisation.

During 1971 and 1972 ETA-V's military actions were quite modest in comparison to their future exploits. Their main targets were the same as those of the 1960s. They planted bombs at the offices of the *Sindicatos* and other official buildings and destroyed monuments to the victory of the nationalist forces in the Spanish Civil War.[100] They also attacked the property of supporters of Franco's regime and buildings such as the Yacht Club at San Sebastián, which were said to belong to the oligarchy.[101] Such actions were similar to those unleashed by Escubi in 1968 and 1969, although they did not, until nearly the end of 1973, rival the scale of that campaign. ETA-V was at great pains to stress the socialist nature of its activities. The bombing of *Sindicato* buildings was presented as complementary to the struggle which the workers were waging against that institution, and an alternative to the 'revisionist' attempt by the PCE to capture the places of workplace representation in the *Sindicato* elections.[102] In practice ETA-V saw workers' agitation as a mere adjunct to the military struggle.

ETA-V's leaders agreed with those of many left tendencies that the *Sindicato* elections should be boycotted, that those who occupied such posts should resign, and threatened to shoot those who refused to do so. The group's sparse propaganda on the workers' struggle was written in very general terms, and the reasons given for its actions were often obscure. For example, ETA-V destroyed the Fishing Club in the coastal town of Lekeitio, on the grounds that it was used exclusively by bourgeois visitors, who were converting Lekeitio from a fishing into a tourist town.[103] The burning down of the tourist office in the fashionable seaside resort of Zarauz in Guipúzcoa was justified in similar terms.[104] ETA-V's military strength was growing continually, but its choice of targets often appeared arbitrary. Sometimes the organisation's violence was directed at more relevant targets. For example, in early 1972 ETA-V destroyed shops belonging to the Mayor of Ondarroa, in Vizcaya, who was alleged to have participated in beating up nationalist priests, and to a San Sebastián municipal councillor, alleged to be a police informer and a member of the fascist group the *Guerrilleros de Cristo Rey*.[105]

According to ETA-V's theory, such actions were the first steps in a guerrilla war, where the people would themselves take up arms. In reality, ETA-V's actions did not lead to mass struggle, although a fair number of people approved of them. The strategy of armed struggle had its own dynamic, which produced police retaliation and counter-retaliation, so that ETA-V's targets became more indiscriminate. For example, in August 1972, in Galdácano in Vizcaya, ETA activists killed a municipal policeman and wounded a Civil Guard, in a successful attempt to avoid arrest.[106] The police response led, four days later, to the deaths of two ETA members in Lekeitio in the same province. ETA-V alleged that their members had been murdered, as they had been given no chance to surrender.[107] Anger at police violence was, eventually, to lead ETA-V to consider that any member of the security forces was a legitimate target.

The belief that the organisation should intervene to assist the workers' struggle, led in January 1973, a year after the kidnapping of Zabala, to the seizure of Felipe Huarte, an important Navarrese industrialist. The action was very similar to the Zabala affair, in that Huarte's firm, Torfinasa, was involved in a dispute with its employees. ETA-V's condition for Huarte's release included the granting of the workers' demands, as well as payment of a ransom of 50 million pesetas.[108] When Huarte's relatives agreed to ETA's terms he was freed. From ETA-V's viewpoint the action was a successful application of its strategy of armed intervention being used to assist the workers' struggle.[109] The payment of the ransom unleashed a quarrel among the regime's supporters, when the Falangist Emilio Romero, editor of *Pueblo*, criticised the family's surrender to ETA-V's demands.[110] The Huarte kidnapping certainly demonstrated ETA-V's ability to undertake difficult military operations. The organisation's claim that it was supplementing the workers' actions rather than substituting for them was not accepted by Huarte's employees, who suspended their strike, or by the Workers' Commissions in

Navarre, who issued a declaration that they were quite capable of defending their interests, without the intervention of ETA-V.[111]

Huarte's kidnapping led to a large number of arrests. Inevitably, such an action, although carried out by *liberados*, required a large-scale back-up by people who provided them with information and assistance. Such people were much more vulnerable than the *liberados* operating from France, so a spectacular exploit would generally result in the arrest or flight into exile of many 'legal' activists. The priority given to armed struggle meant that such people were never able to develop the consistent work in the factories to which ETA-V was, in theory, committed. The fact that the Huarte kidnapping did not occur in a context of an apathetic and weak trade union movement was demonstrated, later in the same year, when Pamplona was the centre of a general strike where ETA-V's rivals, ETA-VI, played a significant part. The kidnapping had not been preceded by any campaign of agitation in the workers' movement. ETA-V's Workers' Front remained a pale appendage of its Military Front, which did little more than call on the workers to support ETA-V's military actions. Nevertheless ETA-V's leaders thought that they had developed a viable strategy which combined military activities and mass struggle. Txikia, the main architect of that strategy, was not to survive long enough to see the consequences of the campaign which he had launched, as he was killed in April 1973. Txikia noticed, while travelling by train, that he was being observed. On arrival at Algorta, he ran off with the police in pursuit and was shot dead when trying to start a car which he had commandeered.[112]

Txikia was a man of enormous drive and daring, who according to his predecessor Etxabe lacked the caution which was a necessary part of the make-up of a military leader.[113] Txikia himself actively participated in activities such as the kidnapping of Huarte. As no single person had the prestige to replace him, the differences between ETA-V's Fronts sharpened, eventually producing new splits in the organisation. Txikia's death and the effects of the other losses suffered by ETA-V, produced the by now familiar phenomenon of people with very little experience having to take over the leadership. As very few members of ETA-V had joined before the Sixth Assembly in 1970, these leaders came either from EGI or from those who had joined ETA-V following the Burgos trial. One such person, who was to become a dominant figure, was Eduardo Moreno Bergareche (Pertur).[114] Some of these new leaders began to advocate that priority be given to political as well as to military activities. Such ideas were eventually to produce splits in ETA-V, just as similar demands in the past had led to the formation of the tendencies which had become ETA-Berri and ETA-VI. Leaders such as Pertur, apart from emphasising mass struggle and socialist doctrine, now saw ETA-V's fight as part of a worldwide struggle against imperialism. Their ideology was heavily influenced by the Maoism which their rivals in ETA-VI had recently abandoned.

In 1972 and 1973 ETA-V, anxious to establish its internationalist credentials, moved away from the extreme chauvinism which had been one of the main reasons for its split from ETA-VI. ETA-V's use of Marxist phraseology was one indication of this changing perspective. Another was its participation in conferences held to support liberation movements throughout the world. ETA-V's appeals to the immigrants were now couched in very different terms from those of Etxabe and Krutwig.[115] So did its attitude to support from outside Euskadi. Whereas, at the time of the Beihl kidnapping, Monzón had expressed the view that the Basque people could liberate themselves without foreign aid, ETA-V now stressed that people throughout the world were fighting for liberation and that a blow struck against national oppression in any part of the world helped oppressed nations elsewhere.[116] ETA-V began to benefit from the sympathy of sections of the Spanish left, which had been aroused by the Burgos trial. The PCE's search for agreement with liberal capitalists caused a section of its intellectual and middle-class base to become disaffected. Some became attracted to Maoism, while others became involved in efforts to aid the Basque resistance. The leaders of ETA-VI, who had devoted considerable efforts to promoting solidarity with the Burgos prisoners, both in Spain and in other countries, were not the long-term beneficiaries of these efforts, as the armed struggle of ETA-V was more romantic, and therefore more attractive to people such as the playwright Alfonso Sastre, a former member of the PCE Central Committee, and his wife Eva Forest. One expression of non-Basque support for ETA was the formation in Madrid of a 'Committee of solidarity with oppressed peoples', some of whose members were to become involved in ETA's activities.[117]

Once ETA-V had strengthened its organisation and increased its numbers it started to prepare an Assembly which could ratify its leadership positions. The Assembly, held in September 1973 in

Hasparren in the French Basque country, was described as the
first part of the Sixth Assembly, as the last Assembly which ETA-
V recognised as legitimate was the Fifth held in 1966 and 1967.
In the period between Txikia's death and the Assembly, ETA-V
was led by an Executive Committee which functioned as a loose
coordinating body of autonomously functioning Fronts, each with
its own leadership.[118] Once more, those who wished to develop
mass activity found themselves at the mercy of whatever action the
Military Front might undertake, irrespective of its effects on the
rest of the organisation.[119] The Military Front members' ability
to escape to France, after striking at their targets within Spain,
ensured their own survival, but resulted in the repression being
borne by the other Fronts, whose members remained in the
interior. Inevitably, those who tried to develop mass activities
wished to exercise some control over the Military Front, although
no-one in ETA-V called for an end to military activities.[120]

In August 1973, the leaders of the Workers' Front were reluctant to attend the Sixth Assembly, because there had been no
debate on ideology, no study of the resolutions which were to be
considered, nor any real thought given to ETA-V's organisational
problems.[121] They demanded that a discussion should be
organised on the basis of written statements, and although they
were persuaded to attend the Assembly, the atmosphere there was
tense, as the Military Front representatives indulged in personal
abuse, instead of discussing principles or policies. In spite of the
differences and mutual distrust the Assembly ended without any
split, except for a small group of supporters of the journal *Gatzaka*,
who supported the libertarian ideas of Beltza, and who refused to
accept ETA-V's adoption of the principles of 'democratic
centralism'.[122] The leaders of the Workers' Front remained
within ETA-V, in spite of their dissatisfaction at their inability to
control the Military Front. A new Biltzaar Ttippia (BT) was
formed with representatives from the various Fronts which was
intended to be an effective leadership rather than a mere coordinating body like the previous Executive Committee. However,
in practice the Military Front continued to dominate.

This dominance was convincingly demonstrated when, on 20
December 1973, the organisation carried out what was easily its
most striking military feat: the assassination of the Prime
Minister, Admiral Carrero Blanco. Technically the operation was
enormously successful. An ETA-V action group based in Madrid
had hired a basement flat on Calle Claudio Coello on the Prime

Minister's route home from his daily attendance at Mass. The team dug a tunnel under the road and planted a powerful charge of explosives, which they detonated when the Prime Minister's car passed over it. The explosion was so powerful that the car was blown high into the air, coming to rest in a balcony. Carrero Blanco, his bodyguard and his chauffeur were killed instantly.[123] The technical brilliance of the operation aroused suspicion in some quarters that those responsible for it must have had the assistance of some agency of a foreign power, perhaps the CIA.

Santiago Carrillo expressed suspicions, shared by many people, when he suggested that the people who had carried it out had been trained professionals, with powerful backing.[124] Such suspicions were aroused not only by the technical difficulties of the operation, but by its timing. The trial of the national leadership of the Workers' Commissions was due to open on the same day.[125] For the PCE, and for others on the left, one of the main effects of the assassination was to make a public demonstration of support for the Workers' Commissions almost impossible. The laxity of the security forces also aroused comment, as no measures to prevent people leaving Madrid were taken until several hours after the killing.[126] Leizaola, the President of the Basque government in exile, at first refused to believe that such a crime could have been committed by Basques. ETA-V responded to speculations on whether it was really responsible for the assassination with brutal humour, declaring that its activists were quite capable of connecting a fuse to an explosive charge.[127]

Doubt about whether ETA-V had really been responsible for the killing was ended when the organisation arranged a press conference in south-west France, where four hooded men claimed to have carried it out, and gave a detailed description of how it had been done.[128] The assassination marked a new departure for ETA-V which had, up until then, confined its activities to Euskadi. In the future it was to undertake further actions in Madrid and other parts of Spain. For the moderate sectors of the opposition the assassination was an act of lunacy, which was likely to frustrate Spain's hoped-for evolution towards democracy by encouraging a backlash by right-wing elements, and perhaps even a military takeover after Franco's death.[129] ETA-V argued that, on the contrary, the assassination was an essential part of its strategy for preventing Francoism continuing after Franco's death. Carrero Blanco, it maintained, was the only person who could have ensured the success of that transition, because no-one else had Franco's absolute confidence and the trust of the most reactionary element in the regime, the so-called 'Bunker', particularly in the army, and of the technocratic big business sectors headed by Opus Dei. With Carrero's death, an orderly transition to Francoism without Franco was said to be immensely more difficult.[130]

Carrero's death ensured that the controversy on what would have happened if he had survived Franco could never be settled. Most of the discussion on the succession to Franco assumed that Prince Juan Carlos was a cypher who was unlikely to have much of an independent position. The crowds at Carrero Blanco's funeral who booed the Bishop of Madrid, but cheered Juan Carlos, could not have seen him as a liberal.[131] Surprisingly, in view of their support for mass action rather than the violence of an armed minority, ETA-V's rivals, ETA-VI, now united with the LCR, approved of Carrero's assassination. Its journal castigated the PCE and the PSOE for sending their condolences to Carrero Blanco's family, and compared their regrets with the jubilation with which, it claimed, the execution had been received by the working class.[132]

ETA-V's estimation of the crucial importance of Carrero Blanco would seem to have been overstated. It was certainly true that Carrero had Franco's confidence, and that he was unusual in combining a very right-wing past, which endeared him to the 'Bunker', with patronage of Opus Dei. However, Carrero was 70 years old and was not a commanding or charismatic figure. His successor as Prime Minister, Arias Navarro, shared sufficient of Carrero's qualities to ensure the transition from Franco to Juan Carlos. ETA-V's original plan had been to kidnap the Prime Minister, and to offer to release him in exchange for all of their own imprisoned members.[133] The effects of such an achievement would have been quite different from those which followed the assassination. So the claim that the elimination of Carrero was part of a considered strategy was hardly plausible. However, the organisation continued to maintain that the assassination had been the most powerful blow ever struck against the Francoist system, and that those left-wing parties who, in the post-Franco era, criticised ETA were able to exist because of the organisation which they then attacked.

The assassination gave ETA-V a prestige unmatched by its rival ETA-VI, which on amalgamating with the LCR had abandoned the nationalist tradition. It thereby lost ground in the ethnically Basque community, while failing to build a large enough base in the 'Spanish' working class to challenge the PCE. The leaders of ETA-V could, plausibly, claim that there was now only one ETA, although this was not to be so for long. ETA-V was to follow up the Carrero Blanco assassination with a campaign of violence which was more intensive than anything which it had achieved in the past. In so doing, it was to draw further away from most of the opposition, which put its hopes in a peaceful dismantling of the dictatorship and a gradual transition to a parliamentary democracy. As the world entered an economic slump, exacerbated by the rapid increase in oil prices, the dominant sections of Spanish capitalism became anxious that Spain should be transformed into a parliamentary democracy, rather than risk the potentially revolutionary consequences of a combination of economic and political strikes. Key sectors of the Franco regime were becoming reconciled to making an accommodation with the opposition. ETA-V resisted the temptation to compromise with the system. Its anti-capitalist line was justified by the Maoist rhetoric which had been so useful in justifying its nationalism and lack of involvement in workers' struggles. Yet ETA-V's Maoism was of a very individual variety, which was to enable it to survive in a period when 'Spanish' Maoist groups were to disintegrate.

REFERENCES

1. Author's interview with Patxo Unzueta, Bilbao, 13 March 1980.

2. Interview with three ETA-VI spokesmen, *Politique Hebdo*, 17 Jan. 1971 in *Documentos Y*, Vol. 10, pp. 195–7.

3. *Comunicado de Aclaración*, *Documentos Y*, Vol. 9, pp. 460–4.

4. *Kemen*, No. 4, undated.

5. *Comunicado* in *Documentos Y*, Vol. 11, p. 58.

6. 'Segunda Conversación', 16 Feb. 1971, *Garai*, 1977, reprinted in *Documentos Y*, Vol. 11, pp. 88–89.

7. *Berriak*, No. 3, 27 Jan. 1971.

8. *Berriak Lanak-H III KO*, April 1971, and *Kemen*, No. 6, April 1971.

9. *Sexta Conversación*, 8 May 1971, *Documentos Y*, Vol. 11, p. 62.

10. *Cuarta Conversación*, 27 March 1971, *Documentos Y*, Vol. 11, pp. 90–91.

11. Both ELAs were in practice political groups, not trade unions. See 'José Antonio Ayestarán y la historia de ELA-STV', *Muga*, No. 3, Feb. 1980.

12. *Primera Conversación*, 16 Jan. 1971, *Documentos Y*, Vol. 11, pp. 88–89.

13. Report by ETA-VI cell in Bayonne, 22 May 1971, in *Documentos*

Y, Vol. 11, pp. 131–37.

14. 'Sobre la VI Asamblea', *Zutik*, No. 52, 1 May 1971.

15. *Saioak*, No. 2, Dec. 1970.

16. 'ETA: Balance de un año. 1970–July 1971', *Saioak*, No. 3, undated.

17. A. Buendía (Patxo Unzueta), *En torno a Saioak No. 3*, Feb. 1972, in *Documentos Y*, Vol. 13, pp. 88–107; author's interview with Patxo Unzueta.

18. 'Tres meses de luchas', *Berriak*, No. 12, March 1972.

19. 'Frente a la represión y el crimen: una gran huelga', *Mundo Obrero*, 2 Oct. 1971.

20. *Berriak*, No. 12, March 1972; *Mundo Obrero*, 15 April 1972.

21. *Iruña: huelga general*, a 38-page booklet published by ETA-VI; also *Berriak*, No. 16, August 1973.

22. *Mundo Obrero*, 20 March, 3 April, 30 April and 30 May 1971.

23. *Berriak*, No. 6, 12 April and No. 8, 28 July, 1971; also *Zutik*, (ETA-VI) No. 52, May 1971.

24. Fernando Jáuregui and Pedro Vega, *Crónica del antifranquismo*, Vol. 2 (Barcelona, 1984), pp. 320–23; also Areilla interview in Ramón Chao, *Después de Franco España* (Madrid, 1976), pp. 77–83.

25. For ETA-VI's criticism of the PCE see *Berriak*, 13 Jan. 1973, and *Zutik*, No. 58, June–July 1973.

26. 'ETA-V y el activismo minoritario', *Zutik*, No. 57, April–May 1973.

27. *Zutik*, No. 54, Dec. 1971.

28. A. Buendía, *En torno a Saioak*, No. 3.

29. *Agur Iraulzaileak*, in *Documentos Y*, Vol. 11, pp. 22–31.

30. *Zutik*, No. 54, Dec. 1971.

31. Author's interview with 'Goiherri', San Sebastián, 5 August 1984.

32. *Apuntes de Economía*, Lección No. 7, March 1972; *Apuntes. . .* was a continuation of ETA-VI's internal journal *Kemen*.

33. *Apuntes de Economía*, Lección No. 9, May 1972.

34. *Berriak*, No. 6, 12 April 1971; *Berriak*, No. 8, 28 July 1971.

35. 'Aprende de los hechos', *Berriak*, No. 10, 15 Nov. 1971.

36. Jesús A. Buendía (Patxo Unzueta) made an exhaustive criticism of ETA-VI's eclecticism in *Apuntes de Economía*, Lección 11, July 1972.

37. *La Gaceta del Norte*, 23 March 1971.

38. See *Comunismo*, No. 1, May 1970; also interview with LCR leader Miguel Romero, *Viejo Topo*, No. 37, Oct. 1979.

39. Pelai Pagés, *El movimiento trotskista en España 1930–1935* (Barcelona, 1978), passim; also Jesús Pérez (ed), *Comunismo* (Barcelona, 1978).

40. Wilebando Solano, *The Spanish Revolution. The life of Andrés Nin* (London, undated), passim; Andrés Nin, *Los movimientos de emancipación nacional* (Barcelona, 1977).

41. Leon Trotsky, *The Spanish Revolution, 1931–39* (New York, 1973), passim.

42. G. Munis, *Jalones de derrota. Promesa de victoria* (Bilbao, 1977), passim.

43. 'Nuestra Táctica de transformación' in *Actas de BT ampliado*, July

1972, *Documentos Y*, Vol. 13, pp. 263–285.

44. *El Militante*, No. 9, Jan. 1976: for the PTE see Ramón Lobato, 'Sobre la dictadura del proletariado', *Hacia el socialismo*, No. 6, Aug. 1976.

45. *Zutik* (ETA-VI Mayos), No. 56, Feb–March 1973.

46. *Actas del BT ampliado*, in *Documentos Y*, Vol. 13, pp. 263–85.

47. *Zutik*, No. 55 (ETA-VI Minos), March 1973.

48. 'Declaraciones de la segunda parte de la VI Asamblea', *Zutik* (ETA-VI Minos), No. 55.

49. *Iruña. Huelga general*, 1973.

50. Ortzi, *Historia*, p. 389.

51. *Zutik* (ETA-VI-LCR), No. 61, Jan. 1974.

52. *Zutik* (ETA-VI), No. 56, Feb.–March 1973.

53. *Zutik* (ETA-VI), Feb.–March 1973.

54. *Zutik* (ETA-VI-LCR), No. 61, Jan. 1974.

55. *Zutik* (ETA-VI-LCR), Jan. 1974.

56. 'Contra el eclecticismo', *Zutik* (ETA-VI-LCR), No. 61, Jan. 1974.

57. 'Resolución sobre la lucha . . .', *Zutik*, No. 61.

58. See *Zutik* and *Combate*, the LKI/LCR's weekly paper, 1977–1986.

59. J.J. Etxabe, 'Carta abierta a todos los militantes de E.T.A.', in *Kemen* (ETA-V); interview with Etxabe in *Garai*, 10 March 1977.

60. *Comentarios y proposiciones ante la próxima asamblea* in *Documentos Y*, Vol. 11, pp. 109–15.

61. *Berriak*, No. 1, Dec. 1970.

62. Author's interview with one such activist (Goiherri), San Sebastián, 5 August 1984.

63. *Aberri Eguna*, in *Documentos Y*, Vol. 12, pp. 405–6.

64. Etxabe interview in *Garaia*, 10 March 1977; *Comunicado de ETA al pueblo vasco*, August 1971, *Documentos Y*, Vol. 12, p. 298.

65. *Estrategia y táctica*, in *Documentos Y*, Vol. 12, pp. 10–16.

66. *Estrategia y táctica*, in *Documentos Y*, Vol. 12, pp. 12–13.

67. Author's interview with Goiherri.

68. *Principios de nacionalismo revolucionario*, in *Documentos Y*, Vol. 12, pp. 20–21.

69. *Principios* . . ., pp. 18–24.

70. *Notas para una teoria del nacionalismo revolucionario* in *Documentos Y*, Vol. 12, p. 73.

71. *Notas para* . . ., p. 73.

72. Author's interview with Jon Querejeta, a participant in the attempt, San Sebastián, 30 July 1984.

73. *Fines y Medios*, supplement to *Iraultza*, Nov. 1970, passim.

74. ETA-V's version of *Zutik* was numbered 57, although the last issue published before the split was *Zutik*, No. 51, published in the spring of 1970.

75. *Zutik* (ETA-V), No. 57.

76. *Zutik* (ETA-V), No. 58.

77. J.-P. Sartre, 'El proceso de la descentralización', *Zutik* (ETA-V), No. 61, undated.

78. *Zutik* (ETA-V), No. 60.

79. *Zutik* (ETA-V), No. 60.

80. *Zutik* (ETA-V), No. 60.
81. Author's interviews with Sabino Arana, Vitoria, 16 March 1980; Iñaki Sarasketa, San Sebastián, 26 March 1980; I. Garcia Arranberri, Ondarroa, 19 March 1980.
82. See *Al comité executivo de ETA*, in *Documentos Y*, Vol. 7, p. 101, 14 April 1967.
83. *A todos los Makos*, announced Beltza's resignation, *Documentos Y*, Vol. 9, pp. 374–5.
84. Author's interview with Garcia Arranberri.
85. *Zutik* (ETA-V) (Caracas, undated).
86. *Zutik* (ETA-V), No. 63, undated.
87. *Zutik* (ETA-V), No. 63, undated.
88. See Chapter 4, p. 96.
89. Author's interview with I. Garcia Arranberri.
90. Author's interview with Goiherri.
91. See a joint statement in *Llamamiento al pueblo vasco*, following the killing of ETA *liberado* Jon Goikoetxea at Easter 1972, *Documentos Y*, Vol. 12, p. 401.
92. For ETA's hopes of incorporating EGI in 1970 see *A todos los makos*, *Documentos Y*, Vol. 9, pp. 368–70.
93. See *Carta Envíada por ETA a los medios de difusión prensa y radio*, *Documentos Y*, Vol. 12, pp. 373–4.
94. *Zutik*, No. 63 (French edition), Jan. 1972; *España: unidad en la represión*, in *Documentos Y*, Vol. 15, pp. 56–8.
95. *Al 15° Congreso de los estudiantes Kurdos. Intervención de ETA*, Bucarest, Feb. 1972, *Documentos Y*, Vol. 12, pp. 379–82.
96. *¿Que es ETA?*, *Documentos Y*, Vol. 15, pp. 31–8.
97. *Liberación nacional e internacionalismo* (undated), *Documentos Y*, Vol. 15, pp. 142–8: *Puntos mínimos ideológicos de ETA* (undated), *Documentos Y*, Vol. 15, pp. 117–25.
98. *Comunicado de ETA*, *Documentos Y*, Vol. 12, pp. 415–6.
99. ETA leaflet: *Aberri Eguna 72*, '*Txapela*' *asesinado*, *Documentos Y*, Vol. 12, p. 418.
100. 'Acciones militares de ETA en 1972', *Hautsi*, No. 2, 1973.
101. 'Acciones . . .', *Hautsi*, No. 2, 1973.
102. *Hautsi*, No. 2, 1973.
103. *Comunicado de ETA ante los últimos acontecimientos*, *Documentos Y*, Vol. 12, p. 441.
104. *Comunicado de ETA ante . . .*
105. *Comunicado de ETA ante . . .*
106. 'Galdacano', *Hautsi*, No. 3, undated.
107. 'Lekeitio', *Hautsi*, No. 3, undated.
108. *Comunicado a la prensa internacional*, *Documentos Y*, Vol. 15, p. 173; *Zutik Berriak* (ETA-V), Feb. 1973.
109. *Información*, No. 101, *Documentos Y*, Vol. 15, p. 177.
110. 'El arresto de Felipe Huarte', *Hautsi*, No. 3.
111. 'ETA-V y el activismo minoritario', *Zutik* (ETA-VI) (Mayos) No. 57, April/May 1973.
112. *Eustakio Mendizabal Benito* '*Txikia*' *asesinado por la policía secreta*, *Documentos Y*, Vol. 15, p. 182.

113. Interview in *Garai*, 10 March 1977.
114. Angel Amigo, *Pertur, ETA 71-76* (San Sebastián, 1978), passim.
115. See leaflet *A los inmigrantes*, *Documentos Y*, Vol. 12, p. 429.
116. *Liberación nacional e internacionalismo* (undated), *Documentos Y*, Vol. 15, pp. 142–8.
117. See *Información*, No. 85 (Madrid, April 1972), *Documentos Y*, Vol. 15, pp. 69–75.
118. Amigo, *Pertur*, p. 30.
119. *Sugarra*, No. 1, 1975, passim.
120. See *Comentario a 'La lucha armada'* (undated), *Documentos Y*, Vol. 16, pp. 379–81.
121. Amigo, *Pertur*, p. 53.
122. See *A la clase trabajadora . . .*, *Documentos Y*, Vol. 15, pp. 161–2.
123. *Le Monde*, 22 Dec. 1973; Julen Aguirre (Eva Forest), *Operación Ogro* (Hendaye, 1974), passim.
124. *Mundo Obrero*, 29 Dec. 1973; *L' Humanité*, 21 Dec. 1973, quoted in *Zutik* (ETA-V), No. 64.
125. *Le Monde*, 23–24 Dec. 1973.
126. *Le Monde*, 26 Dec. 1973.
127. *Le Monde*, 22 and 25 Dec. 1973.
128. *Le Monde*, 30–31 Dec. 1973.
129. Santiago Carrillo, *L' Humanité*, 22 Dec. 1973.
130. See Julen Aguirre, *Operación Ogro*; also *Zutik*, No. 64; *Kemen*, No. 2, Jan. 1974.
131. *Le Monde*, 23–24 Dec. 1973.
132. *Zutik* (ETA-VI-LCR), No. 62, Jan. 1974.
133. *Zutik* (ETA-V), No. 64, 1 May 1974.

6
The Twilight of the Dictatorship, 1974–1977

Carrero Blanco's assassination showed that ETA-V's organisation was stronger than ever before. So too was its claim to ETA's heritage as its rival ETA-VI had, by merging with a 'Spanish' group, abandoned its claim to be the heir of ETA's nationalist tradition. ETA-V's leaders saw Carrero's assassination as an exemplary illustration of the importance of the armed struggle, just as the overthrow of the Allende government in Chile, in September 1973, was taken as exposing the foolishness of those in the opposition who believed that it was unnecessary.[1] Carrero's killing confirmed the dominance of the Military Front over the other, theoretically equal Fronts. The tensions created by this dominance were soon to lead to further splits, the first of which involved most of the members of the Workers' Front.

The leaders of the Workers' Front had been informed of the original plan to kidnap Carrero Blanco, but not of the decision to substitute assassination for kidnapping. The assassination and the consequent police repression, directed against the whole organisation, disturbed the fragile agreement reached during the first part of ETA-V's Sixth Assembly. At the meeting of the Biltzaar Ttippia (BT) held early in December, the Workers' Front representatives had been personally insulted by representatives of the Military Front and accused of 'Spanish' deviations, causing the Workers' Front leaders to demand an apology.[2] The assassination of Carrero Blanco, later in the month, accentuated an already existing climate of mistrust. A rupture was perhaps inevitable as ETA-V could not find a way to combine military actions with mass activity. Before the Assembly, the Military Front representatives had suggested that those attempting to organise mass activity should not publicly identify themselves as part of ETA-V;

149

thus they could avoid some of the repression which adherence to the organisation provoked. The proposal was not acceptable to the Workers' Front members as, in effect, it would have transformed them into a group of sympathisers, leaving the Military Front with a monopoly of the status which the name of ETA conferred. The proposal made sense for the Military Front, whose limited need for mass support need not be organised by people in the same organisation.

The suggestion that the Military Front should become the real ETA-V was also unacceptable to people in the Political Front, and to some members of the Military Front itself. Some ETA-V leaders, including Moreno Bergareche (Pertur), saw that there would be a need for a political organisation if ETA-V's military activities were not to benefit the PNV in the post-Franco period. In May 1974, following an angry meeting of ETA-V's Biltzaar Ttippia (BT), the Workers' Front broke away to form Langile Abertzale Iraultzaileen Alderdia (LAIA) (the Revolutionary Patriotic Workers' Party).[3] LAIA declared that it was impossible to transform ETA into the revolutionary party which the Basque workers needed. The Military Front's insistence on carrying out its activities divorced from mass participation, LAIA's members declared, had persuaded them to abandon ETA, although not to condemn armed struggle as such.[4] LAIA's criticism of ETA-V's practice was less thoroughgoing than that made previously by ETA-Berri and ETA-VI, nor did LAIA make any attempt to extend its sphere of operations outside Euskadi, or to unite with 'Spanish' groups. The new party, although oriented towards industrial struggle, had no clear attitude to trade unions. LAIA was divided between a Marxist tendency, led by Joken Apalategi, and a libertarian one influenced by Beltza's journal *Gathazka*, which advocated a system of worker' assemblies as an alternative to trade unions.[5]

The split, although mainly about organisation, did reflect differences about the likely development of Spanish political life after Franco's death. ETA-V's insistence that armed struggle was the only way to overthrow the dictatorship isolated it from the rest of the opposition. In the aftermath of Carrero Blanco's assassination, people feared that there would be an intensification of repression, which would take them back to a situation resembling the early years of Franco's rule.[6] Such fears were hardly allayed by Franco's choice of premier, Arias Navarro, a long-serving functionary who had a record of toughness in a number of positions dating from the Civil War. In the event, such fears proved over-pessimistic. Arias made a broadcast to the nation on 12 February 1974 where he promised reform and a move towards greater democracy. Arias' government did, on the whole, attempt a partial reform of the Francoist system, albeit hesitantly, and with a good deal of backsliding. The 'Spirit of 12 February', as it came to be called, was greeted by a combination of hope and scepticism by the illegal opposition.[7]

An indication that many of the regime's traditional supporters distrusted the intentions of the Arias government was provided by the violent activities of ultra-right groups, whose presence had been so evident in the pro-Franco demonstrations at the time of the Burgos trial. After the death of Carrero Blanco, these groups, popularly believed to be composed mainly of off-duty policemen, stepped up their violent attacks on members of the opposition. Their activities, combined with the brutal and panic-stricken behaviour of the police, which caused the death of a number of innocent civilians, helped to create a climate of insecurity which to many people seemed worse than the situation before Franco's rule had been seriously challenged.

Many people in the Basque country saw such developments as indicating a hardening of official repression. In fact, before the rise of mass opposition to the regime, the authorities exercised a monopoly of repression and had no need to resort to the help of the so-called *incontrolado* groups, which were illegal and, theoretically, clandestine, but whose members were never arrested or prosecuted. Their emergence showed the fear of the more reactionary supporters of the regime that they were being betrayed by a government which was prepared to consider the legalisation of trade unions and political parties.[8] The power which the right-wing continued to exercise within the government was demonstrated when, in March 1974, a Catalan anarchist, Puig Antich, was executed after being condemned by a military court for killing a policeman in 1973. The execution showed, in ETA-V's leaders' view, that the government was engaged in a war to the death against revolutionaries, and that the reformists who thought that it would allow the Francoist system to be peacefully dismantled were deceiving themselves.[9]

The PNV leaders took a different view and continued quietly to build up the Party's organisation and to take advantage of such freedom as existed to make its existence known to the public. At Easter 1974 Leizaola, the head of the exiled Basque government, attended the Aberri-Eguna celebrations, a visit which he repeated in 1975. The PNV's press claimed that Leizaola's visits were clandestine,[10] but ETA-V members were certain that the elderly Leizaola had been given permission to enter Spain. The PNV leaders' hopes for a peaceful dissolution of the Franco regime which would enable Basque freedom to be granted were encouraged by signs of liberalisation from sectors of the regime. For example, late in 1974, the 'family' representatives in the Cortes for the Basque provinces, who were elected on a limited franchise, announced that they would ask that Guipúzcoa and Vizcaya should be given back their privileges embodied in the *Conciertos Económicos*, which had been taken away in 1937 as a punishment for supporting the Republic.[11] ETA-V's leaders' attitude to such developments was to welcome them as partial victories, obtained by a combination of mass struggle and their own armed activity, so they were encouraged to step up their campaign. The organisation's leaders were aware that conditions had changed, and that the mass activity, which they had always recognised as necessary, was not actually taking place. However, unlike most of the opposition, ETA-V's leaders were not seeking to use mass struggle as a lever to force a compromise on the government. On the contrary, they saw the vacillating policy of the Arias government as a sign of the weakness of the regime which increased the scope for armed struggle, rather than as a reason for abandoning it. When several of their members were killed, wounded or captured in clashes with the police, ETA-V's leaders' own attitude hardened. A qualitative change came in April 1974, when ETA-V activists shot and killed a Civil Guard corporal, Gregorio Posadas, at Azpeitia in Guipúzcoa.[12]

The police killed by ETA-V members up until then had generally met their deaths as a result of clashes with ETA-V commandos, who were attempting to cross the border or to escape arrest. The major exceptions to this were the planned assassination of Melitón Manzanas in 1968, and later of Carrero Blanco. However, both had been special cases, as Manzanas was a notorious torturer, and Carrero, it was argued, had been the key man in the regime's attempt to make the transition to Francoism without Franco. Posada's killing was also presented as a special case, as it was alleged that not only was he distinguished for his brutality and fanaticism, but was responsible for collecting information on ETA-V. However, in a communiqué accepting responsibility for the shooting, ETA-V made it clear that the act was a reprisal for the killings of its activists and announced that, in the future, all sections of the security forces were considered legitimate targets.[13] Throughout 1974, ETA-V action groups carried out a campaign of robberies and bombings, which rivalled the one mounted in 1968/69 and had a similar effect on ETA-V's organisation, causing many arrests and flights into exile. ETA-V's leaders did not regard Carrero Blanco's killing as an isolated operation. In 1974 they planned to kidnap some leading people including Gómez Acebo, the cousin of Prince Juan Carlos, as well as Franco's daughter and her husband, The Marqués de Villaverde.[14] These plans were unsuccessful but ETA-V did succeed in carrying out a number of robberies and bombings, and in rescuing one of their prisoners, José Urzelay, from hospital in San Sebastián.[15] These exploits incurred a heavy cost. In August two leading ETA-V members, José Antonio Garmendia (Tupa) and José María Arruabarrena (Tanke), were gravely wounded and captured after a clash with the Civil Guard near San Sebastián.[16] Urzelay was killed in October when the police raided the house where he was hiding.[17] The capture of leading ETA members made it necessary for many people to flee into exile.

Some ETA-V leaders, particularly Pertur, were determined that the organisation should adopt a structure which would enable it to build a political base. In practice, as priority was given to the military struggle, carried out by the *liberados* in the Military Front, the 'legal' members working and living in the interior had to subordinate their efforts to assisting the *liberados* by providing information, shelter and other support. As the *liberados* moved on after carrying out their missions no permanent organisation could be built up.[18] Pertur, supported by Goiherri, Múgica Arregui and Garayalde (Erreka), proposed a form of organisation which, they hoped, would allow ETA-V to build a firm local organisation. They suggested that in a given region there should be a leader who would have responsibility for all work in the area. The division into Fronts should be maintained at the level of the local working groups, but political unity would ensure a unified direction.[19] The proposals, which were given a trial in a few zones, were a serious attempt to put some flesh on the Front structure, but they inevitably aroused opposition from the *liberados* in the Military Front as they would end their virtual independence and would, by blurring the distinction between Fronts, endanger security.

ETA-V's leaders were once more faced with the perennial

problem of the conflict between the needs of a highly secretive armed vanguard and those of an organisation trying to encourage mass activity. Pertur and his co-thinkers could see that powerful forces within the Spanish ruling class were eager to dismantle the structures and institutions of the Franco regime. The possibility of achieving this was uncertain in Spain as a whole. In Euskadi, the signs were even more contradictory, as increased levels of struggle produced increased repression, arrests, States of Emergency, and more brutality by police and *incontrolados*. While mass struggle extorted concessions from the regime, ETA-V's leaders thought there was a real danger that, in the absence of a revolutionary leadership, the main beneficiary of that struggle would be the PNV.[20] ETA-V's leaders shared the interest of the rest of the Spanish opposition in the coup which in April 1974 overthrew the Portuguese dictatorship, and ushered in a process which was to lead to the abandonment of the Portuguese empire, to substantial nationalisations, and eventually to the creation of parliamentary democracy. Inevitably, some right-wingers saw the coup as a reason to intensify the repression, but a more general reaction was to consider the Portuguese events as further proof that the Francoist system had outlived its time. Liberal elements in business and the administration intensified their links with the moderate elements in the opposition, in an attempt to prepare a transition to parliamentary democracy which would be more controlled than the events in Portugal.

Arias Navarro's policy of instituting reforms while maintaining the basic structure of the regime was frustrated in February by an incident involving Mgr. Anoveros, the Bishop of Bilbao, who had ordered the clergy in his diocese to read a sermon protesting about the persecution of the Basque language and culture. Anoveros' well-timed initiative was a clear challenge to the authorities, much more so than had been the Basque bishops' plea for clemency for the Burgos prisoners in 1970. The government confined the bishop to house arrest and attempted to make him leave Spain.[21] Such a conflict between Church and State was a clear indication that a sector of the Church thought that there was no long-term future for the Franco regime, and was anxious to take its distance from it.

Those who still hoped that the Arias government would be able to oversee a transition to a more democratic system were disappointed when, in October 1974, Arias dismissed Pío Cabanillas, the Minister of Information and Tourism, one of the most liberal members of the Cabinet, prompting the Minister of the Economy, Barrera de Irimo, to resign in sympathy with his colleague.[22] One reason for false optimism on the likelihood of substantial reform was that Franco was thought to be dying, and had provisionally delegated his powers to Prince Juan Carlos, when he entered hospital in July 1974. However, this surrender of his powers was temporary, as he recovered and resumed his exercise of full powers in September. Foreseeing that the dictator's death could not be delayed for long, most of the opposition forces were building their organisations in preparation for the transition to the more democratic system which, they hoped, would follow.

The departure of ETA-V's Workers' Front did not end the quarrels between those who wanted ETA-V to follow a purely military policy and those such as Pertur who wanted ETA-V to take the lead in initiating mass activities. The disagreements within the leadership were brought to a head following the explosion of a bomb in the Calle del Correo in Madrid on 13 September, which killed a number of both police and civilians. The bomb had been placed in the Café Rolando near police headquarters, a popular rendezvous for police and ultra-right elements. A month later, an ETA-V communiqué denied planting the bomb,[23] and there was speculation that it might be the work of the Frente Revolucionario Antifascista y Patriótico (FRAP) (the front of a formerly Maoist, pro-Albanian group), or of the ultra-right. The police accused several ETA-V members, together with a number of Madrid leftists, such as Eva Forest, some of whom had been associated with the PCE, of being responsible.[24] The affair was never clarified, as an amnesty declared in 1977 ensured that those accused of carrying out the bombing were not brought to trial. However, Lidia Falcón, one of those arrested, stated that ETA-V, with the assistance of non-Basques including Eva Forest, had carried out the bombing.[25]

ETA-V split into two separate organisations almost immediately afterwards. Although the bombing was not one of the reasons given by either faction for the split, it determined its timing.[26] The divergences within ETA-V had been very sharp since Txikia's death in Spring 1973, and only a series of compromises between the Fronts had prevented the organisation dividing at the first part of ETA-V's Sixth Assembly in August 1973. When the split occurred it was caused by a familiar problem — the inability of the organisation to exert collective control over the Military Front. In September the Executive Committee of the

Military Front had informed the rest of ETA-V's leadership that it was having its annual meeting to decide on strategy. When the rest of the leadership went to the meeting with the intention of arguing for ETA-V's official position, that military actions should be determined by political decisions, the leaders of the Military Front refused to admit those who were members of other Fronts.[27] At a meeting of the Biltzaar Ttippia (BT) held in October the organisation split when the Military Front leaders refused to be bound by majority decisions.[28] They justified their departure by arguing that the attempt to combine mass work and armed struggle within the same organisation should be abandoned.[29]

The Military Front (henceforth ETA-Militar, or ETA-M) declared that in the future it would confine itself to the practice of armed struggle. This, its leaders insisted, did not imply that mass activity was unnecessary, merely that it should be carried out by bodies which were organisationally separate from those involved in the military struggle.[30] ETA-M at the time of the split consisted of about thirty people, mainly *liberados* living in the French Basque country. Their leading figure, Argala, had been one of the main people responsible for Carrero Blanco's assassination. Others, such as Pérez Revilla and Imanol Pagoaga, a former member of *Las Cabras*, were veterans compared to the leaders of the faction which opposed them. ETA-M, initially, did not try to expand its numbers and refused to recruit very young people.[31] Its split was a declaration that it was confining itself to the specialist role of armed struggle. While it called on the working class and patriotic forces to form a common front to fight for national liberation, ETA-M itself made no attempt to carry out mass work, either in the labour movement or in the cultural sphere. It produced very little written material, and in practice based itself in the French Basque country, entering Spain to carry out its activities and returning to France when its missions were accomplished. This strategy was similar to that employed by Etxabe when he was leader of ETA's Military Front in 1970, but ETA-M's military capacity was far greater than had been available to Etxabe.

The main branch of ETA after the split of the Military Front adopted the name ETA-Político-Militar (PM). The name described the formula with which ETA-PM attempted to solve the organisational crisis which ETA-PM had described. ETA-PM's leaders accepted that combining mass work and armed struggle presented problems for the people engaged in both types of activity. However, they had also experienced disasters such as the Calle de Correo bombing, which had followed the failure to control a Military Front whose leaders insisted on their own autonomy. Some of those who became the leadership of ETA-PM had argued, inside the united organisation, for a division at the base according to functions, combined with a leadership at local level which would supervise all the different activities. Thus, it was hoped, the risks arising from the mixing of activists belonging to different Fronts would be avoided, as would the danger of the Fronts becoming autonomous bodies, pursuing different policies from each other, as had happened before the split.[32] The lack of clearly expressed political differences between ETA-M and ETA-PM contrasted sharply with the splits which had produced ETA-Berri and ETA-VI. The suddenness of the emergency produced by the Calle del Correo bombing, the low political level of ETA-M's criticisms, and the clearly nationalist ideology of both organisations which issued from the split made it seem that the differences between them were merely concerned with ETA-V's own structure. Yet political differences did exist, even if they were not adequately explained by either ETA-M or ETA-PM. These differences arose from ETA's social composition and origin and were to be exacerbated by political developments after Franco's death.

ETA-V, like the original ETA, was part of a larger radical middle-class revolt against the PNV's moderation and inactivity. Radical middle-class nationalists were quite prepared to accept ETA-V as allies, in spite of the group's declarations of commitment to Marxism-Leninism. Radical nationalists such as Txillardegi continued to see ETA-V and its successors as valid partners for a Basque National Front. On the other hand, ETA-PM leaders, such as Pertur, who were serious about their commitment to socialist revolution, to internationalism, and to their own peculiar version of Marxism-Leninism[33] identified with the working class, irrespective of its ethnic origin.

ETA-PM's claim to be a working-class organisation, while sociologically unfounded, made it suspicious of nationalist groups which, in spite of having socialist titles, had no presence in the labour movement. ETA-PM's frequent statements of support for the working class compelled it to have a fairly respectful attitude to the 'Spanish' Marxists who had some strength in the factories. ETA-PM's leaders continued to advocate their own version of the

Pueblo Trabajador Vasco (PTV) alliance, which was to include both immigrant workers and radical nationalists. The alliance was, by its nature, difficult to build. In contrast, the nature of ETA-M's activity enabled it to ignore the actual problem of work in the labour movement. Its need to draw support from a nationalist milieu made it turn to people, who, whatever their political differences, belonged to the same nationalist community.

ETA-PM's leaders continued, in spite of their political concerns and the loss of most of the Military Front *liberados*, to insist on the need for armed struggle. After the departure of the Military Front, ETA-PM held the second part of its Sixth Assembly in January 1975, where it abandoned the structure based on Fronts into which ETA had, in theory, been organised since the Fifth Assembly in 1967, and adopted the Political-Military form of organisation.[34] ETA-PM retained the allegiance of the great majority of ETA-V's membership. However, as the split resulted in the defection of a number of military cadres, it had to promote very inexperienced young members such as Miguel Angel Apalategui (Apala) and Juan Paredes Manot (Txiki) to the status of *liberados*. ETA-PM's leaders were aware that some version of bourgeois democracy would probably be installed after Franco's death, and that unless mass socialist organisations were built, the beneficiaries of liberalisation would be the PNV and other right-wing tendencies.[35] Consequently, ETA-PM's leaders formed an alliance with some recently formed small nationalist groups, in spite of its doubts about their socialist credentials. In addition ETA-PM, as a declared Marxist organisation, saw the need for alliances with 'Spanish' left groups such as the MCE, and the ORT which was strong in Navarre. ETA-M also wished to create a common front of left Nationalists, so there was a basis for partial agreement on that issue, but not on the desirability of alliances with 'Spanish' forces.

A wide spectrum of nationalist opinion despised the PNV's passivity and suspected that it would be prepared to abandon the struggle for independence if a democratic Spanish government offered a measure of autonomy. Some of these radical nationalists were members of ELA-Berri which, although nominally a trade union, was actually a political club. Others, some of them former ETA members, supported Txillardegi's journal *Branka*. In addition, a number of managers employed in the Mondragon co-operatives wished to create a more modern party than the PNV. In 1976, following a complicated series of realignments, the till then fragmented radical nationalists formed a political party, Euskadi Sozialista Biltzarrea (Basque Socialist Convergence), henceforth ESB.[36] ESB's influence was reflected in the journal *Garai*, which was published legally in 1976 and 1977. ESB combined a moderate social and economic programme with a virulent hatred of the PSOE and an ambiguous attitude to the immigrants. The party's leaders, who included Txillardegi, hoped that a wide-ranging autonomy could be achieved through a pact with the Crown, which would grant a modern version of the *Fueros*. The seemingly archaic nature of such a strategy was the product of ESB's desire to avoid making alliances with 'Spanish' parties.[37]

The fact that ESB was supported by former ETA leaders such as Txillardegi and Etxabe showed that it was an expression of the radical nationalism which had led to ETA's formation. ETA-PM's leaders' intention to unite the national and the social struggle required alliances with the social forces which ESB represented as well as with groups such as the MCE. However, such an alliance would have been anathema to ESB which had been formed specifically to combat the 'Spanish' left. ESB's leaders saw their party as an expression of one section of the nationalist spectrum. The PNV as well as both branches of ETA represented, they considered, equally valid components of the nationalist community. ESB's leaders saw themselves as complementary to, rather than being in competition with, the PNV.[38]

Although ETA-PM's failure to create the political alliance it wanted was to be a long-term difficulty, its most immediate problem was to strengthen its ability to carry out armed struggle which had been gravely weakened by the defection of ETA-M. ETA-PM created an action group, the *Bereziak*, for particularly difficult operations. The formation of this group would seem to have conceded ETA-M's point that military activities should not be carried out by people who were also undertaking mass work. However, the *Bereziak* were not intended to undertake all of ETA-PM's military tasks, most of which were to be carried out by 'legal' activists living in Spain.[39] It was hoped that the arrangement would avoid the danger of a military tendency developing activities outside ETA-PM's control.[40] The secession of ETA-M did not prevent ETA-PM from developing its military offensive. In March 1975 the *Bereziak* killed a police officer in San Sebastián,[41] and began the now traditional armed campaign in preparation for the Aberri Eguna celebrations at Easter. The increased tempo of ETA-PM's actions produced the familiar result of the capture and death of a number of its activists. In April Goiherri was captured after being wounded in an encounter with the police, in which a companion was killed.[42] The increase in violent activities caused the government to arrest hundreds of people, to impose a State of Emergency in Guipúzcoa and Vizcaya, the sixth since 1967, and to pass a decree-law giving the police further powers throughout Spain.[43]

In the summer of 1975 ETA-PM reacted to the increased repression in the Basque country by sending detachments of the *Bereziak* to Catalonia, Galicia and Madrid, where they planned to carry out a number of operations, including the organising of an escape from the prison of Segovia.[44] The campaign was a disaster, as leading members of ETA-PM were arrested in Madrid, Barcelona and Galicia, where members of a Galician nationalist organisation with which ETA-PM *liberados* were trying to carry out joint military activities were also seized.[45] In late July the authorities ended the State of Emergency in Guipúzcoa and Vizcaya, a good indication that they believed that both branches of ETA were greatly weakened.[46] In spite of these heavy losses, ETA-PM continued to try to mount a campaign in Barcelona and Madrid. The attempts led to yet more captures and deaths, which included leading members of the organisation, such as Múgica Arregui, so that by late 1975 ETA-PM's capacity to carry out armed activities was greatly reduced.[47]

ETA-M, at the start of its independent existence, had no organisation comparable to its rival, as it consisted mainly of a small number of *liberados* based in the French Basque country. Few of its members had much political understanding or experience, although they were on average older than those in ETA-PM. ETA-M's dominant figure, José Miguel Beñarán (Argala), who had participated in the assassination of Carrero Blanco, was one of the few who had been in the organisation in the 1960s, before the Sixth Assembly.[48] Under his leadership ETA-M's first steps consisted in killing members of the Civil Guard in both Guipúzcoa and Vizcaya.[49] This was followed up by the shooting of a number of alleged police informers, including, in November, the Mayor of Oyarzun in Guipúzcoa.[50] ETA-M's campaign was less ambitious than ETA-PM's, as it did not operate outside the Basque country and selected easier targets. Although ETA-M suffered casualties as a result of its campaign, these amounted to much less than those borne by ETA-PM. Shortly after the killing of the Mayor of Oyarzun, ETA-M ordered all mayors in the Basque country to resign, stating that otherwise they, too, would be killed.[51] Such actions did not need the elaborate structure of organised militants inside Spain required by the strategy favoured by ETA-PM's leaders, as ETA-M's main requirement from sympathisers was information about the existence and movements of enemies of the Basque people. Such a method of operation sometimes produced mistakes and obliged the organisation to apologise for killing an innocent man.[52]

Most people in the Basque country saw the violence of both branches of ETA as much less of a threat than the behaviour of the security forces, who in 1974–75 killed 22 people during demonstrations or at police checkpoints in the four Basque provinces. In 1974 alone, 105 people were injured by police bullets.[53] The victims were sometimes sympathisers of one of the branches of ETA, but more often they were people unfortunate enough to be in the vicinity of trigger-happy policemen. For example, in July 1975 in Ondarroa, a young man on his way home from a party with a group of friends who were singing Basque songs was called into the local police station. The next day his parents were informed of his death, which the police alleged had been accidental.[54] In May 1975 in Bilbao, the police tortured and killed a priest suspected of being a ETA sympathiser. Such incidents provoked demonstrations and renewed brutality by the police when dispersing them. They also inspired a steady flow of recruits to both branches of ETA.

Although ETA-M developed no political activity, it did begin to adopt political attitudes, first of all through a criticism of ETA-PM, made nearly a year after the split which had produced the rival organisation. The criticism was very mild compared to that which had followed previous splits in ETA, and it admitted that the differences in ideology and objectives had been quite insufficient to justify the division which had occurred in ETA-V, and that the pressures of working in clandestinity had produced intransigent attitudes on their part as well as in ETA-PM. In essence, ETA-M's criticism of its rival was that ETA-PM had embarked on a bigger military campaign than it could sustain, and that the Political-Military structure which it had adopted was unsuited to a group engaged in armed struggle.[55] In view of the greater losses suffered by ETA-PM during 1974 and 1975, the criticism would seem justified in military terms. However, most of ETA-PM's leadership drew different conclusions, which led them to examine their organisation's weakness in other spheres, besides the military one.

The loss of so many experienced militants left Pertur in summer 1975 as the leading strategist in ETA-PM and strengthened his determination to broaden the scope of the group's activity, in preparation for the new situation which would follow the death of Franco, when ETA-PM would need to have political and trade union organisations. Pertur, in spite of his political and intellectual dominance, was not typical of ETA-PM's membership as he was from a cultured, non-Basque-speaking family in San Sebastián. His activity in ETA-V and ETA-PM had consisted of organisational, literary and educational tasks, and he had taken no direct part in violent action. Pertur's determination that ETA-PM should have a political as well as a military presence made him begin work on a plan to create a political party. The conclusion of his thinking was the document *Otsagabia* which was produced in 1976 and was eventually to lead to a split in ETA-PM's ranks.[56]

The weakness of the Workers' Front — compared not only to the PCE, but even to the MCE, ORT or ETA-VI — had led ETA-V in 1974 to consider how to organise workers who sympathised with the aim of Basque independence but were not prepared to join the Workers' Front and thereby expose themselves to the full weight of repression which was directed against all ETA members. ETA-V decided that it needed a nationalist equivalent of the Workers' Commissions, a mass organisation not formally linked to a political organisation.[57] The departure of most of the Workers' Front to form the political party LAIA had weakened ETA-V's tiny industrial base, while at the same time it showed the necessity of collaborating with LAIA and similar organisations in the building of a nationalist trade union. LAIA, in 1974, tried to construct a nationalist version of the Workers' Commissions, the Comisiones Obreras Abertzales (COA), which would be committed to national liberation as well as class struggle.[58]

In 1975 ETA-PM and LAIA formed Langile Abertzaleon Batzaedeak (Patriotic Workers' Committee) (LAB). LAIA wanted the organisation to be committed to independence for Euskadi, but ETA-PM preferred the weaker formula of a commitment to national liberation in order to attract a wider layer of support.[59] LAB provided radical nationalism with the embryo of a trade union which was, apart from being small, internally divided from the beginning. An anarchistic faction of LAIA wanted LAB to be a kind of Soviet, but most of LAIA's members agreed with Pertur that it would probably become a militant trade union.[60]

The weakness of the left nationalism in the trade union sphere was also apparent in the political arena. As the moderate opposition waited for the liberation which it believed would follow Franco's death, it began to prepare alliances with those elements in the regime which wanted a parliamentary system. The PCE took the initiative by forming such an alliance, the Junta Democrática, in July 1974.[61] The best known non-communist member of the Junta was Calvo Serer, a monarchist and former editor of the newspaper *Madrid*, who had been linked to Opus Dei. Achieving unity within the opposition was more difficult than making agreements with those who had formerly been part of Franco's regime. The recently revived PSOE[62] responded to the creation of the Junta Democrática by forming an alliance, the Plataforma de Convergencia Democrática, with Liberal, Christian and other forces in the spring of 1975. The Junta programme called for the recognition of the 'political personality' of the Basque country, but also called for the unity of the Spanish state, a more centralist position than that previously held by the PCE.[63] The Plataforma was slightly more in favour of the right to independence.

Both organisations were to win support from a wide area of the political spectrum, ranging from conservatives to Maoists, but neither enjoyed wide support in the Basque country. The PNV was prepared to welcome such initiatives at the level of the Spanish state, but insisted on the legitimacy of the Basque government in exile and on its role as a political mediator. Radical nationalists were even less prepared to support bodies which did not concede the right of Euskadi to choose independence. Nevertheless, the formation of both alliances highlighted the fact that radical nationalism had no equivalent of its own. This vacuum was filled in the summer of 1975 with the creation of the Koordinadora Abertzale Socialista (Patriotic Socialist Co-ordination), henceforth KAS, an organisation which was to outlast its 'Spanish' rivals by many years.[64] The components of KAS were ETA-PM, LAIA and a few tiny left nationalist political parties. KAS's original purpose was to campaign against the death sentences which were likely to be imposed on three ETA-PM members. ETA-M, consistent with its avoidance of mass activity, did not formally join KAS, but did support it. The different left nationalist groups were unable to agree on what the functions of KAS should be. It was variously seen as a potential mass organisation, a consultative committee of all left nationalist groups, or an alliance which would determine the strategy of the Basque revolution.[65]

Forming alliances was extremely difficult because, while most nationalists would not agree to be part of any organisation which included 'Spanish' parties, the 'Spanish' left was tempted either to join the Junta or the Convergencia, or was reluctant to ally with non-Marxist parties. The leaders of both ETA-PM and LAIA wanted an alliance with both the Spanish left and with radical nationalists, which would attract people away from the PCE and the PSOE on the one hand, and the PNV, ELA and similar tendencies on the other.[66] KAS remained too narrowly based to constitute a viable alliance, but any attempt to reach out to make agreements with either the 'Spanish' left or the nationalist right was bound to tear it apart. Yet alliances were necessary if the left nationalist forces were to play any part in negotiating a transition to democracy. Coalitions would also be an essential part of any future participation in elections.

The need to form a left nationalist bloc was accentuated when, in December 1975, the PCE formed a local equivalent of the Junta, the Asamblea Democrática de Euskadi (ADE), which called on the Basque government in exile to transform itself into a representative institution. Such a call was unwelcome to the PNV, which saw the Asamblea as an attempt to undermine the authority of the government in exile.[67] The modest success of the Asamblea created problems for the ORT and MCE, the main Maoist groups in the Basque country. Both had supported the PSOE's Plataforma as a rival to the PCE's Junta. The MCE, in an attempt to create a counterweight to the PCE, had initiated the formation of Euskadiko Herrikea Batzarra (the Basque People's Assembly), which was also supported by the ORT and ETA-PM. The Asamblea did not include representatives from Navarre and was, for that reason alone, unacceptable to most nationalists.[68] The PCE leadership knew that to accept Basque nationalism's claim to Navarre would antagonise forces which it was trying to ally with elsewhere in Spain. Nevertheless, Navarre's omission from the Asamblea constituted a weakness which was seized on by its rivals on both left and right. ETA-PM's leaders tried to compete with the PCE by proposing an alliance which would include both the forces within KAS and within the Spanish left. Such an alliance was unacceptable to ETA-M's leadership who wanted KAS to develop into a Front of all the *Abertzales* (left nationalists). If the project for creating a Basque left alliance including 'Spanish' groups had succeeded, ETA-M would have been isolated.

ETA-PM needed allies for specific and immediate purposes, as well as in the future when Juan Carlos was to replace Franco. From the summer of 1975, ETA-PM concentrated its efforts on a campaign to save the lives of three of its members, who were to be brought to trial on charges likely to result in death sentences.[69] Two of them, Garmendia and Otaegui, were accused, among other offences, of being involved in the killing of the Civil Guard, Posadas, whose death had marked ETA-V's leaders' decision to attack policemen generally, rather than on the grounds of individual conduct. Otaegui was, in fact, condemned to death, but Garmendia's sentence was commuted to life imprisonment on the grounds that a head wound, inflicted when he was arrested, impaired his mental capacity. In a separate trial, another ETA-PM militant, Juan Paredes Manot (Txiki), was sentenced to death for the murder of a policeman in the course of a bank robbery.[70] Txiki and Otaegui, together with three members of FRAP convicted of killing two policemen earlier that year, were executed on 27 September.

Txiki, who, apart from Otaegui, was the only one of ETA's members to be legally executed, became one of ETA's most significant martyrs.[71] His family had come from Extremadura to seek work in Guipúzcoa when he was nine years old. The fact that someone from such a background should sacrifice his life for Euskadi showed, in ETA-PM's view, that immigrants could be integrated not only into Basque life, but also into the struggle for national liberation. Txiki's life and death were, in ETA-PM's opinion, a disproof of allegations that Basque nationalism was inherently reactionary, as well as being a reproach to those chauvinistic elements which did exist in Basque society.[72] However, even the most chauvinistic nationalists were prepared to accept ETA's martyrs as posthumous Basques.

The campaign to save Txiki and Otaegui was widely supported in the Basque country, particularly in Guipúzcoa.[73] Elsewhere in Spain the demonstrations did not approach the level of those organised during the Burgos trial in 1970. Nationalists felt that the PCE had betrayed the prisoners by refusing to support a general strike throughout Euskadi. This accusation could not be levelled at the groups to the left of the PCE, particularly the MCE, which was influential in mobilising considerable support for the general strike held on 29 and 30 September in protest against the executions. ETA-PM's own efforts were much weaker as, like other nationalist organisations, it did not have the MCE's industrial strength, which in parts of Guipúzcoa rivalled that of the PCE. Franco himself died on 20 November, less than two months after the executions of the members of ETA and FRAP. King Juan Carlos, on assuming power, granted a partial amnesty. This gesture was welcomed, but the general impression among the opposition was that the king would remain a prisoner of the system.

An ETA-PM statement declared that, whatever his personal intentions, Juan Carlos was a puppet in the hands of the extreme right and a prisoner of the Francoist institutions, a view which was shared by the PCE.[74] However, Franco's death awakened hopes of change, and produced a movement for total amnesty involving hundreds of thousands of people. In the Basque country, where the proportion of political prisoners was higher than in other regions, the campaign was particularly strong, and many people were arrested for taking part in amnesty demonstrations. Political refugees were also affected by the amnesty provisions. In March 1976, 848 refugees, 839 of whom were Basques, were told that they could return to Spain without having to face charges;[75] many chose not to do so, fearing that they would suffer police persecution. In July 1976 there was a second amnesty which, eventually, freed most of Spain's political prisoners who had been sentenced for peaceful activities, while many of ETA's members, who had been sentenced for actions connected with violence, remained in prison. Consequently, by early 1977, the amnesty campaign became centred more and more on the Basque country, where it reached unprecedented heights of mass mobilisation.

ETA members would, on being released, be met with huge demonstrations of welcome, and would themselves join in the campaign to free those of their comrades who remained in prison.[76] The release of the great majority of the prisoners, far from damping down the campaign, intensified it as people felt that a complete amnesty could be won. In March 1977 there was an amnesty week when large-scale strikes and demonstrations were held.[77] The government was forced to recognise that the campaign would continue as long as any ETA members remained

in prison. Yet it was not easy for the government to persuade the
military to accept the release of people who had carried out spectacular acts of violence. In March 1977 a third amnesty freed
everyone except for those convicted of, or awaiting trial for,
crimes involving bloodshed. Both branches of ETA suspected that
both the Basque government in exile and the PCE-led Asambleas
Democráticas would, in order to reach an agreement with the
government, be prepared to settle for less than a complete amnesty
and the legalisation of all political parties.

ETA-PM's distrust of both of these forces led it to propose the
formation of a United Front of left nationalists and 'Spanish'
revolutionary forces, Herrihko Batasuna (Popular Unity). This
platform demanded the release of all prisoners, the return of all
exiles, complete political and trade union freedom, the dissolution
of the existing police forces, and the punishment of policemen and
others guilty of crimes against the people. ETA-PM refused to
subordinate itself to any of the platforms which, at an all-Spanish
level, were trying to create a common front. Instead, the organisation called for the setting up of a network of patriotic committees,
open to all who supported its programme. These would come
together to form a common organisation which would be
supported by the entire Basque left.[78] This position was quite
unacceptable to ETA-M, which by spring 1976 had become
concerned at ETA-PM's efforts to develop a united Front between
Abertzale and 'Spanish' organisations. ETA-M maintained that,
while it was possible to have co-operation with 'Spanish' forces on
specific issues, any agreement on strategy ran the risk that
nationalists would lose their independence. It was desirable,
argued ETA-M, that the *Abertzale* forces create alliances among
themselves which could then make specific agreements with the
'Spanish' forces.[79] This apparently minor difference in strategy
was to lead, eventually, to a growing division between the rival
branches of ETA. As ETA-PM wished to develop a left-wing
alliance as a counterweight to the PNV, it could hardly ignore the
only left-wing forces which were prepared to co-operate with it.
ETA-M, for its part, was aware of the weakness of the *Abertzale*
forces in the workers' movement, and feared that any close co-
operation with 'Spanish' forces would weaken the nationalist
alliance.[80]

ETA-PM's leaders recognised that, at the beginning of 1976,
their organisation was very weak. The arrest of a number of its
leading members, the executions of Txiki and Otaegui and the

failure to organise a mass escape from Segovia prison, were severe blows for an organisation which had not recovered from the loss of both its Workers' and Military Fronts in 1974. Nevertheless, ETA-PM's leaders were determined to continue the armed struggle. One of the main activities which they were to pursue was kidnapping for ransom, while ETA-M put more emphasis on attacking the security forces. In January 1976, in separate incidents, ETA-PM action groups kidnapped two industrialists. One of the kidnapped men became violently ill and was immediately released. The other victim, Señor Arrasate, was the son of a prosperous industrialist in Berriz, Vizcaya, who had no political connection and was not involved in any industrial dispute.[81] These circumstances produced speculation that the incident might have been a case of mistaken identity. ETA-PM did not immediately, contrary to its usual practice, accept responsibility for the act, as the *Bereziak* had carried it out without informing ETA-PM's leadership beforehand.[82] Once more, the problem of keeping military activists under control, which had bedevilled ETA from its early years, re-emerged. The incident did not produce an immediate crisis in ETA-PM, as four days after Arrasate was seized, the ransom was paid and he was freed.[83]

The kidnapping of Arrasate, unlike that of Zabala and Huarte, was a straightforward case of economic ransom. ETA-PM was concerned by the criticisms of ETA-M and other left nationalist organisations that the Arrasate family were not part of the 'oligarchy'.[87] However, ETA-PM showed it was unrepentant by kidnapping another industrialist, Angel Berazadi, in March. When, in early April, the ransom offered by Berazadi's family was judged insufficient, he was killed.[85] Although the number of killings by both branches of ETA had risen steadily, Berazadi's execution was a new departure. Up until then the victims of either branch of ETA had been policemen, suspected informers, or known right-wingers, or had been killed by accident. Berazadi did not fall into any of these categories, so it was hardly surprising that his killing precipitated a sharp crisis in ETA-PM. The victim seemed a very inappropriate target, as he was of impeccably Basque background, and a sympathiser of the PNV. The action was sharply condemned by that party as well as by the Basque government in exile, which expressed its disapproval by cancelling the annual *Aberri Eguna* demonstration.[86]

ETA-PM, stung by the PNV's claim that Berazadi was a patriot, claimed that he had not taught *Euskera* to his children, and had only given 5,000 pesetas to the Zarauz *Ikastola*. ETA-PM's leaders did accept that the decision to execute Berazadi had been a mistake, and blamed the interference of the Basque right wing (Presumably the PNV) for encouraging Berazadi's family to take an unco-operative attitude.[87] From a PNV standpoint, describing Berazadi as an 'oligarch' was absurd, while the failings imputed to him in ETA-PM's publications were grotesquely trivial as reasons for killing him. The killing accentuated an already tense situation within ETA-PM, as the leadership had been divided over whether to proceed with it. After the decision had been carried out, Pertur, the organisation's main theoretician, resigned from the leadership, but was persuaded to return.[88] Berazadi's killing indicated that the *Bereziak* had lost touch with nationalist opinion. Significantly, the much more theoretically primitive ETA-M never made the mistake of killing or kidnapping people whom the nationalist population saw as members of their own community.

The tensions within ETA-PM produced a state of internal violence, greater than that experienced in previous disagreements. In April, Pertur was kidnapped by members of the *Bereziak*, who alleged that he was endangering security by communicating with ETA-PM's imprisoned members.[89] When the rest of ETA-PM's leadership heard of the kidnapping, they ordered that he be released. In July 1976 Pertur disappeared,[90] and his presumed death was never satisfactorily explained. It was originally held to be the work of the Spanish police, or the *incontrolados*, but suspicion was also cast on the *Bereziak* because of their refusal to co-operate with his family by testifying to what happened.[91] The family's suspicions that Pertur had been murdered by his own comrades were not taken up at that time by ETA-PM, but in the future the affair was to be a source of friction between rival groups claiming ETA's tradition.[92]

The last people to acknowledge seeing Pertur were two members of the *Bereziak*, one of whom was Apala. Opponents of ETA-M, which Apala later joined, were to accuse him of being Pertur's killer, on the grounds that the *Bereziak* had kidnapped Pertur in April. Shortly before his death Pertur had written a letter alleging that the *Bereziak* had created 'a police state where everyone suspected his comrades' among ETA-PM's refugees in France. Apala's defenders replied that the allegations that he was the killer were first made in the right-wing press and only later taken up by Pertur's family and the ETA-PM. The differences between the two tendencies were basically the same as those which had split ETA so often in the past, concerning as they did the relationship between the armed struggle and mass activity. Although Pertur's thesis, *Otsagabia*, was to lead to the creation of a political party and to an alliance with 'Spanish' forces, he did not go nearly as far as either ETA-Berri or ETA-VI in substituting political for military action. Pertur and Apala represented the two opposed tendencies in ETA-PM in their background as well as their ideas. Pertur was an educated man from an urban, culturally Spanish background, whereas Apala was an accomplished military activist from the Basque-speaking area of Goiherri in Guipúzcoa, one of the areas which gave ETA most support throughout its history.[93] Apala was 21 years old in 1976, about the same age as most of the *Bereziak*, so he had not been an influential figure at the time of the split in ETA-V in 1974.

Pertur's disappearance deprived ETA-PM of its most competent political leader. In the months before he vanished, he had been working with his close associate Javier Garayalde (Erreka) on the project of founding a political party which would be able to take advantage of increased liberties in ways in which an armed organisation could not. *Otsagabia*, his key document, adopted by ETA-PM at its Seventh Assembly in September 1976, declared that the organisation should create a political party to fight for the same ends as itself.[94] A number of ETA-PM members would work to build the new party, which was not to be merely a Front for ETA-PM, but an autonomously functioning body. Agreement between the two bodies was to be ensured by the high level of political education which was to be required of the leaders of both. *Otsagabia* was the latest of the many attempts throughout ETA's history to resolve the thorny problem of how to combine mass activity with armed struggle.

Formally, ETA-PM's solution to the problem agreed with those adopted by both LAIA and ETA-M, in separating political and military struggles. ETA-M, while confining itself to military activity, strongly approved of the creation of a political party to fight for ETA's programme. As ETA-PM wanted the party which was to be created to recruit people who had no previous connection with itself, it seemed that although ETA-M had more populist and less Marxist politics, the new party might be supported by both branches of ETA. However, ETA-PM's decision was not universally welcomed. The formation of a party, Euskadi Iraultzaraka Alderdia (henceforth EIA), the Party for the Basque Revolution, backed by ETA-PM and potentially by ETA-M, created a problem for LAIA, as the two parties would have the same ideology, and would be in direct competition. From LAIA's leaders' point of view, the correct procedure for ETA-PM to adopt would have been to consult all the left nationalist forces, instead of unilaterally deciding to form the party itself.[95] As EIA was to be based on Marxist-Leninist principles rather than the socialist-populist ones, which had been proposed in an alternative document by Tomás Goikoetxea,[96] LAIA would in the future find it difficult to justify its own separate existence. ETA-PM's leaders' decision was also a blow for the small groups of independents who had been trying for several years to create a left nationalist party, which both branches of ETA might support. The leaders of both ETA-M and ETA-PM had expressed goodwill towards such efforts, although neither had given them any real backing.[97] ETA-PM's leaders' decision forced independents such as Natxo Arregi to look towards ETA-M; the independents had no power base of their own, as they were people linked to Basque cultural life rather than being political activists.

The *Bereziak*, who were developing the same militaristic, apolitical tendencies which had led the Military Front to split in 1974, had an ambivalent attitude to the decision to form a political party. On the one hand, if the political part of ETA-PM's work was devolved to such a party, and those most involved in political work left the armed organisation, the *Bereziak* hoped to inherit the leadership of ETA-PM. On the other hand, the proposed party was the brain-child of Pertur, their main opponent inside ETA-PM, and its formation might, eventually, lead ETA-PM to abandon armed struggle. Pertur's document had argued that, although ETA's theory of action/repression/action had been partially valid, the repression had crippled the vanguard whose task it was to seize power and establish an independent socialist *Euskadi*. It was essential that this vanguard should make full use of the opportunities provided by bourgeois democracy without falling into the error committed by the Italian Communist party of accepting the rules of the game established by that system.[98] The revolutionary party which Pertur had wished to establish would participate in the institutions established by bourgeois democracy, but would place more importance on the building of autonomous, popular mass organisations. It would seek to build a patriotic united Front of all those committed to national liberation. Such a Front should not demand a completely independent *Euskadi*, as that would narrow its base of support.[99]

Pertur insisted that the minimum conditions for such a regroupment must include a commitment to the formation of a reunified Basque state, the creation of a revolutionary party dedicated to the taking of power by the working class, to the building of popular autonomous bodies rather than to electoralism, and to the adoption of the principles of democratic centralism for the party's organisation. Those conditions effectively ruled out the participation of the members of ESB who hoped for a peaceful evolution towards Basque independence, and who favoured a less centralised, more populist kind of party, and wished to give priority to electoral work. *Otsagabia* was certainly not an attempt to liquidate the armed struggle in the way that ETA-Berri and ETA-VI had done. Pertur's recognition that some kind of democracy would soon be instituted was realistic, but elsewhere his analysis had little relationship to ETA's real situation. As ETA-PM had little weight in mass organisations, the priority to be given to building popular organisations over electoral work could not be implemented. Neither could the intention of organising according to ETA-PM's understanding of the principles of democratic centralism. EIA, throughout its brief history, was to recruit its members from the ethnically Basque middle class which had always formed the core of all of ETA's branches. As it never became a working-class organisation with mass participation and debate, centralism inevitably prevailed over democracy.

The biggest omission of *Otsagabia*'s formula lay in the description of the measures which would ensure agreement between the party and the armed organisation. In a separate document, Pertur and Erreka had attempted to show that this agreement would be achieved by giving all the activists in ETA-PM a solid education in both political and military matters.[100] The military group was to be closely linked to the masses and was to have the assistance of trained political advisers. Once ETA-PM had shed its political functions, it was hoped that the way would be open for reunification with ETA-M. ETA-M's friendly attitude towards the creation of the new party would, it was argued, facilitate this development.[101] Some members of ETA-PM saw the proposal to create a political party as an underhand way of liquidating the organisation, and suspected that the party would be infiltrated by members of other groups. They proposed, unsuccessfully, that the organisation should return to a structure based on Fronts, as decided at the Fifth Assembly.[102] The *Bereziak* never really accepted the decision of the Seventh Assembly in spite of the fact that they had presented no clear alternative to the proposals of the

dominant tendency, now led by Erreka. The *Bereziak* began to act
as an autonomous force, in much the same way as had the
Military Front in 1970 and again in 1974. The discovery by ETA-
PM's leadership that the *Bereziak* had their own separate treasury
brought the dispute to a head and caused a split.[103] Most of the
Bereziak were simple nationalists, but some had anarchist beliefs.
Their social origins did not differ from that of the majority of
people in ETA-PM. Their youth meant that most of them had not
been closely involved in the split within ETA-V in 1974, so they
were not hostile to ETA-M.[104] Their failure to present a clear
opposition to the formation of EIA had been due partly to the
support which ETA-M had given to that proposal.

As the military capacity of ETA-PM declined, ETA-M's
increased, as was shown by the lengthening list of informers,
policemen and right-wingers whom it killed. In October 1976, in
the main street of San Sebastián, an ETA-M action group shot
dead Araluce Villar, the President of the Diputación (provincial
government) of Guipúzcoa, together with four of his escorts.[105] It
was the most spectacular action since the killing of Carrero Blanco
in December 1973, and it provoked outbreaks of rioting by the
incontrolados, and frightened local supporters of the regime.
Araluce Villar had been implicated in the killing of Carlist
supporters of Prince Carlos Hugo in May of that year.[106] The
increase in ETA-M's military capacity took place at a time when
ETA-PM was greatly weakened and was preparing to put more
of is efforts into building the political party.

In the summer of 1976 the long-delayed efforts to reform
Spain's political system began to bear fruit, so that ETA-PM's
project for building a party became more urgent. Shortly after
Franco's death Manuel Fraga Iribarne, who had been widely
tipped as the man to inaugurate a transition to a democratic
Spain, was made Minister of the Interior, while José María
Areilza, who had been the first mayor of Bilbao after Franco's
victory, became Foreign Minister. Areilza had been one of the
regime's diplomats, but had moved into opposition in the
1960s.[107] The Arias government's mixture of reform and repression appeared less and less viable in the year and a half after
Franco's death. The government's failure to control the police was
demonstrated when on 3 March 1976 five people were killed after
police opened fire on a group of strikers who had occupied a
church in Vitoria, the capital of Alava.[108] The killings provoked
a general strike in Euskadi, and Fraga caused a general outcry

when he blamed the deaths on agitators who organised demonstrations.[109] ETA-PM's publications argued that the Vitoria killings showed that the government had no intention of reforming the regime, which would have to be overthrown by the people.[110]

The credibility of the Arias government and of Fraga in particular was further weakened when on 9 May the police allowed an ultra-right group to fire into a crowd attending a Carlist rally in Montejurra, Navarre, killing two people.[111] King Juan Carlos became more and more dissatisfied with the Arias government's inability to democratise, and after an official visit to the United States in June asked for Arias' resignation. Liberal opinion was dismayed by the King's choice as Arias' successor of Adolfo Suárez, a functionary who had been General Secretary of the Movement.[112] The impression that the new Prime Minister was a man of the same type as Arias was soon shown to be mistaken, as Suárez was to achieve a remarkable feat of replacing the Francoist system by a parliamentary democracy within a year, while keeping a tight control over the process, and limiting the opposition's participation in the transition.

Suárez effectively started the liquidation of the Francoist institutions when, in November 1976, the Cortes passed the Law of Political Reform which provided for the establishment of a parliament elected by universal suffrage. The decision was ratified by a referendum held in December. The voting figures were not falsified, as they had been in Franco's time, but the government used radio and television to campaign for a vote in favour, while the opposition parties remained illegal, and were not allowed to campaign openly against Suárez's proposals.[113] Most of the opposition parties urged abstention, although their campaigns were rather muted. In Spain as a whole, the results were a success for the government, as 77 percent of the population voted, the great majority of them in favour of the government's proposals. In the Basque country, however, the level of abstentions was much higher, reaching 55 percent in Guipúzcoa.[114] The parties who had urged abstention then had to consider whether they would participate in the elections which the referendum had authorised. If EIA stood in the elections, its organisational weakness practically compelled it to do so in partnership with others. An EIA spokesman declared that the party was prepared to make alliances with 'Spanish' forces, based on a clear programme, but believed that a National Front which would include the PNV was invalid. On the other hand, he argued that it was justifiable to make alliances with groups such as the ORT and the MCE, which, although 'Spanish', had supported the struggle of the Basque people.[115] In another interview an ETA-PM spokesman declared that ETA-PM would continue the armed struggle, as a bourgeois democracy would not be able to liquidate the oligarchy and that ETA-PM, not the new political party, would continue to decide what armed actions were necessary.[116] He did not give any explanation of how political coordination between the party and the armed wing of the movement would be maintained. As no adequate mechanism to ensure agreement between the two organisations existed, relationships between them were to cause problems in the future.

EIA made its first public appearance in April 1977 at Gallarta in Vizcaya. The location showed EIA's intentions of seeking support outside the ethnically Basque community, as Gallarta, the place where the first general strike in the Basque country had started, and the birthplace of Dolores Ibarruri (La Pasionaria), had socialist rather than nationalist associations.[117] The meeting demonstrated the contradictions which were to recur throughout EIA's existence, as the party proclaimed its organisational and political independence from ETA-PM, but announced that it based itself on ETA's heritage. EIA was declared to be a proletarian, not a populist party, but the meeting included a speech by the mother of an ETA-PM martyr, tape recordings made by imprisoned leaders, patriotic music, and slide projections of photographs of ETA's martyrs. The walls were covered with posters carrying a picture of Pertur. The main speaker, Francisco Letamendía, who had been a defence lawyer at the 1970 Burgos trial and later the main theoretician of the 'Mino' faction of ETA-VI, declared that the struggle against capitalism demanded a struggle for independence and vice versa. Arantza Arruti, one of those tried at Burgos, attacked the government for the limited amount of freedom which had been granted. EIA declared its support for the trade union LAB, and for the workers' struggles.[118]

EIA aspired to be a party of the working class, but its lack of a base among organised workers, combined with its considerable support elsewhere, was to create tensions in the future, as EIA's official ideology came into conflict with its real opportunities. Such problems were eventually to lead to the failure of EIA to achieve its original objective. However, in the short run the party had to make the more urgent decision of whether or not to participate in the elections which the Suárez government had called. The PSOE, PCE and PNV decided to take part, although they had urged abstention in the December referendum. By their participation they implied acceptance of the government which would be elected although many nationalists were reluctant to grant this legitimacy to any Spanish government. However, if the nationalist forces abstained while the 'Spanish' ones participated, the nationalists might be left at a disadvantage. This problem was discussed at a series of meetings attended by nationalist groups and parties which included the PNV and both branches of ETA. The leaders of ETA-M argued, in January, that the elections should be boycotted, on the grounds that it would be paradoxical to vote for a parliament which had been created by a government which had emanated from Francoism, and to accept elections whose legitimacy had been ratified by a referendum which nationalists had boycotted.[119] It was pointed out that the elections had been prepared without the people being consulted, at a time when many prisoners had still not been freed, and some nationalist political parties remained illegal. ETA-M's leaders maintained that if nationalists did participate they should stand on the programme of KAS; ETA-PM would have preferred to win the support of the other components of KAS for a united front to contest the elections. Ideally, KAS would then form part of a broader alliance which would include revolutionary 'Spanish' groups.[120]

As it became clear that failure to grant a complete amnesty in the Basque country could ruin Suárez's plans to hold the elections which would usher in parliamentary democracy, the government decided to get in touch with both branches of ETA, in order to discuss the possibility of a cease-fire, in return for a more extensive amnesty. Contact with both ETAs was made early in 1977 through a Bilbao journalist, José María Portell, who had written a book on the organisation[121]. Discretion was essential because right-wing opinion would have been outraged to hear that the government was negotiating with an organisation dedicated to smashing the territorial integrity of Spain. Yet the government had little choice, if it were to achieve the kind of understanding with the opposition in the Basque country which was being created elsewhere in Spain.

The main opposition parties in the Basque country, particularly the PNV, were reluctant to participate in the elections while there were still Basques in prison for political crimes. The

PNV's leaders were aware that if the party stood in elections which were boycotted by other nationalists, its credibility might be damaged. It was in the government's interest to provide the conditions which would allow the PNV to stand, but it would have been difficult simply to grant an amnesty while violence continued. The government was, however, prepared to do so if a halt to ETA's violence could be negotiated. Such an arrangement had its attractions for ETA-PM, whose capacity to carry out armed struggle in early 1977 was very slight.[122] A complete amnesty would allow it to rebuild its own shattered organisation, as well as constructing EIA, as ETA-PM's leading members would be released. ETA-M's leaders were much cooler towards the idea of a cease-fire, although its representatives met government emissaries in Geneva, while insisting that they were there merely as observers.[123] ETA-PM's leaders demanded that all the prisoners should be freed, democratic liberties granted, the violence exercised by the police ended, and *Abertzale* political parties allowed to function.[124] ETA-M's leaders insisted that KAS, the coordinating body of the left nationalist forces, was the appropriate agency for the negotiations. By negotiating with the government ETA-PM was bypassing KAS and was therefore, ETA-M's leaders claimed, undermining nationalist unity. An ETA-M statement declared that if the government wanted to negotiate, it could do so by talking to its members in prison.[125]

In May, as ETA-M renewed its attacks on its preferred target, killing a policeman in San Sebastián and shooting at others in Pamplona, the police contributed to the climate of violence by shooting and beating up demonstrators and bystanders. The demonstrations demanding a complete amnesty continued, involving very large numbers of people. The government finally released the last of ETA's prisoners in May, though a number of them were sent abroad and forbidden to return to Spain. ETA-PM's representatives agreed on a truce on condition that all their prisoners were freed, although they became increasingly irritated at the government's slowness in implementing the prisoners' release. In late May, only a few weeks before the elections, ETA-PM threatened to resume the armed struggle if all the prisoners were not freed immediately.[126]

The *Bereziak* thought that parties which participated in the masquerade were helping Suárez deceive the people.[127] They were incensed at ETA-PM's leadership for negotiating with emissaries of the government, without the knowledge of most of their members, at a time when their activists were being killed by Civil Guards. In May 1977 the *Bereziak* proclaimed their split from ETA-PM and announced their wish to unite with ETA-M. They alleged that ETA-PM's leadership, behind the back of its members, was carrying out a different policy from that agreed at the Seventh Assembly.[128] When the government decided to release all Basque prisoners before the elections, ETA-PM maintained the truce and authorised EIA's candidates to stand, as part of the electoral alliance Euskadiko Eskerra (The Basque Left).[129] The *Bereziak*, in contrast, announced that as a total amnesty and democratic liberties had not been granted, they would launch an armed offensive and call for the boycott of the elections.[130]

Although the defection of the *Bereziak* greatly weakened ETA-PM, its members did not question the need for the armed struggle to continue. Some of its members argued that, while the spectacular feats carried out by ETA's *liberados* had their place, there was a need to develop a broader, low level military activity based around such things as the defence of neighbourhoods against the violent activities of the *incontrolados*.[131] This desire to implement ETA's original conception of armed activity, which would eventually involve masses of people, did not prosper. ETA-M and the *Bereziak*, as fairly small groups of *liberados*, based in the French Basque country, had no such objectives. The *Bereziak* carried out their first important independent action in May 1977, when they kidnapped the prominent industrialist Javier de Ibarra. The ransom they demanded was not paid and Ibarra was killed.[132] Such an action carried out on the eve of the election added to public confusion, as the *Bereziak* claimed to be the legitimate ETA-PM.

ETA-M defended the *Bereziak* action and bitterly attacked the PCE and PSOE for condemning the killing.[133] This was hardly surprising as the two groups were in the process of arranging the unification which was formally announced in September. The accession of the *Bereziak* brought ETA-M reinforcements of between thirty and sixty people, many of them in their teens and early twenties, an average age significantly younger than that of ETA-M's members. This increase in ETA-M's strength was to enable it to mount a considerable offensive in late 1977. The *Bereziak*, apart from their youth, differed little from ETA-M's existing members, or from ETA's traditional social base. They tended to be ethnically Basque, often from rural areas which traditionally supported the PNV, and with a low political level.[134] In spite of its criticism of ETA-PM, ETA-M had continued until 1977 to regard the other branch of ETA as a revolutionary *Abertzale* organisation. However, the *Bereziak* split and EIA's decision to contest the elections made ETA-M much more hostile to both EIA and ETA-PM. Until the spring of 1977, EIA's leaders had been hopeful of organising an electoral alliance, to be named Euskal Erakunde Herritarra (EEH), Basque People's Alliance, which would include both *Abertzale* and revolutionary 'Spanish' parties, but this prospect crumbled as ETA-M decided to support a boycott.[135] The main revolutionary groups such as the ORT, PTE and LCR-ETA-VI decided to stand alone or to form their own mini-alliances.

As ETA-PM had already agreed to a cease-fire during the electoral period, there would have been no point in EIA refusing to contest the elections. EIA therefore stood as part of Euskadiko Ezkerra (henceforth EE), together with the MCE.[136] The pact was a marriage of convenience, as EIA-ETA-PM had the prestige of its prisoners and martyrs, while the MCE had a solid presence in the working-class movement, particularly in Guipúzcoa, the result of ten years' work since its leaders had been expelled from ETA at the Fifth Assembly. Such an alliance with an 'imperialist' group was unthinkable for ETA-M which, if it had favoured participation, would have been more at home with groups such as EHAS and ESB, which combined radical nationalism with moderate reformist social policies. ETA-M considered that EIA and ETA-PM had broken the discipline of KAS, the forum where the *Abertzale* parties were supposed to agree on tactics towards 'Spanish' forces.[137] Furthermore, ETA-M alleged that ETA-PM's manipulation of EIA had frustrated the growth of that party and driven many of its potential supporters into the arms of ESB.

The breach between ETA-M and ETA-PM destroyed the possibility of having one *Abertzale* party supported by both ETA branches. LAIA was not a suitable partner for ETA-M, as LAIA's leaders saw their organisation as a Marxist party opposed to populism. ETA-M's need for a political arm made it look to Euskal Herriko Alderdi Socialista (EHAS), which had been founded in 1975 by intellectuals such as Natxo Arregi. ETA-PM's decision to form EIA and to give it a Marxist-Leninist programme had been bitterly disappointing to EHAS's leaders, who continued their efforts to form a broad, populist, nationalist party. Tomás Goikoetxea, who had resigned from ETA-PM when his plan for such a party had been rejected in favour of Pertur's Marxist-

Leninist model, also joined EHAS, which was almost alone in backing ETA-M's plea to boycott the election.[138] The relationship between ETA's branches worsened as EIA, in its attempt to create a left alliance, was impelled towards co-operation with 'Spanish' forces and ETA-M, also looking for allies, turned towards the kind of radical nationalists who had helped at the birth of ETA-V in 1970 and 1971.

The election results in most of Spain were a qualified success for the Unión del Centro Democrático (UCD), the party which Suárez had forged out of the more liberal elements of the state apparatus. The UCD did not stand at all in Guipúzcoa, and in Vizcaya it came third, behind the PNV and the PSOE. In the four Basque provinces 19.4% of the electorate voted for the PSOE and 18.8% for the PNV. The abstention rate was 22.6%, almost the same as for Spain as a whole, although in Guipúzcoa, the most nationalist province, it was 34.4%. EE stood in Alava, Guipúzcoa and Vizcaya, but not in Navarre, where nationalist feeling was weak. In Alava it received only 2.1% of the votes cast, but in Vizcaya its share was 5.8% and in Guipúzcoa, 9.5%. Letamendía was elected to Congress, while Bandrés was returned to the Senate.[139] ETA-PM and EIA thought that, in view of their lack of forces and organisation, the result showed that EIA was accepted as ETA's heir.

The core of EIA's leadership was formed by a combination of veterans of the Burgos trial, such as Mario Onaindía and Eduardo Uriarte, men such as Ignacio Múgica Arregi and Javier Garayalde (Erreka), who had led ETA-PM's desperate campaign in the last year of Franco's life, and lawyers such as José María Bandrés and Francisco Letamendía, who were well known as defenders of ETA prisoners. Significantly, EIA's leadership included no-one who had been in ETA before the Fifth Assembly or had been active in the virulently chauvinistic ETA-V of 1970 and 1971. Leaders from those periods, such as Etxabe and Txillardegi, were often supporters of ESB. A number of ETA's most famous prisoners who had been jailed in the late 1960s, such as Sabino Arana, Iñaki Sarasketa and Andoni Arrizabalaga, remained members of the LCR-ETA-VI, although that group had little popular support. Some of EIA's leaders, such as Mario Onaindía, had literary gifts, but they were not capable of making a political analysis equal to that of ETA-VI's Unzueta or the MCE's del Río. The election results were disappointing to ETA-M's leaders whose call for a boycott had been a failure. Although abstention was greater in Guipúzcoa than in Spain as a whole, there was no nationalist boycott on the scale seen during the 1976 referendum. ETA-M's leaders would in time come to realise that participation in elections was a necessary part of the nationalist struggle. By that time, however, the breach with ETA-PM/EIA would have gone too far to be healed. When ETA-M came to accept the need to build an electoral front it would be as a rival, not as an ally of ETA-PM/EIA.

REFERENCES

1. *Hautsi*, No. 4, Sept./Oct. 1978.
2. *Kemen*, No. 1, 1974.
3. For ETA-V's viewpoint see 'Resolución del BT sobre la crisis obrerista', *Kemen*, No. 3, Sept. 1974.
4. *Sugarra*, No. 1, 1975.
5. Author's interview with J.M. Larrazábal, a member of LAIA's executive, San Sebastián, 8 March 1980; interview with LAIA spokesman, *Punto y Hora*, 10–16 March 1977.
6. Marcel Neidergang, *Le Monde*, 1 Jan. 1974.
7. 'Editorial', *Hautsi*, No. 5, Jul 1974.
8. 'El movimiento nacional ante los partidos políticos', *Fuerza Nueva*, 10 Aug. 1974.
9. ETA-V leaflet, 'Una pena de muerte en Barcelona', *Documentos Y*, Vol. 15, p. 463.
10. *Euskadi*, April, 1974.
11. *Doblón*, 14 Dec. 1974.
12. *Comunicado de ETA*, 4 April 1974, *Documentos Y*, Vol. 15, p. 467.
13. *Primero de Mayo* (ETA-V leaflet), *Documentos Y*, Vol. 15, p. 472.
14. Amigo, *Pertur*, pp. 71–2.
15. Amigo, *Pertur*, p. 73.
16. *Comunicado de ETA*, *Documentos Y*, Vol. 15, pp. 481–2.
17. *A los familiares de Jon Urzelay Imaz*, *Documentos Y*, Vol. 15, p. 486.
18. Author's interview with Kepa Aulestia, San Sebastián, 31 July 1984.
19. Interview with Kepa Aulerstia, 31 July 1984.
20. 'Editorial', *Hautsi*, No. 5, July 1974.
21. Ortzi, *Historia*, pp. 405–7.
22. *Doblón*, 2 and 9 Nov. 1974; *Cambio 16*, 11–17 Nov. 1974.
23. *Declaración de la dirección nacional de ETA*, 17 Oct. 1974, *Documentos Y*, Vol. 15, p. 489.
24. 'Operación Jaulas', *Cambio 16*, 7–13 Oct. 1974.
25. Lidia Falcón, *Viernes y 13 en la Calle del Correo* (Barcelona, 1981), pp. 156–8.
26. See 'Historia organizativa desde la escisión del Frente Obrero, hasta in 2ª parte de la VI Asamblea', *Documentos Y*, Vol. 17, pp. 249–57.
27. 'Historia organizativa . . .' *Documentos Y*.

28. *Planteamiento del grupo escindido. Análisis y crítica, Documentos Y*, Vol. 15, pp. 312–21.

29. *Zutik Agire* (unnumbered, undated).

30. *Zutik Agire* (unnumbered, undated).

31. 'Complemento a nuestras posiciones políticas expresadas', *Zutik*, No. 65, Aug. 1975.

32. 'Unas sugerencias para nuestras estructuras', *Kemen*, No. 2 (undated).

33. 'A la izquierda vasca', *Langile*, No. 2, May 1975.

34. *Kemen*, No. 5, April 1975.

35. *Comunicado de la segunda parte de Sexto Biltzaar Nagusi de ETA, Documentos Y*, Vol. 17, pp. 302–4.

36. See *ESB — Un Programa socialista para la autonomía de Euskadi*, (Bilbao, 1977), passim; author's interview with Ildefenso Iriarte Otermin, former member of ETA and ESB, San Sebastián, 24 July 1980.

37. 'Batasuna — un clamor popular', *Garaia*, 9–16 Sept. 1976.

38. Interview with ESB leader Carlos Caballero; Eugenio Ibarzábal, *Euskadi: Diálogos en torno a las elecciones* (Zarauz, 1977), pp. 141–55.

39. In ETA jargon a 'legal' activist was someone pursuing an apparently normal life and using his or her own name.

· 40. Author's interviews with Kepa Aulestia, a former ETA-V *liberado*, San Sebastián, 31 July 1984, and 'Goiherri', 5 August 1984.

41. 'Semana Vasca', *Cambio 16*, 7–13 April 1975.

42. Author's interview with 'Goiherri; Amigo, *Pertur*, p. 99.

43. *Cambio 16*, 5–12 May and 2–8 June, 1975.

44. 'A tiros por España', *Cambio 16*, 11–17 Aug. 1975.

45. *Hautsi*, 6 Sept. 1975.

46. *Cambio 16*, 4–10 Aug. 1975.

47. 'Comunicado de ETA', *Hautsi*, 7 Oct. 1975.

48. See *Le Monde*, 25 Dec. 1973; see Argala's prologue to Apalategui, *Los Vascos*.

49. *Cambio 16*, 26 May–1 June, 1975.

50. See ETA-M's leaflet 'Campaña anti txibatos', 25 Nov. 1975, *Documentos Y*, Vol. 16, pp. 299–300.

51. 'Alkatee Kontraka Campaina', 9 Feb. 1976 and 'Por qué la campaña anti-alcaldes' (undated), *Documentos Y*, Vol. 16, pp. 296–300.

52. See untitled leaflet produced in Februrary 1976, *Documentos Y*, Vol. 16, p. 303.

53. Luis C. Núñez, *La sociedad vasca actual* (San Sebastián, 1977), p. 128; Miguel Castells, *Radiografía de un modelo represivo* (San Sebastián, 1982), p. 82.

54. *Información Mensual* (IM), June 1975, the journal of the Carlist Party.

55. 'Situación politica en Euskadi Sur. B-La organización politico militar', *Zutik*, No. 65 (ETA-M), Aug. 1975.

56. *Otsagabia, Documentos Y*, Vol. 18, pp. 107–27.

57. 'Por un movimiento obrero vasco y abertzale', *Langile*, July 1974.

58. 'Comisiones obreras abertzales', *Sugarra*, No. 1, 1975.

59. 'Tesis sobre LAB', *Kemen*, No. 6, 1975.

60. *Organización de Masas LAB* (undated), *Documentos Y*, Vol. 17, pp. 403–6.

61. 'La Junta Democrática de España', *Información Española*, 119, Sept. 1974.

62. J.L. Hollyman, 1976, 'The Spanish Socialist Party 1939–76', MA Thesis, University of Reading, passim.

63. Santiago Carrillo, *Demain l'Espagne* (Paris, 1974), p. 202.

64. *Comunicado de fundación del KAS, Documentos Y*, Vol. 17, p. 482; Natxo Arregi, *Memorias del KAS 1975–1978* (San Sebastián, 1981), passim.

65. For ETA-PM's conception of KAS see 'Informe No. 2 sobre la alternativa', *Documentos Y*, Vol. 17, pp. 507–13.

66. *Hautsi*, No. 9, Feb. 1976.

67. 'Habla el PNV', *Cambio 16*, 12–25 Jan. 1977.

68. *Zutik*, No. 66 (ETA-M), March 1976.

69. *Hautsi*, No. 6, Sept. 1975.

70. 'Txiki condenado', *Cambio 16*, 29 Sept.–5 Oct. 1975.

71. Javier Sánchez Erauskin, *Txiki-Otaegui: El viento y las raíces* (San Sebastián, 1978), pp. 7–187.

72. 'Juan Paredes Manot, Txiki', *Hautsi*, No. 7, Oct. 1975.

73. 'Tupa, Otaegui, Zutik', *Hautsi*, No. 6, Sept. 1975; 'Euskadi otra vez en pie', *Hautsi*, No. 7, Oct. 1975.

74. 'Editorial', *Hautsi*, No. 8, Dec. 1975; *Mundo Obrero*, 18 Nov. 1975.

75. José María Portell, *Euskadi: Amnistia arrancada* (Barcelona, 1977), p. 69.

76. Sabino Arana, 'Amnistía total y ahora', *Zutik* (LCR), No. 89, 18 May 1977.

77. *Cambio 16*, 26 March 1977.

78. *Hautsi*, No. 9, Feb. 1976.

79. *Zutik*, No. 65 (ETA-M), Aug. 1975.

80. *Zutik*, No. 66 (ETA-M), March 1976.

81. 'La vuelta a la violencia', *Cambio 16*, 26 Jan.–1 Feb. 1976.

82. Amigo, *Pertur*, p. 121.

83. 'Secuestrado por error', *Cambio 16*, 1–7 March 1976.

84. See 'Arrasate', *Hautsi*, No. 10, March 1976.

85. *Cambio 16*, 19–25 April 1976.

86. *Cambio 16*, 26 April–2 May 1976.

87. 'Berazadi, una aclaración necesaria', *Hautsi*, No. 13, July 1976; 'Sobre el impuesto revolucionario', *Hautsi*, No. 6, Sept. 1975.

88. Amigo, *Pertur*, pp. 126–7.

89. Amigo, *Pertur*, pp. 127–28.

90. *Cambio 16*, 2–8 Aug. 1976; 'Pertur', *Hautsi*, No. 14, Aug. 1976.

91. *Cambio 16*, 23–9 Aug. 1976.

92. See *Egin* 20, 22, 24 and 28 Jan. 1978.

93. Miguel Castells, *El Mejor Defensor, El Pueblo* (San Sebastián, 1978), pp. 48–51, 57–64.

94. *Otsagabia, Documentos Y*, Vol. 18, pp. 107–27.

95. Author's interview with LAIA Executive Committee member J.M. Larrazábal.

96. *Sobre socialismo abertzale, Documentos Y*, Vol. 18, pp. 129–54: author's interview with Tomás Goikoetxea, San Sebastián, 10 Aug. 1981.

97. Arregi, *Memorias del KAS 1975–78*, passim.

98. *Otsagabia*, p. 120.
99. *Otsagabia*, p. 124.
100. *Formas de coordinación entre la lucha armada y la lucha política*, Documentos Y, Vol. 18, pp. 107–205.
101. *Formas de coordinatión* ——, Documentos Y, pp. 107–205.
102. *Ponencia retirada en el VII B.N.*, Documentos Y, Vol. 18, pp. 207–19.
103. *Kemen*, No. 15, May 1977.
104. Author's interviews with Tomás Goikoetxea, Kepa Aulestia, and Goiherri.
105. 'Araluce Villar ejecutado', *Zutik*, No. 67, Nov. 1976.
106. 'Interpelación, Montejurra', *Garaia*, 20–7 Jan. 1977.
107. For Areilza see interview in Chao, *Después de Franco España*, pp. 77–83.
108. *Gasteiz-Vitoria. De la huelga a la Matanza* (Paris, 1976), pp. 117–32 (no authors named); *Hautsi*, No. 10, March 1976.
109. *Gasteiz*, p. 154.
110. *Hautsi*, No. 11, 15 March 1976.
111. Josep Carles Clemente and Carles S. Costa, *Montejurra 76* (Barcelona, 1976), pp. 101–30.
112. Samuel D. Eaton, *The Forces of Freedom in Spain 1974–79* (Stanford, 1981), p. 40; Gregorio Morán, *Adolfo Suárez, Historia de una ambición* (Barcelona, 1979), pp. 13–61.
113. *Cambio 16 Internacional*, 19 Dec. 1976.
114. *Cambio 16 Internacional*, 26 Dec.–2 Jan. 1977.
115. *Punta y Hora*, 1–15 Oct. 1976.
116. *Punto y Hora*, 3–10 Feb. 1977.
117. 'Presentación de EIA en Gallarta', *Punto y Hora*, 13 April 1977.
118. 'Presentación de EIA . . .', *Punto y Hora*, 13 April 1977.
119. Anexo 5. 'Cara a las elecciones, posición de ETA-M', *Kemen*, No. 10 (undated).
120 'Anexo 7 E.', *Kemen*, No. 10 (undated).
121. Portell, *Euskadi*, pp. 9–11; Portell, *Los hombres de ETA* (Barcelona, 1974), passim.
122. See interview with ETA-PM leader José Etxegarai Gastearena (Mark) in *Deia*, 27 Dec. 1977.
123. Portell, *Euskadi*, p. 189.
124. Portell, *Euskadi*, pp. 172–4.
125. *Hautsi*, No. 15, July 1977.
126. 'Comunicado de ETA', 28 May 1977, Documentos Y, Vol. 18. pp. 524–7.
227. 'Informe a la militancia (Interno)', Documentos Y, Vol. 18, pp. 497–501.
128. 'Informe a la . . .', Documentos Y, Vol. 18, pp. 497–501.
129. Ortzi, *El no vasco a la reforma* (San Sebastián, 1979) Vol. 1, p. 13.
130. 'ETA ante las elecciones' (undated), Documentos Y, Vol. 18, p. 529.
131. 'Informe de una reunión de Herrialdeburus', *Kemen*, No. 15 (undated).
132. 'A la clase trabajadora y a todo el pueblo de Euskadi', Documentos Y, Vol. 18, p. 526.

133. *Zutik* (ETA-M), No. 68, July 1977.
134. *Deia*, 27 Dec. 1977: 'El oligarca y los adolescentes', *Cambio 16*, 4–10 July 1977.
135. *Zutik* (ETA-M), No. 68, July 1977.
136. *Hautsi*, No. 15, July 1977.
137. 'La evolución de la organización PM y sus consecuencias en EIA', *Zutik*, No. 68 (ETA-M), July 1977.
138. Author's interview with Tomás Goikoetxea.
139. *Diario Vasco*, 17 June 1977; see Luis C. Nuñez, *Euskadi sur electoral* (San Sebastián, 1980).

7

From the Election to the Constitution: June 1977–December 1979

The election results convinced both the PNV and ETA-PM/EIA that the decision to participate was justified although it had been bitterly opposed by other nationalist forces. From ETA-M's point of view, standing in the elections gave credibility to the fraudulent dictatorship of Suárez and Juan Carlos, while doing so in the company of 'Spanish' partners offended against nationalist principles.' ETA-M's sense of betrayal was exacerbated by the success of the EE coalition and the failure of the call for abstention, compared to the December 1976 referendum. Although all of ETA's prisoners had been freed, many refugees were afraid to return to their homes because of fear of persecution. In addition, the last group of prisoners to be released had been deported to various European capitals, while the police who had oppressed the Basque people for forty years continued to occupy the country. ETA-PM, although far from enthusiastic about the semi-democracy which Suárez had instituted, thought the time was ripe to change the emphasis of the struggle from armed activity to the creation of a mass movement. EIA had been formed as a consequence of the realisation that powerful forces, in business and elsewhere, were preparing to phase out the dictatorship. The Suárez government had needed a diminution of armed violence in order to make elections in the Basque country plausible. ETA-PM had been in a strong bargaining position and had made the release of prisoners a condition for its ceasefire. ETA-PM could, after the elections, congratulate itself on having two supporters in parliament, and on the return to activity of its former prisoners, whose enormous prestige was EIA's main asset.[2]

However, the balance sheet was not entirely positive. ETA-PM's military capacity had been severely weakened by the losses which it had incurred in a spectacular campaign of killings and armed robberies and it had lost Pertur, its most capable leader. The internal disagreements which had produced the resignation of most of the *Bereziak*, some of whom were suspected of complicity in Pertur's disappearance, had also weakened the group. The release of ETA-PM's prisoners strengthened EIA, the movement's political arm, rather than ETA-PM, although some leaders, such as Goiherri and Kepa Aulestia, moved to France to reinforce ETA-PM's leadership. As known activists could not generally be reincorporated into armed struggle, ETA-PM would, in the future, be led by young men, who would act in political sympathy with the ex-leaders now in EIA, but not under their organisational guidance. In spite of ETA-PM's temporary military weakness its leaders believed that ETA-PM was the genuine heir of ETA's tradition. It had an organisation of several hundred people inside Spain and the support of most of the prisoners and refugees, especially the 'historic' leaders. ETA-PM's structure had been devastated by the repression during 1975 and 1976, but its leaders considered that the organisation possessed a theory and a political capacity which would enable it to play a key part in the Basque revolution. ETA-PM's and EIA's leaders believed that violent activities were only one form of struggle and that in future they would be able to use the division of labour instituted at the Seventh Assembly, to carry out the class struggle more effectively. In contrast, in ETA-PM's view, ETA-M consisted of a fairly small group of *liberados* with hardly any roots inside Spain and no idea of how the armed struggle fitted into an overall revolutionary perspective. The *Bereziak*, who throughout most of 1977 claimed to be the genuine ETA-PM, had even fewer political cadres. According to Pertur's analysis, the initiative should now pass to EIA, as the slackening of repression would enable the kind of mass struggles which had been almost impossible under Franco to flourish.[3] ETA-PM's leaders believed there was no possibility of achieving either socialism or independence by peaceful means. The armed force had to be prepared to act when the activity of the mass movement reached its limit.

Whatever the theoretical justification for ETA-PM's continuing existence, there were sound practical reasons for it. If ETA-PM had dissolved, the prestige of the armed struggle would have been monopolised by ETA-M and the forces which were gathering round it, to the detriment of EIA. The leaders of both EIA and ETA-PM were concerned that radical nationalist politics should not be monopolised by the conservative and chauvinistic tendencies forming around Monzón and Txillardegi. The tensions which existed between ETA's rival branches were hardly understood by many of those who identified with their struggle, and in the aftermath of the elections there was a feeling of solidarity among nationalists which extended even to supporters of the PNV. This friendly atmosphere was evident at a rally in San Sebastián held on 29 July 1977 by EIA to commemorate the first anniversary of the disappearance of Pertur. Miguel Castells, who had been an unsuccessful EE parliamentary candidate, outlined EIA's attitude towards the immigrants, stating that the party did not demand that they give up their own culture, or accept Basque culture. All that EIA asked of them was that they join in the struggle for Euskadi's freedom. Castells' speech was strongly applauded, by an overwhelmingly nationalist audience. During the meeting the final ETA prisoners to be released from prison to various European countries mounted the platform, accompanied by the dissident former PNV senator, Telesforo Monzón. These men, the famous *Extrañados*, had returned illegally to Spain, to the embarrassment of the authorities who tried to ignore their presence in the country.[4]

The apparent unity was shattered by a violent clash between radical nationalists and other groups, which took place during a demonstration for an extension of the amnesty, in San Sebastián on 8 September 1977. The demonstration had been called by a coalition of parties, ranging from EIA and others on the revolutionary left to the Basque Christian Democracy. The march was led by the members of parliament elected on 15 June, followed by the *Extrañados*. At the beginning of the demonstration there were clashes between the participants and a group of 2,000, mainly young, people attending a meeting in honour of Josu Zabala, an ETA-M member who had been killed by the police a year before. The meeting had been called by local amnesty committees and by various political parties, several of whom were also sponsors of the main demonstration. A PNV parliamentary deputy, Andoni Monforte, was assaulted, while the loudspeakers on the car of PSOE parliamentary deputy J.A. Maturana were destroyed. The counter-demonstrators shouted 'Out with the opportunists', 'The PNV is bourgeois' and other hostile slogans.[5]

In essence, the clashes arose because of differences over the scope of the amnesty conceded by the government. For the radicals, an amnesty which did not give guarantees to the exiles was of little value. In contrast, the 'Spanish' parties were reasonably happy about the amnesty which had been granted, while the PNV's position was ambivalent. The demonstrators divided in two as the group headed by the parliamentarians took one route, and the ex-prisoners with Telesforo Monzón another. The counter-demonstrators waited for the main demonstration to return, then blocked its way for more than fifteen minutes and attacked and injured several participants. When the leaders of the main demonstration entered the offices of the *Diputación* (provincial government) as a refuge from the counter-demonstrators, a group of young men followed them, after clashes with the stewards. Once inside, they hung a banner saying 'ETA, the people are with you' from the balcony, while outside in the street the counter-demonstrators destroyed placards carrying slogans of which they disapproved.[6]

The stupefied supporters of the parties who had called the demonstration held a meeting immediately afterwards. They were particularly annoyed by the fact that there had been people carrying ESB and EIA slogans among the counter-demonstrators, even though these parties had been sponsors of the main march. The incident put EIA in an embarrassing position, and it announced next day that it would open an investigation to discover whether its members had participated in the violence. EIA's parliamentarians, Letamendía and Bandrés, both denounced the attack and offered their sympathy to their colleagues of the PSOE and PNV. ESB also condemned the violence, although more grudgingly. The 'Spanish' left reacted to the attack on their representatives with indignation. The PSOE parliamentary deputy, Enrique Múgica, made a press statement blaming 'a gifted actor', Monzón, the ex-prisoners and 'groups of fanatics' called KAS and ESB who wanted to destabilise the country.[7]

Monzón and the *Extrañados* also condemned the violence, although at a meeting in Vitoria they blamed the organisers for altering the agreed route of the march, and forbidding slogans supporting ETA and calling for independence.[8] Anger at the limitations on slogans and the presence of a strong force of stewards (the police were absent throughout the demonstration) may have been the specific incidents which enranged the counter-demonstrators. However, the more general cause for their anger was that the moderate parties, which they considered had done so little in the fight against Franco, were abandoning the amnesty campaign after benefiting from ETA's struggle. The demonstration was a turning point for both EIA and ESB. EIA's role in it had been ambiguous. While several of the 'exiles' marching with Monzón were prominent EIA members, their party's strong criticism of what had happened was an indication of the moderate parliamentary direction it was now taking.[9] In contrast, ESB, which in June 1977 had been a clearly social-democratic party, followed a course which was eventually to unite it with the radical nationalist supporters of ETA-M. The confrontation showed that EIA was not acceptable to all of the *Abertzale* forces, especially to ETA-M whose lack of a political arm was remedied in July 1977, with the creation of Herriko Alderdi Sozialista Iraultzailea (the Revolutionary Socialist People's Party) (HASI). HASI represented the culmination of the efforts of people such as Natxo Arregi and Alberto Figueroa to found a Basque socialist party. Formally, HASI was the product of the fusion of Euskal Herriko Alderdi Sozialista (the Basque People's Socialist Party) (EHAS) and Euskal Alderdi Sozialista (the Basque Socialist Party) (EAS) with a number of independents. In reality, groups such as EHAS and EAS were political clubs supported by intellectuals.

Although Arregi and his associates had been dissatisfied by ETA-PM leadership's decision to form its own Marxist-Leninist party, they had continued their efforts to create a party which would be able to compete with the PNV and ESB. They were joined by Tomás Goikoetzea, who had resigned from ETA-PM after his project for a broad socialist party had been rejected, in favour of Pertur's Marxist-Leninist model.[10] However, at HASI's first conference in May 1978 an influx of people loyal to ETA-M and the *Bereziak* elected Txomin Ziluaga as General Secretary and threw out the original leaders, most of whom eventually joined EIA.[11] The other *Abertzale* parties disagreed with EIA's decision in October to take part in the Consejo General Vasco (henceforth CGV), a body set up by the government and composed of the MPs from the Basque country, to act as a caretaker body until an autonomous Basque parliament was elected.[12] EE participated and Bandrés, their Senator, became its Minister of Transport. HASI called on other parties to reject the pre-autonomy arrangements.[13] At a press conference in September 1977 EIA proposed that after the municipal elections which were expected soon, the councillors who were elected should co-operate with neighbourhood associations and amnesty committees to create a popular assembly, which should organise a Basque police force and administration.[14] However, EIA gradually abandoned such ideas in favour of participation in parliamentary and municipal institutions.

EIA's and ETA-PM's leaders' desire for an alliance which would include both radical nationalists and the revolutionary 'Spanish' groups was never to be realised. HASI and LAIA agreed with ETA-M that the radical nationalists groups should come to an agreement within KAS before allying with 'Spanish' parties. However, ETA-M and ETA-PM did not agree on what KAS' functions should be. ETA-PM had, in 1975, wanted KAS to be a mass organisation which would recruit members and carry out activity which could not be undertaken by either branch of ETA. ETA-M's leaders were opposed to an organisation of which they were part carrying out semi-open work, as it would have repeated the problems which the Military Front had experienced in working with people who were not engaged in armed struggle. ETA-M's leaders saw KAS as a forum for settling differences and working out agreements. ETA-PM's leaders had never been happy about the way KAS functioned and so the decision that EIA would participate in the elections had been taken independently. Nevertheless, the leaders of both ETA-PM and EIA were, throughout 1977, in favour of their organisations remaining inside KAS, which was thought to represent some of the social forces which could form a left alliance. The left alliance which EIA and ETA-PM's leaders advocated had to include the 'Spanish' groups which did have some working-class support.[15] The desire for an alliance with 'Spanish' forces was not shared by the other components of KAS, so EIA and ETA-PM began to see it as a relic of the past.[16] The relationship between the party and ETA-PM appeared harmonious in the year following the elections. ETA-PM carried out no armed activities for several months after the expiry of the truce negotiated for the pre-electoral period, which seemed to indicate the ceasefire might become permanent.

This impression was strengthened by ETA-PM's analysis of the changed situation and the strategy deriving from it, which were outlined in an interview given to the new daily newspaper *Egin* at the beginning of October 1977, where an ETA-PM spokesman declared that the main result of the end of the dictatorship was that the masses now became the main protagonists of the struggle.[17] The armed struggle was relegated to a secondary plane, whose function was to support the mass movement and to act when popular actions failed to achieve its objectives. According to ETA-PM the concepts of struggle held by, on the one hand, the moderate mass parties — the PNV and the PSOE — and, on the other hand, the radical nationalists were both mistaken. The PNV and PSOE, it was claimed, believed that the struggle was essentially confined to parliament, while the radical nationalists, who supported ETA-M, concentrated exclusively on holding demonstrations. ETA-PM's leaders, in contrast, believed that the people had to mobilise at all levels. Demonstrations had a place, but were the least solid type of political struggle. The spokesman announced that ETA-PM was to suspend the collection of the 'revolutionary tax' (money extorted from businessmen to finance the organisation's activities), because the split into two ETA's made it difficult to control its collection. The police were able to pose as ETA and thereby create confusion. In addition, big business could afford to hire security men to prevent the tax being levied, which resulted in it being paid mainly by small and medium businesses.

The ETA-PM spokesman also denounced the demonstrators who had attacked PNV and PSOE parliamentarians in San Sebastián on 8 September. Such conduct, it was claimed, allowed the PNV and PSOE to appear as the only serious political forces, harmed the whole Basque left and damaged the fight to achieve a Statute of Autonomy.[19] ETA-PM's statement was a logical development of the ideas which had led to the founding of EIA, and which had been announced in its founding Congress in the spring of 1977. Significantly, the interview said little about what ETA-PM would actually do. This was a problem which was to perplex the organisation, and to which no adequate solution was ever found. ETA-PM's efforts to maintain a profile of armed struggle and at the same time differentiate itself from ETA-M were to lead to a vacillating and incoherent policy and to actions which were often bizarre. In the future these were to range from kidnapping for ransom, closure of cinemas showing erotic films, killing of people alleged to be involved in the drug trade, shooting of the managers of factories involved in industrial disputes, and the placing of bombs in railway stations.[19] ETA-PM was to become an organisation committed to armed struggle, but at a loss to find appropriate targets. Inevitably, the tensions between ETA-PM's actions and EIA's increasingly moderate politics brought the two organisations into conflict. EIA remained illegal, although it had been allowed to function quite openly since 1977, because its statutes declared a commitment to an independent Euskadi. EIA's lack of the legal status which would have enabled it to stand in the elections had been one of the reasons why ETA-PM had taken the initiative in forming the EE coalition. EE's fairly good electoral performance seemed to indicate that, in future elections, many of those who had then abstained would wish to participate. An alliance of all the *Abertzale* forces seemed to be possible and the former PNV leader, Telesforo Monzón, was working towards its creation.[20] Although EIA declared itself to be a revolutionary Marxist-Leninist party, the indications were that most of the people who had voted for EE had much less radical social ideas. Their vote had been cast because of their identification with ETA's nationalist struggle, rather than attraction to Marxist-Leninism.[21]

The party's founding documents declared that EIA's objective was the creation of a socialist society, but allowed for an intermediate stage where capitalists and working class would co-operate in establishing an independent Euskadi.[21] In spite of this the party's ideology and structure were declared to be Marxist-Leninist and to be based on democratic centralism. Such a party, based on the model of the Communist International, was intended to provide the leadership for mass organisations such as trade unions, neighbourhood associations, and a youth movement. In practice, EIA was very far from being the kind of party which its founding statement described. It was essentially the political heir of ETA-PM and its fairly good electoral performance was not matched by any comparable influence in trade union activity or other forms of mass work. Nor did EIA acquire a substantial base of activists which could rival either the left parties or the PNV. In the aftermath of the June 1977 elections, EIA spokesmen were prepared to accept that their party's active support was quite limited, but claimed that this was due to their history as a clandestine armed group. In time EIA would, they were convinced, play the kind of directing role which communist parties had done in Lenin's time.[22]

The discrepancy between EIA's ideology and its social base was soon to produce important divisions within it. The principal representatives of the radical and the moderate tendencies were to be Francisco Letamendía (Ortzi), the party's only representative in Congress, and Mario Onaindía, the hero of the Burgos trial, who became EIA's General Secretary in October 1977.[23] Onaindía realised that the Basque country was far from being ripe for a socialist revolution and that the absence of class-consciousness, combined with the existence of a cross-class opposition to the

Franco regime and subsequently to Spanish centralism, produced a very difficult terrain for socialist activity. The experience of the Franco dictatorship had created a peculiar situation in Euskadi as the level of political involvement was very high, while the level of political understanding was abysmal. Political allegiances were often based on nothing more than following the lead of the most dominant member of the *cuadrilla*. In these circumstances Onaindía considered that the immediate task of socialists was not to carry out a socialist revolution, but to create real political parties, trade unions and similar organisations, which would prepare the way for a socialist future. The mindless radicalism of many nationalists hindered the creation of a united working class which must include the immigrant sections of the Basque population.[24] Onaindía's realisation that the immigrant sector of the Basque population would be antagonised by the chauvinism which was so deep-rooted in Basque nationalism was foreshadowed by the support he had expressed for the Spanish working class during the Burgos trial. The moderate tendency within EIA, which Onaindía represented, was soon to clash with the radical nationalism which existed both within EIA itself, and among the supporters of both ETA-M and ETA-PM. Neither branch of ETA saw the election as disproving their own estimate of the political situation. ETA-M's leaders thought that little had changed, as those who had oppressed Euskadi for so long continued to do so, although they now justified their right to rule by a fraudulent election, where parties whose statutes declared their commitment to Basque independence were still deprived of legal status. ETA-M's leaders considered that the presence of the Spanish police, and fear of a military coup, prevented people from exercising their real choice, and that lack of guarantees against persecution caused patriots to remain in exile. The fact that the left parties and the PNV had chosen to participate in the elections and thereby give political cover to the Suárez regime hardly surprised ETA-M's leaders, but ETA-PM's endorsement of what was seen as a charade was bitterly resented.[25] Not only had ETA-PM declared an indefinite truce, but EIA had formed an electoral alliance with the 'Spanish' MCE, the descendant of the ETA-Berri group, which had been expelled at ETA's Fifth Assembly, thus abandoning the armed struggle and breaking with the united front of patriotic forces formed by KAS.

ETA-M, unlike ETA-PM, had continued its military activities throughout the electoral period, with a campaign of bombings against radio and television stations and attacks on the police. The birth of a parliamentary system, however fraudulent, did have the advantage that it made police repression less effective. After the election, there was a lull in ETA-M's activities, although no truce was called. It seemed for a time that ETA-M was following the path of ETA-PM but such expectations were shattered by the dramatic killing on 8 October of Unzueta Barrenechea, President of the provincial government of Vizcaya, together with two of his bodyguards.[26] This action was to be the beginning of a campaign which was to be more extensive than anything carried out before. It was followed in November by the killing of the commander of the Pamplona police[27] and in December by that of a member of the municipal council in Irún.[28] In a clash with the police in Pamplona in January 1978 two ETA-M members and a policeman were killed,[29] causing the Interior Minister, Martín Villa, to remark 'two to one for us'. ETA-M's campaign produced deaths and imprisonments in its own ranks, and the demand for a further amnesty gathered force as the number of prisoners rose. Another focus for ETA-M's activity was produced by the government's decision to build a nuclear power station, at Lemóniz in Vizcaya, which met with considerable local opposition. ETA-M's attempts to sabotage the construction work were to cause several deaths, the first of whom, David Alvarez, an ETA-M activist, died as a result of planting explosives at the site.[30] The campaign fitted perfectly into the traditional ETA theory of action/repression/action, as it followed a peaceful movement of citizens who were opposed to an enterprise which had been started without legal consultation and had allegedly broken planning and safety regulations. As the citizens' protest had failed to prevent the plant being constructed, ETA-M's action was, according to its theory, a legitimate way of complementing rather than replacing mass activity. The tempo of ETA-M's campaign increased throughout 1977, producing a number of spectacular killings. The targets varied from high ranking military officers to Civil Guards, known right-wingers and suspected informers. There were also a number of robberies, one of the most spectacular of these being the seizure of 900 kilograms of plastic explosive in December 1977.[31] A number of ETA-M members were killed and injured during shoot-outs, produced when police intercepted the organisation's attacks or tried to make arrests.

Most members of organisations which had fought against the Franco regime had, while disagreeing with ETA's methods, accepted that they were a response to the much greater violence exercised by the state. It might have been expected that, with the disappearance of the dictatorship, ETA-M's violence would cease. In fact, both branches of ETA were to achieve a much greater level of violence under a parliamentary democracy than they had done under Franco. For example, in 1975, the last year of Franco's life, the number of people killed by both branches of ETA was six. In 1976 the figure rose to fifteen, in 1977 went down to twelve, but in 1978 it reached sixty-four. By early 1978 it had become obvious that ETA-M was not going to disappear with the dictatorship which had produced it. Right-wing politicians saw the wave of violence as a proof of the inability of a parliamentary democracy to deal with the problem of public order. Both the PSOE and the PNV leaderships argued that it was necessary to negotiate with both branches of ETA in order to bring about an end to violence.[32] The PNV's leadership was far from confident that the autonomy promised to the Basque country by the Suárez government would be adequate, and believed that until a substantial measure of autonomy was obtained, and the police ceased to harass the Basque population, the problem would persist.

The fusion of the *Bereziak* and ETA-M, formally announced in September 1977,[33] strengthened the organisation considerably, while police violence directed at the general population made ETA-M's actions legitimate in many people's eyes. In February 1978 alone, ETA-M shot up several police barracks, wounded six occupants of a police vehicle, wounded a municipal policeman linked to the ultra-right, and set off bombs at a number of offices of Iberduero, the company which was building Lemóniz.[34] In March more police barracks were fired on, two policemen were killed and others wounded in an ambush, a retired Civil Guard sergeant was killed, and a bar owner seriously wounded, all in separate incidents.[35] In addition to such deliberate attacks, two construction workers were killed and fourteen wounded when ETA-M planted bombs on the site of the Lemóniz nuclear power station.[36] However, ETA-M seemed in danger of becoming politically isolated, as the PNV began to make the kind of criticism of it which the 'Spanish' parties had been making for some time. Nevertheless, ETA-M's attacks continued throughout 1978. The victims were mainly policemen, known right-wingers and people accused of being police informers.

ETA-M shocked public opinion when, in June 1978, one of its commandos killed José María Portell, the journalist who had been an intermediary between the Suárez government and ETA-PM in the talks which had produced the pre-election ceasefire.[37] ETA-M's communiqué acknowledging the killing accused Portell of being a police informer, but no evidence was provided for the charge. More significantly perhaps, the communiqué accused Portell of being a 'specialist in intoxication', an indication that ETA-M resented his generally liberal pacificistic writing, and his role in helping to arrange ETA-M's ceasefire. Portell's killing aroused the protests of most political parties, including the PNV, which nevertheless refused to take part in meeting jointly with the 'Spanish' parties to condemn the act.[38] However, ETA-M's campaign was worrying for the PNV and was eventually to cause it to make a vigorous protest, which was to shatter the unity of the nationalist community. The persistence of the campaign produced varying responses from different political forces. Some in the PSOE as well as the PNV continued to argue that it was necessary to negotiate with ETA. More right-wing forces saw ETA-M's wave of violence as a proof that a Spanish democracy was unable to cope with the problem of Basque nationalism and urged that more repressive measures should be taken against violence. The government responded to such pressure in July by passing an 'anti-terrorist' law which gave the police further powers.[39]

The police's lack of success in combating ETA-M's activities provoked it to resort to an indiscriminate repression against the Basque population. In addition, ultra-right terrorist squads made a number of attacks on sympathisers of ETA, both in Spain and in the French Basque country. A pattern emerged of police brutality, protest demonstrations often subjected to violent attacks by the police, and ETA-M retaliation against the police, in a seemingly never-ending circle. Such a pattern had been predicted in the theory of action/repression/action developed by Krutwig in the 1960s, except that the spiral of violence did not reach the stage of the people taking up arms and launching a guerrilla war.[40] ETA-M's considerable support among a section of the population was regularly shown by the demonstrations when its activists were killed, but this had not yet produced a solid organisation.

After the pre-electoral truce negotiated in the spring of 1977, it appeared that ETA-PM had abandoned armed struggle in favour of political action. EIA's fairly good election result and the prominence of well-known ETA-PM veterans in EIA had strengthened the impression, as had the announcement made in September 1977 that the organisation would cease to extort the

197

'revolutionary tax' from industrialists. However, although ETA-PM had negotiated a truce, it had no intention of dissolving. The proposal adopted at the Seventh Assembly, that a number of activists abandon the armed organisation to form the core of EIA, had explicitly provided for the continued existence of ETA-PM. ETA-PM's inactivity throughout 1977 was due partly to the heavy losses it had suffered during 1976. The defection of the *Bereziak* had left ETA-PM with very little manpower or weapons,[41] so its first actions, after a prolonged truce, were designed to remedy the deficiency. In December 1977 one of its action groups attacked a lorry and stole 300 kilograms of explosive, and in another incident in the same month, in Elgoibar, ETA-PM seized 265 guns.[42] The truce enabled ETA-PM to rebuild its organisation, but left unresolved the question of what the functions of an armed organisation in a democracy were, and what should be its relationship with its political associate, EIA. Neither Pertur's original document, *Otsagabia*, nor the resolution adopted at the Seventh Assembly gave really satisfactory answers to these questions. As ETA-PM continued to exist it was inevitable that it would eventually reopen a campaign of violence. As money was necessary to maintain the organisation, funds were obtained, starting with a robbery from the Spanish General Electric Corporation in October 1978.[43] The resumption of the collection of the 'revolutionary tax' which was announced in November 1978 put ETA-PM's finances on a sounder basis,[44] but left unresolved what the purpose of the group's armed activities should be. The resolutions adopted at the Seventh Assembly had stated that the armed organisation should intervene when working-class struggle had reached a limit. ETA-PM was to be the military arm of the working class.[45] If ETA-PM had dissolved, ETA-M reinforced by its fusion with the *Bereziak*, would have the monopoly of ETA's tradition, which would have had disastrous effects on EIA's support among the nationalist population. ETA-PM had, therefore, no choice but to continue in existence, and to maintain the armed struggle. ETA-PM had always criticised what it saw as the indiscriminate nature of ETA-M's violence, and contrasted it with its own carefully selected and planned operations. ETA-PM displayed considerable ingenuity in selecting 'legitimate' targets. In June 1978 it planted a bomb at a government building in Bilbao in protest at the delay in handing over functions to local Basque administration, and in September it succeeded in freeing one of its prisoners from hospital.[46]

During the debate on the proposed constitution, which was opposed by ETA-PM and EIA, ETA-PM's action groups attacked radio stations and cinemas and compelled the staff to transmit communiqués denouncing the constitutional proposals,[47] perhaps an unnecessary action as EIA was able to make such announcements legally, both in parliament and outside. ETA-PM's stress on ideological correctness was apparent even in its choice of people invited to contribute to its 'revolutionary tax', which, a press statement announced, was being levied on those businessmen who were exporting capital from Euskadi.[48] ETA-PM's activities in 1977 and 1978, although involving the use of arms and explosives, produced no deaths and both ETA-PM and EIA condemned ETA-M's more spectacular and bloody actions. When ETA-PM exploded a bomb at the office of the Ministry of Education in San Sebastián it was presented as a protest against the government's refusal to draft a constitution which would devolve administration into Basque hands,[49] and when in November 1978 an official of the Ministry of Education was seized and later released unharmed, the action was justified by the government's failure to assist Basque education.[50] Such actions were very different from the escalation of attacks against policemen and army officers being carried out by ETA-M. ETA-PM partially solved the problem of finding suitable targets by intervening in industrial disputes. Early in December 1978, the organisation kidnapped and wounded an industrialist, José Elícegui, whose workers were on strike.[51] This type of action, combining the 'socialist' and nationalist strands in the organisation's ideology, which became increasingly common for ETA-PM, had a number of precedents in ETA's history, going back to the kidnapping of Zabala and Huarte in 1972 and 1973. Such actions were, not surprisingly, very unpopular with the PNV and with businessmen, uncertain whether membership of the *Pueblo Trabajador Vasco* gave them immunity against such attacks.

In spite of ETA-PM's renewed offensive, relations between it and EIA remained friendly throughout 1978. EIA continued to proclaim itself the heir of ETA, while ETA-PM criticised the activities of ETA-M. EIA's leaders were to make no criticism of ETA-PM until the summer of 1979. The relationship between a legally functioning political party and an illegal armed organisation remained, necessarily, obscure, as contacts between the groups could take place only at an informal level. The amnesty which had freed ETA-PM's prisoners benefited EIA more than

ETA-PM. Veterans such as Goiherri, who remained leaders of the armed group, moved to France,[53] as people with police records were unsuitable for work in the interior. The new activists, young men swept into activity as a result of the mass struggle of the mid 1970s, were impatient of the constraints which EIA's leaders tried to impose on them. When ETA-PM's leaders had decided in 1976 to create EIA they were aware that the militaristic tendency inherent in those participating in an armed struggle would be more likely to lead them to reject advice from the political party than from the 'political' members of ETA-PM. Before the creation of EIA, the 'political' members of the organisation had considerable prestige as they shared much of the risks with the 'military' activists, although they did not themselves engage in armed struggle. Political members provided money, obtained 'safe houses' and transported members of the military wing in their cars. The members of EIA had no such relationship with the ETA-PM's military commandos. The plans for the separation into ETA-PM and EIA had, in order to avoid militaristic deviations, specified that ETA-PM was to retain its own trained political staff, whose presence was evident only in the contents of the communiqués which the organisation issued. Even when ETA-PM's actions became more like those of ETA-M the organisation continued to justify its activities in 'Marxist' terms. As time passed and the familiar cycle of arrests produced a turnover in leadership, ETA-PM's actions became less considered and the new leadership became more distant from EIA.

However, in 1977 and 1978, EIA's main problem was not its relationship with ETA-PM, but with the other *Abertzale* groups. Although disagreement on whether or not to participate in the June elections had split the nationalist forces, it did not end the endeavour to achieve a measure of unity. KAS remained in existence, although ETA-PM/EIA's unilateral decision to stand in the elections showed that it did not function in the way it was supposed to. However, KAS had never been more than a consultative committee, as it lacked any mass base.[54] ETA-M, although it continued to give priority to armed struggle, recognised the need for mass organisations. EE was unsuitable as it did not include most of the left nationalist forces, and did include the 'Spanish' MCE. An alliance to displace EE was needed for the municipal elections to replace the local administration appointed by the government. There was far less nationalist resistance to participation in municipal elections than there had

200

been to standing for the Spanish parliament. The electoral performance of both the PNV and EE seemed to indicate that the
parliamentary elections had been widely accepted, so continued
abstention did not seem an intelligent tactic. Telesforo Monzón
took the lead in trying to organise the electoral coalition, which
eventually became Herri Batasuna (People's Unity). The search
for nationalist unity was not a new initiative for Monzón as within
the PNV he had been a consistent supporter of unity with ETA,
as shown by his sponsorship of Anai-Artea, the centre for Basque
refugees in St. Jean de Luz,[55] and his assistance to ETA-V at its
formation, by acting as spokesman during the Beihl kidnapping.
His expulsion from the PNV in November 1977 freed him from
organisational restraints and made him an ideal figure to promote
the unity of all radical nationalists, which he had tried, unsuccessfully, to create before the June election.[56]

In November 1977, HASI, LAIA, ESB and ANV attended a
meeting called by Monzón in Alsasua in Navarre, which consequently became known as the Mesa de Alsasua.[57] The meeting,
which agreed to form an electoral coalition, was to have far-
reaching consequences for the political life of the Basque country.
The parties coming together were extremely varied and seemed,
on the face of it, unlikely partners. The core of the agreement
accepted by the participants was rejection of the pre-autonomy
institutions created by the Spanish government as an interim
arrangement, until an autonomous Basque parliament could be
elected. The prospect of early municipal elections demonstrated
the need for alliances but did not bring agreement on which allies
to choose. EIA declared that it saw KAS as the nucleus of alliance
of the whole left,[58] while ETA-M also saw the need for a group-
ing which would be wider than KAS and would include groups
such as ESB, which combined social-democratic policies with
radical nationalism, but would exclude 'Spanish' groups such as
EIA's ally the MCE. When in April 1978 the Mesa de Alsasua
was transformed into Herri Batasuna,[59] EIA, while not actually
denouncing the alliance, considered that the project, as conceived
by Monzón and ETA-M, was dangerously exclusive. Mario
Onaindía had, in January 1978, proposed the slogan 'Unity of the
Basque left', rather than 'Unity of the left *Abertzales*', a formula
which expressed the desire to ally with 'Spanish' groups such as
the ORT and the MCE. Onaindía was concerned about the
dangers of ignoring the feelings of immigrant workers who did not
identify with the nationalist tradition.[60] His opinion that Herri

Batasuna was a ragbag of incompatible tendencies, without much of a future, seemed justified, yet that organisation prospered even when some of the parties who formed the alliance went out of existence.

The emergence of Telesforo Monzón as Herri Batasuna's main spokesman surprised some of his ex-colleagues, but was consistent with his long-held beliefs. Since joining the PNV in the early 1930s Monzón had been insistent that everything else must be subordinated to the attainment of Basque independence. Thus, although he had been part of the conservative wing of the PNV, he had always been prepared to make alliances with whoever would help to achieve that end. While sharing leadership of Herri Batasuna with radical 'Marxist-Leninists' he proudly proclaimed himself a *Jelkide* (a 'follower of God and the old laws').[67] During the Civil War he had been deeply resentful at the Spanish republican government's attempts to prevent the Basque forces signing a separate peace with Franco and in the late 1940s he had been in favour of the PNV coming to an agreement with Don Juan, the Pretender to the Spanish throne, independently of the Spanish republican forces.[62] When the PNV and the Basque government in exile preferred to maintain its alliance with the Spanish republicans, he resigned from the government. Helping to form Herri Batasuna was the latest step in consistent attempts to achieve unity of all those whom he considered to be patriotic Basques.

Herri Batasuna's main organiser was ESB's General Secretary Inaki Aldecoa.[63] The leaders of ETA-PM and EIA were deeply suspicious of ESB, for what they considered as its murky antecedents.[64] ESB was essentially an attempt to widen the range of Basque nationalist appeal by obtaining votes from those who would not be attracted by the PNV and might otherwise vote for the PSOE. ESB's performance at the 1977 election was disappointing, but not catastrophic (it got 5.5% of the vote in Guipúzcoa),[65] so in the aftermath of the election its activists were not despondent. They claimed that their vote combined with that of EE was a better indication of the sociological base of support for their politics than their own vote alone, as the support for EE was a vote for ETA's heroes. The fact that some of EIA's leaders had Marxist-Leninist notions was irrelevant, while their alliance with the 'Spanish' MCE was absurd.[66] ESB claimed it would not present parliamentary candidates who were not Basque speakers, an attitude which contrasted sharply with that of EE, whose best known candidates in 1977 did not speak *Euskera*.[67]

Aldecoa was convinced that there was a social base for a broad nationalist coalition.[68] As a Navarrese, he was acutely conscious of the need for Basque nationalists to form a united front. In Navarre, where nationalists of all tendencies were in a minority, neither ESB nor EE had stood candidates in the 1977 elections. Similar considerations influenced another moderate political party, Acción Nacionalista Vasco (ANV), to join Herri Batasuna. ANV was the moribund left nationalist party of the 1930s, revived in 1976 by a former ETA member, Valentín Solagaistu. ANV's leaders had considered before the election that older people would not be prepared to vote for new parties,[69] and that the forces round KAS would disappear, whereas ANV would benefit from its main political asset, the support of a number of former commanders in the Basque army during the Civil War. However, the ANV's leaders were proved wrong.

The most left-wing component of Herri Batasuna was LAIA, the organisation formed by the members of ETA's Workers Front after its split from ETA in 1974. While LAIA's positions on the need for a mass movement, which was not subordinate to an armed group, were similar to those which had produced ETA-Berri and ETA-VI it, unlike these earlier splits, had formed a Basque revolutionary party, rather than uniting with groups outside the Basque country.[70] LAIA had adhered to the 'assemblyist' conceptions common on the Spanish left during the 1970s, which advocated that all important decisions should be made at meetings of the entire workforce. It had been divided over whether to support the left nationalist union, LAB, or another organisation, Langile Abertzale Batzordea (LAK) (Patriotic Workers Committee) based on assemblyist principles.[71] As a consequence of these divergences, LAIA itself suffered a split in 1976. The LAIA faction, EZ, (meaning no) which rejected what it saw as the majority's reformism, was anarchistic and soon disintegrated, some of its members uniting with a splinter from the *Bereziak* to form the Comandos Autónomos Anti-capitalistas (CAA),[72] a group which was to distinguish itself by killing a number of its political opponents.

The founding of EIA by ETA-PM in late 1976 had put LAIA in something of a dilemma, for while EIA's creation implicitly acknowledged that the Workers' Front had been right to create a political party in 1974, it also occupied LAIA's 'political space'. Incorporation into Herri Batasuna, while surprising, given

LAIA's history and principles, was understandable in the light of its failure to establish a strong presence of its own. In March 1977 a LAIA spokesman had expressed similar political ideas to those of EIA,[73] but LAIA's leaders disagreed with EIA's decision to stand in the elections, rather than abide by the collective decision of the groups in KAS. As a small party, LAIA had looked to KAS as an important forum for its ideas, and had always been critical of what it saw as ETA-PM's and EIA's casual attitude to it. LAIA wanted KAS to be a genuine forum and decision-taker, not just a meeting place for ETA's two rival branches.[74] LAIA's loyalty to KAS and subsequently to Herri Batasuna was to lead it to come full circle, by becoming part of a support group for ETA-M, in spite of its own origin in 1974 as a rejection against domination by an armed organisation. Formally Herri Batasuna was merely an electoral alliance, created to fight the municipal elections which were, in the event, not held until April 1979. Some kind of electoral alliance was a necessity for left nationalists if they were not to be crushed by the PNV and the PSOE. However, ESB and LAIA found that Herri Batasuna had destroyed the basis of their own separate existence as it was dominated by ETA-M, although that organisation was a sympathiser, not an actual member. LAIA in particular found that discussion was pointless as the political line was decided by the absent partner, ETA-M.[75]

As for the other political parties in the alliance, the ANV barely existed, while HASI acted merely as a spokesman for ETA-M, and did not develop any of the activities normally associated with a political party. In theory the constitution of Herri Batasuna provided radical nationalism with an elaborate network of organisations which instituted a division of labour and formed alliances at different levels. HASI provided ETA-M with a sympathetic political party which was supposed to play the same role as did EIA in regard to ETA-PM. The next level of alliances was provided by KAS, which united those groups which accepted ETA's tradition. Herri Batasuna was, in theory, a fairly broad alliance whose members need not be unconditional supporters of ETA-M. LAB, the nationalist trade union created by LAIA and ETA-V, had an uneasy relationship with the radical nationalist network, as many of its members supported the line of EIA and ETA-PM. The system of alliances was very flexible and could incorporate bodies such as neighbourhood associations, a youth movement and committees formed to fight for the release of ETA's prisoners. The comprehensive nature of the organisations and the absence of the bureaucratic structures typical of political parties was supposed to provide a model of democratic functioning.

Opponents of Herri Batasuna maintained that the theoretically elaborated organisational structure was merely a façade, and that Herri Batasuna's real structure consisted of a number of personalities who issued statements, or called demonstrations, according to ETA-M's wishes.[76] Certainly, the division of labour between the various components of the radical nationalist alliance was unclear in principle, and non-existent in practice. For example, demonstrations might be called by Herri Batasuna, KAS, HASI or the amnesty committees either separately or jointly. However, even if the organisational structure which ETA-M's supporters described was imaginary, or fraudulent, Herri Batasuna was able, from 1978 onwards, to mount demonstrations which were much larger than those of either the 'Spanish' Left or EIA/EE. The formation of Herri Batasuna, by including chauvinistic and reformist parties such as ESB and excluding the revolutionary 'Spanish' left, was seen by ETA-PM and EIA as an obstacle to their long-held desire to unite the national and the social struggle. ETA-PM/EIA's project of overcoming the traditional division in Basque society between a nationalist movement which was reactionary on social and economic issues, and a socialist movement which was blind to the reality of national oppression, made it particularly hostile to ESB, which had been formed precisely to provide nationalism with a modern image which would help it to resist the 'Spanish' menace.

EIA's rejection of Herri Batasuna was part of a gradual drawing away from radical nationalism, which was soon to produce dissension in its own ranks. Mario Onaindía, who was appointed General Secretary of EIA in September 1977, realised that a revolution which would establish an independent socialist Euskadi was unlikely in the foreseeable future. He and his co-thinkers Múgica Arregui, Uriarte and Erreka thought that it was possible to obtain a substantial statute of autonomy and to build a Basque socialist party.[77] This perspective, which led EIA to accept the need to work within the CGV was only the first of the post-election decisions which widened the distance between EIA and the other radical nationalist tendencies. In spite of the fact that the CGV had no real power, EIA spokesmen continued to insist that revolutionaries had an important job to do there. ETA-M's followers, in contrast, saw the main function of the CGV as legitimating the exclusion of Navarre from Euskadi. EIA's spokesmen declared that it was necessary to work within the CGV, even though it covered only three of the four Basque provinces.[78] EIA, in January 1978, took another step which was to outrage most radical nationalists when it decided to amend its statutes in order to become legally recognised.[79] EIA had been able to operate quite freely, but a legal status had obvious advantages.

EIA's willingness to alter its statutes contrasted with LAIA's and HASI's refusal to do so, and provoked criticism from those parties,[80] as did EIA's attitude to the Mesa de Alsasua. It was clear that EIA's political orientation was diverging more and more from the other components of KAS. ETA-PM/EIA's decision to form the EE coalition with the MCE had been taken partly because of its disillusion with KAS. By the spring of 1978, EIA spokesmen were announcing that KAS was a relic of the past,[81] while still proclaiming a desire to be part of a left nationalist electoral alliance. There were, however, some remaining areas of agreement between EIA and the other *Abertzale* parties. For example, they were all united in opposing the centralist elements in the proposals for a new Constitution, which was being debated in parliament throughout 1978. EIA's parliamentary representatives, Letamendía and Bandres, proposed amendments which would have permitted Basque independence.[82] However, the growing antagonism between EIA and Herri Batasuna was based on disagreement on whether the June 1977 elections had made any fundamental change in either Spain or the Basque country. The leaders of ETA-M and Herri Batasuna believed that the elections had not ended the dictatorship or abolished the political system instituted by Franco. This belief seemed absurd to the Spanish left, while EIA and ETA-PM's attitudes were ambiguous. EIA's actions became increasingly contradictory as it participated in Parliament and the CGV, while at the same time continuing to give political support to ETA-PM. The claim that nothing had really changed was largely based on the behaviour of the police, whose attacks on nationalist sympathisers continued, just as they had done in the last years of the dictatorship.

One such attack occurred in May 1978 when hundreds of armed men in civilian clothes rioted in the centre of Pamplona, attacking the offices of left-wing and nationalist parties,[83] and assaulting bystanders, in a response to the deaths of two Civil Guards at the hands of ETA-M. Another even worse incident occurred in July in the same city, during the festival of San Fermín, the high point of the year in Pamplona, when after a bullfight a group of demonstrators took the opportunity to parade with banners demanding amnesty. The police opened fire, killing Germán Rodríguez, a member of the LCR-LKI (the successor to ETA-VI), and pursued the demonstrators beyond the bullring, firing indiscriminately, injuring scores of people, and causing the festival to be abandoned.[84] Typically, such incidents produced protest demonstrations, violent repression by the police, and sometimes the killing of police by ETA-M as a reprisal, a pattern of events which seemed to illustrate the action/repression/action theory. There were often strikes in protest against the police action, but these were smaller than those of the last years of the dictatorship, an indication of the growing hostility of the left parties to ETA-M's actions.

A particularly bizarre example of police misbehaviour occurred in July 1978 in the town of Renteria, near San Sebastián, where police fired rubber bullets at the balconies of houses and damaged and looted property. Pictures of the police eating cakes looted from a baker's shop appeared in the newspapers and created widespread resentment.[85] Such incidents ensured that the campaign *Que se Vayan* launched by EIA for the withdrawal of the police was popular among large sections of the population. In addition to police violence the nationalist population was subjected to attacks by armed ultra-right groups on people suspected of being sympathetic to either branch of ETA. The ultra-right actions included the murder of a taxi driver in Guipúzcoa in October 1977[86] and an attack on Etxabe, the former leader of ETA-V's Military Front, in St. Jean de Luz in July 1978, which wounded him and killed his wife.[87] Paradoxically, police violence was seen as more of a threat than it had been under Franco, when, as demonstrations were generally forbidden, there was less likelihood of the clashes which became common in 1977 and 1978. The left parties, and the PNV, criticised the government for not imposing discipline and removing known ultra-right officers, and proposed that the police in the Basque country should be brought under the control of the CGV.[88] The PSOE and the PCE believed that the violence on both sides was a hangover from the Franco era. If ETA would cease its attacks on the police, and there was a purge of ultra-right officers, combined with an exercise of discipline by the government, they believed the spiral of violence and reprisals would be broken.

, For supporters of ETA-M, this approach was a superficial one, which concentrated on the personalities of some policemen instead of emphasising their roles as an army of occupation. ETA-M became particularly angry at the increasingly critical attitude to it of the PNV, PSOE and PCE. The argument that there were historically two stages to ETA's activity, one justifiable under Franco, and a later one which was not, appeared hypocritical to ETA-M's supporters. A Herri Batasuna leader, Miguel Castells, claimed that the parties which now celebrated a very limited democracy were able to do so as a result of ETA's struggle, which remained as necessary, and valid, under Suárez as under Franco.[89] The PSOE's leaders thought that Spain's infant democracy faced a very real problem in having a police force bitterly distrustful of democracy, but believed that ETA-M and the policemen belonging to ultra-right groups complemented each other in creating a spiral of violence, which endangered the democracy which both detested.[90] The PSOE's growing hostility to both branches of ETA was shared by the PCE, so that the rift between nationalists and the left began to re-create the situation which had existed before the Civil War. The hostility of the 'Spanish' left was not a surprise to ETA-M which had always regarded it as social-imperialist. As the 'Spanish' left had little strength in the areas where ETA-M had its main support its comments could be ignored. The criticisms made by the PNV, although expressed in much more cautious terms, constituted a much greater problem.

Although the June 1977 election results had, for the first time, given the PSOE more votes than the PNV in the Basque country and Navarre, the PNV's success in establishing itself as the leading political force was to astonish both the revolutionary and the moderate left. If the founders of Ekin in the early 1950s had considered the PNV as a spent force, this had seemed even more so in the period before June 1977. Yet the PNV had received a very much higher vote than any of the nationalist forces which sought to replace it and claimed to have 83,000 members.[91] The party benefited from the prestige of historic leaders such as Leizaola and Ajuriaguerra, who had participated in the Civil War and had maintained the Basque government in exile, but its effective leadership had been transferred to younger men such as Javier Arzallus, a former Jesuit, and Carlos Garaicoechea, a Navarrese businessman, in March 1977 at a party congress held legally in Pamplona. Although these men had played almost no part in the resistance to Franco they proved capable politicians. Much of the PNV's success was due to its promotion of social and cultural activities. Throughout 1977 and 1978 the PNV established *Batzokis* (PNV headquarters) in towns and villages all over

Euskadi. Some were little more than bars, others were the local administrative headquarters of the party, with an extensive network of cultural activities consisting of dancing, folklore and music. The PSOE's attempt to revive its own *Casas del Pueblo* was much less successful.

The PNV also exercised a strong influence in a variety of organisations, ranging from eating clubs and savings banks to chambers of commerce. It soon became apparent that the party held a crucial position as arbiter in the struggle between radical nationalism and the central government. The PNV leaders hoped for an autonomy statute as generous 'as that granted in 1936, but knew that its scope would be affected by the government's awareness that concessions to regional nationalism might provoke a military coup. The violent actions of ETA-M, and later of ETA-PM, were a major factor in provoking a backlash from elements in the army who suspected that a statute of autonomy might be merely a stage on the secession of Euskadi from Spain. The majority of the PNV leaders had no intention of trying to set up a completely independent Euskadi, and were well aware of the overwhelming obstacles to doing so. Nevertheless, in response to the pressure from their own rank and file, the PNV leaders did sometimes demand independence.[92] The PNV's leaders also knew that both branches of ETA had wide support among the Basque population. Sensitivity to these factors made them reluctant to condemn either branch of ETA too harshly or to show themselves willing to accept the Constitution which the Spanish parliament was debating throughout 1978. The PNV leaders' caution, combined with occasional nationalist rhetoric, made it seem to 'Spanish' political forces that the party was playing a double game, in presenting a public face of a moderate, conservative party, anxious to play its part in building a democratic Spain, while at the same time acting as a respectable cover for ETA's terrorism.

The 'Spanish' parties' criticism of the PNV sharpened as, in late 1978, parliament came close to agreement on a Constitution which would permit a considerable degree of Basque autonomy. The PNV's objection to the Constitution seemed, from the viewpoint of the 'Spanish' parties, to be based on archaic and irrelevant criteria.[93] For example, the PNV leaders and the press they controlled demanded the restoration of both the Foral rights which had been abolished in 1876 and of the *Conciertos Económicos* which had replaced them and had existed up till Franco's victory. PNV spokesmen's revival of the formula of a pact between the Basque people and the Crown as a way to achieve Basque autonomy seemed, to 'Spanish' politicians, to be an absurd way to approach modern problems. In parliament the PNV's representatives voted for a constitutional amendment moved by EE's congressman Letamendía, which would give autonomous regions the right to federate, while the PSOE voted against.[94] The PNV leaders took the campaign for the restoration of the *Conciertos Económicos* outside parliament by organising a massive demonstration, in Bilbao in June 1978, which was supported by other nationalist groups, but not by the PSOE or the PCE.[95] The unity of the anti-Franco forces was crumbling, as the left-wing parties became more willing to compromise with the UCD, particularly on the question of regional autonomy. The PNV's commitment to the *Conciertos Económicos* was reflected in its press which carried numerous articles on that theme.[96]

The PNV leaders' conviction that they now had to fight against all the 'Spanish' parties was shown at the end of September 1978, in simultaneous demonstrations called in Bilbao, San Sebastián and Vitoria, demanding the reintroduction of the *Fueros*. The slogans carried stressed the prosperity of the Basque country and alleged that Basque wealth was subsidising Spain.[97] As the fragile unity of the anti-Franco parties dissolved, the PNV now saw the PSOE, which was now broadly in agreement with the UCD on the acceptable limits to Basque autonomy, as its principal enemy.[98] The PNV leaders were particularly resentful of the PSOE's claim to be the majority party in Euskadi. The fact that the PSOE had received more votes than the PNV was from a nationalist viewpoint irrelevant, given the large immigrant component of its vote. As the PNV's grass-roots organisation was immeasurably stronger than that of the PSOE, the PNV's leaders were confident that, when municipal elections were held, the PSOE would not make up for its lack of suitable candidates and local organisation.

The PNV leadership had to recognise that their amendments to the Constitution designed to permit a semi-independent Euskadi could not succeed against the opposition of nearly all the other parliamentary forces. Yet the PNV's leadership could not formally abandon their historical objective of achieving independence without antagonising their own members. The apparently archaic nature of the PNV's demands were, actually, a means of presenting an acceptance of autonomy within the Spanish state as a renewal of ancient rights, and thereby satisfying the more radical members of the Party. The PNV leadership responded to internal disagreement by calling a special conference to decide if the party should vote in favour of the Constitution.[99] The crucial role of the PNV was highlighted by the fact that the debates in parliament were supplemented by direct negotiations between itself and the government. As relations between the PNV and PSOE worsened, in the autumn of 1978, its journal *Deia* published articles almost every day, refuting the PSOE allegation that the PNV's lack of enthusiasm for the new Constitution made it an enemy of democracy.[100]

The PNV's special conference held on 29 October gave the parliamentary leaders freedom to decide on how to vote on the Constitution.[101] A vote against the Constitution would be interpreted, by the 'Spanish' parties, as an indication that the PNV was unwilling to accept the new democratic Spain. A vote in favour, on the other hand, would be seen by many PNV members as an abandonment of the party's historic aims. However, the PNV leaders were in a strong position to bargain. The Suárez government needed the PNV's approval, or at least benevolent neutrality, if the Constitution and, eventually, the autonomy provisions were to be accepted by the majority of the Basque population. Tough negotiation by the PNV would affect the extent of the autonomy to be granted. The activities of ETA-M had a more questionable effect. On the one hand, they enraged the army and thereby reduced the government's possibility of making concessions to Basque aspirations. On the other hand, they showed the danger of trying to impose a solution which would be unacceptable to the mainstream of Basque nationalism. To that extent, the actions of both wings of ETA and the PNV were complementary. The PNV disapproved of ETA's methods but argued that the police methods favoured by the Interior Minister played into ETA-M's hands.[102]

As the final stage of approving the constitution approached, Carlos Garaicoechea, the PNV chairman, announced at a Madrid press conference early in October, that the PNV would find it very difficult to vote for the Constitution as it stood, minus his party's amendments, reclaiming the Basque country's traditional rights.[103] Garaicoechea's anger had been provoked by the UCD's action in introducing additional clauses into the Constitution, which strengthened its centralist content. The PSOE abstained on the UCD's amendments, which from the PNV's point of view amounted to supporting the government's proposals and made the

PNV leaders fear that the UCD and PSOE might come to an agreement which would be unacceptable to the PNV. The PSOE wanted to dissolve the Basque government in exile,[104] but the PNV knew that as long as the exiled government existed, it could plausibly be claimed that the Suárez government and its local Basque representatives were not legitimate. In mid-1978, the PNV press accentuated its support for the exiled government and its president Leizaola, and attacked the non-Basque character of the 'Spanish' parties. The PSOE, for its part, regarded such attacks as illustrations of the PNV's traditional chauvinism. Its voters were, they considered, as Basque as were the PNV's. The PNV leaders' insistence on the 'Spanish' nature of its rivals necessarily meant an accentuation of the party's own ethnic character. The PNV leaders constantly repeated that the 'Madrid' politicians could not be expected to understand Basque reality. Arzallus suggested that the Basque institution, the *cuadrilla*, could be a method of saving the Basque language, because while the presence of a single Spanish speaker in a group of people forced bilingual members of the group to speak Spanish, the closed circle of the Basque speaking *cuadrilla* could create an environment where only *Euskera* need be spoken.[105]

The PNV's emphasis on historical rights rather than modern needs bewildered and annoyed the 'Spanish' parties, but apparently archaic demands such as those for the restitution of the *Fueros* were in fact an intelligent way to make a good bargain with the central government, while remaining responsive to the doubts of the PNV's own constituency. The PNV leaders' tactics in dealing with the problems caused by ETA-M's violence were based on the knowledge that many of its own members felt an emotional identification with ETA, seeing it as a group of heroic young men carrying on the fight against 'Spanish' oppression, rather than as a hostile political tendency. Many PNV members wanted a complete amnesty including the return of exiled members of ETA, as a step towards achieving an independent Euskadi, and continued to support the committees which campaigned on behalf of those imprisoned after the expiry of the 1977 amnesty. Nevertheless, the PNV could not fail to be concerned at the effects of ETA-M's killings and robberies, which in 1978 reached a higher level than ever before. Bank robberies and the extortion of a 'revolutionary tax' levied on business and professional people were not popular with a party which realised that ETA's violence could strike at its own ranks. Angel Berazadi, who had been kidnapped and murdered by ETA-PM in the summer of 1976, had been a PNV sympathiser, while Carlos Garaicoechea, the PNV's chairman, had had business and professional connections with Huarte, who had been kidnapped by ETA-V in 1973. The PNV consistently issued statements condemning ETA killings and could claim to be more genuinely opposed to violence than the government was, since it also condemned the killings[106] by ultra-right groups such as the *Batallón Vasco-Español*, which were widely believed to be linked to the security forces.

ETA had originated in the PNV and had been strengthened by subsequent recruitment from the PNV's youth movement and by individuals from PNV families. ETA was part of the nationalist community and its members were linked to PNV sympathisers by ties of blood and friendship. While specific actions of ETA might provoke hostility, it was not seen as an enemy of the Basque community as the 'Spanish' parties were. Even its 'Marxism' could be forgiven, if it did not lead to a renunciation of nationalism. In contrast, the PNV did see the 'Spanish' Marxist groups as enemies intent on ruining the Basque economy.[107] The PNV was however concerned at the escalation of ETA-M's campaign, which jeopardised the prospect of achieving Basque autonomy. The party decided to make a sharp public demonstration of its condemnation of the methods of both branches of ETA by calling a mass demonstration in Bilbao against all political violence, on 28 October 1978.[108] Characteristically, the PNV, rejecting the PSOE's suggestion that the demonstration should be called by the Consejo General Vasco, convened it in its own name, in order to emphasise its own hegemonic position, and to deflect charges from supporters of ETA-M and Herri Batasuna that it was breaking the unity of the nationalist community, in the face of the 'Spanish' enemy. While some other political forces were allowed to support the demonstration, it was to remain the PNV's responsibility.

The decision to make such a strong public demonstration against ETA's violence was unpopular with many PNV supporters, so the party launched a massive campaign in the newspaper *Deia*, which for several weeks was turned into a campaigning vehicle for the demonstration, sometimes carrying several articles on the subject in a single day.[109] The 'debate' over supporting the demonstrations was rather one-sided in that *Deia*, which was controlled by the liberal tendency, then led by Arzallus, did not generally carry articles reflecting the view of the more intransigent nationalists. The PNV leadership made it clear that in calling the demonstration it was not accepting the Spanish Constitution, but the fact that 'Spanish' parties were allowed to participate aroused fears among some of the party's supporters that the PNV was uniting with opponents of the nationalist community to attack other nationalists. The PNV's leaders attempted to calm such fears by public speeches and articles in *Deia*.[110] In a meeting in Tafalla, in Navarre, where both Arzallus and Garaicoechea explained the need for the demonstration, Garaicoechea insisted that the PNV had a clear position of condemning all violence, not just that of ETA, while Arzallus argued that the demonstration would halt the government's offensive against Basque rights.[111] When the decision to hold the demonstration was strongly attacked in statements by ETA-M, Herri Batasuna and KAS spokesmen,[112] the PNV replied by stating that it would consider cancelling it if ETA-M would announce a ceasefire.[113] ETA-M repeated its request to call off the demonstration, pointing out that it had never sought confrontation with the PNV as it had always recognised that the party represented the interests of a part of the *Pueblo Trabajador Vasco*. ETA-M stated that it also supported the slogan of the demonstration 'Euskadi free and at peace', but that it would not halt the armed struggle until the government agreed to accept a five-point negotiating platform proposed by KAS.[114] The PNV's determination to proceed opened up a breach in the nationalist community which greatly disturbed Herri Batasuna supporters who were unconcerned about attacks from the PSOE or PCE. Txillardegi, for example, stated that the Basque people would 'experience 28 October as a tragedy', and criticised the PNV for not consulting its base.[115] The party was, he alleged, abandoning its nationalist principles and behaving in the same way as it had done in parliament in the 1930s, when it had compromised with 'Spanish' forces. Garaicoechea remained adamant, declaring that those who wanted the demonstration to be cancelled should demand that ETA-M, which was, he complained, still extorting money from businessmen, should call a ceasefire. He also denied that the decision to go ahead with the demonstration had caused internal revolt in the PNV.[116] There were however hints of the internal struggle going on; for example, an article in *Deia* by Sabin de Zubiri, a member of the PNV's Vizcayan provincial committee, which admitted that the decision to call the demonstration had initially caused surprise among the rank and file.[117]

While the PNV's action was a severe blow to those who wanted unity of all the nationalist forces, it allowed Herri Batasuna to exploit the resentment of the PNV's rank and file. Herri Batasuna called its own demonstration, also in Bilbao, on the same day. The belief that the PNV leadership was under internal attack seemed plausible, judging from the stream of articles in *Deia* supporting the demonstration by veteran PNV leaders and intellectual figures.[118] Luis de Arredonda, who had been a leader of the party in the 1930s, went so far as to claim that the decision to call the demonstration was comparable in importance to the one forcibly to oppose Franco's rising.[119] While the dispute with Herri Batasuna bewildered and troubled many PNV members, ETA-M's continuing military escalation throughout October made it necessary for the PNV to condemn a campaign which had reached frightening proportions. More than a dozen people, including two naval officers, were killed by ETA-M and the CAA during October.[120] The government's unwillingness to proceed with the granting of Basque autonomy, while policemen and others were being killed on such a scale, was reiterated in a statement made by Suárez' right-hand man, Abril Martorell, that no autonomy statute would be granted while the violence continued. Garaicoechea, still anxious not to appear to be uncritically supporting the 'Spanish' forces, insisted that the PNV did not want a confrontation with Herri Batasuna's rival demonstration, and asked that the police should not attack it.[121]

The PNV's condemnation of ETA's violence did not go far enough to satisfy the 'Spanish' parties. PSOE spokesman Txiki Benegas continued to regret that the Consejo General Vasco (CGV) had not itself called the demonstration.[122] The PCE regretted the PNV's hostile attitude to the Constitution which was nearing the final stage of agreement, and wanted a large-scale popular mobilisation in its support when it would be submitted for approval in a referendum.[123] The right-wing 'Spanish' parties were even more critical. A spokesman for Alianza Popular (AP), the party led by Fraga Iribarne, announced that it would not participate in the demonstration because it objected to the allegedly secessionist nature of its main slogan — 'Euskadi free and at peace'.[124] The decision could only be welcome to the PNV as the idea of marching together with the supporters of Fraga, who was held responsible for the killing of a number of innocent people in his period as Minister of the Interior in 1976, would have been quite unacceptable to most PNV supporters. Even the UDC was unwelcome as the PNV national committee asked that it stay away, in a press statement which stressed that the party's own stewards would maintain order, and that the slogans carried would stress opposition to violence from whichever direction it came, not just that of ETA.[125] Such even-handedness did nothing to mollify Herri Batasuna which, together with the amnesty committees, had organised the counter-demonstration which would march from Bilbao to the mountain of Archanda, where in 1937 the last battle against Franco's army had been fought, before the surrender of Bilbao. This demonstration's main slogan was 'With the fighters of yesterday and today', linking the struggle of the Basque army in 1937 with that of ETA, to the annoyance of those ex-soldiers who supported the PNV's demonstration.[126]

The conflict presented difficulties for ETA-PM and the political organisations — EIA and EE — which had sprung from it. ETA-PM and EIA argued that both demonstrations provoked an unfortunate division in the nationalist camp, and that neither should be supported.[127] EIA itself was torn by internal disputes, between the tendencies led by its General Secretary, Mario Onaindía, who was moving towards a policy of accepting the limitations of parliamentary democracy, and EE's Congressman Letamendía's more radical intransigent line. The PNV's demonstration was a massive success as the number of participants was claimed as 60,000, the great majority of whom were its own supporters. The route of the demonstration was changed to avoid clashing with the rival march, which was broken up, violently, by the police. The PNV leaders were exultant, as the headline 'Mission Accomplished' in *Deia* showed.[128] The party had, by its extraordinary mobilisation, shown that despite the low level of activities under the dictatorship, it had deep roots in Basque society. The PNV, rightly, saw the demonstration as a proof that it was the most important political force in Euskadi. Herri Batasuna's leaders drew different conclusions from the event, and especially from the violent dispersal of their own demonstration by the police. The PNV was seen as finally having become a 'Spanish' party, by having come .out against ETA-M's struggle. The mobilisation for Herri Batasuna's demonstration was also impressive, for although it was smaller than the PNV's the participants were younger and included leading members of EIA, such as Letamendía, López Irasuegui, one the heroes of the Burgos trial, and leading independents such as Periko Solaberría, a worker-priest who had stood as an EE parliamentary candidate in Vizcaya.[129] It seemed to ETA-M supporters that as the PNV had definitely abandoned the struggle for Basque independence, and the political formations inspired by ETA-PM were fragmenting, Herri Batasuna and ETA-M were the only legitimate heirs of the nationalist tradition. Herri Batasuna's leaders knew that the PNV was deeply divided by the decision to hold the demonstration and that the traditional conservative members of its *sabiniano* tendency were suspicious that the party's doctrine was being abandoned.[130] If both the PNV and EIA were to accept the rules of the game, as laid down by the Constitution, ETA-M and Herri Batasuna would have no rivals in their efforts to lead the movement to gain independence for Euskadi.

When, three days after the PNV's demonstration, both houses of the Spanish parliament approved the final draft of the Constitution, the PNV abstained. In a measured statement during the final debate, Arzallus insisted that his party had no wish to adopt attitudes which might appear aggressive. It was clear that the PNV's leaders, while unable to vote on the Constitution, were prepared to work within the boundaries of the political system set by it, an attitude which was in marked contrast to that of EE Congressman, Letamendía, and Senator Bandrés, both of whom voted against the Constitution. Letamendía, during the final debate, delivered a harsh attack on what he saw as the treason of the PNV, while Bandrés was much more conciliatory.[131] The different emphasis was an indication of the differences which were growing within EE/EIA and which shortly afterwards caused Letamendía to give up his seat in Congress. The PNV members of Parliament denied that their abstention showed an unwillingness to work for an end to violence in Euskadi and argued that pacification could not be achieved by the police methods employed by the UCD government. In a Congress debate on violence, the PNV representatives presented a 15-point programme for pacification, the key points of which included a restoration of the *Conciertos Económicos*, the creation of an autonomous Basque police force, measures to promote *Euskera* and a government assurance not to delay the promised municipal elections.[132]

Although the PNV's opponents charged that its failure to vote for the Constitution gave implicit support to ETA-M, such criticism had little influence on the party. Its abstention did not prevent the Constitution from coming into operation, while an open acceptance that Euskadi was to be permanently denied independence would have been opposed by the intransigent nationalists among its own members, and would have perhaps strengthened the appeal of Herri Batasuna among sectors of the population who might otherwise vote for the PNV. In addition, the PNV leaders knew that the degree of autonomy granted would depend on many factors, not least on the struggle carried on by the PNV itself, as there were powerful forces in Spanish society which were unhappy about conceding Basque autonomy. They also knew that the Spanish government was torn between the need to concede enough autonomy to satisfy the majority of the Basque population, and therefore reduce support for ETA, and the fear that too many concessions to Basque nationalism would encourage a military coup. As the PNV had abstained in the vote in parliament on the Constitution, it urged its supporters to abstain in the referendum which was held on 6 December.[133] The Constitution was overwhelmingly approved, but abstention was nearly twice as high in the Basque country as in Spain as a whole, arguably a good indication of the PNV's influence. In Guipúzcoa and Vizcaya, the most nationalist provinces, the abstention rate was around 56%. In addition, there were a large number of spoiled and blank ballot papers throughout the Basque country, which could plausibly be considered as indicating an abstentionist position.[134] The referendum result, combined with the PNV's earlier success in mounting the demonstration against violence, showed that, despite the misgivings of its more traditional supporters, the PNV was well placed to benefit from the new political situation. The numbers voting against acceptance of the Constitution gave little indication of the weight of either branch of ETA, both of whom had urged rejection, as the extreme right had advocated the same position.

PNV leaders reacted angrily to critics such as Felipe González who accused it of hypocrisy, alleging that it would have voted for the Constitution if it had thought that approval depended on the PNV's own support.[135] The PNV daily, *Deia*, took great satisfaction from an editorial in the Madrid journal *El País*, which recognised that the party had shown itself to be the hegemonic force in the Basque country and expressed the hope that, having made its demonstration of strength, the PNV would now accept the Constitution and democracy, rather than joining the 'rejection front' of the *Abertzale* parties.[136] Herri Batasuna and ETA-M continued to oppose the PNV, while benefiting from the fact that that party's dominance showed the strength of nationalism in Euskadi. ETA-PM and EIA were in much more difficult positions as the split between nationalist and 'Spanish' communities showed the impossibility of uniting the national and social struggles.

REFERENCES

1. 'ETA frente a las elecciones legislativas', *Documentos Y*, Vol. 16, p. 319.
2. See interview with ETA-PM leader José Etxegarai Gastearena (Mark) in *Deia*, 27 Dec. 1977.
3. 'Communicado de ETA a la clase trabajadora y a todo el pueblo vasco', *Documentos Y*, Vol. 18, p. 526; 'ETA ante las elecciones', undated, *Documentos Y*, Vol. 18, p. 529.
4. Personal observation by author.
5. *Deia*, 9 Sep. 1977; *Punto y Hora*, 15–21 Sep. 1977.
6. *Deia*, 10 Sept. 1977.
7. *Punto y Hora*, 15–21 Sept. 1977.
8. *Deia*, 10 Sept. 1977.
9. *Deia*, 10 Sept. 1977.
10. See *Egin*, 30 Sept. 1977, for HASI's origins.
11. Author's interview with Tomás Goikoetxea, San Sebastián, 10 Aug. 1981.
12. *Egin*, 15 May 1978.
13. HASI statement, *Egin*, 4 Jan. 1978.
14. *Deia*, 9 Sept. 1977.
15. See statement by Mario Onaindía. *Egin*, 8 Jan. 1978.
16. Statement by EIA leader Serrano Izco, *Egin*, 7 April 1978.
17. *Egin*, 2 Oct. 1977.
18. *Egin*, 2 Oct. 1977.
19. See below, Chapter 8.
20. Interviews with Monzón in *Punto y Hora*, Dec. 1976 and *Garaia*, Feb. 1977.
21. For analysis of EE's electoral performance see Luis Núñez, *Egin*, 30 Oct, 2,3,4 and 5 Nov. 1977; also, Núñez, *Euskadi sur electoral*, passim; *Arnasa*, No.1, Dec. 1976.
22. Author's interview with EIA spokesmen, Aug. 1977; also *Kemen*, No.11, Anexo 5, Feb. 1977.
23. *Egin*, 13 Oct, 1977. For Letamendía's version of the disagreements in EIA see, Ortzi, *El no vasco a la reforma* (San Sebastián, 1979), pp. 130–40.
24. Statement by Mario Onaindía, *Egin*, 8 Jan. 1978.
25. Interview with ETA-M spokesman, *Egin*, 29 Sept. 1977.
26. *Egin*, 10 Oct. 1977.
27. *Egin*, 27 Nov. 1977.
28. *Egin*, 17 Dec. 1977.
29. *Egin*, 12 Jan. 1978.
30. *Deia*, 20 Dec. 1977.

31. *Egin*, 29 Dec. 1977.
32. See statement by Peces Barba, a PSOE member of parliament. *Egin*, 2 July, 1978.
33. *Egin*, 29 Sept. 1977.
34. *Egin*, 12, 20, 25 and 29 Feb. 1978.
35. *Egin*, 4, 6, 14 and 20 March 1978.
36. *Egin*, 18 March 1978.
37. *Egin*, 29 June 1978.
38. *Egin*, 19 July 1978.
39. *Egin*, 2 July 1978.
40. For the action/repression/action theory see Chapter 2, pp. 42-4.
41. Interview with ETA-PM leader Mark, *Deia*, 27 Dec. 1977.
42. *Egin*, 29 and 30 Dec. 1977.
43. *Egin*, 1 Nov. 1978.
44. *Egin*, 1 Nov. 1978.
45. Interview with ETA-PM spokesman, *Viejo Topo*, No.42, March 1980.
46. *Egin*, 13 June 1978 and 28 Sept. 1978.
47. *Egin*, 17 June 1978 and 12 Nov. 1978.
48. *Egin*, 2 Nov. 1978.
49. *Egin*, 13 Nov. 1978.
50. *Egin*, 29 Nov. 1978.
51. *Egin*, 10 Dec. 1978.
52. Senator Bandrés at a meeting in Pamplona. *Egin*, 9 April 1978.
53. Author's interview with Goiherri, San Sebastián, 5 Aug. 1984.
54 Arregi, *Memorias*, passim.
55. See 'Ayuda a los refugiados vascos', *Documentos Y*, Vol. 9, pp. 66-7.
56. EIA's comment 'El PNV expulsa a Telesforo Monzón', *Bultzaka*, Nov. 1977, was very complimentary to Monzón.
57. *Egin*, 26 Nov. 1977.
58. *Egin*, 8 Jan. 1978.
59. *Egin*, 28 April 1978.
60. *Egin*, 8 Jan. 1978.
61. Interview, *Punto y Hora*, 23 Nov. 1977.
62. See Monzón article, 'Qué horror', *Egin*, 26 Oct. 1978.
63. Author's interviews with former ESB parliamentary candidate, Ildefonso Iriarte Otermín, San Sebastián, 24 July 1980.
64. See Mario Onaindía *La lucha de clases en Euskadi, 1939-80* (San Sebastián, 1980), pp. 112-33, 137, 149.
65. *Diario Vasco*, 17 June 1977.
66. Author's conversations with ESB activists, July 1977
67. *ESB, Un programa socialista para la autonomía de Euskadi* (Bilbao, 1977), p. 107.
68. Author's interview with Iriarte Otermín.
69. Interview with ANV spokesman, *Punto y Hora*, 15–30 Sept. 1976.
70. 'LAIA, el por qué de su creación', *Sugarra*, No.1, 1975.
71. Author's interview with LAIA leader J.M. Larrazábal, San Sebastián, 10 March 1980; *Egin*, 9 Nov. 1977; *Punto y Hora*, 10–16 March 1977.
72. Interview with ETA-PM leader 'Mark', *Deia*, 27 Dec. 1977.

73. Interview with LAIA spokesman, *Punto y Hora*, 10–16 March 1977.

74. Author's interview with J.M. Larrazábal.

75. Interview with Larrazábal.

76. Author's interviews with Mario Onaindía, Vitoria, 26 March 1980; Enrique Casas, San Sebastián, 31 March 1980; J.M. Larrazábal, San Sebastián, 8 March 1980; Angel García (PSOE leader), San Sebastián, 30 March 1980.

77. Author's interview with Mario Onaindía.

78. *Deia*, 15 Nov. 1977.

79. *Egin*, 20 Jan. 1978.

80. *Egin*, 20 Jan. 1978.

81. Statement by EIA leader Serrano Izco, *Egin*, 7 April 1978.

82. *Deia*, 15 June 1978; *Egin*, 13 May and 5 Oct. 1978.

83. *Egin*, 11 May 1978.

84. *Egin*, 9 July 1978.

85. *Egin*, 13 July 1978; *Diario Vasco*, 13 July 1978.

86. *Egin*, 8 Oct. 1977.

87. *Egin*, 3 July, 1978.

88. For the attitudes of the PNV, the PSOE and EIA to the police see *Cambio 16*, 30 July 1978.

89. *Egin*, 20 April 1978.

90. Author's interview with PSOE leaders Enrique Casas, Luis Arbella, Angel García.

91. Letter to author from the PNV press office, 29 Nov. 1978.

92. See Arzallus in *Egin*, 3 May 1978.

93. See statement criticising the PNV by UGT leader Jaime San Sebastián, *Deia*, 13 Dec. 1978.

94. *Deia*, 15 June 1978.

95. *Deia*, 11 June 1978.

96. *Deia*, 9 Nov. 1977; 1 and 21 June 1978.

97. *Deia*, 1 Oct. 1978.

98. *Deia*, 1, 2 and 7 Oct. 1978.

99. *Deia*, 5 Oct. 1978.

100. *Deia*, 1, 2, 5, 7 Oct. 1978.

101. *Egin*, 30 Oct. 1978.

102. Javier Arzallus, *Deia*, 1978.

103. *Egin*, 10 Oct. 1978.

104. See statement by Benegas, *Deia*, 22 Oct. 1978.

105. *Deia*, 8 Oct. 1978.

106. See *Deia*, Editorial, 13 Nov. 1977.

107. See statement by the PNV's Vizcaya Provincial Committee, *Egin*, 18 March 1979.

108. Press statement: Ref. EBB 029/78. 10 Oct. 1978; also *Deia*, 11 Oct. 1978.

109. *Deia*, 12, 13 Oct. 1978.

110. *Deia*, 12, 17 Oct. 1978.

111. *Deia*, 14 Oct. 1978.

112. *Egin*, 17 Oct. 1978.

113. Press statement by PNV National Committee (EBB 033/78).

114. *Egin*, 24 Oct. 1978.
115. *Egin*, 24 Oct. 1978.
116. *Deia*, 17 Oct. 1978.
117. *Deia*, 18 Oct. 1978.
118. See *Deia*, 12, 19, 25, 26 Oct. 1978.
119. *Deia*, 20 Oct. 1978.
120. *Egin*, 3, 4, 10, 14, 15, 23, 26, 27, 30 Oct. and 1 Nov. 1978.
121. *Egin*, 28 Oct. 1978.
122. *Egin*, 22 Oct. 1978.
123. *Deia* 24 Oct. 1978; *Mundo Obrero*, 8–14 Dec. 1978.
124. *Deia*, 25 Oct. 1978.
125. EBB 034/78, 25 Oct. 1978.
126. *Deia*, 25, 27, 28 Oct. 1978.
127. EIA press statement, *Deia*, 22 Oct. 1978.
128. 'Objetivo Cumplido', *Deia*, 29 Oct. 1978.
129. *Egin*, 29 Oct. 1978.
130. See *Egin*, 12 Oct. 1978 for letter from a PNV member protesting against the demonstration.
131. *Egin*, 1 Nov. 1978.
132. *Deia*, 9 Nov. 1978.
133. *Egin*, 1 Nov. 1978.
134. *Deia*, 22 Dec. 1978.
135. *Deia*, 9 Dec. 1978.
136. *El País*, 8 Dec. 1978.

8

ETA in a Parliamentary Democracy

Although agreement on the need for a statute giving a considerable degree of autonomy to the Basque country did not in itself settle the question of the precise powers which the autonomous Basque government would have, it represented a considerable narrowing of the political gulf between the PNV and the 'Spanish' parties. In the view of ETA-M's leaders, the PNV's guarded acceptance of a Constitution which denied the Basque people the right to full independence was a betrayal of Euskadi, and any measure of autonomy promised by a Spanish government was largely irrelevant. The PNV leaders, having urged their supporters to abstain in the referendum which approved the Constitution, were placed in the difficult position of trying to obtain a statute which would be acceptable, and yet fall within the terms of the Constitution. Such ambivalence was in the following years to bring charges of hypocrisy against the party from both 'Spanish' and *Abertzale* critics. Yet the PNV leaders did not see the statute as merely a measure of autonomy to be granted by a sovereign Spanish state, but as an agreement to be negotiated between representatives of the Basque people and the Spanish government, just as the incorporation of the Basque country into Spain had, allegedly, been negotiated with the Spanish crown. In this way, the sovereign rights of the Basque people would be reconciled with Euskadi remaining part of Spain.

The supporters of the right-wing Alianza Popular, led by Fraga Iribarne, had been reluctant to countenance Basque autonomy, but realised that it was inevitable. The PNV's leaders' differences with the 'Spanish' parties concerned both the form and the content of the proposed statute. The PNV leaders not only wanted a greater degree of autonomy than did the 'Spanish' parties, but

223

they also wanted the statute to be presented as a recovery of historic Basque rights.[1] The stress on historic rights was not merely a device to enable the party to reconcile its doctrines with political reality. It was also aimed at strengthening the PNV's electoral position, since a statute which emphasised the rights of municipalities and historic areas would have favoured the PNV because of its strength in rural districts. However, the most important difference between the 'Spanish' and the nationalist parties was whether Navarre should be included in the Basque autonomous community. The 'Spanish' right in Navarre was strongly opposed to such a proposal and the 1977 election had produced a clear majority for the non-nationalist parties there. Yet the PNV could not accept that Navarre was never to be part of Euskadi. The party's leaders needed a formula which would allow them to accept an autonomous community consisting of three provinces, while maintaining in principle that Navarre was part of Euskadi. EIA's policies demonstrated a similar mixture of strict doctrinal orthodoxy and practical flexibility. Bandrés summed up his party's attitude, and at the same time antagonised intransigent nationalists, when he declared that the statute was 'the last train to solve Euskadi's problems'.[2] As EIA and ETA-PM became committed to support for a statute which had originated in a Constitution they had once opposed, their opponents accused them of inconsistency. The fact that the discussions on the precise wording of the statute were complicated and little understood by the general population made for considerable confusion. Even Herri Batasuna, while remaining committed to achieving Basque independence, announced in November 1978 that as long as Navarre was not definitely excluded from the provisions for Basque autonomy, then negotiations with the Spanish government were legitimate.[3]

Any doubts ETA-M's leaders might have had that Euskadi was still at war with Spain must have been dispelled on 21 December 1978, when Argala was killed in St. Jean de Luz, by an explosive charge which went off when he tried to start his car.[4] Nothing could have been more calculated to strengthen ETA-M's leaders in their determination to continue with the armed struggle. Argala died the day after the fifth anniversary of Carrero Blanco's assassination. The right-wing group which had carried out the attack was generally thought to be controlled by the Spanish police. Accordingly, throughout 1979, ETA-M continued with a campaign of retaliation which was much more extensive than that carried out under Franco. The targets of the violence were generally policemen, suspected informers and known right-wingers. In a particularly horrifying incident in January, a Civil Guard and his fiancée were shot dead.[5] Most of the victims were shot, but a number of policemen were killed or injured when removing booby traps. Early in January ETA-M commandos killed the assistant military governor of San Sebastián, and the military governor of Madrid.[6] These were merely the most spectacular of the numerous actions which showed that ETA-M's military capacity was strengthened by the changed conditions of a parliamentary democracy. ETA-M's intensified campaign caused dismay among both government and moderate opposition supporters. It showed that the violence which had begun under the Franco dictatorship was not going to end automatically with the advent of democracy. Apart from ETA-M's ability to kill high-ranking officers, even outside Euskadi, no prominent supporter of the previous regime could feel secure in the light of the steady toll of right-wing victims of the organisation, which included such people as Pilar Careaga, the former mayor of Bilbao, who was shot and seriously wounded in March.[7]

The police, unable to prevent ETA-M's attacks, responded with their customary brutality to demonstrations in support of ETA's prisoners. However, the most striking counter-attack against ETA-M was made by the *incontrolados*. The killing of Argala was followed in January 1979 in Donibane, France, by an attempt on the life of ETA-M's treasurer, José Manuel Pagoaga, which left him gravely injured.[8] In May in Biarritz an *incontrolado* action group fixed a bomb on the car of Txomin Iturbe, who had become ETA-M's main leader on Argala's death.[9] Such actions, combined with continuing repression by the police, gave credence to the belief held by ETA-M's supporters, that there had been no meaningful transition to democracy in June 1977, and that police repression and killings carried out by ultra-right-wing groups were part of a concerted policy to keep Euskadi subject to Spanish rule. Nationalist parties such as EIA and the PNV, whose senior echelons believed that the government's promise to grant autonomy would lead to serious change, were regarded by Herri Batasuna leaders, such as Miguel Castells, as either gullible or treacherous.[10] Such an interpretation of the transition to parliamentary democracy appeared absurd to the leaders of the PSOE and the PCE, although they remained concerned about the government's inability to bring ultra-right elements in the armed forces under control. The Suárez government did proceed to carry out its promise to grant the autonomy for the Basque country which it was hoped would bring about the acceptance of the Constitution, already achieved elsewhere in Spain. In the fifteen months after the referendum ratifying the Constitution the Suárez government was to hold parliamentary elections, a referendum to approve a Basque autonomy statute and elections for the Basque parliament. These measures, which seemed to both the PSOE and the UCD to meet all legitimate Basque demands, did not however end the violence of either branch of ETA. Such activities provoked a large number of arrests, the number of prisoners rose, allegations of police torture multiplied, police harassment of peaceful activities continued, and the campaign of armed struggle intensified.

The attempt to persuade the French government to act against either branch of ETA by extraditing activists to Spain, or withdrawing their status as political refugees, met with little success. Although the French authorities sometimes imprisoned ETA members or confined them to inaccessible places such as the French Alps or the island of Yeu,[11] the reputation of the Spanish police for torturing suspects made it politically difficult for it to obtain co-operation from France. When the French courts did take action against ETA-M's activists the organisation retaliated, as in April 1979, when one of its commandos planted a bomb which damaged the French consulate in San Sebastián and seriously wounded two policemen.[12]. The Spanish government's failure to get French support in its attempt to combat ETA-M was matched by its inability to get such backing from either the PNV or EIA, neither of which could be persuaded to condemn violence unreservedly. Indeed, violence intensified as ETA-PM stepped up the level of its armed struggle, although ETA-PM's leaders did not wish to emulate the bloody attacks on policemen and right-wingers which were the stock in trade of ETA-M. Nevertheless, ETA-PM's activists had by 1979 the resources they had lacked in 1977. Furthermore, the political theory which they shared with EIA stipulated that an armed organisation remained necessary in a parliamentary democracy.

As the theatrical gestures made by ETA-PM's activists during the debate on the constitutional referendum were insufficient to justify the group's existence, they began to be supplemented by more serious acts of violence. Many of these arose out of industrial disputes, since ETA-PM's leaders saw their organisation as the military arm of the working class.[13] As ETA-PM had no organised base in the factories, armed attacks on factory managers and businessmen were its main way to demonstrate its socialist credentials and to show that its version of armed struggle was very different from the indiscriminate violence of ETA-M. A good example of ETA-PM's strategy was provided by its intervention against the management of the Michelin company which was involved in a lengthy dispute with its employees. On several occasions, ETA-PM commandos kidnapped Michelin executives, who were generally released shortly afterwards, having been shot in the leg.[14] Such actions were intended to force the company to adopt a more conciliatory attitude to their workforce, and therefore were, in ETA-PM's leaders' opinion, a contribution to the class struggle. Sometimes the punishment of managers was combined with kidnapping for ransom, as in February 1979 when the managing director of Michelin's factory in Vitoria was seized and held for several weeks.[15] Other sources of finance were the collection of the 'revolutionary tax' and the practice of armed robbery. ETA-PM's commandos acquired material as well as money in this way. In one robbery alone, a commando seized a thousand kilogrammes of plastic explosive.[16]

ETA's resumption of armed struggle was insufficient to prevent EIA, its political arm, from losing ground to Herri Batasuna. Many leading supporters of EIA, such as Ortzi and the radical priest Periko Solabarría, transferred their allegiance to Herri Batasuna, alleging that EIA had become inactive and reformist.[17] With the consolidation of Herri Batasuna, ETA-M obtained the backing of a force which was more capable of launching a political campaign than were the amnesty committees which had hitherto provided its main support. Throughout 1979 Herri Batasuna launched a series of spectacular actions which included occupations of public buildings, marches, hunger strikes and acts of civil disobedience, which resulted in the imprisonment of its leaders. No party, apart from the PNV, could match Herri Batasuna's level of activity. The mass participation component of the action/repression/action cycle assumed a greater importance than hitherto in ETA's history. Typically, Herri Batasuna would hold a demonstration, which would be broken up by the police, and ETA-M members would retaliate by killing policemen or right-wingers.[18] When ETA-M members were killed in clashes with the police, their funerals would be the occasion for angry demonstrations and subversive speeches by Herri Batasuna spokesmen, which would in turn result in criminal charges against them. ETA-M's growing body of prisoners played their part by going on hunger strike and holding demonstrations, which brought severe punishment on their heads and increased the anger of their supporters.[19] ETA-M and Herri Batasuna had created an extremely effective strategy of tension which helped to ensure that the political demobilisation which had been achieved throughout the rest of Spain did not occur in Euskadi.

The continuing support for ETA-M presented the government with a considerable problem. Right-wing politicians claimed that ETA's violence could be ended by military measures, whereas the PNV's supporters believed that the problem would be overcome through the hastening and extension of Basque autonomy.[20] The government continued with the measures which were to lead to the election of an autonomous Basque parliament in March 1980. The criticism of the government made by the PNV and to a lesser extent by the Catholic Church was partially compensated for by the growing consensus on the Basque question between the UCD, the PSOE and the PCE. When in February 1979 the Basque PSOE leader, Enrique Múgica, agreed in a television discussion with the UCD minister of the interior, Martin Villa, that Spain needed a more effective police force, radical nationalists were confirmed in their belief that the 'Spanish' left and right were equally imperialist.[21] As the parliamentary and municipal elections approached, Herri Batasuna's candidates seized the opportunity afforded by the election campaign to publicise the plight of ETA-M's prisoners, by making inflammatory speeches proclaiming the need to continue the armed struggle for the liberation of Euskadi. Such speeches resulted in arrests, criminal charges against Herri Batasuna's leaders, hunger strikes by those arrested, demonstrations by their supporters and declarations of support by ETA-M's prisoners.[22] During the parliamentary election campaign, Telesforo Monzón, Herri Batasuna's leading public figure, was imprisoned, gravely ill, in a military hospital. Such incidents produced a colourful and dramatic campaign which contrasted with the sober conduct of the 'Spanish' parties' candidates and even with those of EE. Herri Batasuna's candidates had declared that they would, if elected, decline to take their seats in the Madrid parliament.

The parliamentary elections held in March 1979 strengthened the government's position in Spain as a whole, as the UCD remained the largest party. However, in the Basque country the

UCD did badly, as did all the 'Spanish' parties. The PNV received nearly 280,000 votes in Alava, Vizcaya and Guipúzcoa, and succeeded in having seven candidates elected to Congress and eight to the Senate, but remained weak in Navarre, where it stood as part of a coalition which received only 21,000 votes.[24] The election results were also a triumph for Herri Batasuna which, in its first electoral contest, received over 170,000 votes, more than half those obtained by the PNV. Both Monzón and Letamendía were elected to parliament, in spite of the coalition's announcement that its candidates would not take their seats. EE's candidates also did well, considering that they were now competing with Herri Batasuna for the radical nationalist vote. Onaindía replaced Letamendía as the party's representative in Congress, while Bandrés retained his seat in the Senate. As the PSOE's vote fell to 252,000 the PNV became the majority party. In the long awaited municipal elections, held the following month, the nationalist victory was even more pronounced. The PNV obtained more than twice as many votes as the PSOE. Herri Batasuna also polled votes and had one hundred more councillors elected than did the PSOE.[25]

The PSOE had been expected to do badly in the municipal elections, where a sophisticated propaganda machine and television coverage could not compensate for its lack of competent and popular candidates. In addition, many immigrants who might vote for a 'Spanish' candidate in a parliamentary election could be expected to abstain, or even vote for a nationalist, in elections which were seen as a local issue. Even if a decline of the PSOE vote was expected, the extent of its defeat was staggering, as it was left with a very weak presence outside its traditional immigrant strongholds. For example, Rentería, a heavily immigrant and industrial town in Guipúzcoa, returned a majority of nationalist councillors, who then chose an Herri Batasuna mayor. Success in the elections strengthened the PNV's hand in the negotiations to approve a Statute. In June, when the main parties in the Basque country agreed on the contents of a Statute which the government would be asked to accept, a huge demonstration was organised in Vitoria where municipal representatives attended in an effort to recreate the atmosphere of 1931 when the Statute of Estella had been adopted by these municipal authorities influenced by the PNV.[26] The agreement demonstrated the key position held by the PNV whose success in getting parties as diverse as the UCD and EIA to agree on the contents of the Statute was indeed remarkable. Yet the apparent consensus concealed disagreement which was soon to lead to conflict. EIA saw the Statute as a stage towards achieving independence, while the UCD and Alianza Popular were in favour of a more restricted Statute than was the PNV. Such disagreements did little to weaken the PNV's position. As it was the strongest party in the Basque country and held a position midway between EIA and the 'Spanish' parties, it was probable that it would be able to achieve many of its aims.

Predictably, ETA-M denounced the contents of the Statute as merely a measure of decentralisation which did nothing to advance the cause of Basque independence. Throughout 1979 the organisation continued with a campaign in which policemen, army officers and private individuals were killed. In May an ETA-M commando opened fire on an army vehicle in Madrid, killing General Gómez Hortiguela, two colonels and an army chauffeur.[27] The alarm caused by the assassination was intensified when, on the following day, a bomb exploded in a restaurant next to the headquarters of Fuerza Nueva, killing eight people, which the police attributed to the Maoist Grupos de Resistencia Antifascistas Primero de Octubre (GRAPO).[28] Such acts produced enormous resentment among the officer corps, and inevitably raised the spectre of an armed coup. The attitudes of many former supporters of the Franco regime were expressed by Fraga Iribarne, who continued to insist that ETA's violence could be ended if more resources were given to the police. For the PNV's spokesmen such attitudes exemplified the habitual blindness of 'Spanish' parties to the problem of Euskadi. In speeches, press statements and declarations in Parliament, the PNV's leaders declared that ETA's violence was a response to national oppression and would cease when steps were taken to end that oppression, starting with the granting of an adequate Statute of Autonomy.[29]. Such statements, which seemed to the right-wing parties to be a thinly veiled apology for terrorism, were seen by Herri Batasuna and ETA-M supporters as acquiescence in the continuing oppression of the Basque people by the Spanish enemy.

The government was torn between its need to placate the army and its desire to come to terms with mainstream nationalism, as a means of isolating both branches of ETA. Although police brutality and right-wing attacks continued, they did not form part of a coherent strategy, as the government became convinced that it had to grant many of the PNV's demands if it were to prevent that party's supporters from defecting to Herri Batasuna. The difference between Basque and 'Spanish' concepts of where the responsibility for violence lay was vividly illustrated in June 1979 when a policeman shot dead a young woman, Gladys del Estal, who was taking part in a peaceful anti-nuclear demonstration in Tudela, Navarre.[30] Seen from Madrid, the killing was a regrettable incident, but to many people in the Basque country the incident showed the government's inability, or unwillingness, to bring the police under control. The killing provoked a wave of strikes and demonstrations throughout Euskadi, which won support from a wider range of people than those who would generally support Herri Batasuna.[31] In the weeks following the death of Gladys del Estal, ETA-M's commandos killed a number of people who included ultra-rightists, alleged police informers and a retired army officer.[32] The action/repression/action cycle was functioning as ETA-M's theory postulated.

The leaders of Herri Batasuna, while pleased with their electoral success, were not content to be merely an electoral coalition, but gave priority to demonstrations and mass mobilisation. The decision that those of its members who were elected to parliament should not attend avoided the problems which could have arisen from the coalition's disparate composition and the lack of agreement on political issues other than Basque independence. Its representatives on municipal councils were a trickier problem as ESB members believed that the efficient management of municipal life was a good way of demonstrating Basque superiority over the rest of Spain. LAIA's leaders also believed that the municipalities should be used as arenas in which the advantages of libertarian socialism could be demonstrated.[33] In places such as Rentería, where Herri Batasuna became the largest group in the council, it took over the local administration, while in some areas Herri Batasuna councillors boycotted the institutions to which they had been elected. In either case LAIA, ESB and ANV, supposedly independent parties, lost all control over the decisions to be adopted, even when councillors were members of their parties. For example, in San Sebastián a 'popular assembly' of Herri Batasuna ordered its representatives not to attend council meetings. When, in September 1979, Tomás Alba, an eccentric councillor and former Falangist who disagreed with that decision, was shot dead,[34] the action at first appeared to be ETA-M's way of ensuring that councillors complied with the decisions of the 'popular assembly'. However, when ETA-M denied the responsibility for the killing which had been carried out by an ultra-right group, the Batallón Vasco Español, Alba was accepted as a patriotic martyr.

Herri Batasuna did not attempt to expand the Autonomy Statute provisions in the way that EIA and the PNV did, because of a conviction that any improvements which would have narrowed the gap between the PNV and the government, would have weakened support for Basque independence. In opposition to the negotiations being carried on by the other parties, Herri Batasuna's national committee proposed that an alternative Statute should be drawn up by an assembly composed of sympathetic local councillors and representatives of 'popular' movements ranging from amnesty committees to feminist and anti-nuclear-power movements. A meeting to set up Euskal Herriko Batzarre Natzionale (EHBN) (The Basque People's National Assembly) was called for June 1979 in Alsasua, Navarre, but the police prevented the participants from gathering.[35] EHBN's structure and composition was as fluid and uncertain as those of the other organisations which supported ETA-M. Although presented as an attempt to form a representative body, which was planned to be the embryo of an independent government, its structure was confused with that of Herri Batasuna itself. In addition to the attempt to launch an alternative National Assembly, Herri Batasuna produced its own Statute, an elaborate document which outlined the rights and obligations of citizens of the future independent Euskadi. The Statute proposed three different criteria for acquiring Basque citizenship according to descent, place of birth and time of residence in Euskadi. It would have made *Euskera* the main language in teaching and would have compelled all government and local authority functionaries to learn that language.[36]

The combined effect of Herri Batasuna's refusal to compromise and of ETA-M's military offensive was to increase the division of the Basque people into two antagonistic camps. The effects of this were opposed by both EIA and ETA-PM whose leaders made many statements criticising what they saw as a counterproductive strategy.[37] ETA-PM's commandos continued to practise armed struggle, which its public statements presented as a complement to EIA's policies. Until June 1979 the relationship between EIA and ETA-PM maintained the formula laid down by Pertur which stipulated that, although the organisations were in political agreement, neither should dictate the other's tactics. EIA campaigned

for the autonomy which was regarded as irrelevant by Herri
Batasuna and when the Spanish government was slow to respond,
ETA-PM would intervene with a judicious display of violence. In
June, for example, when ETA-PM's activists bombed administrative buildings in San Sebastián, the actions were presented as
measures to aid attainment of a comprehensive Statute.[38] Until
EIA's leaders were confident that the government would actually
implement a Statute which would satisfy their demands, both
political and military actions were seen as valid methods of struggle. Once agreement on the Statute was reached, EIA had
achieved its immediate demands. Nonetheless, the party remained
committed to the establishment of an independent Euskadi, which
would include both Navarre and the French Basque country. The
socialist content of EIA's policies were never clearly defined, and
the social origin of its activists and of those who voted for it
encouraged a moderate reformist practice. For such a party to
maintain a partnership with an armed group had been
incongruous even before the Statute had been agreed. The relationship came under strain when, in June 1979, ETA-PM
commandos exploded bombs in Benidorm, Fuengirola and other
tourist resorts, which killed two people,[39] in an attempt to hit at
economic targets, and to bring pressure on the government to
grant a further amnesty. Such actions brought muted criticism by
EIA spokesmen.

The difficulty of combining armed struggle and political action
was demonstrated when disagreements arose between the Basque
nationalists and the UCD over the scope of the forthcoming
autonomy Statute. The PNV and EIA organised massive
demonstrations demanding greater autonomy, while, in July,
ETA-PM intervened by attempting to kidnap Gabriel Cisneros,
a UDC parliamentary deputy and member of the Constitutional
Commission, who reputedly represented the more centralist sector
of his party. Cisneros managed to escape from his assailants but
was shot and gravely wounded.[40] ETA-PM's attack, which
appeared to non-nationalists as identical to the tactics of ETA-M,
was in fact in line with the strategy outlined when the division of
labour between EIA and ETA-PM had been decided, where mass
activity and armed struggle were both declared to be necessary.
The nationalist parties were playing their part by demonstrating
and debating in parliament, and ETA-PM's attempt to kidnap
Cisneros was not intended to substitute for this. In practice, EE's
Senator Bandrés was in the unenviable position of being in

political sympathy with a group which had tried to kidnap a fellow member of parliament. In July, relations between EIA and ETA-PM were brought to breaking point when ETA-PM commandos planted bombs in Madrid's two main railway stations and airport, killing five people and injuring more than a hundred.[41] EIA spokesmen demanded that ETA-PM should apologise and make a self-criticism and Bandrés declared that the bombings had been 'atypical and clumsy'.[42] Relationships between EIA and ETA-PM improved when ETA-PM spokesmen announced that the organisation was calling off its armed campaign. However, the rapprochement could only be temporary as an armed group could not justify its existence while maintaining a permanent cease-fire. ETA-PM's leaders' attempt to find credible targets for selective violence (and thereby to distinguish their action from those of ETA-M) was extremely difficult. Although ETA-PM made no general attack on either the police or right-wing individuals, its chosen method of working had produced results which were just as horrifying. ETA-PM's supposedly more sophisticated theory, which had not prevented blunders such as the killing of Angel Berazadi in 1976,[43] did nothing to prevent the massacres at the railway stations.

The Madrid bombings were sharply attacked by EE's parliamentary representatives, Bandrés and Onaindía, who once again, demanded successfully that ETA-PM should apologise for its action.[44] EIA's leadership did not however demand that ETA-PM should dissolve, because ETA-M would then have an unchallenged claim to be the heir of ETA's tradition. The process of disassociating EIA from ETA-PM's armed struggle was extremely difficult as many of ETA-PM's members were imprisoned for activities which had taken place after the expiry of the 1977 amnesty. The most satisfactory solution to the problem would have been for ETA-PM's leadership to declare that they would terminate the armed struggle, and for EIA to negotiate an amnesty for ETA-PM's prisoners. Some of ETA-PM's leaders, such as Goiherri and the brothers Kepa and José Aulestia, who were in political agreement with Bandrés and Onaindía, were trying to get their commandos to make such an orderly withdrawal.[45] ETA-PM responded to the criticism aroused by the massacre at Madrid's railway station by calling off its bombing campaign, but renewed its offensive in September when one of its commandos wounded two policemen in San Sebastián.[46] ETA-PM's attempts to conduct an armed campaign which would supplement EIA's political struggle were failing miserably as its actions appeared more and more irrational. ETA-PM's practice of kidnapping industrialists and shooting them in the leg[47] was highly embarrassing for EIA's leaders who were becoming convinced that the progress which was being made towards achieving Basque autonomy made such violence counter-productive. In July 1979, the prolonged negotiations between the government and most of the Basque parties ended with agreement on an autonomy Statute, which the PNV leader, Arzallus, declared was better than that obtained in 1936.[48] Mario Onaindía was equally enthusiastic as was the prominent 'Spanish' conservative, Areilza, who declared that the agreement did nothing to endanger the unity of Spain.[49] According to EIA leaders Onaindía and Iñaki Martínez, the agreement would force Herri Batasuna to end its policy of sterile confrontation.[50]

The leaders of Herri Batasuna and ETA-M disagreed. According to Patxi Zabaleta, a leader of Herri Batasuna in Navarre, the document, which he described as the 'Statute of Moncloa', was a victory for the supporters of centralism, and had, he claimed, been welcomed enthusiastically by the right-wing in Navarre.[51] Navarre was not included in the proposed Basque autonomous community, although provision was made for future incorpora-tion if the people of the province so desired. The exclusion of Navarre, an understandable concession given that the nationalists of all shades were a minority there, was nevertheless to cripple both the PNV and EE in that province and to lead to splits in their organisations there. In an interview, an ETA-M spokesman condemned the left-wing parties and EIA for welcoming a Statute which excluded both Navarre and the French Basque country, which discriminated against *Euskera* in favour of Castilian, and had been produced behind the backs of the people.[52] ETA-M consequently continued with its armed attacks, undeterred by an agreement which its leaders considered farcical. Five policemen were killed by its commandos in two separate incidents in late July,[53] and the military governor of Guipúzcoa was shot dead in September, only a few days after two army officers had been killed in Bilbao.[54]

Once agreement had been reached among the majority of political forces on the contents of the Autonomy Statute, legisla-tion was passed by Parliament and a referendum was held on 25 October 1979, in Alava, Guipúzcoa and Vizcaya. All the main political forces except Herri Batasuna urged the electorate to approve the Statute. Nearly 54% were in favour, while only 3% voted against. However, abstention at just over 40% was high.[55] Herri Batasuna's leaders, who had urged voters to abstain, interpreted the result as a victory for their politics. From a radical nationalist point of view, the majority in favour was fraudulent, as neither Navarre nor the French Basque country had been included in the referendum.[56] The parties which favoured the Statute interpreted the high abstention rate as due mainly to weariness with politics, for since December 1976 there had been three referendums and two parliamentary elections, as well as municipal ones. Adherence to the Autonomy Statute by EIA, ETA-PM and the PNV broke the unity of the nationalist community and accepted the continued separation of Navarre and the French Basque country from Euskadi. If the conflict between Euskadi and Spain could be overcome, ETA-M might be reduced to an armed group representing a small minority of the population. Accordingly, ETA-M made the campaign on the referendum the occasion to launch an offensive which killed two police officers early in October and a civil guard at the end of the month. Some of its own members were killed in clashes with the police.[57] Its prisoners held a hunger strike and called on the population to abstain in the referendum.[58] ETA-PM's prisoners for their part called for a vote in favour of the autonomy statute.[59]

Hostility between the 'Spanish' parties and the radical nationalists increased when, two days after the referendum, a commando of the CAA, the body formed by a fusion of fragments of the Bereziak and LAIA, killed Germán González, a photographer and member of the PSOE, alleging that he was a police informer.[60] The PSOE and the UGT reacted by calling a general strike which was supported by the PCE and the Workers' Commissions. The importance which PSOE leaders attached to the killing was shown by Felipe González' attendance at the victim's funeral.[61] In a statement to the press, a PSOE leader, Benegas, treated the attack as a declaration of war against his party and suggested that the CAA was merely a cover used by one of the branches of ETA to carry out particularly distasteful crimes. Ramón Rubial, the veteran PSOE leader, suggested that the government might retaliate, employing similar methods. Both branches of ETA issued press statements denying that they had any connection with the CAA, and accused the PSOE of taking advantage of the killing to discredit the nationalist cause. The PNV's leaders condemned the murder of González, but in a much milder tone than that of the PSOE. An editorial in *Deia* criticised the suggestion of Rubial that the killers of González might have to be attacked by their own methods, in the way that de Gaulle had done when he created a secret force to fight against the OAS.[62] The main nationalist trade union, ELA-STV, firmly refused to support the protest strike called by the UGT and the Workers' Commissions. *Egin* and *Punto y Hora,* journals which supported Herri Batasuna, did not take any position on whether the killing of González was justified, but concentrated on what they saw as the treachery of the 'Spanish' parties in using González' death to attack ETA-M.[63] The LCR-LKI's journal took a similar line, although denying that there was any evidence indicating that González had been a police informer.[64] The CAA issued a press release stating that its commandos had killed González because he was a police informer, not because of his membership of the PSOE, but declared that it did not rule out actions against the PSOE's leaders.[65]

Approval of the Statute appeared to bring the Basque country nearer to an end to armed conflict. EIA's supporters in particular were moving towards an acceptance of parliamentary democracy, and a dissolution of their theoretically vanguard party into a broader political formation. EE was to be transformed from an electoral alliance into a political party which in 1981 was to unite with the Euro-communist faction of the Communist Party in Euskadi, led by its General Secretary Lerchundi.[66] Such a perspective made EIA's connection with an armed group even more of a liability. The relations between EIA and ETA-PM again came near to breaking point in November 1979, when an ETA-PM commando kidnapped Javier Rupérez, a UCD Congressman, and held him hostage for several weeks as a means of obtaining the release of a number of imprisoned ETA-PM members, and ending the practice of torture by the police.[67] It was, therefore, presented as a rational use of violence, to achieve a specific end, not as a relapse into a general campaign of terror. Such a differentation was lost on most of ETA-PM's critics, who thought the organisation was behaving in a similar way to ETA-M.

The Rupérez kidnapping placed EE's members of parliament, Bandrés and Onaindía, in an impossible position. As Bandrés negotiated with the government on ETA-PM's conditions for the release of his colleagues, it appeared to most of the Spanish press that EIA and its parliamentary representatives were merely a legal front for ETA-PM, and that EIA and ETA-PM were still pursuing essentially the same strategy. Photographs released by Rupérez' kidnappers, which showed him reading EIA's theoretical journal *Arnasa*,[68] strengthened the mistaken impression that EIA and ETA-PM functioned as wings of the same organisation, although ETA-PM's Seventh Assembly had, on establishing EIA, explicitly declared that the party and the armed group should be organisationally separate.[69] There was therefore no reason for EIA's leaders to be aware of ETA-PM's plans. Bandrés, in a letter to the President of Congress, reacted angrily to suggestions that he had been a party to Rupérez' kidnapping.[70] Rupérez was freed on 12 December, when ETA-PM's leadership was satisfied that its conditions (the release from prison of some of its members) would be met.[71] ETA-PM made no apology for the action, which fitted into the organisation's strategy and had achieved its objective.

However, even partial political agreement with a group which indulged in kidnapping was not in the long term a feasible position for an increasingly moderate political party. The embarrassment caused to EIA by such actions was shown by an article written by Bandrés in January 1980, where he spoke of his anguish at the time that Gabriel Cisneros 'hovered between life and death'.[72] Yet Rupérez kidnapping, however embarrassing to Bandrés, was successful in attaining its ends. Twenty-six Basque prisoners, most of whom belonged to ETA-PM, were freed in January in what was generally seen as the fulfilment of an agreement made for the release of Rupérez.[73] Judging by a communication from a group of ETA-PM members in Martutene prison, the whole episode was seen as a successful application of ETA-PM's strategy of supplementing legal action with armed struggle.[74]

By the end of 1979 the division between those who accepted the fact that Euskadi would remain within Spain while enjoying considerable autonomy, and those intransigent nationalists who still favoured independence, was evident within parties and coalitions as well as between them. In December the conservative *sabiniano* leadership of the PNV in Vizcaya produced a statement attacking Arzallus, the party's parliamentary spokesman, and expelled five of his supporters from their executive. The national committee revoked the decision and held a conference which elected Arzallus as chairman of the party in Vizcaya.[75] The conference was denounced as fraudulent and manipulated by the *Sabinianos*, most of whom did not attend. The realism of the

PNV's moderate tendency was demonstrated in December when the Basque government in exile was dissolved and its president, Leizaola, handed over the archives to the Consejo General Vasco, and declared that independence would bring a hundred years of misery for Euskadi.[76] Such an indication of the PNV leaders' willingness to come to terms with the Spanish government was combined with a determination not be be outflanked by Herri Batasuna. In January the PNV representatives abandoned the Cortes in protest at the government's delay in proceeding with the autonomy measures,[77] and stayed away until shortly before the elections to the Basque parliament, held on 9 March, which established the conditions for a genuine autonomy.

The tensions which racked the PNV had their counterpart in Herri Batasuna, where ESB's resentment at the coalition being dominated by ETA-M was expressed in a press statement complaining that the national leadership of Herri Batasuna, which had originally been formed partly by representatives of the component parties, was now 'elected' in a totally uncontrolled manner by general assemblies.[78] HASI's branch in San Sebastián argued that a democratic organisation should always be able to recall its leadership and therefore it supported the procedure which ESB's leaders objected to.[79] Aldecoa, ESB's general secretary, reiterated that Herri Batasuna was an electoral coalition, that ESB did not approve of candidates being selected in a general assembly, and that it might leave the alliance.[80] Before the elections to the autonomous Basque parliament Herri Batasuna disintegrated, as LAIA and ESB abandoned the coalition, leaving ETA-M in full control. A LAIA spokesman declared that Herri Batasuna had destroyed the parties which had originally formed the alliance, but this realisation came too late to preserve LAIA.[81] The leaders of both ESB and LAIA had thought that ETA-M's prestige could be used to strengthen support for their parties, but once they denounced the manipulation of Herri Batasuna by ETA-M and abandoned the coalition, they promptly collapsed, as did the even more shadowy ANV. The departure of most of its original components did little to weaken Herri Batasuna, which ETA-M now controlled through HASI and 'independents' such as Monzón, Castells and Ortzi. Disagreement on whether to accept parliamentary democracy also affected other organisations which had originally been supported by both wings of ETA. ETA-PM's prisoners began to complain that the amnesty committees had become sectarian organisations, dominated by supporters of ETA-M.[82] A similar development occurred in LAB, which was incapable of combining the function of a trade union with that of support for armed struggle. EIA's militants remained committed to Pertur's project of creating a genuine trade union, but their social background and experience did not fit them for that task. Inevitably the disagreements between EIA and Herri Batasuna emerged inside LAB and as early as 1978 EIA's supporters complained that LAB did not function as a union, but as a transmission belt for Herri Batasuna and ETA-M. As EIA's leaders abandoned their hopes for revolutionary change, so they gave up 'assemblyist' conceptions of trade union direct democracy in favour of more traditional bureaucratic structures, which were acceptable to Herri Batasuna's supporters. EIA's adherents decided that coexistence with those who backed Herri Batasuna was impossible and consequently split the union as a preliminary to dissolving their trade union faction into ELA-STU, thereby abandoning the Marxist and 'assemblyist' strands of the union's ideology. Herri Batasuna supporters maintained their own version of LAB (sometimes known as LAB-KAS) which functioned as an auxiliary to Herri Batasuna but, according to its critics, had no real trade union structure.[83]

The elections for the autonomous Basque parliament, held on 9 March 1980, showed the advantage which Basque nationalism derived from the polarisation produced by confrontation with the Spanish government. Nationalists gained forty-two seats, compared with eighteen for the 'Spanish' parties. Herri Batasuna obtained eleven seats and EE nine,[84] but the real winner was the PNV, with twenty-five seats and the knowledge that it could count on the support of fellow nationalists in any conflict with the enemy in Madrid.

As the self-government provisions of the autonomy statute compared favourably with that of 1936, it now seemed to most 'Spanish' political observers that the Basque problem was nearly settled. The precise implementation of the transfer of powers still had to be worked out and were soon to provide grounds for conflict between the PNV and 'Madrid'. However, the PNV's leaders seemed finally to have accepted that the Basque country would remain part of Spain, and that governing the Basque autonomous community fulfilled most of the party's aspirations. Although in 1980 few functions had been transferred from the central to the autonomous government, the PNV could look forward to exercising very extensive powers. Herri Batasuna

spokesmen, knowing that many PNV activists remained committed to the idea of an independent Euskadi, constantly criticised the
PNV for having abandoned its nationalist principles and having
become a regionalist party.

To its opponents the PNV seemed to display a systematic
hypocrisy, epitomised by its call for abstention in the December
1978 referendum on the Constitution, which provided the
framework for the autonomy statute, but the party's motivations
were more complex. It was indeed ambivalent about the Constitution and even over whether Basques owed any loyalty to the
Spanish State, but this ambiguity had existed ever since Sabino
Arana had first accepted the formula of regional autonomy within
the confines of that State. The question of whether autonomy was
a step towards independence, or on the contrary, whether its
acceptance presupposed Basque loyalty to the Spanish state and its
king, was never settled. Indeed, the party's peculiar structure
prevented the PNV from carrying out any public discussion of the
matter, so that its political life was a closed world to outside
observers.

The post-Franco PNV was able to attract the votes of large
numbers of conservative people, who were neither ethnically
Basque nor particularly nationalist. This made a striking contrast
to the 'Spanish' right, which was after 1982 unable, either in the
Basque country or elsewhere, to present a serious challenge to the
PSOE. It seemed, for the first few years of the PNV's regional rule
that the effects of power and the real privileges that accrued from
being a PNV member would hold the party's undeclared factions
together. As all sections of the PNV were united in wanting a
greater degree of autonomy than the Spanish state was willing to
grant, the struggle to widen the contents of the autonomy statute
could delay the decision over whether or not the statute was a step
on the way to independence. Such ambivalence inevitably condi-
tioned the PNV's attitude to the activities of ETA-M and its
competitors, whose campaign of violence was at the same time a
warning to 'Madrid' that peace could not be achieved unless
nationalist aspirations were met, and a dangerous provocation
which could unleash a military coup. ETA-PM's justification for
its campaign of violence was less and less obvious, now that its
political partner, EIA, had representatives in both the Spanish
and the Basque autonomous parliament. Although the formula
outlined in Pertur's document *Otsagabia* had provided for ETA-
PM's continued activity, to supplement the activities of its

political partner, the recipe had not worked well. Arguably, the kidnapping of Rupérez in November 1979 was a successful example of the careful use of violence for political aims, as it had resulted in the freeing of some ETA-PM prisoners,[85] but it had undermined the democratic credentials of EIA's members of parliament. Many of ETA-PM's other actions were so bizarre or vicious that they endangered its relationship with EIA. After the formation of an autonomous parliament these strains were to be increased.

The planting of bombs in tourist resorts in the summer of 1979 had been highly embarrassing for EIA, so when such actions were repeated in 1980 the dominant faction in its leadership moved decisively towards liquidating the armed organisation. This proved extremely difficult, as the attraction of armed struggle once more frustrated the efforts of ETA-PM's more sophisticated members to escape from the cycle of violence. Pertur's plan for both a political and a military organisation, organisationally separate but in political sympathy, was now seen to be unworkable. It seemed monstrous to EIA's opponents that its leaders could conduct normal political activity, and even make pacifistic declarations, while 'their' military wing continued to shoot and bomb its opponents. ETA-PM's spokesmen declared that the campaign would be ended if the prisoners were released and a referendum was held in Navarre, to decide if the province should be incorporated into the Basque autonomous community. Such demands showed, in the opinion of ETA-PM's leaders, that their carefully modulated campaign had nothing in common with the indiscriminate violence of ETA-M, but the claim seemed bizarre to most Spaniards and increasingly to the leadership of EIA. Onaindía, Bandrés and Garayalde (Erreka) increased their pressure on ETA-PM to institute a cease-fire and, eventually, to dissolve. The more nationalist *Nueva Izquierda* faction of EIA, led by Múgica Arregui, was less eager to wind up ETA-PM, but nevertheless refused to act as the political arm of those ETA-PM leaders determined to carry on the armed struggle.

The belief that EIA's leaders were the real inspirers of the armed violence led to the arrest of several of them on the occasion of ETA-PM's attacks.[86] EIA's difficulties were illustrated when Bandrés abstained on a parliamentary resolution condemning ETA-PM's activities.[87] ETA-PM's particular theory of political violence was used to justify behaviour which was more absurd and cruel than those of the rival branch. Its activists killed a manager of the Michelin factory in Vitoria in June 1980, in an unsolicited contribution to the workers' struggle.[88] ETA-PM also carried out attacks on UCD candidates, killing José Ignacio Usterán in Vitoria in September and Juan de Dios Doval in San Sebastián in October. Such actions, which were supplemented by others carried out by the CAA, showed a mindless brutality, as the UCD had very little strength in the Basque country; neither were its activists extreme right-wingers. ETA-PM became more and more divided between those such as 'Goiherri' and José Aulestia who sought a way out of the spiral of violence, and others such as Jesús Abrisketa, one of the defendants at the Burgos trial, who insisted that the armed struggle must continue. The supporters of the EIA leadership in ETA-PM included a majority of the veteran militants,[89] but the hard-line militarist faction had the support of most of the younger members who had joined after 1977. Understandably, as the advocates of dissolution were unwilling merely to resign, leaving the name and organisation in the hands of their opponents, ETA-PM entered a long period of factional struggle. EIA's leaders' anxiety to end the embarrassment of a link with an armed organisation was accentuated by their decision to dissolve EIA into Euskadiko Eskerra, unite with the Euro-communist wing of the Communist Party in the Basque country led by its General Secretary Roberto Lerchundi, and abandon the communist model of organisation for a more electoralist parliamentary one.

As ETA-M's military structure left dissidents with no option but individual desertion, it showed no sign of slackening its campaign of violence after the elections to the Basque parliament. Its actions included kidnapping for ransom; assassination of businessmen who refused to pay the 'revolutionary tax'; killing of political opponents, alleged police informers and retired army officers; bank robberies, the planting of bombs in public buildings, and the machine-gunning of bars and police barracks. Initial optimism about the decline of violence was disappointed very soon after the elections. On 25 March 1980 the Count of Aresti was killed in Bilbao for refusing to pay the 'revolutionary tax', four days later a child died in Azkoitia when a bomb intended to blow up a Civil Guard car exploded and, in Madrid on 18 March, General Manuel Esquivias was wounded in an attempt on his life which succeeded in killing a soldier.[90] Alarm at the escalation of violence led to the growth of a movement for peace which drew support from wider sections of the population than ETA's usual opponents. On 14 November all of the main political parties, except Herri Batasuna, issued a call for peace and reconciliation. For Herri Batasuna such efforts were hypocritical as, in its opinion, they ignored the actions of the ultra-right groups and the police use of torture. The PNV, while joining the 'Front for Peace', remained suspicious of the Madrid government's intentions of implementing the transfer of powers to the autonomous government which the PNV now led. In the opinion of Mario Onaindía the PNV, while disapproving of some of ETA-M's actions, was glad to have a constant threat of violence as a lever to extort concessions from the Spanish government.[91]

Nevertheless, the PNV could not be happy that its own supporters were forced to pay the 'revolutionary tax' and were, on occasions, kidnapped when they refused to do so. The kidnapping of a businessman, José Garavila, a PNV sympathiser, in Bermeo on 25 October[92] caused great resentment among party activists, who threatened reprisals against ETA-M supporters. The municipal council passed a resolution condemning the act, with the abstention of the representatives of Herri Batasuna, but Garavilla was released only after a ransom had been paid. The kidnapping which caused most horror was carried out in January 1981 when an ETA-M commando seized José María Ryan, the chief engineer at the Lemóniz power station. The action, a logical consequence of ETA-M's sustained attack on the construction of the plant had an inevitably tragic outcome as the conditions of Ryan's release included a demand that work on the station should be stopped. The PNV took the lead in organising massive demonstrations demanding Ryan be set free, but when on 6 February he was killed after a week of captivity, ETA-M's prestige was at one of its lowest points ever as its leaders had seriously miscalculated the effect of killing a person not involved in political activity or linked to the security forces. PNV spokesmen, in an example of the constant ebb and flow of that party's hostility to ETA, criticised ETA-M in some of the harshest terms ever.[93] ETA-M was rescued from a position of dangerous isolation when, a week after Ryan's death, one of its activists Joseba Arregi, died under torture in the police headquarters in Carabanchel prison in Madrid. The Basque parliament suspended its activities in protest and there were violent demonstrations all over the Basque country.[94] On 29 January, when Adolfo Suárez resigned as Prime Minister, military dissatisfaction at his government's failure to win the fight against terrorism was seen as one of the main reasons for his departure. The deteriorating situation was highlighted by the scenes when King Juan Carlos came to the Basque country, on a visit which had been arranged before Suárez's resignation, when the situation appeared more hopeful. On 4 February, as the King rose to address the parliament, the Herri Batasuna representatives rose to their feet and drowned out his words by singing *Eusko Gudariak*, the anthem of the Basque troops in the Civil War, before being ejected by security guards.[95]

Events in the Basque country were overshadowed by the attempt at a military coup on 23 February when Civil Guard units under the command of Colonel Antonio Tejero seized control of parliament and held the members prisoner. Simultaneously, Tejero's accomplices were declaring their support for a new dictatorship. After a tense night, when the King telephoned all the main army commanders demanding their loyalty, the rebels surrendered and Spain's parliamentary democracy survived. The army's dissatisfaction with the government's inability to defeat terrorism had been one of the motives for the failed coup. Curiously, Herri Batasuna and the wider nationalist community remained passive during the crucial period when the outcome of the coup was in doubt. Herri Batasuna held no demonstrations and prominent members stayed in hiding. A successful coup would have been, perhaps, advantageous to ETA-M as it would have removed what was seen as the façade of parliamentary democracy and revealed the unchanged nature of Spanish oppression of the Basque people. The PNV, in contrast, was shaken by the attempted coup and adopted a more conciliatory attitude to the government of Calvo Sotelo, who had succeeded Suárez. The PNV remained dissatisfied with the pace of the transfer of powers to the Basque government, but the coup was a reminder that Spanish governments were not free agents and that fear of military reactions was a powerful factor in inhibiting the transfer to regional autonomy. Calvo Sotelo's government tried to appease the army's dissatisfaction at the devolution of power to regional government, by cutting these down through the *Ley Orgánica de Armonización del Proceso Autonómico* (LOAPA) which was presented to the Cortes on 29 September 1981.[96] LOAPA was seen, accurately, by the PNV as reneging on the understanding that the rhythm of transference of powers which had prevailed under Suárez would be maintained. The PNV organised large demonstrations against LOAPA and both the Basque and Catalan autonomous governments appealed, successfully, to the constitutional tribunal, arguing that it was unconstitutional. The fact that the provisions of LOAPA had been agreed on by the UCD and PSOE leaderships strengthened Basque nationalist suspicions that all the 'Spanish' parties maintained their traditional commitment to centralist rule. The PNV strongly resisted the LOAPA in its passage through parliament, but no amendments were accepted by the government which retained the support of the PSOE on that issue.

The Tejero coup had a temporarily sobering effect on the now deeply divided ETA-PM which, on 28 February, announced an indefinite truce and released the consuls of Uruguay, El Salvador and Austria who had been kidnapped a week before in reaction to Arregi's death.[97] It seemed that the leaders of EE were succeeding in their attempt to get ETA-PM to lay down its arms, as a truce only made sense as a preliminary to dissolution. The bitter internal struggle made ETA-PM actions even more contradictory than usual. A few weeks before the announcement of the truce one of its commandos had kidnapped the Valencian industrialist Luis Suñer who remained a prisoner despite the truce. The fact that an ETA-PM spokesman had previously denied responsibility for the kidnapping caused surprise, as did the announcement that the truce might be ended if the other parties particularly the PSOE, did not cease their obstruction of the progress towards implementation of the autonomy Statute. Suñer was freed on 14 April after three months' captivity, on payment of a huge ransom.[98] The hard-line faction in ETA-PM, while determined to maintain the armed struggle, tried to demonstrate its 'measured' use of violence by concentrating on economic actions, such as the kidnapping for ransom of the father of the pop singer Julio Iglesias in December 1981. The police freed Iglesias and captured a number of his kidnappers on 17 January 1982, in a village in Aragón near the border with Navarre.[99] Even if the outcome of the kidnapping had not been such a disaster it would have harmed EIA's already deteriorating relationship with ETA-PM. Onaindía made one of his strongest attacks on ETA-PM on the eve of its Eighth Assembly, held in France in February 1982, where the expected split took place, with considerable ill-feeling but without internal violence.[100] There were now two organisations claiming to be ETA-PM, but the minority, now known as ETA-PM (VII), which announced that it would maintain a truce, was merely waiting until the good offices of EIA's leaders made it possible for its members to be given guarantees which would allow them to re-enter Spain and incorporate themselves into normal political life. In a press statement the group, which included most of the experienced political leaders, announced that they wished at all costs to escape from the cycle of action/repression/action.[101]

The majority faction, ETA-PM-VIII, declared its determination to carry on the armed struggle, but was soon to disintegrate. With the end of its association with EIA there was now very little to distinguish the two branches of ETA. However, past conflicts, and resentments over events such as the death of Pertur, made it difficult for ETA-PM-VIII members to merge with a group which included Pertur's presumed assassins, from the Bereziak. In the event, as ETA-PM declined, many of its members who wanted to continue the armed struggle joined the rival branch. The debate within ETA-PM had not been purely internal. PNV leaders attended discussions where, according to the minority faction, Javier Arzallus urged ETA-PM to continue the armed struggle as a means of bringing pressure on Madrid to amplify the scope of the autonomy statute and speed up the transfer of responsibilities to the autonomous Basque government.[102] The activities of ETA-PM-VIII were, however, of minor importance compared to those of ETA-M, to whom the creation of an autonomous government was not a fundamental question. As ETA-M was committed to fight for independence, the precise degree of power devolved to the autonomous parliament was important only to the extent that it created better conditions to pursue that struggle. The role of Herri Batasuna in the Basque Parliament was confined to making propaganda. The difficulties of remaining in parliament, while offering no clear alternative to the PNV majority, apart from the demand for independence, caused the Herri Batasuna representatives to withdraw in February 1981.

While ETA-M continued with a series of attacks which in March 1981 included the killing of policemen and army officers and bombings of public buildings, the ultra-right '*Batallón Vasco Español*' retaliated with attacks on nationalists and leftists.[103] Mass activity was most striking at funerals of nationalist heroes. On 9 March, when Telesforo Monzón died in Donibane in France, the passage of his corpse to the family seat in Vergara was an occasion for massive demonstrations, interruption to the funeral procession by the police, and demonstrations of protest at the police actions.[104] Herri Batasuna's ability to profit from such an event demonstrated yet again that it was able to tap reserves of emotion unavailable to conventional political parties. ETA-M's actions culminated on 8 May with an attack on the chief of the king's military household, General Joaquín de Valenzuela, when a bomb placed on his car roof by a motor-cycle passenger injured him and killed three of his companions.[105] ETA-M's ability to operate with impunity in Madrid enraged army officers and encouraged fears of another coup. On 18 October 1981 the police shot dead two leading ETA-M members and captured others during the same month. Government hopes that ETA-M's strength was being broken were shown to be mistaken as ETA-M returned to the offensive in November with shootings of policemen and bombings of electrical installations belonging to Iberduero, the developers of Lemóniz.[106] The death or arrest of leading members of the group merely braked ETA-M's activities for the time it took to rebuild its organisation.

In 1974 ETA-V, when beginning its attacks on the police, had stressed that these were to be confined to appropriate targets. Gradually, the definition of what constituted a justifiable target widened until the victims included alleged informers, all military officers and police, former policemen, families of Civil Guards, political opponents, people alleged to be involved in the drug trade, and anyone who refused to pay the 'revolutionary tax'. A considerable proportion of the Basque population fell into one or other of those categories. In addition, ETA-M, which had originally confined its activities to the Basque country, now acted frequently in other parts of Spain, particularly Madrid. When ETA-PM had pioneered kidnapping for ransom, planting bombs in tourist resorts and killing alleged drug pedlars, its actions had been criticised by ETA-M, but all these measures were adopted by it as its rival grew weaker.

On 28 October 1982 parliamentary elections produced a sweeping victory for the PSOE. The party's performance in the Basque country also improved dramatically from the poor results it had obtained in both local and parliamentary elections in 1979.[107] Now that Spain had a government led by one of the losers in the Civil War, it might seem that the way was clear to a settlement of the Basque problem. Such optimism failed to appreciate the nature of the nationalist feeling in the Basque country. The PSOE was a more formidable enemy than the UCD had been, because of its support among immigrant workers, who in the eyes of both ETA-M and the PNV constituted a potential fifth column. The new PSOE government made it clear even after the Supreme Court ruled, in August 1983, that LOAPA was unconstitutional that it remained committed to the content of the law. The change of government did not halt the offensive of ETA-M, as two days after the election an anti-tank grenade was fired at the Civil Guard post in Pasajes, Guipúzcoa, and the following day a car bomb exploded in Vitoria, killing a policemen and wounding twelve others. On 4 November an ETA-M commando killed General Lago Román, head of the Brunete armoured division in Madrid, and followed that up by a series of bombings and shootings of civilians in the Basque country.[108]

The new government continued with the slow transfer of responsibilities to the autonomous Basque community which had been agreed by its predecessor. The *Ertzantza* began to take over some responsibilities from the police, and the government released a number of prisoners who supported the dissolved ETA-PM-VII Assembly, following an agreement worked out by Juán José Rosón, the former UCD Minister of the Interior.[109] Tensions within the Basque country mounted as a demonstration supported by most political parties, protesting against ETA-M's shooting of three young men in Rentería on 18 October, was attacked by supporters of Herri Batasuna. ETA-M had accused the men of being informers, but had produced no evidence for a charge which was strongly denied by the two survivors and the relatives of the man who died. Felipe González, the new Prime Minister, could expect that his government would be more successful than its predecessors in getting support from the French authorities, as the election of a socialist government surely demonstrated that the Franco dictatorship had indeed ended and would encourage the French government to end its long-standing policy of giving refuge to opponents of the Spanish regime. The PSOE also hoped for better relationships with the moderate nationalist parties than those enjoyed by their UCD predecessors. The first encounter between Felipe González and the *Lendakari*, Carlos Garaicoechea, on 13 January 1983 seemed encouraging, although Garaicoechea insisted that there had to be a dialogue which should include Herri Batasuna, as well as the PNV and PSOE.[110]

The developments in the fragments of ETA-PM were contradictory. A press conference of ETA-PM-VII Assembly held in the French Basque country on 13 February 1983 declared its members' wish to abandon the armed struggle and return to Spain to work peacefully for the objectives of Euskadiko Ezkerra.[111] A spokesman declared that they had been threatened with reprisals by their former colleagues, now known as ETA-PM VIII, which was itself disintegrating as it was torn between those who wanted to join ETA-M, those who wished to continue as an independent group, and others who were becoming convinced that the armed struggle no longer served any useful purpose. Hopes of a better understanding between the PSOE government and the PNV than there had been with that of the UCD soon faded. Nationalists were strongly critical of González's Minister of Interior José Barrionuevo, a former official of the Francoist student union, whose vigorous support for the security forces, and conviction that ETA's violence was a police rather than a political problem, was anathema to nationalists of all sectors. Nor was Barrionuevo's strategy effective, as ETA-M's actions continued throughout 1983 and were supplemented by those of ETA-PM which was making a desperate attempt to recover its strength and cohesion, and by the CAA which carried out bombings and kidnappings and burned down a factory in Oyarzun in February. The even more shadowy Iraultza group (apparently a split from MC/EMK) joined in with a number of bombings.[112]

ETA-M's ability to kidnap rich people for ransom provided it with finance. In Madrid on March 25 1983 one of its commandos seized financier Diego de Prado, a friend of the king, and kept him in captivity for 72 days until his family paid an undisclosed ransom.[113] The organisation appeared to be able to act with impunity as the police force's few successes in freeing kidnap victims were at the expense of other terrorist groups. ETA-M's continuing ability to carry out an armed struggle was reinforced by the evidence of popular support provided by municipal elections held in May 1983. Once again the PNV was the victor, demonstrating the advantage it had over the PSOE at the grass roots. Herri Batasuna gained only slightly less votes than it had done in the previous municipal elections in 1979, so that the overall nationalist victory was striking proof in nationalist eyes that most Basques were in their camp.[114] The PSOE government antagonised the PNV by delaying and circumscribing the process towards autonomy, and seemed to be making little effort to stamp out police torture or to curb the activities of the extreme-right terrorist groups who were thought to be controlled by the police. The hostility felt towards the PSOE was shown in graffiti painted on walls all over the Basque country, equating it with the ultra-right terrorists. One of the government initiatives which most outraged nationalist opinion was the creation of the *Zona Especial del Norte* (ZEN), announced with great publicity in May 1983, which outlined a series of security measures and reinforcement of the police.[115] For Basque nationalists of all stripes the ZEN plan was yet one more example of 'Madrid's' inability to appreciate the political basis of the Basque problem.

The symbolic content of the conflict between the nationalists and others was vividly illustrated by the bitter polemics which erupted in the summer of 1983 in a number of towns over the apparently trivial matter of whether the *Ikurriña* or the Spanish flag should be displayed during local fiestas. Herri Batasuna, with ambivalent support from the PNV, was able to get a number of municipalities to declare that the *Ikurriña* only should be flown. The government-appointed civil governors would typically intervene, demanding that the Spanish flag should also be displayed. Attempts to reach a compromise by displaying neither flag, or both, generally failed as Herri Batasuna councillors would personally raise the *Ikurriña*, while if a local council decided to fly both flags, hooded men would lower the Spanish one. The 'war of the flags' which lasted over the summer of 1983, and was continued the following year, combined confrontation with the absence of dialogue and allowed Herri Batasuna to derive strength from a seemingly ludicrous issue. The depth of nationalist feeling was shown when Bandrés dismissed the conflict as a 'battle over rags'. His remarks were greeted with fury and denounced as unpatriotic by the press of the PNV as well as by Herri Batasuna, in a display of nationalist unity which transcended 'left' and 'right' labels.[116]

The PNV was itself divided between those who wanted to create a modern state organisation overcoming provincial separatism and those who wished to restore Foral rights. The Foralists were most strongly entrenched in Vizcaya, which as it had the largest population would have given them considerable power within a federal set-up. Although PNV members who tended to be more sympathetic to ETA were also those who supported traditional dialects and Foral rights, ETA had from its inception been an advocate of a modern Basque state, and had welcomed the creation of *Batua*, the modernised version of *Euskera*, as an instrument of modernisation and of unified Basque identity.

In 1984, after the second elections to the Basque autonomous parliament confirmed the PNV's dominance, the socialist party leader, Txiki Benegas, met with Garaicoechea to agree on a legislative pact that would avoid clashes between the regional and central administrations, and would facilitate the transfer of power to the Basque government.[117] Without the agreement, the PNV, despite its control of the autonomous government, would find its powers constantly blocked if it remained locked in an endless conflict with the central authority. On the other hand, the González government had accepted the letter, but not the spirit, of the Supreme Court's ruling that LOAPA was unconstitutional. A pact with the enemy, in the eyes of radical nationalists, made the PNV an accomplice in accepting a watered down version of the autonomy state. PNV leaders were very sensitive to such criticisms from Herri Batasuna, as they knew that they found an echo in the ranks of their own party. The legislative pact was to be the cause of constant tension as it was not a single easily specified matter, but rather a kind of non-aggression agreement. Garaicoechea's attempts to obtain greater powers for the Basque government led to sharp clashes with the PSOE leaders, particularly Felipe González, and also antagonised the upholders of provincial autonomy within the PNV.

Such complicated problems would have been difficult for any political party to deal with. In the PNV, given its lack of structured debate, disagreements inevitably took the very personal form of a quarrel between Arzallus and Garaicoechea, which had become evident in 1983. Arzallus, a superb controller of the party apparatus, had been largely responsible for promoting Garaicoechea, a charismatic figure much more attractive to the electorate than himself. The division of labour between a *Lendakari* who represented the whole Basque people, and therefore adopted a more conciliatory tone towards the party's enemies, and a party apparatus which represented the PNV's traditional aspirations for independence seemed to work well for a time. However, what started out as a division of labour became a choice of different political options. The situation became inflamed when, in April 1984, the national leadership of the PNV ordered its Navarrese members to vote for the conservative UPN candidate J. Luis Monge as president of the provincial government in preference to the PSOE candidate. The PNV, given its weakness in Navarre, had to form alliances, but the UPN, for the most part very right-wing former Francoists, were unattractive partners. The great majority of PNV activists refused to support the UPN, so in June the national leadership removed their leaders and imposed a committee of those loyal to themselves.[118] Garaicoechea, a

Navarrese, while not directly involved, did not conceal his sympathy for the expelled members.

Garaicoechea had to reconcile the demands of the more conservative and foralist sections of his own party with the need to come to some agreement with the PSOE. In an attempt to give some room for manoeuvre the PNV had freed him from party discipline in January 1984, but relations between Garaicoechea and the PNV's national leadership continued to deteriorate. During September rumours grew about a possible split within the party, but he denied that he would be forced to resign.[119] The *Lendakari* had considerable support within the PNV as was shown by the applause he received when he attended the celebrations of the day of the party in October. However, the Arzallus leadership, after consolidating its control of the party apparatus, held an Assembly on 20 November where the leadership's foralist line was accepted against the opposition of most of the party in Guipúzcoa and the expelled section in Navarre.[120] The circle was closing on Garaicoechea, and on 19 December he was forced to resign, although on the previous day he had denied that he would do so. The PNV installed José Antonio Ardanza, a colourless bureaucrat, as the new *Lendakari*.[121] Garaicoechea could have refused to go and called elections to the Basque parliament, but instead, he chose to pursue his fight within the party, in the belief that his support among the membership was greater than among the apparatus. Inevitably, Garaicoechea was forced to call for a reform of the PNV's internal organisation, in a political struggle which soon led to his followers expulsion, as an archaic voting structure gave a majority control to an apparatus which had only minority support among the members. The PSOE, both nationally and in the Basque country, took the surprising step of welcoming Garaicoechea's ousting and made it clear that Ardanza would get the co-operation which had been denied to his predecessor. Such co-operation with the most conservative and nationalist wing of the PNV surprised many observers,[122] but it helped to divide the PNV and deprived it of a leader who had given the party a modern and liberal image.

The prolonged struggle within the PNV was seen as secondary by ETA-M which continued to pursue its essentially military strategy. Even when severe flooding in Vizcaya in August 1983 killed more than fifty people and caused immense damage, the armed struggle continued, as ETA-M killed a policeman and a bar owner in separate incidents in September. The remnants of ETA-

PM-VIII added to the violence by carrying out a number of bombings in September, and in October kidnapped an army pharmacist, Alberto Martín, in Bilbao. Inevitably, given the government's refusal to accept ETA-PM's demands that an ETA-PM communiqué should be televised, Captain Alberto Martín was killed. A telephone call to the Red Cross in Bilbao on 18 October told them of the abandoned hut where his body would be found.[123]

That killing was hardly a qualitative step in the escalation of violence, as both wings of ETA had long since regarded any army officer as a legitimate target. Nevertheless, the death of someone whose duties, in spite of his military status, were hardly warlike caused some unfavourable reaction. Carlos Garaicoechea attended Martín's funeral, where ultra-right mourners shouted insults at him. In an attempt at excusing the murder an ETA-PM communiqué alleged that Martín had been an intelligence officer, but produced no evidence for the claim. Garaicoechea's reception at Alberto Martín's funeral showed that the climate of violence was hardening as members of the security forces, enraged by their inability to counter the attacks on them, prepared to create a counter-terrorist force. A few days before Martín Barrios's killing, two young Basque refugees had disappeared in Bayonne, and on 19 October two Spanish policemen were arrested in Pau, France, accused of attacking an alleged ETA member, José María Larretxea. On 22 October thousands of people demonstrated against the presumed killing of the two missing Basque refugees.[124] Nationalist opinion was becoming incensed at the calls of Alianza Popular leader Manuel Fraga for a 'dirty war' carried out by illegal means against ETA. All sections of nationalist opinion suspected that the government was contemplating such measures.

The attacks on refugees in France continued when, on 5 December, Segundo Marey, who worked for the Sokoa Cooperative, which employed many Basque refugees, was kidnapped in Hendaya. As Marey, who was released nine days later near the Spanish border, appeared to have no connection with any branch of ETA, it seemed that he had been mistaken for an ETA-M member. The event would not have appeared very significant but for the fact that the kidnappers called themselves the *Grupo Antiterrorista de Liberación* (GAL), initials which were soon to become notorious as part of the dirty war against ETA. As GAL continued with what was to be a very sustained and bloody compaign by

killing another Basque refugee in the bar where he worked in
Bayonne, on 20 December, nationalist conviction that the
González government was behind its activities was illustrated
when a mob attacked the PSOE headquarters in Orereta and
when the CAA attempted to destroy PSOE headquarters in
Lasarte and Hernani.[125] GAL shot an ETA member Mikel
Goikoetxea in St. Jean de Luz on 28 December, and he died on
New Years' Day.[126] The spokesmen of Herri Batasuna, and the
journals *Egin* and *Punto y Hora*, continually alleged that the GAL
was a creation of the Spanish government, acting with the
complicity of the French authorities. In fact, there was evidence
that the French government was angry at GAL's activities, as a
number of its members were arrested by French police following
attacks on Basque refugees. The basis of the charge that the
French authorities encouraged GAL was that the assassins,
mainly French and North African members of the criminal under-
world, possessed their victims' addresses and photographs. Such
documentation could, presumably, have been obtained at a fairly
low level of the police hierarchy by criminals through established
police contacts.

As the struggle between ETA-M and the Spanish government
became more bitter, ETA-M's choice of targets became more
indiscriminate. On 29 January 1984 one of its commandos shot
dead Lieutenant-General Guillermo Quintana Lacaci, as he
returned from mass in Madrid.[127] Quintana Lacaci was an odd
choice of victim for a movement which had started out as a struggle against Fascism, as he had, as Captain-General of Madrid
military region, been one of the key people in defeating the coup
of 23 February 1981. The wave of killings by GAL and ETA-M
members embittered the election campaign to the second
autonomous Basque parliament which was called for 26 February.
A GAL commando killed two ETA-M members in Hendaye on
8 February, and Basque refugees in France held a hunger strike
at Bayonne cathedral in protest at the authorities' failure to
protect them. Three days before the elections a unit of the CAA
shot dead Enrique Casas, who led the PSOE list for Guipúzcoa,
at the door of his home in San Sebastián.[128] The murder
outraged the ranks of the PSOE, and Herri Batasuna's first reaction was to denounce it as yet another dirty trick by the security
forces, designed to discredit ETA-M. The only previous PSOE
sympathiser to be killed by any Basque nationalist organisation
had been accused of being an informer although no evidence for

the claim was ever produced. As no such claim was made against
Casas, the killing indicated that all PSOE activists were possible
targets for the CAA. Herri Batasuna spokesmen deplored the
attack but without any of the fervour which they reserved for the
death of ETA activists. The killing had little effect on the results
of the elections. The PNV continued to improve its position; so,
to a lesser extent did Herri Batasuna and Euskadiko Ezkerra. In
Guipúzcoa the general trend was slightly more favourable to the
PSOE.[129]

Increased co-operation between the French and Spanish
governments took the form of deporting ETA activists to various
countries in Central America and Africa, which were persuaded
to take them by concessions on aid or trade. If ETA violence had
indeed been primarily a police question such measures would
have gone a long way to solving it. The PNV's leaders believed
that the PSOE was committing a tremendous error in following
traditional centralist policy and in refusing to meet Basque
aspirations for autonomy. The government's strategy of removing ETA's operational base in French Basque country by expulsions produced protest demonstrations and were grist to Herri
Batasuna's mill. In the long-drawn-out struggle over the extent
of the transfer of powers from the central to the autonomous
government, the PSOE government continually tried to delay
and reduce the extent of the autonomy granted. Given the PNV's
close identification between party and government, the conflict
became one between the two parties and even between the two
ethnic groups within the Basque population. Euskadiko Ezkerra's
contention that the Basque nation had yet to be built, on the basis
of co-operation and mutual respect by both ethnic groups, made
very little headway against the rancour produced by ETA and
GAL.

Basque nationalists believed that GAL was the brainchild of
Francisco Alvarez who, in 1983, was chief of police for Bilbao, and
was later information officer for the Directorate of State Security.
Alvarez worked closely with leading police officers such as Saenz
de Santamaría, who refused to disclose information on the
participants of a shooting which led to several deaths in
Hendaya.[130] GAL was undoubtedly much more successful than
any official police action in killing ETA members. From its beginning in late 1983 until March 1986, when pressure by the new
French Chirac government halted its activities, it killed twenty-
four people and wounded twenty-five, including both ETA

members and innocent people. GAL's actions were undoubtedly regarded with complacency by some PSOE leaders, such as García Damboronea, but the effect of the campaign was devastating for the negative effect it had on nationalist opinion. One of GAL's greatest coups occurred on 19 June 1984 when its activists planted a bomb on a motor-cycle and seriously injured Román Orbe and Tomás Pérez Revilla, a veteran leader of ETA-M, who died six weeks later.[131] As the French government continued with its policy of deporting ETA members to a variety of countries and placing more restrictions on remaining Basque refugees, ETA-M's activities became more difficult. GAL, which had begun by attacking ETA members in France, now moved against Herri Batasuna in Spain. On 20 November 1984 a GAL commando entered the Bilbao office of Santiago Brouard, a paediatrician and Senator for Herri Batasuna, and shot him dead. Herri Batasuna supporters interpreted the killing as an indication that the government intended to launch an indiscriminate attack on them, pointing out that a police guard on an embassy adjoining Brouard's office had been removed shortly before his killing.[132]

Herri Batasuna spokesmen alleged that Brouard's death was directly authorised by the Spanish government and proved that the change from Francoism to a constitutional monarchy with a socialist government was merely cosmetic. Suspicion accentuated when the magistrate in charge of the investigation was refused permission to question police witnesses and removed from the case. ETA-M retaliated the next day by ambushing and severely wounding General Luis Rosón and his chauffeur in Madrid.[133] The General may have been selected because he was the brother of Juan José Rosón, the former UCD Minister of the Interior, who had pioneered the system of pardon which had helped persuade ETA-PM-(VII) to abandon the armed struggle. Herri Batasuna responded to Brouard's assassination with a call for a general strike through Euskadi on 22 November. The PNV backed the call for the strike, but asked its supporters to attend separate demonstrations from those organised by Herri Batasuna, where support for ETA-M was strongly expressed. Herri Batasuna spokesmen made it clear that representatives of the 'Spanish' parties and of Euskadiko Ezkerra would be unwelcome at the funeral service. In Vizcaya, apart from the larger factories which were strongholds of the Left, most schools, shops and commercial premises closed.[134] GAL attacks on ETA sympathisers continued throughout the early months of 1985 but the government's main strategy was to destroy ETA-M's base in France through the co-operation of the French government in deporting ETA members to Africa and South America. Some ETA leaders were also handed over to face charges in Spain, despite strong opposition from the Basque government and the PNV, but that did not halt ETA-M's attacks, although the PSOE government hoped that it would eventually do so. The deportations did have a radicalising effect on the leadership of the PNV which once more began to support the demand for negotiations between ETA-M and the Government and to call for independence, through the formula of a return to the situation which prevailed before the end of the first Carlist War in 1839.[135]

Both the PNV and Euskadiko Ezkerra were extremely critical of central government delay in handing over police functions to the autonomous police, the *Ertzantza*, who were still mainly engaged in guarding public buildings and carrying out traffic duties. Nevertheless, it was the government's declared intention to hand over most routine policing to the autonomous police. An army officer, Lieutenant-General Carlos Díaz Arcocha, a native of Bilbao from a Carlist family, was named head of the *Ertzantza* early in 1985, a measure which marked the type of compromise which the central government saw as necessary to establish an autonomous police. On 7 March 1985 he was killed when an ETA-M commando planted a bomb in his car parked at a petrol station, next to the cafeteria where he was having his customary breakfast. Díaz Arcocha had taken no precautions whatsoever, and had obviously believed that his position as a functionary of the Basque government ensured that he would not be attacked. Such a belief had been shared by many and his death produced consternation among moderate nationalists.[136] Although Díaz Arcocha had not been threatened, he knew that ETA-M had in 1978 killed the army officer who commanded the provincial police force of Alva, the *Miqueletes*. On that occasion ETA-M had stated their respect for the *Miqueletes*, as a genuine Basque institution, which should not be disfigured by the leadership of a Spanish army officer, so in killing Díaz Arcocha ETA-M were not creating a precedent, nor starting a general offensive against the autonomous police. The Basque government issued a ten-point statement condemning the killing which, although it did not specifically mention ETA,[137] was greeted with gratitude by the Spanish government.

Such declarations did nothing to check ETA-M's violence

either in the Basque country or in Madrid, where on 12 June 1985 one of its commandos killed an army colonel, his chauffeur and a policeman.[139] ETA-M now resumed what had become a regular summer campaign of planting bombs in Mediterranean holiday resorts. GAL continued with its attacks on nationalists, mainly in France where they killed the local agent of the pro-ETA newspaper *Egin*, Javier Galdeano, on 31 March and continued to make bloody and indiscriminate attacks throughout the year. On 25 September four Basque refugees were shot dead in an attack on a bar in Bayonne.[139] As the PSOE government completed its third year in office it was no nearer solving the Basque problem. Basque rejection of the security forces mounted when the body of Mikel Zabaltza, who had been arrested on 26 November, was found in the Bidasoa river three weeks later, as the police story that the prisoner had escaped from custody was widely disbelieved. GAL's activities slackened in late 1985, but it returned to the offensive on 4 December when its activists wounded a Basque refugee in Heleta in the French Basque country. A few days afterward a Basque cultural centre in Bayonne was bombed. In Biarritz a French citizen died on 3 January after he was shot on Christmas Eve. On 8 February 1986 a Basque refugee was shot in Donibane and on 17 February two French citizens were killed in Bidarrai.[140] GAL faded from the scene in spring 1986, partly because of the retaliations by ETA-M which killed several of its leaders, but mainly because of the Spanish government's response to French pressure.

In March 1985 a GAL leader, Jean Pierre Cherid, had died when trying to plant a bomb in Miarritze and on 17 August another leading member, Clement Perret, was killed by ETA-M.[141] As adverse publicity from journals in both France and Spain giving details of GAL members' links with the Spanish police made the GAL tactic counter-productive, the French government's declared willingness to return ETA members to Spain to stand trial, or where no specific charges were available, to deport them to African or Latin American countries, was now a much greater threat to ETA-M. A court decision on 13 March 1986 that ETA was an 'association of evildoers' made it much easier to proceed against its members even when there were no specific charges against them. Conservative Spaniards had often charged that the French government had feared to take decisive action because of fears of ETA retaliation, but neither ETA-M nor its sister groups acted against targets in France and ETA-M had always tried to restrain the actions of Iparraterrak, its French Basque disciples, understandably so, in view of the consequences of endangering ETA-M's French base. The Spanish government looked forward to the elimination of ETA given the new co-operation with France. Such optimism was, at the very least, premature, as the deportations soured relations with the PNV and the autonomous Basque Government, provided material for a wave of demonstrations by Herri Batasuna, and provoked the burning of cars belonging to French tourists. Even more alarmingly, the deportations seemed not to affect ETA-M's ability to continue its struggle, not only in the Basque country but in Madrid. On 6 February 1986, shortly before the referendum on whether Spain should remain in NATO, ETA-M's commando *España*, based permanently in Madrid, machine-gunned the car of vice-admiral Cristóbal Colón de Carvajal, a direct descendant of Columbus, killing him and his chauffeur and wounding another officer.[142] Colón de Carvajal, in spite of his high rank, was a naval museum keeper, not an active service officer. Two days before, in Rentería, a civil guard and his nine-year-old daughter had been gravely wounded when a bomb had been planted in the father's car.[143]

The inability of the police to prevent ETA-M's actions or capture those responsible confirmed conservative leaders such as Manuel Fraga in their opinion that tougher measures involving suppression of civil liberties were necessary, while liberal opinion became dissatisfied with the spectacular inefficiency of security forces, who had become so reliant on the use of torture and generalised repression that they were ineffectual in a democracy. Criticism of the police eased temporarily when there were a few successes in the anti-terrorist struggle. On 14 March an ETA-M member, Angel María Gallaraga, was shot dead in San Sebastián in an encounter where a policeman also lost his life. In March the police arrested a number of members of ETA-M's organisation in Navarre and claimed to have broken it up completely. Also in March, six people who were alleged to be responsible for the killing of the head of the *Ertzantza*, Díaz Arcocha, were arrested. The most heartening event of all occurred on 11 January 1986 when the Bilbao industrialist José Pedro Guzmán, a director of the football club Atlético de Bilbao, was freed by a police unit from his place of captivity, a disused hut near Bilbao, where he had been held since being seized on 30 December.[144] The freeing of Guzmán was the first occasion where the police had succeeded in frustrating an ETA-M kidnapping, although several victims of ETA-PM and the CAA had been freed on previous occasions. Three of the kidnappers were seized and the repercussions of the event lead to twenty-six arrests,[145] so it seemed that ETA-M was losing its immunity and that the police were at last capable of obtaining information on its activities. Guzmán was an apolitical figure, but the kidnapping was strongly criticised by the press and by the directors of Atlético de Bilbao. The police success was however an isolated event. Subsequent actions of ETA-M both in the Basque country and Madrid showed that the police had no success in infiltrating ETA-M, nor reliable information on its intentions or the identity of its activists.

The freeing of Guzmán did not indicate that ETA-M was no longer capable of undertaking similar actions, as on 10 March in San Sebastián one of its commandos seized an industrialist, José María Egaña, who was released after 19 days in captivity on payment of a ransom.[146] The Spanish government strategy for defeating ETA-M depended more and more on gaining French co-operation in dismantling its base in the French Basque country. Such hopes seemed fulfilled when Domingo Iturbe Abasolo 'Txomin' was arrested in late April and on 15 May sentenced to three months' imprisonment, although that action was unwelcome to the PNV. The attack on ETA-M's French base had little immediate effect on its military capacity as it continued to carry out assassinations of policemen and others in the Basque country, and, in Madrid on 8 May, made an attempt on the life of Antonio Hernández Gil, President of the Supreme Court, by firing anti-tank grenades from a specially adapted car.[147] The fact that ETA-M commandos could operate in this way in the capital showed that, at least in the short term, the government's campaign was not working. The failure of the government to halt ETA-M's violence was a minor factor in the parliamentary elections held on 22 June, as no other party had a credible alternative. The PSOE was comfortable winner, giving Felipe González four more years in office. In the Basque country the election campaign was affected by the sudden death on 10 June of an ETA prisoner, twenty-seven-year-old Joseba Asensio, in the prison of Herrera de la Mancha, from undiagnosed tuberculosis.[148] Asencio's burial was the occasion for violent demonstrations, when the police charged the funeral possession when it took an unauthorised route. The effects of Asensio's death probably increased Herri Batasuna's vote and helped increase its representation in Congress from two to five. However, a more important factor was the disarray in the ranks of the PNV where supporters of Garaicoechea, who had been excluded from the lists of candidates, either abstained or voted for other parties. The PNV's representation in Congress dropped from eight to six, and in Navarre their vote was derisory. Euskadiko Ezkerra improved its performance and succeeded in getting a second member elected to Congress. The PSOE's leaders had to balance their satisfaction at the PNV's disarray with the realisation that Herri Batasuna's base showed no sign of weakening, in spite of revulsion at ETA-M's violence.[149]

The French authorities continued with their harsher line, imposing sentences of up to seven years' imprisonment on ETA-M leaders in June. In the same month a French court sentenced four Spanish policemen in their absence to eighteen months in prison for attacking an ETA-PM leader in France in October 1983, but the Spanish authorities refused to hand over the convicted men.[150] ETA-M continued with what was to be its main tactic in the coming period, a series of car bombings which on 28 June in Madrid killed a Civil Guard and injured eleven others. When the French government deported ETA-M's main leader Iturbe Abásolo to Gabon relations between the Spanish and the Basque government worsened as, unknown to Madrid, agents of the autonomous government, including García Andoain, head of the *Ertzantza*, had been engaged in discussions with Iturbe, said to be a moderate within ETA-M, over the conditions for a ceasefire. Arzallus accused the Spanish government of being more intransigent than ETA-M.[151] As if to show that its ruthlessness and military capacity were greater than ever, ETA-M's Madrid commando exploded a car bomb in the centre of Madrid on 21 July, killing eleven young Civil Guards who had been undergoing a course in traffic control. Exactly a week later ETA-M returned to the attack by firing six anti-tank grenades at the offices of the Ministry of Defence, causing substantial damage to the building and to cars parked nearby.[152] The ability of ETA-M's Madrid commando to act with such impunity and to escape without arrests or casualties showed the security forces in a bad light. However, the Spanish government could take comfort from the fact that the French authorities continued to co-operate by handing over suspected terrorists. On 23 July another ETA-M member, Juan Ramón Nafarrete, was delivered to the Spanish police, to the dismay of the Basque government and PNV leaders, who were convinced that such actions would not bring peace any nearer. Although ETA-M carefully refrained from carrying out reprisals in France, which would have put their supporters under yet greater pressure, its leaders were unable to control their French equivalents in *Iparraterak*, who on 25 July gravely wounded a policeman in an attack on the courthouse at Bayonne where ETA members had recently been sentenced.[153]

The French government continued systematically to expel ETA activists. ETA members who had broken the law by carrying arms or breaking the terms of their residence had formerly been sentenced to fairly short terms of imprisonment, but were now deported. A good example of the new approach was shown when Koldo Dorbarán was arrested on 29 July in St. Jean de Luz, accused of carrying a firearm. Dobarán was taken to a magistrate, who released him provisionally until September when he was to be tried for the alleged offence, but the police immediately took him to the border and handed him over to the Spanish police, in spite of the fact that he had previously been granted right to residence and given a work permit.[154] A consistent application of such a principle would have led to the deportation of all known ETA members and would have been a greater menace to them than GAL had been. French Basque nationalists, organised in the defence group *Herriarekin* ('with the people'), mounted a campaign against the deportations which had considerable support among the local clergy, and in Spain a number of French-registered cars were set on fire by ETA sympathisers. However, ETA-M's main hope of reversing the now unfavourable position was to mobilise mass support in the Spanish Basque country where the new measures were unpopular among all nationalists. Ardanza, the leader of the Basque autonomous government, criticised the deportations and was in turn criticised by Javier Solano, the central government representative in the Basque country. Herri Batasuna activists organised a march in protest against the French government's deportations. Detachments set out from different points in the four Basque provinces and from the French Basque country and converged on San Sebastián. There were frequent clashes with the police during the march and on 26 July, its final day, two Civil Guards were killed by a bomb in Aretxabaleta, in Guipúzcoa. The marchers were brutally attacked by the police after the civil government banned its finishing rally.[155] The summer season of demonstrations had ended in the same way as in previous years, and the struggle between ETA-M and the Spanish government was as far from a solution as ever.

Throughout 1986 ETA-M's calls for negotiations with both the government and the *Poderes Fácticos* who allegedly ran Spain under the camouflage of a parliamentary democracy increased. The government denied that it was prepared to negotiate, or recognise the negotiations undertaken by the head of the *Ertzantza* on behalf of the Basque government and the PNV, claiming that effective policing and increased co-operation with France would lead to ETA's defeat. ETA's renewed emphasis on its willingness to negotiate did, indeed, show that the attacks on its base in France and its inability to show any way out of the impasse presented it with difficulties, which did not however amount to the imminent collapse awaited by the PSOE leaders. ETA-M was still able to attack the security forces, almost as a routine. The desire for a negotiated amnesty, which implied the disciplining of those who sought individual pardons, led ETA-M into a costly blunder in September, when one of its units shot dead Dolores González Catarain 'Yoyes', a leading member of the group until 1980, as she walked with her five-year-old child in her home village of Ordizia. 'Yoyes' had believed that her former comrades would not retaliate against her while she adhered to an implicit agreement to abstain from any public statement or political activity. Her funeral produced the familiar denunciation of terrorism from most political spokesmen, which Herri Batasuna supporters saw as the cynical attempt to make capital from the execution of a traitor.[156]

ETA-M's kidnapping of an industrialist, and PNV member, Lucio Aguinagalde in Vitoria on 15 October, and his subsequent freeing by the *Ertzantza* on 2 November, illustrated the disagreements over the role of the autonomous police, between the PSOE and the PNV. When a unit of the *Ertzantza* located the cave where Aguinagalde was held prisoner, the head of the corps since the assassination of Díaz Arcocha, Genaro García de Andoain, a PNV veteran and personal friend of the kidnapped man, was shot dead in the action which freed Aguinagalde, although one of his captors managed to escape. Arzallus, the PNV's President, hailed the rescue as a triumph for the *Ertzantza* and a refutation of the PSOE's belief that the corps were unwilling to act against ETA-M. The Spanish police thought it absurd that a unit of traffic police, untrained for such operations, led by a man of 67, and armed, contrary to regulations, with shotguns, should undertake such a hazardous task and allow one of the kidnappers to escape, instead of informing the Civil Guard of their discovery.[157]

The decision to hold elections for the Basque parliament on 30 November increased the political tension between nationalists and 'Spanish' forces. The PNV and Garaicochea's party, Nacionalistas Vascos, competed in proclaiming a more fervent nationalism than that which prevailed in the united party prior to the split, so that the differences between them, apart from personal rivalries, concerned preferences for a unitary Euskadi or a restoration of the Foral institutions.

ETA-M showed its capacity to carry out spectacular killings on 26 October, when a motor-cyclist with a pillion passenger drew up beside the car of the Civil Governor of Guipúzcoa, General Rafael Garrido Gil, in San Sebastián and placed a bomb on the roof.[158] The explosion killed the general, his chauffeur and his son and injured a number of bystanders, one of whom, a Portuguese woman, died later. The action showed an indifference to the lives of bystanders, unusual hitherto in actions undertaken within Euskadi. The fact that a predecessor of Garrido had been shot dead by ETA-M in September 1979 showed the scale of casualties among the higher military echelons. The victory over ETA so long awaited by Spanish governments seemed to be brought nearer when, on 3 November, the French police struck the greatest blow ever against ETA-M by raiding the co-operative furniture factory *Sokoa*, which provided work for Basque refugees, in Hendaye, a few hundred yards from the Spanish border, seizing a huge quantity of concealed weapons including ground-to-air missiles, as well as extensive documentations on the collection of ETA-M's 'revolutionary tax'. In line with the French government's harsher treatment of ETA members, six of those arrested after the raid were handed over to the Spanish police.[159] The Spanish government could, once again, persuade itself that victory was in sight although attacks on police continued.

The elections for the Basque parliament, held on 30 November, showed a much more varied picture than the dominance of the PNV produced by the two previous elections. The PNV obtained 17 seats out of 75, Garaicoechea's Nacionalistas Vascos got 13, the PSOE 19 and Euskadiko Ezkerra 9. Herri Batasuna, whose representatives had boycotted the assembly since 1981, obtained 13 seats.[160] However, for most Basque nationalists the concept of a Basque government dominated by non-nationalists was a contradiction in terms, so there could be little hope that the assembly or the government it produced would be able to solve the Basque country's problems. The year ended without the parties being able to agree on the formation of a coalition government. Herri Batasuna's announcement that the party would lift its decision not to participate in parliament, if by so doing the PSOE could be kept out of the government, illustrated the continuing antagonism between the nationalist and non-nationalist communities on which ETA-M's strength ultimately rested.

It had seemed that, as the autonomous Basque government took over the functions in education, security and communications provided for in the autonomy Statute, the grievances which had sustained ETA-M would disappear, and it would be unable to sustain its armed struggle. Yet throughout the first half of the 1980s ETA-M carried out a much more extensive campaign of robberies, bombings and assassinations than that undertaken during the Franco dictatorship. Support for ETA-M was sustained by the brutality of the police, who, even in the 1980s, continued to torture suspects and assault innocent citizens, and were suspected of complicity in the murder of ETA-M sympathisers. The ill-treatment of Basque prisoners and the prospect of refugees in France being returned to face trial in Spain were opposed by many PNV supporters, who continued to extend a tolerance to ETA-M which aroused resentment in Madrid. The PNV leaders' attitude continued to be that, although ETA-M's strategy was mistaken and many of its actions were indefensible, most of its members were motivated by genuine patriotism. The support which some priests gave to ETA-M showed that the PNV members' attitudes were shared by many in the nationalist community.

The PNV's leaders regarded the 'Spanish' parties' criticisms as unreasonable and held that ETA-M's violence was a predictable, if mistaken, reaction to successive governments' delay in transferring powers to Basque hands.[161] Apart from the ambivalent attitude of the PNV, ETA-M could point to Herri Batasuna's electoral support, from 13% of the electorate and considerably more in traditionally nationalist areas.[162] Herri Batasuna was much less successful in becoming either the social movement or the political party which some of its supporters had desired. Ambitious plans for alternative assemblies, which would challenge the official administration, came to nothing. Its youth and women's movements remained shells, while LAB never became a serious rival either to ELA or the 'Spanish' trade unions. The decline of ETA-PM and the failure to create the kind of mass organisation which ETA-M's theory had required left radical nationalism with a structure consisting of Herri Batasuna, the daily newspaper *Egin*, the weekly journal *Punto y Hora*, the amnesty committees, and various ad-hoc organisations. Both Herri Batasuna and ETA-M retained a socialist rhetoric, whose lack of precision was a necessary consequence of radical nationalism's varied base. While right-wing opponents accused ETA-M's leaders of wishing to create an Albanian type of society, PSOE leaders compared radical nationalism's ideology to Peronism, in its combination of rhetoric, fanaticism and absence of any concrete social programme.[163]

The endurance of ETA-M and Herri Batasuna showed that radical nationalism could draw on strengths unavailable to groups such as FRAP, which did not have a base in a community with a strong sense of ethnic solidarity. Basque nationalism was fortunate in possessing an exceptionally potent myth backed by Basque ethnic and linguistic distinctiveness and the memory of the *Fueros*, which were presented as proof that there had once been a golden age when Basque liberty had been acknowledged by the Spanish crown, whose granting of noble status to all Basques in the sixteenth century was seen as further evidence of Basque superiority. The myth of a golden past was supplemented by one describing defeat and oppression, dating from the conclusion of either the first or second Carlist War, the loss of the *Fueros* and the plague of the *Maketo* invasion with its dramatic effect on Basque life and culture. According to nationalistic doctrine the redeemer, Sabino Arana, had awakened the sleeping soul of the Basque nation, taught it to recognise its oppression and called the people to honour its duty to the fatherland. Redemption was never final and the backsliding of the PNV had to be countered by the young men who in 1959 formed ETA and began the long process of national reawakening. The richness of Basque nationalism's symbolic and mythical heritage made it unnecessary for all its themes to be continually deployed. Basque racial superiority was hardly emphasised from the 1930s onwards. Although the PNV continued, even in the 1980s, to stress its Christian character, radical nationalism had a much more ambivalent relationship with religion, combining declarations of Marxism with support from some priests. The development of industry inevitably resulted in a reduced emphasis on the supposedly idyllic life of Basque peasants, which had been an important part of the original nationalist ideology. Instead, the high level of industrialisation came to be seen as further evidence of Basque superiority over backward Spain.

The fairly typical development from an agricultural to an industrial society was seen by nationalists as a thrilling history of a golden past, defeat and renewal. Nor was the story finished; past glories could be recovered and an independent Euskadi established, at the cost of blood, suffering and martyrdom, if each generation played its part in the struggle. The young men who responded to the challenge of winning Euskadi's independence came predominantly from the ethnically Basque middle class, from family backgrounds sympathetic to the PNV. After 1977, election returns showed that the social support of radical nationalism lay in Guipúzcoa and Vizcaya, particularly the former, and that it was strongest in traditional strongholds of the PNV. The evidence of social research and opinion polls confirmed that it was a movement of the ethnically Basque middle class.[164]

The social composition of both activists and sympathisers of radical nationalism explained Herri Batasuna's ambivalent relationship to the PNV. The PNV's leaders were often horrified at the violent language of Herri Batasuna's spokesmen, but nevertheless there were areas of agreement. In contrast, Herri Batasuna's relationship with the PSOE was from the beginning one of unmitigated hostility. The disagreements between Herri Batasuna and the PNV can be best compared to quarrels within a family, which, while they often brought charges of treachery on the one hand and communism on the other, did not destroy the family's unity. Family solidarity was demonstrated when the PNV spokesmen paid tribute to ETA's martyrs or threatened to make common cause with Herri Batasuna if 'Madrid' remained blind to Basque grievances. EIA and EE, the parties which had been supported by ETA-PM, had a much more ambiguous attitude to both the PNV and the 'Spanish' parties. As EIA, and subsequently EE, aimed to end what they saw as the false duality between the national and the class struggle, they had to reach out to the working-class supporters of the 'Spanish' parties as well as to nationalists who backed the PNV. EE's attempt to carry out this task caused it to adopt incoherent and contradictory postures. Perhaps the strongest manifestation of EE's radicalism was the demand that the state schools and the *Ikastolas* should be combined in a unified system of free public education.[165] This was unacceptable to the PNV which shared the commitment of other conservative Spaniards to independent church-run schools. Herri Batasuna, for its part, wisely never risked alienating its more conservative supporters by such a proposal. EE's limited popularity was an indication, not of its success in uniting the national and class struggle, but of the existence of an educated middle class often of mixed Basque and Spanish descent, which found the PNV's clericalism and conservatism unattractive, wished to integrate the immigrants into an autonomous Euskadi and was, consequently, unhappy about Herri Batasuna's chauvinism and intolerance.

The discrepancy between EE's and Herri Batasuna's activities and social base, and their adoption of a Marxist rhetoric, had been a constant of radical nationalist politics ever since ETA had adopted socialist principles at its Fourth Assembly in 1965. For ETA's left-wing critics the organisation's 'Marxism' was at best a confusion produced by the impact of the Cuban and Vietnamese revolutions on ignorant and impressionable young men.[166] Such critics pointed to the emptiness of ETA-M's and Herri Batasuna's social programme, which consisted merely of a demand for the improvement of the living conditions of the working class. Yet the belief of the successive waves of ETA activists who had embraced some version of Marxism, that they were transforming their organisation, had been shared by conservatives such as Txillardegi, who had abandoned ETA for that reason. The main attraction of Marxism for left-wing factions of ETA lay in Lenin's doctrine of 'the right to national self-determination', which seemed to give doctrinal legitimation to the struggle for Basque independence. Indeed, the 'right to national self-determination' was seen by ETA-V, and later ETA-M, as the core of Marxism, and the 'Spanish' left's vacillation on the question as proof of its apostasy. Apart from this concentration on a doctrine never held by Marx or Engels,[167] the most obvious divergence from Marxist concepts consisted of the substitution of the 'nation', or the 'people', for the working class. Those factions such as ETA-Berri or ETA-VI which did begin to make an analysis in terms of social class soon ceased to be nationalist, while ETA-PM was destroyed because of the incoherence of a theory which caused it to vacillate between Marxist and nationalist positions. In the mainstream ETA tradition, reference to the working class was purely rhetorical and its activities bore little resemblance to those of the parties which belonged to the traditional workers' movement.

Just as the working class, the agent of revolution according to Marx, played no independent role in either ETA's theory or practice,[168] so the capitalist class, which Marx saw as the workers' adversary, was singularly absent from ETA's analysis. A movement which based itself on the 'people' could hardly attack a social class most of whose members belonged to the 'people'. The enemy was identified first as 'Spain' and later as 'imperialism'. Where a more precise identification was attempted, the enemy became the 'oligarchy', the small group of Basque capitalists conveniently situated in the Bilbao suburb of Neguri, far from ETA's strongholds, who had, supposedly, betrayed Euskadi because of the benefits which they derived from their involvement in the Spanish economy. The absence of class analysis allowed ETA to include or exclude individuals from the *Pueblo Trabajador Vasco* according to their behaviour or political ideas rather than their class position.

The theory that the Basque country was a colony, although it included some of the most industrialised parts of Spain, provided an attractive blueprint for ETA's leaders and legitimised their own role as the crucial agents in the people's struggle. Few of ETA's leaders were either bourgeois or working-class, and those who had been manual workers were generally from semi-rural backgrounds, with links to the land and to traditional Basque society. ETA's emphasis on the role of an armed elite resulted in the blurring of the concept of class. When in 1976, for example, ETA-PM declared that it was creating a Marxist-Leninist working-class party, there was little indication of the specific content of the proposed party's activities, or concern that ETA-PM had almost no roots in working class struggle.

The content of the socialism which ETA and its successors espoused was never clarified. Neither former ETA leaders nor activists in EE or Herri Batasuna displayed much interest in concrete proposals to change the Basque country's social and economic structure. Socialism was seen in vague terms as a fairer society and the stress was on idealism and self-sacrifice rather than on a distinct political programme.[168] The absence of such a programme explains the paradox of ETA-M and Herri Batasuna's ambitious relationship with the PNV, and the surprising spectacle of a conservative party refusing to condemn wholeheartedly an organisation which extorted money from and kidnapped the PNV's own supporters. Although most of the PNV's leaders seemed satisfied with the main lines of the settlement agreed in 1979, some saw the autonomy Statute as a stage in the achievement of an independent Euskadi. If independence remained the PNV's objective, then its differences with ETA were hardly fundamental. Even if many of the more extreme declarations of PNV leaders were designed to please their base and to extract more concessions from Madrid,[169] such statements made ETA's actions seem less isolated, and indicated that the organisation was still a part of the nationalist community.

ETA has often been declared by its opponents as being on the point of extinction, and has indeed at several times been reduced to a small group of activists with little ability to influence events. Many observers have been surprised at its survival after 1977. The leaders of the PNV remained convinced that if all the security forces were controlled by an autonomous Basque government, so that the main target of ETA-M's violence could only be fellow Basques, violence could be ended and a final amnesty negotiated. Any clash with a Basque administration would have eroded the passive support which ETA-M enjoyed and would have, presumably, resulted in a greater willingness to provide information to the police. However, as no Spanish government was likely to agree to its police being withdrawn from any part of the national territory, that was an improbable development.

The absurdity of ETA's contention that Euskadi was a colony was reflected in its failure to create a guerrilla army to liberate the homeland from the 'imperialist' forces. The violence carried out by ETA-V, ETA-PM and ETA-M had little in common with the strategy proposed by Krutwig and Zalbide, being essentially daring exploits by small groups, which did, however, benefit from information received and shelter given by sympathisers. Many of ETA's leaders realised the difficulties faced by those attempting to undertake mass activity, caused by their identification with an armed group, and proposed various methods of overcoming the problem. However, most of ETA's factions saw this inherent antagonism as a tactical problem. The most consistent position was that taken by ETA-M in 1975, when it confined itself entirely to armed struggle. Almost all of those who practised armed struggle held that it was one strand among others in the fight for national liberation. According to Krutwig and Zalbide, the first theoreticians of armed struggle, the violent acts of an armed vanguard had the objectives of radicalising the mass of the population. Consequently, the distinction between mass struggle and revolutionary violence would disappear as the vanguard became part of the people's army. In the last years of the Franco dictatorship the leaders of ETA-V, ETA-M and ETA-PM all declared that they were in favour of mass struggle, but that in conditions of illegality the actions of the armed vanguard remained necessary. However, ETA was never successful in combining the two forms of struggle in the way which the theory stipulated.

When ETA-PM's commandos intervened in industrial disputes, they did so not as part of a working class industrial strategy, but rather as a kind of Robin Hood attack on businessmen. Similarly, the bombs which ETA-PM's commandos planted in tourist areas were unconnected with mass struggle and detrimental to its development. ETA-M found in Herri Batasuna an organisation which did involve large numbers of people, but as an auxiliary to ETA-M, not an autonomous force. The limited success of EIA/EE in establishing a political party made the armed violence of ETA-PM an embarrassment. It would seem that the various theories of ETA's leaders on the function of the armed struggle do not account for the adoption of a tactic which was from 1967 onwards ETA's defining feature, not one activity among others. Although many Basque nationalists disapproved of violence, neither the cohesion of the nationalist community nor the hegemony of the PNV were threatened by ETA's activities, as they would have been by the development of a political programme which divided Basques on the basis of their class position or political ideas.

Those factions in ETA which did develop a socialist analysis of Basque society, which might have endangered the unity of the nationalist community, soon abandoned armed struggle and, eventually, nationalism itself. Once they did so such groups became much less attractive to militant young nationalists than their rivals who continued to proclaim the need for an armed vanguard. The impact of a gunshot or an explosion was greater than that of illegal propaganda or, later, the tedious work of trade union organisation, educational programmes or electoral campaigns. Armed struggle enabled ETA to appeal to young men who would not have committed themselves to study, discussion or routine political work, but responded to ETA's call to arms. Those branches of ETA which did not produce specific social and economic programmes retained most support. Although ETA-V and its successors needed some political analysis, the apolitical nature of most of their adherents meant that only those, such as the defendants at the Burgos trial or Argala, who had shown themselves to be fighters before they were politicians would be listened to.

ETA's armed struggle was an important factor in accentuating the nationalism of part of the population, and the division of the inhabitants of the Basque country into two communities. That division was not clear-cut, as most people considered themselves to be both Spanish and Basque. Nor was the conflict simply the product of geographical origin or language, as all of the 'Spanish' parties found support among people of Basque descent and (to a much lesser extent) among speakers of *Euskera*, while the nationalist parties had adherents of non-Basque origin, who made little attempt to learn the language. The criteria for being recognised as Basque became allegiance to nationalism itself. In the post-Franco era the PNV conceded that a person of immigrant origin could become a Basque and even a leading citizen, yet for its supporters a native background remained superior to an immigrant one, just as *Euskera* was superior to Spanish.

The PSOE's considerable vote was not matched by comparable cultural or political activity, so in practice it tended to become the party of 'Spanish' workers, where the rights of *Euskera* were accepted, but not strongly felt. The PNV's hegemony in the nationalist community presented the PSOE leaders with strategic difficulties. Benegas, its General Secretary in the Basque country, tended to stress the party's role as the representative of the left of both communities, whereas García Damborenea, its Secretary in Vizcaya, reacted more strongly against the nationalists and emphasised the PSOE's role in defending 'Spanish' Basques against the vexations resulting from nationalist hegemony.[170] These included the need for teachers to learn *Euskera*, even in areas where their pupils would not speak that language. Some nationalist-dominated municipalities tried to make knowledge of *Euskera* compulsory even for street cleaners. However, the general feeling that *Euskera*-speakers had been unfairly treated throughout the period of the Franco dictatorship meant that their preferential treatment was resented less than were the privileges which were thought to accrue from support of the PNV.

In the 1980s Basque feelings of superiority remained strong. The popular stereotypes of Andalusians as lazy, incompetent and dishonest persisted, although Herri Batasuna and EE spokesmen insisted that Andalusians and Galicians were fellow sufferers under the yoke of the Spanish State, and the radical nationalist press gave extensive coverage to the weak nationalist movements of those regions. Herri Batasuna issued many declarations that racial criteria were irrelevant in determining whether a person was Basque or not, and it extolled those ETA martyrs who were of immigrant origin. Election results suggest that some young immigrants voted for Herri Batasuna, in spite of the fact that the organisation advocated policies which would effectively have deprived many immigrants (and natives unable to speak *Euskera*) of their livelihood. The Statute proposed by Herri Batasuna in 1979 would also, like the Statute of Estella backed by the PNV in 1933, have discriminated against immigrants in voting rights. For the PNV, at least in its public statements, the enemy was no longer the immigrants, but 'Madrid', an ambiguous designation which could either be interpreted chauvinistically, or taken to refer to the bureaucratic centralism of Spanish governments. The total effect of the varied nationalist attitudes to outsiders was sufficient to make many immigrants feel uneasy.

The dramatic change in the status of *Euskera* made many Spanish-speaking Basques feel that they were now the victims of linguistic oppression. Now that there was a television channel in *Euskera*, and it was the main vehicle of instruction in some schools, ability to speak it became a considerable advantage in obtaining employment in teaching and public service, even in overwhelmingly Spanish-speaking areas, but to radical nationalists such changes appeared a merely cosmetic exercise. They considered *Euskera* should be the official language of Euskadi just as Spanish was of Castile, and that all schoolchildren should be learning *Euskera* as part of a plan to make it the language of everyday life, even in traditionally Spanish-speaking areas. Such an aspiration appeared totalitarian to non-nationalist parents but it was supported by those who thought that 'Spanish' domination, particularly since the Civil War, had imposed cultural genocide. Herri Batasuna supporters refused to accept that both languages should have equal rights. Nationalist intransigence found new adherents among former supporters of the 'Spanish' left who had been demoralised by its decline during the transition of parliamentary democracy. Both the MCE (formerly ETA-Berri) and the LCR/LKI (formerly ETA-VI) readopted the nationalist positions whose rejection had once led to their expulsion from ETA,[171] without, however, making an analysis of their own evolution.

Basque nationalism would seem to be rooted in the changes produced by industrialisation. Basque cultural peculiarities did not produce nationalism before the 1880s, as Basques were able to find advancement through service with the Spanish state. *Euskera* was not in competition with Spanish, as it was a group of dialects rather than a single written language, and was not therefore suitable for administration or commerce. In the 19th century Spanish conservatism, far from finding Basque particularism a danger, was able to use popular support for the *Fueros* as a weapon against liberalism. Although the defeat of the Carlist forces in 1873 did bring changes which were resented by large numbers of Basques, this was not in itself enough to create a national consciousness. The *Fueros*, in spite of their wide popularity, had been resented by traders and industrialists who were the most dynamic element in Basque society and who needed access to the Spanish market. Basque nationalism was not, therefore, produced by a middle class in an undeveloped region of an existing political unit seeking political independence in order to facilitate economic development.[172] On the contrary, the Basque economy, at least in Vizcaya, was much more developed than that of the rest of Spain. The rejection of Basque nationalism by the largest industrial and banking interests which relied on a Spanish market was to be one of the movement's greatest permanent weaknesses. A movement which had purely political causes would surely have arisen immediately after the abolition of the *Fueros* in 1876, rather than coinciding with the arrival of the immigrants in the 1880s. It seems curious that in a region which had been part of the Spanish state since the sixteenth century, nationalists should date the loss of independence from the defeat of the Carlist forces in 1839, an event which brought few changes to the region.

Basque nationalism originated in Bilbao and the movement's later spread to other parts of Euskadi coincided with the rise of industry, socialism, and the arrival of the *Maketos*. The rise of nationalism has been attributed to the manipulation of regional differences by employers to divide the workforce, yet the response of Basque businessmen to the nationalist movement was ambivalent. For the banking, steelmaking and shipbuilding firms which dominated Vizcayan industry the benefits of the divisive potential of nationalism were outweighed by the threat it posed to their links with the Spanish market. In fact, in the late nineteenth century, Basque industrialists' political allegiance was divided between liberals and conservatives, while the more traditional forces in the countryside, particularly among the clergy, continued to support Carlism. Basque nationalism, backed mainly by smaller business interests, was an uncertain ally of big business.

However, Basque nationalism was a much better instrument for mobilising middle-class conservative opinion than any developed elsewhere in Spain, and until 1932 it functioned as part of a conservative alliance, particularly with the Carlists. Consequently, the dominant tendencies in the PNV advocated not independence but a greater degree of autonomy within the Spanish State. When the Spanish right's refusal to grant Basque autonomy broke the PNV's accord with the Carlists, the nationalist party was thrown into an alliance with its traditional enemies, the socialists and republicans. The defeat of the Spanish Republic in the Civil War made Basque nationalism quite powerless and threatened to reduce it to a nostalgic folklore movement of those who continued to take pride in their Basque identity, but had reconciled themselves to the permanence of the Franco regime.[173]

Basque nationalism was saved from stagnation by the recovery of the Spanish economy in the 1950s, which brought a new invasion of *Maketos*, as once again impoverished peasants from other parts of Spain came to the Basque country to seek work. In the 1960s Basque nationalism benefited from a lessening of repression, as the regime tried to weaken the connection between nationalism and Basque culture by allowing a very limited freedom for *Euskera*. Such concessions failed in their objectives, as they provided a focus for Basque resistance while stopping far short of redressing legitimate grievances. As the PNV was incapable of organising discontent into an effective resistance, successive waves of its youthful supporters were drawn towards ETA, which received a considerable access of strength from the crisis in the Catholic Church, as many young men deserted the seminaries and threw themselves into nationalist politics.[174] The revival of 'Spanish' opposition to Franco, which brought ETA into contact with radical and socialist ideas, increased its members' differences with the PNV.

The transition to a parliamentary democracy and the granting of autonomy to the Basque country would seem to have reduced the basis for radical nationalism. Furthermore, fears that the Basques would be culturally swamped were no longer relevant, as by the 1980s more people were leaving Guipúzcoa and Vizcaya than going there. Yet nationalism, although originally produced by a reaction to the effects of immigration in an economic boom, was sustained by the condition of slump. Just as the immigration of the 1950s and 1960s had been seen by many nationalists as the result of 'Spanish' malevolence, so de-industrialisation was regarded as the result of policies decided in Madrid. ETA-M is unlikely to achieve its aim of establishing an independent Euskadi, but it will probably survive, although perhaps at a reduced level of activity. Most of the factors which gave ETA strength throughout its existence continued after 1980 in a somewhat weakened form. Nationalist feeling remained widespread, as the vote for the PNV, Herri Batasuna and EE showed. Many young people from nationalist families continued to feel that ETA's commitment to armed struggle was legitimate, and the majority of nationalists who disagreed nevertheless respected that view, and refused to categorically denounce ETA.

The mainstream nationalists' preferred solution to the problem of violence consists, in its stronger version, of gaining independence by peaceful and gradual means. A weaker version of that perspective would be for a considerable extension of the autonomy provisions, which would transfer powers of policing, education and the mass media into local, mainly nationalist, hands. Consequently, it would become possible for Basque nationalists to declare loyalty to the Spanish Crown. PNV spokesmen often suggest that, as the institutions of the Common Market become more important, national states become less so and a Europe expressing ethnic diversity can be constructed. Such a claim underestimates the power of the individual states within the Common Market and the unlikelihood of Spain devolving questions of security to a regional government. However, if a Spanish government were to considerably expand the scope of the autonomy provisions, mainstream nationalist opinion would be satisfied, although 'Spanish' Basques would fear the effects of nationalist domination.

Outside Spain, interest in ETA and Herri Batasuna is part of a wider concern with the many other groups which undertake armed struggles. Much has been written about the various 'terrorist' groups ranging from the PLO to the Italian Red Brigade and the IRA. Inevitably, studies of 'terrorist' groups which ignore the social context of their existence and concentrate solely on their internal organisation and training, or the supposed psychological motivation of their members, end up examining either trivial, or at best secondary, features of the phenomenon. I have attempted to show the deep roots of ETA in Basque history and social structure. The persistent belief by some outside commentators that ETA is to be explained in the same terms as an organisation like the German Bader-Meinhoff group[175] should not survive a conversation with moderate members of the nationalist community, whether businessmen, priests, or professional people, to whom ETA members are seen as, at worst, mistaken. From outside the nationalist community it might appear strange that someone who has been convicted for monstrous crimes should be accepted as a well meaning if impetuous patriot, but that is the reality in ethnically Basque areas.

Useful comparison of ETA would be confined to movements in European society which are themselves deeply rooted in a community. In that respect ETA and the IRA are, indeed, comparable organisations. Both grew out of a deeply Catholic culture in societies deeply divided into rival communities. Both the IRA and ETA have been able to move effortlessly from professing a pious, conservative, ideology to the adoption of radical socialist rhetoric, without affecting their practical activity, or losing support in deeply conservative milieux. Both have combined considerable mass support (the IRA more than ETA) with giving primacy to the leadership of an armed elite, acting outside the control of any political structure. Both use a native language as a weapon to differentiate their own community from alien immigrants.

However the chasm between the 'Spanish' and non-Spanish Basques has never been as great as between Irish protestants and Catholics, as many people, from both ethnic groups or from a mixed background, consider themselves both Spanish and Basque. Intermarriage is commonplace and political allegiance is not solely a function of family origin, as it is in Northern Ireland. However, the greatest difference between ETA and the IRA arises from the nature of the ethnic groups upon which they are based. Both arose in bitterly divided societies where one community is more economically privileged than its competitor, but in contrast to the Northern Irish Catholics, the ethnically Basque population from which ETA draws its support is much more privileged than the *Maketos*. The middle-class social composition and higher educational level of radical Basque nationalists has meant that Herri Batasuna has not been so tied to the Church's traditional moral values. ETA itself will remain committed to unobtainable objectives. In 1986, twenty-seven years after the group was founded, the creation of a completely independent Basque state was as unlikely as ever. If ETA's objectives were no nearer achievement its social base seemed to have contracted only slightly. The call for negotiations between ETA and the Spanish state, or directly with the army, which were emphasised during 1986, while certainly not an abandonment of its aim, did represent a shift of emphasis. The existence of large numbers of ETA members undergoing long spells of imprisonment was a source of strength, in maintaining resentment among their families and the wider Basque population. On the other hand, the prospect of a steadily mounting roll of prisoners, exceeding the numbers of active ETA members, was a depressing perspective, harmful to ETA-M's morale, which presented the danger of imprisoned and exiled members seeking individual pardons as 'Yoyes' had done. Moderate nationalists believe that an amnesty and ceasefire are not only a possibility, but a necessary part of a solution to the problem of Basque violence. ETA-M leaders were aware that a ceasefire carried the danger of the eventual dissolution of their organisation in the way that had happened with ETA-PM after 1977. It is highly unlikely that ETA-M will agree under any conditions to dissolve, or to accept a prolonged truce, which in the long run would amount to the same thing. The likely outlook for the Basque country, therefore, is that ETA-M continues to exist and sustain an armed struggle, although at a lower level than in the late 1970s and early 1980s. The loss of its base in the French Basque country, although important, need not be fatal. The constant proclamations by Spanish governments that the problem of ETA is about to be resolved are likely to be continually disappointed.

The moderate nationalist party, Euskadiko Ezkerra, argues that the Basque nation consists of all the people who live in the national territory. The educational system and the mass media must accept that as a majority of Euskadi's inhabitants are not from an exclusively Basque ethnic stock, nor do they speak *Euskera*, that the Basque nation will include a Spanish-speaking component. Navarre is seen as an integral part of the Basque country, but the integration of the province must wait on the willingness of the majority of its inhabitants to agree to that status. Euskadiko Ezkerra's proposals to build the Basque nation include a public education system which would provide instruction in both Spanish and *Euskera*, a system of public administration independent of the patronage of the PNV, and a campaign to strengthen and revive *Euskera*. In short, the achievement of a situation where being Basque is not identical with being nationalist. In Euskadiko Ezkerra's hypothetical Basque society of the future, adherents of the PSOE or of 'Spanish' conservative parties would be able to live as first-class citizens, not as suspect members of a fifth column, each community would accept the others legitimacy, and the achievements of one would not be defeats for the other. In such a situation the question of the precise amount of autonomy which was desirable would be decided peacefully and rationally.

Euskadiko Ezkerra's appealing view is plausible only if one ignores the extent to which Basque, and every other nationalism, draws its strength from distrust and suspicion of outside social groups. In a society without *Maketos* Basque nationalism would weaken into the regionalism which existed before the immigration of the *Maketos* in the 1880s. Both Herri Batasuna and the PNV have an intelligent appreciation that a unified nation, far from being a desirable objective, would destroy the confrontation which is essential to their existence.

REFERENCES

1. See *Deia*, 1, 10 Sept., 9, 15 Nov., 27 Dec., 1977 and 15, 21 June, 1 Oct. 1978.
2. Ortzi, *El no*, Vol. 2, p. 67.
3. Ortzi, *El no*, Vol. 2, p. 68.
4. *Egin*, 22 Dec. 1978; *Deia*, 22 Dec. 1978.
5. *Egin*, 7 Jan. 1979.
6. *Egin*, 3 and 4 Jan. 1979.
7. *Egin*, 26 and 28 March 1979.
8. *Egin*, 14 Jan. 1979.
9. *Egin*, 5 May 1979.
10. See statement in *Egin*, 27 May 1979.
11. *Egin*, 31 Jan. 1979.
12. *Egin*, 7 and 8 April 1979.
13. 'ETA(PM) "Somos el aparato coercitivo de la clase obrera"', *Viejo Topo*, March 1980.
14. *Egin*, 6 and 14 Feb. 1979.
15. *Egin*, 20 and 27 Feb. and 2 March 1979.
16. *Egin*, 7 March 1979.
17. See interview with Periko Solabarría, *La Batalla*, June 1979.
18. *Egin*, 15 and 16 Jan. and 3, 4, 6, 12 Feb. 1979.
19. Hunger strikes had been part of ETA-M's referendum campaign. *Egin*, 28 Dec. 1978.
20. See speech by Arzallus, *Deia*, 13 March 1979; see press release by the PNV's national committee, 7 Feb. 1979, Ref. EBB 002/79.
21. *Egin*, 6 Feb. 1979.
22. *Egin*, 1, 2, 3, 4, 6, 8, 9, 10, 11, 15, 16, 18, 20 Feb. 1979.
23. *Egin*, 25, 26 Feb. and 17 March 1979.
24. *Deia*, 3 March 1979.
25. *Deia*, 4 April 1979; *Diario Vasco*, 4 April 1980; *Punto y Hora*, 4–11 April 1979.
26. *Punto y Hora*, 28 May–4 June 1979; *Egin*, 4 June 1979.
27. *Egin*, 26 May 1979.
28. *Egin*, 27 May 1979.
29. *Ere*, 20–27 Sept. 1979; *Deia*, 26 June 1979.

30. *Egin*, 4 June 1979; *Punto y Hora*, 8–15 June 1979.
31. *Egin*, 5, 6, 11 June 1979.
32. *Egin*, 8 and 20 June 1979.
33. Author's interview with J.M. Larrazábal, San Sebastián, 11 March 1980.
34. *Egin*, 29 and 30 Sept. 1979.
35. *Egin*, 13 June 1979.
36. 'Nacionalidad', *Euskal Herriko Batzarre Nazionala* (Bilbao, undated).
37. See interview with Mario Onaindía, *Viejo Topo*, Nov. 1979.
38. *Egin*, 15 and 16 June 1979.
39. *Egin*, 28, 29, 30 June and 1, 2 July 1979.
40. *Egin*, 4 July 1979.
41. *Egin*, 30 and 31 July and 1 Aug. 1979.
42. *Egin*, 31 July 1979.
43. See Chapter 6.
44. *Egin*, 1 and 3 Aug. 1979.
45. Author's interview with Goiherri, San Sebastián, 5 August 1984.
46. *Egin*, 16 Sept. 1979.
47. *Egin*, 24 Nov. 1979.
48. *Egin*, 19 July 1979.
49. *Egin*, 19 July 1979.
50. *Hitz*, No. 1, July 1979.
51. *Egin*, 19 July 1979; *Punto y Hora*, 19–26 July 1979.
52. 'Habla ETA Militar', *Punto y Hora*, 18–25 Oct. 1979.
53. *Egin*, 29 July 1979.
54. *Egin*, 20 and 24 Sept. 1979.
55. *Punto y Hora*, 1–8 Nov. 1979; *Egin*, 26 Oct. 1979.
56. See Luis C. Nuñez, '¿El Estatuto de la mayoría?', *Punto y Hora*, 1–8 Nov. 1979.
57. *Egin*, 9, 11 and 12 Oct. and 1 Nov. 1979.
58. *Egin*, 23 Oct. 1979.
59. *Egin*, 28 and 29 Oct. 1979.
60. *Egin*, 29 Oct. 1979.
61. *Egin*, 29 Oct. 1979.
62. *Deia*, 30 Oct. 1979.
63. 'Manipulaziao', Editorial, *Punto y Hora*, 1–8 Nov. 1979; *Egin*, 28 Oct. 1979.
64. *Zutik* (LKI), 8 Nov. 1979.
65. *Egin*, 29 Oct. 1979.
66. Santiago Carrillo, *Memoria de la Transición* (Barcelona, 1983), pp. 105–112; see also *Hierro*, 14 Aug. 26, 28, and 29 Sept. and 5, 8, 23, 27 Oct. 1981.
67. *Ere*, 21–28 Nov. 1979.
68. *Ere*, 29 Nov–8 Dec 1979.
69. *Otsagabia — Formas de coordinación entre la lucha armada y la lucha política, Documentos Y*, Vol. 18, pp. 197–205.
70. *Ere*, 29 Nov–8 Dec. 1979.
71. *Egin*, 13 Dec. 1979.
72. *La Voz de España*, 29 Jan. 1980.
73. *La Voz de España*, 11 Jan. 1980.

74. *La Voz de España*, 11 Jan. 1980.

75. *Egin*, 20, 21, 22, 23 and 26 Dec. 1979.

76. *Egin*, 12 and 16 Dec. 1979.

77. *La Voz de España*, 19 Jan. 1980.

78. *La Voz de España*, 6 Jan. 1980.

79. *La Voz de España*, 6 Jan. 1980.

80. *Ere*, 22–31 Jan. 1980.

81. J.M. Larrazábal interview, *Ere*, 20–26 Aug. 1980; author's interview with Larrazábal.

82. *La Voz de España*.

83. 'Un congreso "duro y áspero"', *Punto y Hora*, 17–24 April 1980; author's interview with Koldo Aulestia and Alejandro Vazquez, leading members of EIA in LAB, San Sebastián, 25 March 1980.

84. 'K.O. al centralismo', *Punto y Hora*, 13–20 March 1980.

85. *La Voz de España*, 11 Jan. 1980.

86. *El País*, 1 July 1980.

87. *El País*, 25 June 1980; *La Calle*, 1 July 1980.

88. *El País*, 3 July 1980.

89. Author's interview with 'Goiherri'.

90. *Diario Vasco*, 26 and 30 March 1980; *El País*, 19 March 1980.

91. Interview with Mario Onaindía in *La Calle*, 18–24 Nov. 1980.

92. *Diario Vasco*, 26 Oct. 1980.

93. *Egin*, 7 Feb. 1981; *El País*, 7 and 8 Feb. 1981; *Punto y Hora*, 12–19 Feb. 1981.

94. *Egin*, 11 Feb. 1981.

95. *Egin*, 5 Feb. 1981.

96. *Deia*, 30 Sept. 1981.

97. *El País*, 21 Feb. 1981; *Cambio 16*, 16 March 1981.

98. *El País*, 17 April 1981.

99. *El País*, 18 and 19 Jan. 1982.

100. *El País*, 20 and 22 Jan. 1982.

101. *El País*, 23 Feb. 1982.

102. *Diario Vasco*, 17, 18, 19, 21, 22, 23 and 24 Aug. 1985; *Deia*, 18 and 25 August 1985.

103. *Cambio 16*, 16 March 1981.

104. *Punto y Hora*, No. 218, 20–27 March 1981.

105. *El País*, 8 May 1981.

106. *Cambio 16*, 2 and 23 Nov. 1981.

107. *Diario Vasco*, 29 and 20 Nov. 1982.

108. *Egin*, 31 Oct. and 1 Nov. 1982; *Cambio 16*, 8 Nov. 1982.

109. *El País*, 31 Oct. 1982.

110. *El País*, 14 Jan. 1983.

111. *El País*, 14 Feb. 1983.

112. *La Vanguardia*, 23 Feb. 1983.

113. *El País*, 26 March 1983.

114. *Egin*, 10 May 1983.

115. *Egin*, 20 May 1983; *El Socialista*, 20–26 July 1983.

116. *Deia*, 1, 2 Aug. 1983.

117. *Egin*, 27 Feb. 1984.

118. *Egin*, 4 and 5 April, 7 June 1984.

119. *Egin*, 16 and 18 Sept. 1984.
120. *Egin*, 19, 20 and 21 Oct. 1984.
121. *Egin*, 19, 20, 21 and 22 Dec. 1984.
122. *El País*, 28 Dec. 1984.
123. *Egin*, 6, 22, 29 Sept., 6, 7, 10, 11, 18, 19, 20 Oct. 1983.
124. *Egin*, 19, 20, 21, 22, 23 Oct. 1983.
125. *Egin*, 6, 7, 15, 21, 22, 23 Dec. 1983.
126. *Egin*, 29. 30, 31 Dec. 1983, 2 Jan 1984.
127. *El País*, 30 Jan. 1984.
128. *Egin*, 9 and 24 Feb. 1984.
129. *Egin*, 27 Feb. 1984.
130. *Egin*, 1 Oct. 1986.
131. *Egin*, 20 June and 30 July 1984.
132. *Egin*, 20, 21 and 22 Nov. 1984.
133. *El País*, 22 Nov. 1984.
134. *Egin*, 21, 22, 23 Nov. 1984.
135. *Cambio 16*, 26 Feb.–4 March 1985.
136. *Egin*, 8 March 1985; *El País*, 8 March 1985.
137. *Egin*, 13 March 1985.
138. *El País*, 13 June 1985.
139. *Egin*, 1 April, 10 June and 26 Sept. 1985.
140. *Egin*, 16, 17, 27 Dec. 1985, 4 and 9 Jan., 15 Feb. 1986.
141. *Egin*, 20 March and 18 Aug. 1985.
142. *El País*, 7 Feb. and 14 March 1986.
143. *Egin*, 5 Feb. 1986.
144. *Egin*, 31 Dec. 1985, 12, 18 Jan. and 15 March 1986.
145. *El País*, 13 Jan. 1986.
146. *Egin*, 11 and 30 March 1986.
147. *El País*, 9 May 1986.
148. *Egin*, 11, 12 June 1986; *El País*, 23, 24 June 1986.
149. *Egin*, 23 and 24 June 1986.
150. *El País*, 25 June 1986.
151. *El País*, 29 June 1986; *Egin*, 7 Aug. 1986.
152. *El País*, 22 and 29 July 1986.
153. *Egin*, 26 and 27 July 1986; *Deia*, 27 July 1986.
154. *Egin*, 30 July 1986.
155. *Egin*, 24, 25, 26, 27 July 1986.
156. *Egin*, 11, 12, 13 Sept. 1986.
157. *Deia*, 3 and 4 Nov. 1986.
158. *Diario Vasco*, 27 Oct. 1986.
159. *El País*, 4 Nov. and 6 Dec. 1986.
160. *Diario Vasco*, 1 Dec. 1976.
161. See the PNV's journal *Euskadi*, 21 Oct. 1983.
162. *Egin*, 10 May 1983, 27 Feb. 1984, 1 Dec. 1986.
163. Author's interview with Enrique Casas, San Sebastián, 31 March 1980.
164. Alfonso Pérez-Agote, *La reproducción del nacionalismo. El caso vasco* (Madrid), passim; also José Antonio Garmendia and others, *Abertzales y Vascos* (Madrid, 1981), passim; and Juan J. Linz, *Conflicto en Euskadi* (Madrid, 1986) passim.

165. 'Las Ikastolas, situación actual y perspectivas', *Arnasa*, No. 4 (undated).

166. Luciano Rincón, *ETA 1974–84* (Barcelona, 1985) passim.

167. Marx and Engels, *Collected Works*, Vol. 9 (Moscow, 1977), pp. 299–300, 307, 310, 455–63.

168. *Sugarra*, No. 1, 1975.

169. Author's interview with a group of Herri Batasuna councillors in Renteria, 27 March 1980.

170. For example, Xavier Arzallus declared that 'if Madrid deceives us we will be on the side of Herri Batasuna', *Egin*, 31 Oct. 1979.

171. Ricardo Garcia Damborenea, *La encrucijada vasca* (Barcelona, 1984) passim; Txiki Benegas, *Euskadi, Sin la paz nada es posible* (Barcelona, 1984) passim.

172. Luciano Rincón, 'Etica, ático y reumático', *El País*, 13 Nov. 1984.

173. Ernest Gellner, *Thought and change* (London, 1964), passim.

174. Landaburu, *La Causa*, pp. 115–116.

175. Paulo Iztueta, *Sociología del fenómeno contestatario del clero vasco* (Zarauz, 1981), passim.

176. Editorial in *Cambio 16*, 1 June 1981; Claire Sterling, *The terror network* (New York, 1981), passim; Alfredo Semprún, *ABC*, 22 Aug. 1985, alleged that ETA-M obtained much of its funds by distributing drugs obtained from Eastern Europe.

Bibliography

Primary Sources

Newspapers

ABC (Madrid), daily.
Deia, Bilbao, daily.
El Diario Vasco, San Sebastián, daily.
Egin, San Sebastián, daily.
Hierro, Bilbao, daily.
L'Humanité, Paris, daily.
Le Monde, Paris, daily.
Mundo Obrero, Madrid, weekly, sometimes daily.
El País, Madrid, daily.
The Times, London, daily.
La Vanguardia, Barcelona, daily.
La Voz de España, San Sebastián, daily.

Journals

Acción Comunista, 1967–70, St. Michel sur Orge.
Alderdi, 1959, 1982–1983.
Amaiur, 1974.
Apuntes de Economia (ETA-VI), 1972.
Arkatasuna, 1978–1980, Bilbao.
Arnasa, 1977–83, Hendaye/San Sebastián.
Arriba, Madrid.
La Batalle, 1978–1980, Barcelona.
Batasuna (EGI), 1970.
Batasuna (ESBA), 1968.
Batasuna (ETA), 1967–1970.
Batzkarra, 1978, Bilbao.
Berriak (ETA-VI), 1970–1973.
Bultzaka (EIA), 1977–1978, Bilbao.
La Calle, 1980–1981, Madrid, weekly.
Cambio 16, 1973–1986, Madrid, weekly.
Combate, 1973–1986, Madrid, weekly.
Comunismo, 1970.
Crash, 1978, Madrid.
Cuadernos del Comunismo, 1979–1980, Madrid.
Cuadernos ETA, 1960.
Cuadernos de Ruedo Ibérico, 1966–1972, Paris.
Doblón, 1974, Madrid, weekly.

Bibliography

Ere, 1979–1981, San Sebastián, weekly.
Euskadi, 1981– 1986, Bilbao, weekly.
Euskadi Obrera, 1977, Bilbao.
Frères du Monde
Fuerza Nueva, 1970–1977, Madrid, weekly.
Garaia, 1976–1977, San Sebastián, weekly.
Hacia el Socialismo, 1976.
Hautsi, 1974–1977.
Hemen Eta Orain, 1978–1980, Bilbao.
Herri Batasuna de Donostia, 1979.
Herria 2000 Eliza, 1981, Bilbao.
Hertzale, 1979.
Hitz (EIA), 1978–1983, Bilbao.
Horizonte Español, 1966, 1972, Paris.
Ikastaroak, 1980.
Información, 1972, Madrid.
Información Española, 1974, Brussels.
Información Mensual, 1975.
Intervieu, 1979–1982, Barcelona, monthly.
IPES, 1980–1984, Bilbao.
Iraultza, 1980, San Sebastián.
Iraultzen, 1978.
Kas, 1979.
Langile, 1974–1975.
Lantzen (LAIA), 1978.
El Militante, 1976.
Muga, 1978–1984, Bilbao.
Nuestra Bandera, 1979–1983, Madrid.
Punto y Hora, 1976–1986, San Sebastián, weekly.
Saioak, 1970–1971, Journal of the Red Cells.
Saioak, 1979–1983, San Sebastián, independent scholarly-political journal.
Servir el Pueblo (MCE).
El Socialista (PSOE), Toulouse/Madrid, weekly.
Sugarra (LAIA), 1974–1980.
En Teoría, 1981, Madrid.
Transición, 1978, Barcelona.
Tribuna Socialista, 1960–1962, Paris.
Viejo Topo, 1979–1980, Madrid, weekly.
Zer Egin (MCE), 1969–1984.
Zona Abierta, 1977, Madrid.
Zutik (ETA-Caracas), 1960–1973.
Zutik (ETA), 1960–1970.
Zutik (ETA-Berri), 1967–1969.
Zutik (ETA-VI/LCR), 1971–1984.
Zutik (ETA-VI/Minos), 1973.
Zutik (ETA-V), 1971–1984.
Zutik (ETA Militar), 1974–1977.

Bibliography

Printed documents, interviews, speeches and conference reports

The most valuable source of documents relating to ETA is to be found in the massive 18-volume collection *Documentos Y*, published by Hordago in 1979–1981.

Anua, Javier *et al.*, *La constitución española 1978* (Ediciones Vascas, San Sebastián, 1978).

Arana Goiri, Sabino, *Obras escogidas* (Haranburu, San Sebastián, 1978).

Arteaga, Federico de, *ETA y el proceso de Burgos* (Madrid, 1971).

Bandrés, Juan María *et al.*, *Burgos, juicio a un pueblo* (San Sebastián, 1978).

'Batasuna', *La répression au Pays Basque* (Paris, 1970).

Benegas, Txiki and Díaz, Valentín, *Partido Socialista de Euskadi, PSOE* (San Sebastián, 1977).

Bordegarai, Kepa and Pastor, Robert, *Estatuto vasco* (San Sebastián, 1979).

Castells, Luis, *Fueros y Conciertos Económicos* (Haranburu, San Sebastián, 1980).

Celhay, Pierre, *Consejos de Guerra en España* (Paris, 1976).

Chao, R., *Después de Franco, España* (Madrid, 1976).

Díaz Plaja, Fernando, *La pre-guerra española en sus documentos* (Plaza & Janes, Barcelona, 1969).

Díaz Plaja, Fernando, *La guerra de España en sus documentos* (Plaza & Janes, Barcelona, 1969).

Documentos Y (18 vols.) (Hordago, San Sebastián, 1979–1981).

E.S.B. Partido Socialista Vasco, *ESB. Un programa socialista para la autonomía de Euskadi* (ESB, Bilbao, 1977).

Escudero, Manu and Villanueva, J., *La autonomía del País Vascco, desde el pasado al futuro* (San Sebastián, 1976).

Estornes, Idoia, *¿Que son los partidos abertzales?* (San Sebastián, 1977).

Euskadi y el Estatuto de Autonomía, EREIN (publisher) (no editor given) (San Sebastián, 1979).

García de Cortazar, Fernando and Montero, Manuel, *Historia contemporánea del País Vasco* (Txertoa, San Sebastián, undated).

Garmendia, José María and Elordi, A., *Historia de ETA*, 2 Vols. (Haranburu, San Sebastián, 1979–1980).

Goñi Alzueta, J. and Rodríguez Erdozain, J.M., *Euskadi. La paz es posible* (Bilbao, 1979).

HOAC Ediciones, *El PSOE en sus documentos, 1879–1977* (Barcelona [Madrid] 1977).

Ibarazábal, Eugenio (ed.), *Manuel Irujo* (San Sebastián, 1977).

―――― *Euskadi: Diálogos en torno a las elecciones* (EREIN, San Sebastián, 1977).

―――― *50 años del nacionalismo vasco* (Ediciones Vascas, San Sebastián, 1978).

Irujo, Manuel, *Inglaterra y los Vascos* (Buenos Aires, 1945).

Isaba, Patxi, *Euzkadi Socialiste* (Editions du Cercle, Paris, 1970).

Jiménez de Aberasturi, Luis María and Juan Carlos, *La Guerra en Euskadi* (Plaza & Janes, Barcelona, 1978).

Karlista Alderdia, *Euskadi, Askatasuna, Socialismo, Autojestioa* (No place of publication given, 1975).

LAB, *Ante el movimiento obrero de Euskadi.*

Monzón, Telesforo, *Herri Baten Oihua* (Herri Batasuna, Pamplona, 1982).

Movimiento Comunista, *10 años de lucha por el socialismo* (Madrid, 1978).

Onaindía, Alberto de, *Ayer como hoy* (Axular, St. Jean de Luz, 1975).

Onaindía, Mario (ed.), *Resoluciones. Congreso Constituyente de Euskadiko Ezkera* (Bilbao, 1979).

Orduña, Reballo E., *Estatuto de Autonomía para el País Vasco* (Madrid, 1980).

Orrantia, Mikel and Mendieta, Lander, *¿Euskadi: Pacificación?* (Ediciones Libertarias, Madrid, 1980).

Pastor, Robert, *Euskadi ante al futuro* (Haranburu, San Sebastián, 1977).

Pérez Calvo, A., *Los partidos políticos en el País Vasco* (San Sebastián, 1977).

PNV-EAJ, *El Partido Nacionalista Vasco hoy* (PNV, Bilbao, undated).

—— *Ponencia de organización* (PNV, Bilbao, undated).

—— *138 años de despojo* (PNV, Bilbao, 1977).

—— *¿Conoce a Sabino Arana y Goiri?* (PNV, Bilbao, 1978).

—— *El partido nacionalista ante la Constitución* (PNV, Bilbao, 1978).

Postigo, Carmen, *Los Conciertos Económicos* (San Sebastián, 1979).

PSOE, *II Congreso ordinario des Partido Socialista de Euskadi PSOE* (PSOE, Bilbao, 1979).

Ruedo Ibérico (no author given), *Euskadi: El último estado de excepción de Franco* (Paris, 1975).

Salaberri, Kepa, *Sumarismo/31. El Proceso de Euskadi en Burgos* (Ruedo Ibérico, Paris, 1971).

Sánchez Erauskin, Javier, *Txiki: Otaegui. El viento y las raíces* (Hordago, San Sebastián, 1978).

Vilar, Sergio, *La oposición a la Dictadura* (Barcelona, 1976).

Zutik, *Ez, ez, ez, Konstituzioa horiez* (Bilbao, 1978).

Works by protagonists

Agirre, Julen (Eva Forrest), *Operación ogro* (Ruedo Ibérico, Hendaye, 1974).

Aguirre, José Antonio de, *De Guernica a Nueva York pasando por Berlín* (Ekin, Buenos Aires, 1943).

—— *Freedom was flesh and blood* (Gollancz, London, 1945).

—— *Entre la libertad y la revolucion 1930–35* (Bilbao, 1976).

—— *El informe del Presidente Aguirre al gobierno de la República* (La Gran Enciclopedia Vasca, Bilbao, 1978).

Alonso Zaldivar, Carlos, *Notas sobre el Partido Comunista de Euskadi* (San Sebastián, 1977).

Amigo, Angel, *Operación Poncho: Las fugas de Segovia* (Hordago, San Sebastián, 1978).

—— *Pertur—ETA 71–76* (Hordago, San Sebastián, 1978).

Amilibia, Miguel de, *Los batallones de Euskadi* (Txertoa, San Sebastián, 1978).

Bibliography

Apalategi, Jokin, *Los Vascos de la nación al estado* (Elkar, San Sebastián, 1979).

Apalategi, Jokin and Iztueta, Paulo, *El Marxismo y la cuestión nacional vasca* (Itxaropeno, Zarauz, 1977).

Arenillas, José María and José Luis, *Sobre la cuestión nacional en Euskadi* (Barcelona, 1981).

Arregui, Natxo, *Memorias del KAS 1975–78* (Hordago, San Sebastián, 1981).

Benegas, Txiki, *Euskadi: sin la paz nada es posible* (Argos Vergara, Barcelona, 1984).

Carrillo, Santiago, *Nuevos enfoques a problemas de hoy* (Paris, 1967).

—— *La lucha por el socialismo hoy* (Paris, 1969).

—— *Demain l'Espagne* (Seuil, Paris, 1974).

—— *Eurocommunism and the state* (Lawrence and Wishart, London, 1977).

—— *Memoria de la transición* (Barcelona, 1983).

Castells, Miguel, *Los procesos políticos* (Madrid, 1977).

—— *El mejor defensor, el pueblo* (Ediciones Vascas, San Sebastián, 1978).

—— *Radiografía de un modelo represivo* (Ediciones Vascas, San Sebastián, 1982).

Chiapuso, Manuel, *Los anarquistas y la guerra en Euskadi* (Txertoa, San Sebastián, 1977).

—— *El gobierno vasco y los anarquistas* (Txertoa, San Sebastián, 1978).

Claudín, Fernando, *Documentos de una divergencia comunista* (Barcelona, 1978).

—— *Santiago Carrillo, Crónica de un Secretario General* (Planeta, Barcelona, 1983).

Clements, Josep Carles and Costa, Carles, *Montejurra 76* (La Gaya Ciencia, Barcelona, 1978).

Cruz Unzurrunzaga, Juan, *Infiltración* (Hordago, San Sebastián, 1979).

Elósegui, Joseba, *Quiero morir por algo* (Bordeaux, 1971).

Erroteta, Peru and Vega, Pedro, *Los herejes del PCE* (Planeta, Barcelona, 1982).

Falcón, Lidia, *Viernes y 13 en la Calle del Correo* (Madrid, 1981).

Gaurhauts (Tomás Goikoetxea), *Sobre el nacionalismo revolucionario, socialismo abertzale y marxismo nacional vasco* (Hendaye, 1976).

—— *Hernani I* (Txertoa, San Sebastián, 1978).

Gil Robles, José María, *No fue posible la paz* (Barcelona, 1968).

Ibarruri, Dolores, *They shall not pass* (New York, 1966).

Iztueta, Paulo, *Sociología del fenómeno contestario del clero vasco* (San Sebastián, 1981).

Landaburu, Francisco Javier de, *La causa del pueblo vasco* (Paris, 1956).

Lanegi, Aingeru *et al.*, *Eurocomunismo y Euskadi* (Haranburu, San Sebastián, 1977).

Larrañaga, Policarpo de, *Contribución a la historia obrera de Euskalherria* (2 vols.) (San Sebastián, 1977).

Linz, Juan J., *Conflicto en Euskadi* (Espasa-Calpe, Madrid, 1986).

Onaindía, Alberto de, *Hombre de paz en la guerra* (Ekin, Buenos Aires, 1973).

Onaindía, Mario, *La lucha de clases en Euskadi 1939–80* (Hordago, San

Sebastián, 1980).

Ortzi (Francisco Letamendía), *Historia de Euskadi: el nacionalismo vasco y ETA* (Ruedo Ibérico, Paris, 1975).

―――― *Los Vascos ayer, hoy y mañana* (San Sebastián, 1976).

―――― *Denuncio en el parlamento* (Txertoa, San Sebastián, 1978).

―――― *El no vasco a la reforma* (2 vols.) (Txertoa, San Sebastián, 1979).

―――― *El chivo expiatorio* (Elkar, San Sebastián, 1980) (novel).

Ramírez, Luis (Luciano Rincón), *Nuestros primeros veinticinco años* (Ruedo Ibérico, Paris, 1964).

―――― *Del postfranquismo a la predemocracia* (Barcelona, 1980).

―――― *ETA 1974–1984* (Plaza & Janes, Barcelona, 1985).

Recalde, José Ramón, *La construcción de las naciones* (Siglo XXI, Madrid, 1962).

―――― *Integración y lucha de clases en el neocapitalismo* (Ciencia Nueva, San Sebastián, 1968).

Sarrailh de Ihartza, Fernando (Federico Krutwig), *Vasconia* (Norbait, Buenos Aires, 1962).

Sartorius, N., *El resurgir del movimiento obrero* (LAIA, Barcelona, 1975).

Semprún, Jorge, *Autobiografía de Federico Sánchez* (Planeta, Barcelona, 1977).

Serrano Izco, Bixente, *Navarre, Euskadi* (Hordago, San Sebastián, 1978).

Solano, Wilebando, *The Spanish Revolution: The Life of Andrés Nin* (London, undated).

Uriarte, Eduardo de, *La insurrección de los Vascos* (Hordago, San Sebastián, 1978).

Zumbeltz, K. de (José Luis Zalbide), *Hacia una estrategia revolucionaria vasca* (Hordago, Hendaye, 1974).

Eye-witness accounts

Areilza, José María de, *Así los he visto* (Barcelona, 1976).

Eaton, Samuel D., *The forces of freedom in Spain, 1974–1979* (Hoover Institute Press, Stanford, Cal., USA, 1981).

Echave, Tomás, *Vitoria 76* (Vitoria, 1977).

Escudero, Manu, *Euskadi, dos comunidades* (Haranburu, San Sebastián, 1978).

Fraser, Ronald, *Blood of Spain* (Allen Lane, 1979; Penguin, 1981).

García Damborena, Ricardo, *La encrucijada vasca* (Argos Vergara, Barcelona, 1984).

Gasteiz-Vitoria (no authors given) (Ruedo Ibérico, Paris, 1976).

Gil de San Vicente, Iñaki, *Contra Eurocomunismo, revolución* (Ediciones Vascas, San Sebastián, 1979).

Halimi, Gisèle, *El proceso de Burgos* (Caracas, 1976).

― Portell, José María, *Los hombres de ETA* (Dopesa, Barcelona, 1974).

―――― *Euskadi: Amnistía arrancada* (Dopesa, Barcelona, 1977).

Savater, Fernando, *Contra las patrias* (Tusquets, Barcelona, 1984).

Scheiffler, José Ramón, *Dos años de lucha por la paz* (Iparraguirre, Bilbao, 1980).

Steer, George, L., *The Tree of Guernica* (Hodder and Stoughton, London, (1936).

Secondary sources

Arana, J.A. de, *Presente y futuro del pueblo vasco* (Bilbao, 1968).

Ayestarán, J.A. and others, *Euskadi y el estatuto de autonomía* (San Sebastián, 1979).

Beltza, López Adán E., *Nacionalismo vasco y clases sociales* (Txertoa, San Sebastián, 1976).

———— *El nacionalismo vasco 1876–1936* (San Sebastián, 1977).

———— *El nacionalismo vasco en exilio 1937–1960* (Txertoa, San Sebastián, 1977).

———— *Del carlismo al nacionalismo burgués* (Txertoa, San Sebastián, 1978).

Blas Guerrero, A. de, *Nacionalismo e ideologías políticas contemporáneas* (Espasa, Madrid, 1984).

Blaye, Eduard de, *Franco and the politics of Spain* (London, 1976).

Blinkhorn, Martin, ' "The Basque Ulster": Navarre and the Basque Autonomy Question under the Spanish Second Republic', *The Historical Journal* no. 3, 1974.

———— *Carlism and crisis in Spain 1931–1939* (CUP, Cambridge, 1975).

Bolloten, Burnett, *The Grand Camouflage. The Spanish Civil War and Revolution 1936–1939* (Pall Mall, London, 1968).

Brenan, Gerald, *The Spanish Labyrinth* (CUP, Cambridge, 1936).

Broue, Pierre and Temine, Emile, *La révolution et al guerre d'Espagne* (Minuit, Paris, 1961).

Broussard, Léon, *Jecki, Jecki, Etxentoak ou le défi des Basques* (Paris, 1975).

'Bultzagilleak', *¿Que pasa en el País Vasco?* (Zarauz, 1979).

Busquets, Julio, *El militar de carrera en España* (Ariel, Barcelona, 1967).

Caro, Baroja J., *Los Vascos* (Madrid, 1971).

Carr, Raymond, *Modern Spain, 1875–1980* (OUP, Oxford, 1980).

———— *Spain 1808–1975* (OUP, Oxford, 1982).

Carr, R. and Fusi, J.P., *Spain: dictatorship to democracy* (Allen & Unwin, London, 1979).

Castells, J.M., *El estatuto vasco* (San Sebastián, 1976).

Clark, Robert P., *The Basques: the Franco years and beyond* (University of Nevada, Reno, Nevada, USA, 1980).

———— *The Basque Insurgents. ETA, 1952–1980* (University of Wisconsin Press, USA, 1984).

Corcuera Atienza, Javier, *Orígenes, ideología y organización del nacionalismo vasco, 1876–1904* (Siglo XXI, Madrid, 1979).

Cruz, J. et al., *Franquismo y lucha de clases* (Cedos, Barcelona, 1977).

Davant, Jean Louis, *Histoire du Pays Basque* (Goitziri, Bayonne, 1975).

Domingo, Xavier et al., *De Carrero Blanco a Eva Forest* (Paris, 1975).

Elejabeita, Carmen de, *Lucha política por el poder* (Elias Querejeta, Madrid, 1976).

Ellwood, Sheelagh, *Priestas las filas* (Crítica, Barcelona, 1984).

Elorza, Antonio, *Ideologías del nacionalismo vasco* (Haranburu, San Sebastián, 1978).

Fusi Aizpurua, Juan Pablo, *Política obrera en el País Vasco, 1880–1923*

(Turner, Madrid, 1976).

—— *El problema vasco en la II República* (Turner, Madrid, 1979).

—— *Pluralismo y nacionalidad* (Alianza, Madrid, 1984).

Gallo, Max, *Histoire de l'Espagne franquiste* (2 vols.) (Marabout, Paris, 1969).

Gárate, Gurutz, *Marx y los nacionalismos separatistas* (San Miguel, Bilbao, 1979).

García Venero, Maximiano, *Historia del nacionalismo vasco* (Editora Nacional, Madrid, 1969).

Garmendia, J.A., Parra Luna, F., and Pérez-Agote, A., *Abertzales y Vascos* (AKAL, Madrid, 1982).

Garmendia, J. and Elondi, Alberto, *La resistencia vasca* (Haranburu, San Sebastián, 1982).

Gellner, Ernest, *Thought and change* (Weidenfeld, London, 1964).

—— *Nations and nationalism* (Blackwell, Oxford, 1983).

Genovés, Santiago, *La violencia en el País Vasco y sus relaciones con España* (Universidad Nacional Autónoma de México, Mexico City, 1980).

de la Granja, José Luis, *Nacionalismo y II República en el País Vasco* (Madrid, 1986), passim.

Harrison, R.J., *An economic history of modern Spain.*

Heiberg, Marianne, 'Basque nationalism: its economic, political and cultural determinants and effects' (Ph D Thesis, London, 1982).

Heine, Hartmut, *La oposición política al Franquismo* (Crítica, Barcelona, 1963).

Hermet, Guy, *The Communists in Spain* (Saxon House, Farnborough, 1974).

Hollyman, John, 'The Spanish Socialist Party 1939–1976' (M.A. Thesis, University of Reading, 1976).

Jáuregui, Bereciartu, Gurutz, *Ideología y estrategia de ETA* (Siglo XXI, Madrid, 1981).

Jáuregui, Fernando and Vega, Pedro, *Crónica del anti-Franquismo* (3 Vols.) (Barcelona, 1984).

Jiménez de Aberásturi, J.C. (ed.), *Estudios de historia contemporánea del País Vasco* (Haranburu, San Sebastián, 1982).

Kerman, Ortiz de Zarate R., *El problema revolucionario vasco* (Buenos Aires, 1972).

Larronde, Jean Claude, *El nacionalismo vasco, su origen y su ideología en la orbra de Sabino Arana Goiri* (Txtertoa, San Sebastián, 1977).

Luxemburg, Rosa (edited by H.B. Davis), *The national question* (Monthly Review Press, New York, 1976).

Madariaga, Salvador de, *Spain* (London, 1942).

Medhurst, K.N., *The Basques and Catalans* (Minority Rights Group, London, 1977).

Mogui, Gregorio, *La révolte des Basques* (Paris, 1970).

Morán, Gregorio, *Adolfo Suárez. Historia de una ambición* (Barcelona, 1979).

—— *Los Españoles que dejaron de serlo* (Planeta, Barcelona, 1982).

Munis, G., *Jalones de derrota, promesa de victoria* (Sero XYZ, Madrid, 1977).

Muñoz Alonso, Alejandro, *El terrorismo en España* (Planeta, Barcelona, 1982).

Nin, Andrés, *Los movimientos de emancipación nacional* (Fontamara, Barcelona, 1977).

—————— *La cuestión nacional en el estado español* (Barcelona, 1979).

Noticias del País Vasco, Euskadi: *El último estado de excepción de Franco* (Paris, 1975).

Núñez, L., *Clases sociales en Euskadi* (Txertoa, San Sebastián, 1977).

—————— *La sociedad vasca actual* (Txertoa, San Sebastián, 1977).

—————— *Opresión y defensa del Euskera* (San Sebastián, 1977).

—————— *Euskadi sur electoral* (Ediciones Vascas, San Sebastián, 1980).

(No author given), *La otra Euskadi: el infierno de los Vascos* (St. Jean de Luz, 1975).

Olcina, Evarist, *El Carlismo y las autonomías regionales* (Seminarios y Ediciones SA, Madrid, 1974).

Pagés, Pelai, *El movimiento trotskista en España, 1930–1935* (Barcelona, 1977).

Partido Carlista, *La explotación capitalista* (n.d.).

Payne, Stanley, *El nactionalismo vasco* (Dopesa, Barcelona, 1974).

Pérez Calvo, A., *Los partidos políticos en el País Vasco* (San Sebastián, 1977).

Pérez-Agote, Alfonso, *La reproducción del nacionalismo. El caso vasco* (Siglo XXI, Madrid, 1984).

Preston, Paul (ed.), *Spain in crisis* (Harvester, Sussex, 1976).

—————— *The coming of the Spanish Civil War* (Methuen, London, 1983).

—————— *The triumph of democracy in Spain* (Methuen, London, 1986).

Reinares, F. (ed.), *Violencia y política en Euskadi* (Bilbao, 1984).

Ripley, W.Z., *The races of Europe* (London, 1899).

Robinson, R.A.H., *The origins of Franco's Spain: the Right, the Republic and Revolution, 1931–1936* (David & Charles, Newton Abbot, 1970).

San Sebastián, Koldo, *Historia del partido nacionalista vasco* (San Sebastián, 1984).

Solozábal, Juan José, *El primer nacionalismo vasco* (Haranburu, San Sebastián, 1979).

Sterling, Claire, *The terror network* (Weidenfeld & Nicolson, London, 1981).

Thomas, Hugh, *The civil war in Spain* (Pelican, Harmondsworth, 1971).

Trotsky, Leon, *The Spanish Revolution, 1931–1939* (Pathfinder, New York, 1973).

Ugalde, Martín de, *Síntesis de la historia del País Vasco* (Barcelona, 1977).

Unamuno, M. de, *Paz en la guerra* (novel) (Madrid, 1923).

Vilar, S., *La naturaleza del Franquismo* (Barcelona, 1977).

Williams, C. (ed.), *National separatism* (University of Wales Press, Cardiff, 1982).

'Zubillaga', *Los orígines y frutos del nacionalismo vasco* (Madrid, 1978).

Time Ne
Bold
+ Underlined

Appendix 1
ETA and its Divisions

| 1954 | | EKIN | | | | | |

```
1954                    EKIN

1956        EKIN —   EGI — EG

1959                    ETA

1967                                        ETA-Berri
                                            Kommunistak


1970    ETA-VI
                        ETA-V

1971

1972                            EGI
        Bloque        SAIOAK
        'Minos'
1973    LCR

1974                    ETA-PM          (Workers' Front)
                                            LAIA            ETA(M)


                                        LAIA    (EZ)
1977                                    Commandos Berriak


1982    ETA-PM
        VII Assembly

        ETA-PM
        VIII Assembly      MCE

        LKI                                LAIA            ETA(M)
```

Source: Sullivan. D. " ETA and
    Basque Nationalism: The
294
    Fight for Euskadi 1890-198
    p294

(Comandos autónomos anticapitalistas)

Appendix 2
The Structure of Radical Nationalism

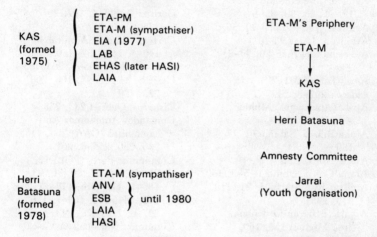

KAS
(formed
1975)
{
ETA-PM
ETA-M (sympathiser)
EIA (1977)
LAB
EHAS (later HASI)
LAIA

ETA-M's Periphery

ETA-M
↓
KAS
↓
Herri Batasuna
↓
Amnesty Committee

Herri
Batasuna
(formed
1978)
{
ETA-M (sympathiser)
ANV
ESB } until 1980
LAIA
HASI

Jarrai
(Youth Organisation)

Additional organisations (for example Mujeres de Kas) appeared and disappeared from time to time

Index